PICTURE
HISTORY
OF THE
U.S. NAVY

THE HILLS OF HOME

PICTURE
HISTORY
OF THE
U.S. NAVY

From Old Navy to   New, 1776 to 1897

Theodore Roscoe ★ Fred Freeman

BONANZA BOOKS · NEW YORK

Printed in the United States of America
Library of Congress Catalogue No. 55-10146
This edition published by Bonanza Books,
a division of Crown Publishers, Inc.,
by arrangement with Charles Scribner's Sons

b c d e f g h

TO ROSAMOND

ACKNOWLEDGMENTS

This volume—a joint endeavor by the book's author and its artist-designer—represents over four years of concentrated effort devoted to the preparation of text, the research and procurement of historical prints and photographs, the composition of unique iconographic layout to accommodate and dramatize the pictorial continuity, and the creation of original illustrations to portray historic scenes or figures otherwise unrecorded by brush, pen or camera. Research and picture procurement alone comprised an undertaking which could not have been accomplished without the support and helping hand of friends, the kindly interest of collectors and cherishers of Americana, information (entirely unofficial) from those versed in naval lore, and the guidance and professional advice of historians, librarians and archivists.

In the foregoing regard, Theodore Roscoe wishes to declare a standing personal indebtedness to those who aided the literary end of this volume's preparation. First acknowledgment must go to that good companion, the writer's wife, who typed the manuscript twice over and who endured the impositions of authorship's midnight oil. Among others who made his endeavors possible, the writer remains most indebted . . .

To Charles L. Martin of Tuckahoe, N. Y., old friend who offered a hand at the outset, who assured support from "launching to completion," and whose generous backing and mainstay encouragement went far to assist the writing of this book. The writer is signatory to a debt in friendship beyond the repayment of any formal acknowledgment.

To Edwin F. Sherwood of Arlington, Va., whose friendly interest supported the research and enabled the procurement of many of the prints and photographs in this volume.

To Emery L. Walker of Wauwatosa, Wisc., who proferred welcome aid and endowed the writer with a family library of Brady albums and military photographs invaluable for reference.

Fred Freeman wishes to acknowledge a debt to the artists of the Navy and outside it, whose work made possible this volume. Especially are we thankful to those artists, names unknown, to whom we cannot give proper specific credit. Too often in our time, mention of the artist is omitted, even when his name is known, and credit for his published work is assigned collectors, museums and even to photographers or units making reproduction copies.

To the artists, then, and those early photographers too, known or unknown, living or dead, whose faithful labor has kept for us all a priceless record of their times, a full measure of acknowledgment and thanks is tendered.

For the contribution of historical data and of privately owned prints, paintings and photographs, with permission to reproduce such material, Theodore Roscoe and Fred Freeman express their appreciation in the Special Acknowledgments section.

Contents

Chapter I

BAPTISM OF FIRE

INTRODUCTION

"Whatever efforts are made by the land armies, the navy must have the casting vote in the present conflict. . . . A constant naval superiority would terminate the war speedily; without it, I do not know that it will ever be terminated honorably. . . . In any operation and under all circumstances, a decisive naval superiority is to be considered the basis upon which every hope of success must ultimately depend." So wrote George Washington, aware from the first musket shot that warships would decide the issue.

What hope, then, could Washington have entertained as the Colonies drifted into war against the world's foremost sea power? Britannia ruled the waves with a giant battle fleet—some 270 warships including over 100 powerful frigates and 131 mighty ships-of-the-line. The Americans did not possess a single warship. Undaunted, Washington organized a mosquito fleet of Marblehead fishing schooners in the autumn of 1775. "At the Continental expense I have fitted out six. These are all manned by officers and soldiers." Six fishing schooners! John Adams saw the need and sponsored the creation of a Navy in November '75. Five homespun ships were commissioned by year's end: *Alfred*, named "in honor of the founder of the greatest navy that ever existed;" *Columbus*, "for the discoverer of this quarter of the globe;" *Cabot*, "for the discoverer of the northern part of the continent;" *Andrew Doria*, "in memory of the great Genoese admiral;" *Providence*, "for the town where she was purchased." Three small naval schooners were simultaneously commissioned. "The first beginning of our navy," wrote John Paul Jones, "was . . . so singularly small that I am of opinion it has no precedent in history." Fortunately the Royal Navy possessed no leader of the intellectual stature of Washington, Adams or Jones. King George's Admiralty had gone to pot; the Royal Navy suffered from softening of the brain. And France sent battle fleets to America's aid. If it had been otherwise, the War of Independence would have been lost. For it was (to quote British historian James) "in all its main features a maritime war." And the issue was decided on the ocean.

1. FIRST MAP OF THE UNITED STATES PUBLISHED IN AMERICA. Legend reads: "NEW and correct MAP of the UNITED STATES of NORTH AMERICA. Laid down from the Latest Observations made by the Authorities agreeable to the PEACE of 1783." Handiwork of cartographer Abel Buell of Connecticut, map is dated 1785. Appearing two years after close of Revolution, it was probably based on British maps used by colonists during war. Comparison with modern projection shows relative accuracy of early-American specimen. Note Virginia, Carolines and Georgia extending from East Coast to Mississippi River; Florida territory belonging to Spain, Louisiana to France. West blurs into Indian country—the "Osages" and "Akansas." And vast strip of Connecticut cuts across Pennsylvania, extends to the Mississippi (territorial claim that caused shooting war between Connecticut and Pennsylvania partisans at time this map was published). Canadian border is vague and Great Lakes somewhat distorted (large islands in Lake Superior were evidently imaginary). But Atlantic coastline and Eastern Seaboard are depicted with fair reliability, as is Appalachian hinterland. Small on paper, this American territory was continentally vast. Fighting Revolutionary America, British admirals and generals were to prove old adage, "You cannot conquer a map."

2. TYPICAL SAIL PLAN *1, Course; 1a, Studding-sails; 2, Fore-topsail; 2a, Studding-sails; 3, Main-topsail; 3a, Studding-sails; 4, Mizen-topsail; 5, Fore-topgallant-sail; 5a, Studding-sails; 6, Main-topgallant-sail; 6a, Studding-sails; 7, Mizen-topgallant-sail; 8, Fore-royal-topsail; 8a, Studding-sails; 9, Main-royal-topsail; 9a, Studding-sails; 10, Mizen-royal-topsail; 11, Fore-skysail-topsail; 12, Main-skysail-topsail; 13, Mizen-skysail-topsail; 14, Fore-topmast staysail jib; 15, Jib; 16, Flying jib; 17, Mizen spanker; 18, Spenser; 19, Main-royal-staysail; 20, Main-topmast-staysail; 21, Mizen-topgallant-staysail.*

Warship Types
COLONIAL PERIOD

3. LINE-OF-BATTLE SHIP (ship-of-the-line)—the 18th century battleship. Two- or three-decked, three-masted, square-rigged, with displacement roughly varying from 1,800 to 3,000 tons, these great naval windjammers were heavy capital ships of their day. Like all warships of period, they were rated according to number of guns in main battery (64, 74, 100, and so on). Gun-ratings were subject to much discrepancy (i.e., a 64-gunner might carry 70 guns, or ship rated as 100-gunner might carry 110.) Crews also varied in number; big "liner" might carry 350 to 800 men. British ships-of-line were characteristically sturdy in hull, blunt-ended, with deep draft; usually slow sailers (6 or 7 knots). French "liners," somewhat less stalwart, were slimmer in body; relatively fast. Spanish were biggest on sea, with high freeboard (tall "castles" fore and aft), elaborate decoration, inferior sailing qualities. As name suggests, big line-ship held the oceanic battle line. Smaller warships (frigates, sloops) served as raiders, escorts and patrol vessels.

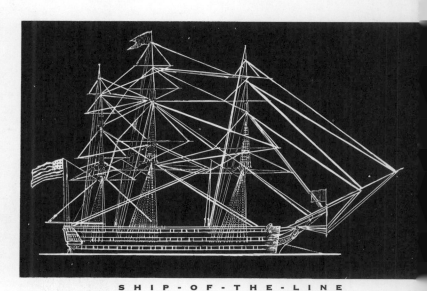

SHIP-OF-THE-LINE

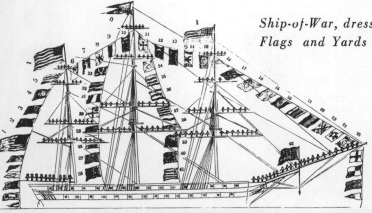

Ship-of-War, dressed with Flags and Yards manned

Ship-of-the-Line on starboard tack

FRIGATE

SLOOP-OF-WAR

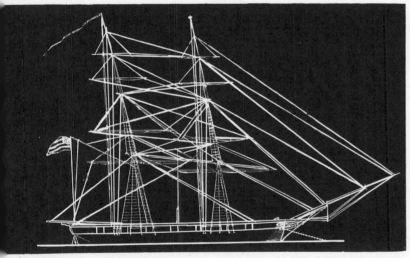

BRIG-OF-WAR

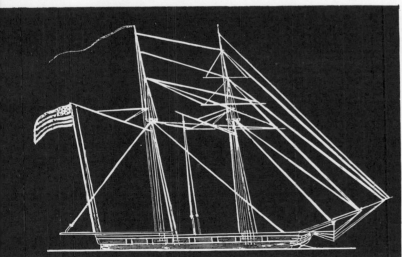

SCHOONER-OF-WAR

4. FRIGATE—the cruiser of the 18th century. A two-decked square-rigged frigate was considerably smaller than average ship-of-the-line; usually faster. Type corresponding to modern heavy cruiser carried 40 to 50 guns. Type corresponding to modern light cruiser carried 26 to 38. British favored 32- and 44-gunners. Average crew: 250 officers, men.

5. SLOOP-OF-WAR (ship-sloop) —the 18th-century destroyer. In Royal Navy, term "sloop" was originally applied to any vessel with guns on one deck; then to any small ship commanded by officer one grade below Captain. Naval sloop common in Revolutionary War period was single-deck two-master, square-rigged like brigantine or snow, or fore-and-aft rigged like ketch. Large sloops averaged 18 to 24 guns; small sloops, 10 to 16. Large ship-sloop would not be a poor match for a small frigate.

6. WAR-BRIG—another 18th-century "destroyer" type. Brig was two-masted, square-rigged vessel, often built flush-decked as shown. About same dimensions as medium naval sloop, similarly armed and similarly employed. Both brigs and sloops were generally classed as corvettes (any man-of-war smaller than frigate). Both were equipped with oar ports and sweeps for rowing. Crew: 150.

7. NAVAL SCHOONER—the 18th-century gunboat. Adopted in British Navy about 1750, the light, fast schooner mounting three or four guns was a Colonial American contribution to naval warfare. By Revolutionary War period, large 8- to 14-gun schooners were not uncommon. Average naval schooner was in category of small warcraft. War-schooners were extensively employed in lake, river and coastal waters; often used as dispatch boats and supply vessels.

8. CORNER OF CAPTAIN'S CABIN (18th-century warship)—reconstructed from remains of British frigate *Charon* sunk off Yorktown during the Revolution. (below right)

Frigate drying sails

Razee or Frigate

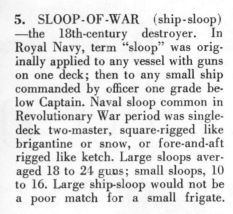

Frigate under full sail

Sloop-of-War under sail

Sloop-of-War hove to

Brig-of-War under full sail

Schooner-of-War getting under weigh

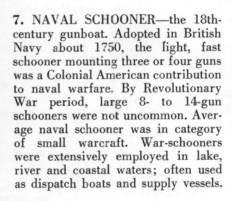

9. BROADSIDE BATTERY (circa 1775). Heaviest fire a warship of Colonial period could deliver was "broadside," with all guns on port or starboard side of the ship letting go in approximate unison. Simultaneous discharges were not easily performed. Heavy "long gun" demanded a crew of 10 or 12 men; required 13 firing operations. Gunnery orders of period were: (1) Cast loose! (2) Level your gun! (3) Middle your breechings! (4) Take out tompions! (5) Take off aprons! (6) Prick and prime! (7) Lay on your aprons! (8) Handle crows and handspikes! (9) Point gun! (10) Level gun! (11) Blow up your matches! (12) Take off your aprons! (13) Fire!

Naval Ordnance

10. TYPICAL NAVAL GUN MOUNT (circa 1775). Average cannon of era were cast-iron, muzzle-loaded smoothbores. They were rated by weight of shot they could throw (i.e., an 18-pounder gun threw cannonball weighing 18 pounds; a 12-pounder threw 12-pound ball, and so on). Short (light) guns were usually installed on vessel's upper ("spar") deck; heavier long guns on lower ("gun") decks. The mount, a wooden carriage, recoiled on wheels. Weapon could be trained by hauling on tackle, or shoving with crowbar. Recoil was controlled by rope called "preventer."

11. NAVAL MORTAR (circa 1775). Small mortars of type shown, called "cohorns" (possible corruption of "cowhorn"), were mounted in warships' tops to lob cannonballs or bombshells. Warships were also armed with small howitzers, swivel guns, blunderbusses and other close-range weapons installed at rail on fixed mounts. Sailors and marine sharpshooters were stationed aloft with muskets, hand grenades and incendiary bombs. Cutlass, pike and broadaxe were the standard naval sidearms of the Revolution. (below)

Early naval uniform button

Exercife of the Great Guns.

UPON Beat to Arms (every Body having immediately repaired to their Quarters) the Midfhipman, commanding a Number of Guns, is to fee that they are not without any neceffary Article, as (at every Gun) a Spunge, Powder-horn, with its Priming-wires, and a fufficient Quantity of Powder, Crow, Handfpike, Bed, Quoin, Train-tackle, &c. fending, without Delay, for a Supply of any Thing that may be miffing; and for the greater Certainty of not overlooking any Deficiency, he is to give ftrict Orders to each Captain under him, to make the like Examination at his refpective Gun, and to take Care that every Requifite is in a ferviceable Condition, which he is to report accordingly. And, befides the other Advantages of this Regulation, for the ftill more certain and fpeedy Account being taken upon thefe Occafions, the Midfhipman is to give each Man his Charge at Quarters (as expreffed in the Form of the monthly Report) who is to fearch for his particular Implements, and, not finding them, is immediately to acquaint his Captain, that upon his Report to the Midfhipman, they may be replaced. The Man who takes care of the Powder is to place himfelf on the oppofite Side of the Deck from that where we engage, except when fighting both Sides at once, when he is to be amidfhip. He is not to fuffer any other Man to take a Cartridge from him, but he who is appointed to ferve the Gun with that Article, either in Time of a real Engagement, or at Exercife. Lantborns are not to be brought to Quarters in the Night, until the Midfhipman gives his Orders for fo doing to the Perfon he charges with that Article. Every Thing being in its Place, and not the leaft Lumber in the Way of the Guns, the Exercife begins with,

1. Silence.

At this Word every one is to obferve a filent Attention to the Officers.

2. Caft loofe your Guns.

The Muzzle lafhing is to be taken off from the Guns, and, being coiled up in a fmall Compafs, is to be made faft to the Eye-bolt above the Port, the Lafhing-tackles at the fame Time to be caft loofe, and the Middle of the Breaching feized to the Thimble of the Pomillion. The Spunge to be taken down, and with the Crow, Handfpike, &c. laid upon the Deck by the Gun.

3. Level your Guns.

The Breech of your Metal is to be raifed, fo as to admit the Foot of the Bed's being placed upon the Axeltree of the Carriage, with the Quoin upon the Bed, both their Ends being even

4. Take out your Tompions.

The Tompion is to be taken out of the Gun's Mouth, and left hanging by its Laniard.

5. Run out your Guns.

With the Tackles hooked to the Upper Bolts of the Carriage, the Gun is to be bowfed out as clofe as poffible, without the Affiftance of Crows or Handfpikes; taking Care at the fame Time to keep the Breeching clear of the Trucks, by hauling it through the Rings; it is then to be bent fo as to run clear when the Gun is fired.

6. Prime.

If the Cartridge is to be pierced with the Priming-wire, and the Vent filled with Powder, the Pan alfo is to be filled; and the flat Space, having a Score through it at the End of the Pan, is to be covered, and this Part of the Priming is to be bruifed with the round Part of the Horn. The Apron is to be laid over, and the Horn put up out of Danger from the Flafh of the Priming.

7. Point your Guns.

At this Command the Gun is, in the firft Place, to be elevated to the Height of the Object, by means of the Side-fights; and then the Perfon pointing is to direct his Fire by the upper Sight, having a Crow on one Side and a Handfpike on the other, to heave the Gun by his Direction till he catches the Object.

N. B. The Men who heave the Gun for pointing are to ftand between the Ship's Side and their Crows or Handfpikes, to efcape the Injury they might otherwife receive from their being ftruck againft them or fplintered by a Shot; and the Man who attends the Captain with a Match is to bring it at the Word, "Point your Guns." and kneeling upon one Knee oppofite the Train Truck of the Carriage, and at fuch a Diftance as to be able to touch the Priming, is to turn his Head from the Gun, and keep blowing gently upon the lighted Match to keep it clear from Afhes. And as the Miffing of an Enemy in Action, by Neglect or Want of Coolnefs, is moft inexcufable, it is particularly recommended to have the Pe ple thoroughly inftructed in pointing well, and taught to know the Inconveniences of not taking proper Means to hit their Mark; wherefore they fhould be made to elevate their Guns to the utmoft Nicety, and then to point with the fame Exactnefs, having caught the Object through the upper Sight at the Word.

8. Fire.

The Match is inftantly to be put to the bruifed Part of the Priming; and when the Gun is difcharged the Vent is to be clofed, in order to fmother any Spark of Fire that may remain in the Chamber of the Gun; and the Man who fpunges is immediately to place himfelf by the Muzzle of the Gun in Readinefs, when at the next Word.

9. Spunge your Guns.

The Spunge is to be rammed down to the Bottom of the Chamber and then twifted round, to extinguifh effectually any Remains of Fire; and when drawn out to be ftruck againft the Outfide of the Muzzle, to fhake off any Sparks or Scraps of the Cartridge that may have come out with it, and next its End is to be fhifted ready for loading; and while this is doing the Man appointed to provide a Cartridge is to go to the Box, and by the Time the Spunge is out of the Gun, he is to have it ready; and at the Word,

10. Load with Cartridge,

The Cartridge (with the Bottom End firft, Seam downwards, and a Wad after it) is to be put into the Gun, and thruft a little Way within the Mouth, when the Rammer is to be entered; the Cartridge is then to be forcibly rammed down, and the Captain at the fame Time is to keep his Priming-wire in the Vent, and, feeling the Cartridge is to give the Word home, when the Rammer is to be drawn, and not before. While this is doing, the Man appointed to provide a Shot is to provide one, or two, according to the Order at that Time, ready at the Muzzle, with a Wad likewife, and when the Rammer is drawn at the Word,

11. Shot your Guns.

The Shot and the Wad upon it are to be put into the Gun, and thruft a little Way down, when the Rammer is to be entered as before. The Shot and Wad are to be rammed down to the Cartridge, and there have a Couple of forcible Strokes, when the Rammer is to be drawn, and laid out of the Way of the Guns and Tackles, if the Exercife or Action is continuing;

FOOTNOTE ON
Tactics
COLONIAL PERIOD

13. TACKING FOR "WEATHER GAUGE"—the key maneuver. In sailing days, tactics were primarily controlled by wind. Everything depended on wind-force and wind-direction. Upon sighting enemy, the attacking ship tried to gain "weather gauge" (i.e., position to windward). Normally ship to leeward, unless much the faster sailer, would soon be overhauled. Windward ship could usually outmaneuver.

12. LINE-OF-BATTLE SHIPS IN COLUMN—typical battle formation of period. Although aggressive, British battle tactics were rigidly dictated by rule-book "Fighting Instructions"; maneuvers were highly conventionalized. On attack, orthodox rule was for line to remain intact as ships bore down in effort to parallel enemy's course and close in with broadsides. In contrast, French favored defensive tactics; usually avoided parallel course, preferred to exchange quartering broadsides. (above)

14. STERN CHASE—typical pursuit of sailing days. Hounding the fugitive, pursuing warship tries to slow her with long-range shots from "chase gun" on forecastle. But long-range hits were lucky.

15. "RAKING"—a deadly tactic in day of sail. Maneuvering across enemy's bow or stern, attacking vessel could sweep the victim's spar-deck from end to end with devastating cannonade, firing broadside guns in succession, while enemy could reply only with bow or stern battery which seldom consisted of more than two guns. The vessel thus raked was usually sorely and sometimes fatally stricken. (at left)

16. "BOARDERS AWAY!"—climax of sailing-ship battle. If possible, assailant would catch victim alongside with grappling hooks. Order for "boarders" sent seamen leaping from ship to ship to fight it out with cutlass, axe and pistol. Murderous scrimmage usually ended with defeated ship in shambles. After formal surrender, enemy survivors were made prisoner, dead were thrown overside, "prize crew" was placed aboard captured vessel. Captors shared prize money. (below)

17. YARD-ARM TO YARD-ARM, ships fought hammer-and-tongs at close quarters in sailing days. Point-blank broadsides were aimed to riddle enemy vessel "between wind and water" (between spar-deck and waterline). Concentrated fire was also aimed at enemy's rigging, sails and masts. Up would go canvas in smoke and flame, set ablaze by bombs and hot shot (cannonballs heated to cherry red in ship's forge). A crashing mast, seriously crippled any sailing vessel. (at left)

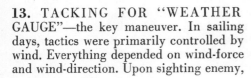
"Exercise of the great guns" in the 18th Century from John Hamilton Moore's Seaman's New Daily Assistant 1784

Colonial American

18. EARLY AMERICAN CRADLE—a colonial merchant ship. Born, bred, sustained by the sea, the original Thirteen Colonies were by nature maritime. Every woodcutter's brother was a sailor. Long before Revolution, New England whalers were roaming the ocean like Vikings in search of the mighty cachalot that provided blubber for candles and sperm-oil lamps. Fleets of British-American sailing ships carried lumber, furs, tobacco and other home-grown products to England; returned laden with cargoes of British goods. The rum, molasses and slave trade engaged scores of American luggers on the West Indies run. Shipbuilding was a pioneer industry. By 1700 some 800 vessels had been built in Massachusetts alone. Early merchantmen (model shown) were English design. But by eve of Revolution, Colonies contained a number of homespun marine architects whose work compared with best—notably, James Penrose and Joshua Humphreys of Philadelphia, James K. Hackett of Portsmouth, Jonathan Greenleaf and Cross Brothers of Newburyport, Benj. Talman and Sylvester Bowers of Providence. As of 1770 almost one-third of merchantmen at sea under British flag were American-made, American-manned. Nucleus for American Navy.

Views of model of 44-gun ship America showing beakhead bulkhead and the carvings, bow and stern and her hull lines.

19. COLONIAL AMERICAN SEA CAPTAIN. Clothes never make the man, and the nautical capabilities of such "sea squires" as at right, were no less genuine for powdered wig, skirt-coat and shoe-buckles. A rough, tough, lusty, roaring lot, these early American skippers, but consummate masters of marlinspike seamanship and navigation. As King's subjects, many had served in sea campaigns against French Canada, had battled the Spaniards at Havana, had fought at Cartagena in the foolish War of Jenkins' Ear. Veterans experienced with naval cutlass and cannon were not lacking for the Revolution. Nor was a seagoing spirit of independence. Not to mention pioneer guts.

Captain Abraham Whipple

Naval Effort

20. DRAUGHT OF COLONIAL FRIGATE *BOSTON* (below)—earliest plan yet found of American-built warship. Wrought by Ben Hollowell at Boston (1747-1748) vessel was 24-gunner, sturdy, fast. Lines and make-up shown were standard for her class and era. As were those of 44-gun frigate *America* built at Portsmouth, N. H. (presumably by shipwright N. Meserve) in 1749. Proof that America could spawn fine naval vessels, these frigates may have alarmed Crown Government which restricted gun manufacture to England, awarded no more warship contracts to Colonials. But Crown could not dampen the dander of such skippers as those shown at the right in contemporary painting, which contains only authentic portrait of Esek Hopkins—future Commander-in-Chief of Revolutionary Navy. However, these Yankees weren't up to the warships built for them.

SEA CAPTAINS CAROUSING. At Surinam (circa 1758). Note seasick celebrant. *Also Esek Hopkins (holding wine glass on table)—future American Navy leader.*

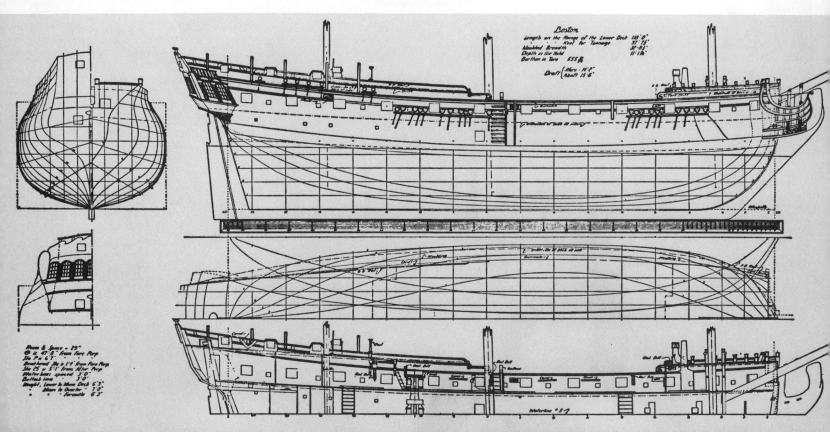

A·VIEW OF PART OF THE TOWN OF BOSTON IN NEW ENGLAND AND BRI...

1 Beaver   5 Mermaid
2 Senegal   6 Romney
3 Martin   7 Launceston
4 Glasgow   8 Bonetta

On Friday Sept.r 30.th 1768, the Ships of WAR, armed Schooners, Transports, &c Came up the Harbor a Spring on their Cables, as for a regular Siege. At noon on Saturday October the 1.st the fourteenth and Train of Artillery, with two pieces of Cannon, landed on the Long Wharf: there Form'd and playing, and Colours flying, up KING STREET. Each Soldier having received 16 rounds of Powd...

Rebellion by

Faneuil Hall (left)

Demolishing statue of George III in New York City (right)

Old Boston building where tea plot was hatched (far right)

and Anchored round the Town: their Cannon loaded, ... twenty-ninth Regiments, a detachment from the 59th Regt. ... Marched with insolent Parade, Drums beating, Fifes ... and Ball.

| | A Long Wharf |
| B Hancock's Wharf |
| C North Battery |

21. TROUBLE-MAKER OFF AMERICA'S EARLIEST LIGHTHOUSE. Mezzotint engraved and published by Wm. Burgis, 1729, nicely pictures situation that became thorn in colonial side—King's revenue man anchored near Boston Light. Ever since founding of the Colonies, Mother Country had imposed heavy duties on settlers, compelling them to pay through nose for privilege of trade with England whilst denying them free trade elsewhere. To impoverished and exploited colonists, His Majesty's cutters came to symbolize tyrannical taxation and overbearing Britannic imperialism. And Boston Light (erected 1716 on Little Brewster Island at entrance of Boston Harbor) became figurative Torch of Liberty in '75.

22. HERE COME THE RED COATS!— as seen by Paul Revere. Famous silversmith himself engraved and published this panoramic view of British fleet unloading "Lobsterbacks" at Boston, 1768. Here was fuel for fiery resistance which had smoldered in Colonies since imposition of Stamp and Quartering Acts in 1765. By Stamp Act (more taxes on colonists) Crown hoped to gain revenue to pay cost of recent war with France. Equally onerous Quartering Act compelled each Colony to furnish King's soldiers with barracks, bedding, candles, vinegar, salt and rum. Storm raised by Patrick Henry, Sam Adams and others against this Royal program invited King's "get tough" policy that eventually touched off rebellion. Red Coats landing in Boston to enforce Crown authority soon had Yankee Sons of Liberty to deal with. Of warships shown in picture, *H.M.S. Senegal* (2), *Martin* (3), *Glasgow* (4), *Mermaid* (5), *Romney* (6), *Launceston* (7) and *Bonetta* (8) would see hot action in Revolution. So would energetic Paul Revere. But historic ride was in future when he engraved above print. This was Colonial Boston.

Sea

Tossing the tea overboard in Boston Harbor

23. GASPÉE EPISODE (June 9, 1772)
—spark to powder keg. While revenues were taxing colonists out of all patience with the Crown, Yankee smuggling (natural reaction to high taxation) was trying patience of Crown Government. After so-called "Boston Massacre" of 1770 (brawl between Red Coats and citizenry ending with death of four proper Bostonians) the situation heated to combustion point. Heat increased in 1772 when British revenue schooner *Gaspée,* aground off Narragansett, was seized and burned by Providence patriots led by Abraham Whipple. (Picture of episode errs in detail if not in mood. Ship was set afire after battle; raiders did not wear Indian disguise.)

24. BOSTON TEA PARTY (December 16, 1773). To bolster England's tea trade (currently stuck with huge surplus) Parliament awarded the great East India Company a monopoly of American markets. As E.I.C. unloaded tons of cut-rate tea in colonial ports, such merchants as John Hancock ("Prince of Smugglers," currently overstocked with smuggled Dutch tea) were faced with ruin. So Boston's Paul Revere and other patriots organized a raid. Dressed as Mohawks, raiders boarded three British ships at Griffin's Wharf; threw tea cargoes overside. Tempest in teapot? Kind that brews naval warfare. (Lithograph left, published 1846, is a shade inaccurate, for the historic affair was staged at night!)

25. FORCING COLUMBIA TO DRINK
TEA. Published in *Royal American Magazine,* 1774, this engraving by Paul Revere (Lord North pours while Columbia gags and Britannia weeps at outrage) was titled "The Able Doctor, or America swallowing the Bitter Draught." Actually, Columbia refused to swallow. Tea riots spread. Americans were denounced in London as "bastards and outlaws." Crown put Boston under martial law, ordered Royal Navy to close the port. War was inevitable. Americans demanded free enterprise. British policy had been candidly set by Cromwellian Admiral Monk during English-Dutch War of previous century: "What matters this or that reason for the war? What we want is more of the trade that they have." So too with Yankee trade.

The Stamp Act riots of New York

26. MINUTE MAN. Citizen of Boston? Farmer of Braintree? Salem sailor? Many hands enlisted in partisan work, secreting powder, storing muskets for showdown. The Minute Man knew it was coming. Perhaps he read valiant speeches of Patrick Henry of Virginia, or Benjamin Franklin of Philadelphia, or homegrown Sam Adams. Perhaps he couldn't read, much less comprehend theories of politics and economy debated by Continental Congress. But he understood the Liberty Tree; the threat to Freedom imposed by army rule and royal warships on blockade. Tea Act repeal came too late. Years later an ancient Yankee was asked why he fought at Bunker Hill? Tea? Hell, he never drank the stuff. Taxes? Didn't often pay any. Trade? Blockade didn't bother him much. "But at town meetin' we'd learnt to think for ourselves, to govern ourselves. We wanted to keep it that way." General Thos. Gage, Military Governor of Massachusetts, called for help.

27. HERE COME MORE RED COATS! (Magnificent illustration by Lynd Ward from *America's Paul Revere*.) Determined to squelch Yankee resistance, British War Office planned to dispatch Lord Clive, conqueror of India, to Massachusetts. When Clive dispatched himself by unobligingly committing suicide, Generals Howe, Burgoyne and Clinton—a glittering trio—were shipped to Boston with Red Coat legion. "The die is now cast," declared the King. "The colonists must either triumph or submit." In spring of 1775, Minute Men answered at Lexington, Concord and Bunker Hill. Revolution was on.

Bunker Hill

28. BATTLE OF BUNKER HILL and burning of Charlestown across Charles River from Boston. In first major battle of Revolutionary War (June 17, 1775), British under General William Howe paid heavy toll to dislodge American militia under General Artemas Ward from hill overlooking Boston Harbor. Early 19th-century lithograph shows Red Coats landing on site of present Navy Yard. In foreground is British ship-of-line *Somerset* (Paul Revere had boated under her stern when he rowed across Charles to start his midnight ride to Lexington). Royal Navy gave Red Coats powerful fire support in Battle of Bunker Hill. And what could colonists do against enemy owning dozens of *Somersets*? Yankees had answer to that one, too. In Maine . . .

Ships at Bunker Hill

29. ANSWER AT MACHIAS, MAINE (June 12, 1775)—Revolutionary War's first naval battle. Month before Bunker Hill, British General Gage sent two sloops and H.M. cutter *Margaretta* to Machias to commandeer load of lumber for King's Boston garrison. Instead of lumber, Red Coats got a load of Jeremiah O'Brien, Scotch-Irish lumberjack with a chip on his shoulder. Leading local partisans, O'Brien seized first sloop to reach Machias Wharf; then attacked and captured the King's surprised naval cutter. (above)

gansett Bay one night in June 1775, Abraham Whipple with armed sloop chased *Rose's* tender hard ashore on Conanicut Island. According to Newport historian, Whipple "is due the honor of discharging the first gun upon the ocean at any part of His Majesty's Navy in the Revolution." But let descendants of O'Brien and Whipple fight it out. (below)

ambush-and-run, privateers waylaid lonely merchantmen or slashed into convoys to seize valuable ships which were taken as "prizes" to be sold at auction in friendly port, the prize money divided between privateer captain and crew. Captive ships that were burdensome would be looted and burned in open sea. By summer of 1775, American privateers were flying like wasps out of Yankee and Southern ports to sting unwary "British bottoms." Coming up were such famous free-lancers as *Phoenix* under William Wattles of Norwich, Conn., and *Pilgrim*, captained by illustrious Johnathan Haradan. To check Yankee privateering, Royal Navy closed in to fetter American ports with blockade. Faced with sea war in earnest, Revolutionary leaders decided to answer King's fleet with an official American Navy.

30. ANSWER AT NEWPORT, R. I. While Maine men cheered capture of *Margaretta*, Rhode Islanders defied Crown authority. When H.M. frigate *Rose* (Captain Wallace) plagued Newport traffic, natives countered by plaguing *Rose*. Smallboat raids (type illustrated) led to deepwater action. Prowling down Narra-

31. ANSWER FROM AMERICAN PRIVATEERS. Privately owned vessel equipped with naval guns and "letter of marque" (official permission from home State or Government to serve as commerce raider), the privateer usually spearheaded naval warfare in day of sail. Half warship, half pirate, lone wolves in fast game of

Victim of an American privateer

Birth of America's Navy

NAVY OF UNITED COLONIES

32. CONGRESS—FATHER OF AMERICAN NAVY. By autumn of '75, with Boston front stalemated and blockade slowly smothering New England seaboard, it was obvious counter naval effort was imperative. On October 13th, Silas Deane, Esq., moved that Congress outfit a 10-gun warship "for intercepting such transports as may be laden

with stores for the enemy." When arguments were finally over, Congress had fathered America's Navy. (Although term "Father" is highly allegorical, it was in Navy's case subject to much dispute in later years. Hoping to shine in reflected glory, several factions claimed the honor for favorite naval heroes. Congress finally kept parent honor for itself.

33. SHORE BOMBARDMENT, ROYAL NAVY STYLE. Continental Congressmen were reluctant to vote for all-out war, but British forced hand by "get tough" policy. Example: on October 7, 1775, Captain Wallace with H.M.S. *Rose, Glasgow* and *Swan* sailed up Narragansett Bay to cannonade Bristol, R. I., manner illustrated. "The night was dark and rainy," says an early historian, "and people were in terror and confusion. For an hour 120 cannon and cascades [fire guns] were discharged upon us, kept up a constant fire on the people. From the town . . . Captain Wallace demanded 100 head of cattle." By such means, Royal Navy subsisted. And stoked the fires of revolution.

34. BURNING OF FALMOUTH settled issue when Congress played reluctant "Father." Many members feared British reaction to American naval resistance. Cried Joachim Zubly of Georgia: "New York is stopped by one ship! Philadelphia says her trade is in the power of the Fleet! . . . In Georgia . . . a small naval force may destroy all the defenses. . . . The navy can destroy our trade!" To others Zubly's plaint was perfect argument for American Navy. When British bombarded and burned Falmouth on Cape Cod (as shown in contemporary woodcut), Congress voted for Navy.

35. FLAG OF NAVY OF UNITED COLONIES. The American Navy was organized in November 1775 by a seven-man Naval Committee. In December, this body was expanded into the "Marine Committee" composed of 13 members and presided over by John Hancock, President of Congress. The ancestor of the present-day Navy Department, the Committee ordered 13 frigates built; it also adopted the naval flag (shown at left). And voted to buy some vessels for immediate use.

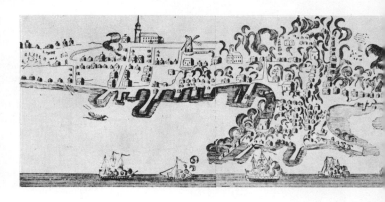

36. GENERAL GEORGE WASHINGTON. For Virginia planter, husbandman, landowner whose chief concerns had been farming and management of enormous tracts of real estate, this nonprofessional soldier appointed to lead the Revolutionary Army (June 14, 1775) showed remarkable appreciation of naval strategy and sea-power's relation to war effort. From first he appealed for naval forces to run blockade, capture enemy supply vessels, transport American supplies and men. When Congress delayed, he himself organized "Washington's Fleet"—six schooners and a brigantine under command of Marblehead fisherman John Manley —a mosquito squadron to harry British fleet off Boston. As President of nation, Washington would one day sponsor "isolationist" policy. But during Revolution he courted allied naval support, refusing to launch Yorktown campaign until assured "the decisive naval superiority . . . upon which every hope of success must ultimately depend." After Yorktown he stated: "whatever efforts are made by the land armies, the navy must have the deciding vote in the present contest." Washington thus showed an understanding of sea-power lacked by King George's generals, by no less a general than Napoleon, and by many generals since. (Interesting footnote: Mount Vernon, original home of Washington's half-brother Lawrence, was named after British Admiral Edward Vernon who died in 1757.)

American Naval Leaders

37. JOHN ADAMS—Braintree "brain" of the Marine Committee. Lawyer, free-thinker, patriot, one of monumental intellects in Continental Congress, Adams of Massachusetts pioneered for the American Navy. At his urging, Silas Deane of Connecticut introduced the subject in Congress. He was immensely proud of his role as Navy's sponsor. "I had at least as great a share in producing (it) as any man living or dead." As infant Navy was launched, Adams wrote: "No great things are to be expected at first, but out of a little a great deal may grow." Man of vision. (at left)

38. COMMODORE ESEK HOPKINS—Commander-in-Chief of Navy of United Colonies. (Spurious portrait, published London, 1776.) His commission wire-pulled by influential brother Stephen of Marine Committee, Hopkins was hapless choice. From outset he displayed unfortunate tendency to quarrel with own rather than England's captains. Apologetic biographers would mention handicaps. His American contemporaries dealt with him more severely. (right)

39. IDEALIZED PORTRAIT OF ESEK HOPKINS. Evidently painted by a sentimentalist, this pensive "Hopkins" is as factitious as the English sham. Hopkins was nearly 58 when appointed Commander-in-Chief. Only authentic surviving likeness shows him as sea-dog merchant skipper (before Revolution) carousing lustily in a tavern. A similar carouse would lead to his undoing in the first major sea battle fought by the American Navy. Strawman admiral. (below)

40. CAPTAIN JOHN BARRY. At Philadelphia in autumn of 1775 was this Wexford-born shipmaster with stout Indiaman, *Black Prince*—a merchant vessel promptly purchased by Marine Committee and converted into frigate *Alfred* to serve as Hopkins' flagship. Offered command of a small naval brig, John Barry accepted with enthusiasm. Combativeness and daring won him subsequent promotion to captaincy of American frigates *Effingham*, *Raleigh* and *Alliance*. (at left)

41. HIS MAJESTY GEORGE III, KING OF ENGLAND (1760 to 1820) —figurehead for Royal Navy. Famous for his green silk coat, protuberant eyes and Germanic manners, third George of the House of Brunswick was more despotic than average product of his time. Dull, stubborn, domineering, more German than English, he sought to strengthen his "divine-right" monarchial power by packing Parliament with sycophants. His reactionary rule and meddling with colonial policy won resentment of British Whig liberals as well as animosity of Americans. His royal decree that all Americans who resisted Crown authority were "traitors" subject to death sentence for treason, and his hiring of Hessian mercenaries to subdue the colonists, solidified American resistance to British rule. Although he was referred to in Parliament as "best of sovereigns," his reign was distinguished by incompetence, corruption, and loss of the American colonies. "The shame of the darkest hour of England's history lies wholly at his door," wrote English historian Green. Perhaps his moral default as a ruler was caused by mental illness. In any case, suffering from dementia in 1780, he went completely insane in 1810. (Popular in contemporary London, the glorified portrait shown at right was work of King's engraver, Wynne Ryland, who was hanged for forgery of banknotes in 1783. Georgian justice — hang a Ryland but elevate a Sandwich.)

Royal Navy, 1775

LORD VISCOUNT SACKVILLE.

44. LORD GEORGE GERMAIN— master mind behind British strategy. Dismissed from Army command (during Seven Years War) for mussy-minded muddling. Returned to saddle in 1775 as Secretary of State for Colonies, he assumed remote control of British war operations in America. Sitting in London War Office, His Lordship planned complex military-naval moves calculated to baffle George Washington. Fortunately for American cause, they baffled Britain's generals and admirals, as well. But on small maps they looked easy. (above)

42. LORD NORTH, PRIME MINISTER OF ENGLAND from 1775 to 1783. Member of distinguished family that contributed many famous statesmen (and Epsom Salts) to British history, Frederick North added brilliant rhetoric and little else to George III's government. His wartime services seem characterized by an exchange with an M. P. who, protesting deterioration of Royal Navy in 1780, bitterly observed that Prime Minister was asleep. "No," North yawned answer, "but would God I were." Late in Revolution he resigned under pressure from English liberals. (at right)

43. JOHN MONTAGU, EARL OF SANDWICH—playboy First Lord of Admiralty. Talented grafter, gambler and master of palace intrigue. Sandwich wire-pulled himself into Admiralty in 1748. During his incumbency as First Lord, Royal Navy morale was riddled by courts-martial of Admirals Byng, Keppel and Sir Hugh Palliser. Through bribery, extravagance and graft he reduced Royal Navy to bankruptcy in 1771, fleet in disrepair, storehouses empty. Sandwich Islands (Hawaii) were named after him. He is probably best remembered as originator of famous snack (slice of meat between two of bread), supposedly his favorite indulgence while at the gaming tables.

Divertisement, 1770

48. CAPTAIN LAMBERT WICKES. Maryland lobsterman appointed skipper of 16-gun sloop *Reprisal,* Wickes proved stellar officer. Marine Committee selected him for extraordinary special mission—carrying of Benjamin Franklin to France. Having delivered Franklin (plus three prizes captured during crossing), Wickes would sweep England's doorstep with raids that panicked Parliament. Then like early star he would be lost in night—disappear in the void of an Atlantic gale. A captain courageous. *(No picture extant)*

49. CAPTAIN JOHN PECK RATHBURN. New Bedford fisherman with reputation as competent mariner. So it was assumed he could handle a war-sloop. Assumption correct. Striking British Bahamas in 1777, he would handle a 12-gun sloop as though it were a fleet; accomplish more than Esek Hopkins in previous venture with entire squadron. With becoming modesty Rathburn fades from history's pages, but in such records as remain he emerges as one of Continental Navy's best commanders. *(No picture extant)*

45. CAPTAIN ABRAHAM WHIPPLE—mariner who led party which burned revenue cutter *Gaspée.* Warned his neck was under shadow of rope (a noose that threatened all American patriots), he advised British, "Always catch a man before you hang him." Outstanding frigate captain in Continental Navy, when British finally caught him he was worth more as hostage than hangee. (He was called "The Informal Commodore." Off duty.) (left)

46. CAPTAIN NICHOLAS BIDDLE. Midshipman in King's uniform when Revolution broke out, Biddle was one of few Americans in Royal Navy who resigned from service to fight under Continental flag. With rare experience (which included early polar expedition), he was sole professional naval officer in original American fleet. Captain of frigate at 27, he displayed exceptional ability at handling of ship and men. He was sailing into stellar career when death overtook him in the form of a 64-gun ship-of-the-line which no 32-gun frigate could withstand. A born leader.

47. CAPTAIN JAMES NICHOLSON. Chesapeake squire with some sailboat experience, he had himself hoisted to first place on promotion list; succeeded Esek Hopkins as Navy's senior officer. Thereafter he was in deep water. After losing two brand-new frigates (one, without firing a shot), he engaged in factional intrigue against Paul Jones. Typical "political" captain (one of several in Continental service), he served as another proof that politics applied to brass could be pernicious corrosive.

50. LIEUTENANT JOSHUA BARNEY. Served as First Lieutenant in frigate under James Nicholson. Captured (no fault of his own) and paroled in prisoner exchange. Risked certain hanging to skipper a privateer. Captured again—escaped—was recaptured—again escaped. Career to rival anything in Dumas. Commanding a war-sloop at Revolution's end, he was one of last Continental captains on sea. In the Navy's galaxy he was a star of first magnitude.

51. "COMMODORE" BENEDICT ARNOLD. Dark star. Strange phenomenon on Navy's horizon. Brigadier General in charge of lake squadron. By Government order, or self-assumed command? No matter. His brilliant naval defense of Champlain would save America's northern frontier. But Arnold himself was lost in dream of ambition that led to nightmare. Star that flashed as a meteorite, then plummeted to earth and burned out to a cinder. (left)

Death of General Warren at Bunker Hill

MAJ GEN BENEDICT ARNOLD

B. Arnold M Genl

52. VICE ADMIRAL LORD HOWE —commander of British naval forces in American waters (1776 to 1778). "Illegitimate grandson" of George I and Baroness Kilmansegge, Richard Howe was second cousin of George III. Thus entitled to peerage and epaulettes, he became Admiral during Seven Years War; was Treasurer of Royal Navy under Earl of Sandwich. In February 1776 he was commissioned jointly with brother, General Sir William Howe, "to treat with the revolted Americans." Considerably brighter than his brother, he resigned in 1778, protesting the American war mismanaged. Popular in the Royal Navy as "Black Dick."

54. REAR ADMIRAL MARRIOT ARBUTHNOT—successor to Lord Howe as commander of British fleet in North American waters. Another rule-book line officer, Admiral Arbuthnot made modicum of headway with blockade; managed to transport Clinton's army from New York for second try at Carolina. But eventually bungled battle with French. Criticized as inefficient by choleric General Clinton, he was recalled home; replaced by Admiral Sir Thomas Graves — who lost a bigger battle.

55. "BUTTERFLY FROM MAGGOT." Contemporary caricature of Georgian Navy commander reflects views expressed by Commodore Edward Thompson, R.N., in letter to young relative about to enter King's naval service. "Low company is the bane of all young men, but in a man-of-war you have the collected filth of jails. The scenes of horror and infamy on board are many. . . . It is a mistaken notion that a youth will not be a good officer unless he stoops to the most menial offices; to be bedded worse than hogs and eat less delicacies. . . . From having experienced scenes of filth and infamy, fatigues and hardships sufficient to disgust the stoutest and bravest, alas! there is only a little hope of promotion sprinkled in the cup. The state of inferior officers in his Majesty's service is a state of vassalage." Observing that junior officers are not prepared for captaincy when promotion does come, Thompson concludes, "the change is at once from a filthy maggot to a shining butterfly." (left)

57. REAR ADMIRAL SIR PETER PARKER. Another naval lord dispatched to deal with American rebels. Capable enough on the blue, at Fort Moultrie in 1776, Peter Parker picked a peck of poisonous palmetto. Britons like to recall him as sponsor and patron of famous Lord Nelson. (left)

53. VICE ADMIRAL SIR GEORGE BRYDGES RODNEY. Commander of West Indies squadron in 1774, he was forced into Paris exile through gambling debts. Restored to rank, he returned to West Indies to defend Jamaica, threatened by French in 1779. Advocate of iron discipline (for everybody but Rodney), he wrote that his eye on his captains "has more dread than the enemy's fire." Eye also on prize money, he seized Dutch St. Eustatius when island's strategic value was negligible—a move that sent him back to England in legal snaggle over booty. Returned to win great victory over French in 1782.

56. REAR ADMIRAL SAMUEL HOOD—second in command under Admiral Graves. One of few "mustangs" in Royal Navy, Hood rose from ship's servant to high rank, his career an outstanding blend of brilliant officership and cutthroat ambition. After criticizing a Fleet Captain for slavish obedience to faulty orders, he himself would follow Graves' orders to the letter in crucial Battle off Virginia Capes—to Graves' undoing and his own advancement. (below)

58. CAPTAIN JOHN PAUL JONES (Painting by Cecilia Beaux). Scotsman born (1747). Schooled at and by sea (cabin boy at 12). Brief service in Royal Navy (not the uniform for an independent lad). Mate on a West Indies slaver (not the job for a freedom-loving stripling). Actor, Jamaica stock company (role in Richard Steele's *Conscious Lovers*). Mate of passenger vessel (the ocean his stage). Shipmaster at 21. Such were the antecedents of the officer (original name: John Paul) who volunteered for American naval service under the name of Jones. Scorned as an "illegitimate" by Tories who touched forelock to a Lady Hamilton or Lord Howe, he was to be snubbed in America for "illegitimacy" as an immigrant with neither social nor political connections. Enemies pro-

nounced him a pirate (for raid on England); whispered he was wanted for murder—with reference to killing of mutineer on lugger at Tobago (as though slaying a mutineer in self-defense were crime). Detractors (themselves ambitious parvenus) denounced him as ambitious parvenu. But John Paul Jones, master mariner, displayed a competence as sailor and battle leader unique in Revolutionary American Navy. Scorning political pull, he entered service as lieutenant. "If I cannot rise by direct dealing, I will not rise at all." Inventive and able strategist, he could plan a campaign. Expert tactician, he could fight it through. Knew naval architecture (could design a ship). Could write (fair verse; an astute critique; a set of officer qualifications that remains standard to this day). He could scorch a malingering crew with words of brimstone, and he could talk the courtly language of diplomacy. At once irascible and humane, introspective and aggressive, sensitive and iron-nerved, humble and proud, he was that rare complexity of thinker and doer, the artist-fighter whose genius forever baffles those who seek a capsule formula for leadership. One of Democracy's pioneer champions, he would stand out as greatest American naval leader of his time.

59. AMERICA VERSUS BRITAIN —early Revolutionary cartoon. Fairer size-up would have shown Yankee Gulliver resisting a Brobdingnagian giant armed with huge blunderbuss. As Crown had carefully restricted ordnance manufacture to British Isles, Americans were hampered by weapons shortage from first to last shot of Revolution. Forays to capture munitions were No. 1 missions on infant Navy's agenda. Soon after war's outbreak precious cannon started coming "underground" from France. But American Navy's first squadron couldn't muster gunpower of two British ships-of-line. And facing Royal Navy possessed of 131 mighty "liners," Americans did not have on sea a single line-of-battle ship throughout entire war. "The first beginning of our Navy," wrote John Paul Jones, "was, as navies rank, so singularly small I am of the opinion it has no precedence in history."

All you that have bad masters,
And cannot get your due,
Come, come, my brave boys,
And join our ship's crew!

The Men

60. RECRUITING, 1776. Who and whence were the Americans who manned the Revolutionary Navy? Candlelight record-keeping such as it was, many of their names were lost to history. And many (for all were revolutionists with price on head) preferred contemporary anonymity. All told, a possible 5,000 served in Continental or State warships, volunteering

for duration of cruise. Perhaps typical Revolutionary naval volunteer is glimpsed in account penned by one who served in an American frigate: "All means were resorted to which ingenuity could devise to induce men to enlist. A recruiting officer, bearing a flag, and attended by a band of martial music, paraded the streets to excite a thirst for glory and a spirit of military ambition. The recruiting officer possessed the qualifications to make the service appear alluring, especially to the young. . . . When he espied any large boys . . . he would attract their attention by singing in a comical manner doggerel [quoted above]." Once the frigate was loaded, it was moved to mid-channel to prevent unruly recruits from escaping. "Upwards of 330 men were carried, dragged and driven on board, of all kinds, ages, and descriptions, in all the various stages of intoxication, from that of sober tipsiness to beastly drunkenness, with an uproar and clamor that may be more easily imagined than described." An untouched portrait of Revolutionary sailor.

61. AMERICAN GUN CREW, 1776. Iron men and iron powder-monkey. Training was largely matter of taming for Yankee Tars of Revolutionary Navy. But there was no shortage of the grit demanded for naval gunnery in day when batteries fired practically mouth-to-mouth. Incidentally, little powder-monkeys, knee-high to grasshoppers, stood (and died) alongside the bravest. Small boys fed powder to American naval guns until well after Civil War. Forgotten heroes. (below)

62. FLOGGING IN ROYAL NAVY. All navies (including contemporary early American) disciplined by cat-o'-nine-tails. But Georgian service was singularly brutal. Men were frequently torn to pieces by being "flogged through fleet"—a barbarous death sentence. Eight hundred lashes were often ordered (350 generally fatal). Keelhauling was also common, the victim thrown overside to be towed under keel where barnacles would lacerate his body. Luckier malefactors, condemned, were blown from mouth of cannon. In day when children were hanged at Tyburn for petty larceny, Draconian punishments in Royal Navy kept step with age. Yet they failed to mend situation exposed during Revolutionary War by wholesale desertion and by mutinies on board H.M.S. *Prince, Defiant, Valiant, Cumberland, Trent* and *Victory*. Brave enough to mutiny in teeth of brutal "cat," British Jack showed no lack of courage. Rather, he lacked Cause. Misled by corrupt Admiralty—beset by command jealousies and courts-martial —officered in main by vain popinjays or sadists of Captain Bligh (H.M.S. *Bounty*) type—manned largely by gallows birds and guttersnipes—Royal Navy of 1775 was more than several decades short of Nelson. Enormous was King George's Fleet. But it would go to prove that ships are no better than crews in them, and crews seldom better than their captains.

63. BRITISH TARS, GEORGIAN ERA. Little different from Jacks of Elizabethan day were seamen in service of George III —meaning Royal Navy was manned by a desperate, bedeviled lot. Uniformed in rags, eating from communal tub in which he stabbed his dirk (or "whinger"), himself mere cannon fodder, Jack was a slave. Brutal flog-and-grog shipboard existence was only dimly brightened by wild carousals in foreign ports when lid was off. On occasion similar to one pictured, Commodore Thompson reported 300 native women romping in orgy aboard one warship. "There's not a vice committed but is practised here," he deplored. An untouched portrait of British sailor of '76.

65. JUNIOR OFFICER ROYAL NAVY. "To pitchfork the knave or fool of the family into a commission was the whole duty of the thoughtful parent," observes H. Belcher (*The First American Civil War*). With social caste system tending to undermine morale of aspirant who had to work for advancement while His Nobs, perhaps a lazy tosspot, received it as birthright privilege, King George's Navy sailed under queer mixture of malcontents, spartans and pedigreed incompetents. (at left)

64. IMPRESSMENT (YOU'RE IN THE NAVY NOW). Early print entitled, "The Press Gang Impressing a Young Waterman on the Day of his Marriage," protests shanghai method of raising crews. However, His Majesty's tipstaffs normally raided waterfront taverns and brothels, sources which crowded British warships with lowest characters imaginable. Crammed into scurvy forecastles, these men and boys, many of them diseased felons, turned warships into floating pesthouses. Admiral Sir Richard Kempenfelt wrote in 1779: "Their appearance in general is a disgrace to the service, very shabby and very dirty." Kempenfelt recommended uniforms, constant drill and "full time for meals and repose." He also urged divine service in fleet. "Religion is particularly necessary in the common people to preserve morals. Our seamen are more licentious than those of other nations. The reason is, they have less religion." Unfortunately "upper class" failed to set good example. And Sir Richard never had chance to try reforms as he was lost with 800 on board in 1782 when flagship *Royal George* capsized off Spithead. However, shanghaied seamen were unlikely subjects for evangelism. (below)

66. AMERICAN FRIGATE *ALFRED*—24-gun flagship for Commander-in-Chief Hopkins. Aboard her Paul Jones served as First Lieutenant, training crew to handle her 9-pounders. Around her, at Philadelphia anchorage, she gathered American Navy's first squadron—makeshift brood composed of sloop *Columbus* (20 guns), brigs *Cabot* and *Andrew Doria* (14-gunners), little sloops *Providence* (12 guns) and *Hornet* (10) and 8-gun schooners *Wasp* and *Fly*. Blunt-nosed, slow, not too "weatherly," *Alfred* led Navy to sea in late February 1776. (at left)

67. FIRST ALL-AMERICAN FRIGATE TO SEA—the *Randolph*. Of 13 new warships ordered by Continental Congress in December '75, *Randolph* was first keel-to-truck home-built frigate to sail for Navy. Wrought by Wharton and Humphreys of Philadelphia, she was 32-gunner, about 133 feet long, 34½ in beam, with 10½ hold. She sailed from Revolutionary capital in February 1777, on her quarterdeck Captain Nicholas Biddle. Was the only one of four Philadelphia frigates to escape blockade and reach ocean. The others (sister-ship *Washington* and 28-gunners *Effingham* and *Delaware*) never made it.

Warships

68. AMERICAN FRIGATE *RALEIGH*—one of 13 frigates ordered by Continental Congress on December 13, 1775. A 697-tonner carrying 32 guns, she was approximately 131½ feet long, with 34½-foot beam, 11-foot depth of hold. Constructed by James K. and William Hackett of Portsmouth, N. H., she was launched on May 21, 1776, and completed by midsummer. Her class (or rate) included frigates *Hancock*, *Randolph*, *Warren* and *Washington*. Five smaller frigates of *Providence* class were simultaneously projected. Built by Sylvester Bowers at Providence, R. I., 28-gun *Providence* was a 632-ton vessel, approximately 126½ feet long, with 33¾-foot beam, 10½-foot depth of hold. Launched in May '76, she was completed and at sea by following autumn. Her class included frigates *Congress*, *Virginia*, *Trumbull* and *Effingham*. (Not all of these 10 "heavy frigates" were completed. And of those that were, not one remained to America at war's end.

69. AMERICAN WAR-SLOOP *RANGER*. One of three ship-sloops built for Continental service, she was 308-ton 18-gunner constructed by James K. Hackett at Portsmouth, N. H. Armed with 6-pounder guns and manned by crew of about 140, she sailed into history on October 31, 1777, as raider under command of John Paul Jones. After stellar war career she was captured (while under another captain) in 1780. Sister sloops *Saratoga* and *General Gates* were to be far less fortunate. (left)

70. AMERICAN LIGHT FRIGATE *BOSTON*—one of three 24-gunners projected in 1775 program. Displacing 514 tons, *Boston* was approximately 114¼ feet long, with 32-foot beam, 10½ depth of hold. Built at Newburyport, Mass., by Johnathan Greenleaf and Cross Brothers, she was launched by summer of '76; sailed into action in '77. Her Revolutionary career was longer than most; she was not captured until 1780. Sister frigates *Delaware* and *Montgomery* never got from their cradles to sea. (above)

71. H.M. SHIP-OF-THE-LINE *VICTORY*. Typical 100-gunner of period. To be famous as flagship of Lord Nelson in later wars, she was built in 1765; survives today at Portsmouth Naval Dockyard, England. About 186 feet in length, with 52-foot beam, 20-foot depth of hold. *Victory* originally carried 18-pounder long guns, long 12-pounders and lighter 9's. Crew of some 360 hands. Average Royal Navy "liner" was smaller 64-gunner of *Yarmouth, Augusta,* or *Raisonable* class. As of 1775, Britain possessed some 131 line-of-battle ships. (Americans possessed none.)

and Weapons

The frigate Rose

72. H.M. FRIGATE *ALARM*—typical 32-gunner of period. Such vessels were about 125 feet in length, with 35-foot beam, 12-foot depth of hold. Armed with 18-pounders, 12-pounders and 9-pounders. Carried some 250 men. Class included H.M.S. *Vestal, Southampton, Minerva, Diana, Niger, Eolas, Stag, Orpheus, Quebec, Milford, Flora* and others. Royal Navy contained numerous larger frigates of 44-gun *Roebuck, Diomede, Rainbow* and *Serapis* class. Also smaller 28-gunners of *Solebay, Unicorn* class. Soon after war's outbreak some 50 to 80 British frigates were maintained on American station. (at right)

73. H.M. WAR SLOOP *DRUID*—typical 14-gunner of period. Royal Navy contained smaller sloops of 10-gun *Racehorse* class, and larger of *Weazel* (16-gun), *Albany* (18-gun) and *Jason* (20-gun) class. The 14-gunners (*Druid, Ceres, Hope, Allegiance* and others) were about 110 feet in length, with 30-foot beam, 10-foot depth of hold. Fleet also contained numerous 14-gun brigs of *Active, Trepassy* class; larger brigs of 20-gun *Sandwich* class; smaller of 10-gun *Egmont* class. The 14-gun brig was about 95 feet long, with 26-foot beam, 11½-foot depth of hold. (left)

Early Carronade

74. PLAN DRAWING, TYPICAL NAVAL GUN MOUNT, Revolutionary Period. When gun was mounted, its trunnions (P) rested under clamp (h-e) in trunnion box of four-wheeled carriage (called a truck carriage). In training the gun, crew used crowbars to shove the carriage to right or left. Wedges were adjusted under gun breech to raise or lower gun's aim. Weapon was sighted by aligning marks on the barrel with a taut length of string pointed in target's direction. Largest naval cannon of standard issue was 32-pounder carried by British ship-of-line. Standard for frigates and corvettes were 24-pounder and 18-pounder (long guns with ranges well over a mile). Warships also carried small hand-aimed swivel guns mounted at rail. Naval cannon were forged cast-iron; the carriages usually made of elm, painted black. (right)

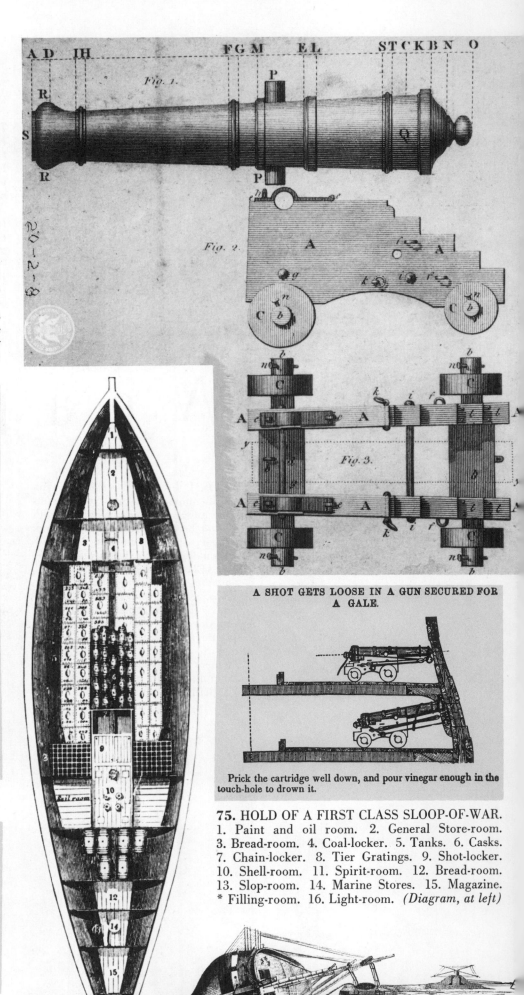

GETTING THE GUNS ON BOARD.

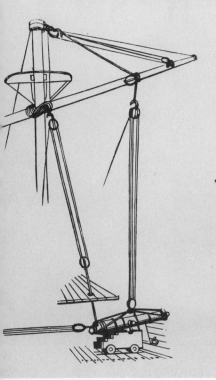

The gun-carriages and all the equipments belonging to the guns are brought alongside in lighters, and hoisted in with the yard & stay. Get them on their respective decks, and reeve the purchase for getting the guns on board.

Securing the main-yard.—To the bolts in the lower cap, hook the double blocks of two burtons. The single ones are hooked to selvagee-straps, round the yard, close to the lifts, and the falls sent on deck, through leading-blocks.

Excerpts from the "Kedge Anchor"

STOWING HAMMOCKS.

Nothing adds more to the smart and favorable appearance of a vessel of war than a neat stowage of hammocks. The superintendants of this necessary duty are often at fault, forgetting that negligence in the performance of this service is seldom permitted to pass unnoticed.

In the stowage of hammocks, the officer should stand on the opposite side of the deck, a position which will enable him to preserve a symmetrical line, and guide and direct the stower in his progress fore and aft the netting; they are also enjoined to be careful that the hammocks of the men be properly lashed up. Defaulters in this particular should be reported to the First Lieutenant. Seven turns at equal distances, is the required number of turns with a hammock-lashing.

Note.—In piping-down hammocks, the officers are cautioned not to permit the men to throw them on the deck.

A SHOT GETS LOOSE IN A GUN SECURED FOR A GALE.

Prick the cartridge well down, and pour vinegar enough in the touch-hole to drown it.

75. HOLD OF A FIRST CLASS SLOOP-OF-WAR.
1. Paint and oil room. 2. General Store-room.
3. Bread-room. 4. Coal-locker. 5. Tanks. 6. Casks.
7. Chain-locker. 8. Tier Gratings. 9. Shot-locker.
10. Shell-room. 11. Spirit-room. 12. Bread-room.
13. Slop-room. 14. Marine Stores. 15. Magazine.
* Filling-room. 16. Light-room. *(Diagram, at left)*

Representation of a frigate hove down to a dock or wh

76. BRITISH FIRE POWER— Revolutionary Period. When ship-of-line let go with 40-gun broadside, blast could be devastating. Although little improved since Tudor days, Georgian naval guns were probably superior to rival specimens extant. In 1775 there were no American-made cannon to assert rivalry. Revolutionary Yankees could carpenter a carriage, but gun-forgings were impossible, as Crown had restricted cannon manufacture to British Isles. While using dummy guns to bluff the Redcoats at Boston, Washington organized a mosquito fleet to raid H.M. munitions ships in Massachusetts Bay. When American Navy was launched, its No. 1 mission was to raid Britain's Bahamas arsenal. Containing some 270 warships (nearly half of them ships-of-line) Royal Navy could have mustered over 8,000 guns against the 110 makeshift weapons of first American Navy squadron. Most of cannon in Continental Navy were either captured from the British or procured from France. (at left)

When freshly blows the northern gales,
Then under courses snug we fly;
When lighter breezes swell the sails,
Then royals proudly sweep the sky.

Lower Gun Deck H.M.S. Victory (below)

THE LOWER GUN DECK

Opening

77. FISHING SCHOONER *HANNAH*—presumably the first American warship. Tradition identifies her as Marbleheader fitted out at Beverly, Mass.; and commissioned by Washington on September 2, 1775. Story has it that she stood to sea under Capt. Nicholas Broughton on September 5th; returned on September 7th with two small supply ships as prizes. (below)

Cant the spritsail-yard to steady the boom; man the halliards and sheet—see the downhaul and brails clear, take in the slack of the sheet to steady the sail; "hoist away;" and as the sail goes up, ease off the sheet—when taut up, haul aft the sheet.

from the "Kedge Anchor"

78. ATTACK ON BRITISH CONVOY OFF BOSTON. Best authorities identify six small craft of "Washington's Fleet" as schooners *Lee, Franklin, Harrison, Hancock, Lynch* and *Washington,* under Commodore John Manly. Raiding enemy off Boston, they were aided by privateers of the type pictured attacking Redcoat convoy. Patrol frigates *Tartar* and *Raven* won this particular scrimmage. But Manly's codfish group bagged some 35 vessels that fall. Then came squabble over prize money. The many quarrels over spoils finally impelled Washington to appeal for disciplined unified naval service. (below)

Operations

81. COMMANDER-IN-CHIEF COMES ABOARD—Hopkins in a gamming chair. Navy historians favor portrait of "young" Hopkins wearing pensive smile, parson-collared uniform. As he was old sea dog and old skippers often were too gouty to climb Jacob's ladder, sketch (modern) seems most realistic. "Mr. Hopkins," Paul Jones noted, "lost so much time at outset that his squadron was frozen in the Delaware." (above)

82. ATTACK ON NASSAU—Navy's first strike. On February 18, 1776, Continentals sailed from Philadelphia. In squadron were flagship *Alfred* (Capt. Saltonstall), sloop *Columbus* (Whipple), brigs *Doria* (Nicholas Biddle) and *Cabot* (J. B. Hopkins), sloop *Providence* (John Hazard) and schooners *Wasp, Hornet, Fly*. They reached Bermuda night of March 2nd. Then Hopkins telegraphed punch with daylight attack (against advice of First Lt. Paul Jones). Some 71 cannon, 15 mortars were seized. But delay gave enemy chance to ship off big powder supply.

79. "I HOISTED WITH MY OWN HANDS THE FLAG OF FREEDOM the first time it was displayed on board *Alfred* in the Delaware." So Paul Jones proudly recalled ceremony of December 3, 1775, when he raised first official American flag to fly for Navy. Washington hoisted similar "Jack and Stripes" at Boston following January. *Alfred* also flew Rattlesnake Flag as broad pennant of Commodore Esek Hopkins. (left)

80. AS ENGLISH SAW HOPKINS—from "Impartial History of the War in America," pub. London, 1780. War in America? London gossip was more concerned with the capers of Jack Rann ("Highwayman of 16 Strings") and the androgynous doings of Chevalier d'Éon (man or woman?). But Yankee Navy roused some Fleet Street interest—hence this portrait of a walleyed "Robert" Hopkins who never existed. (right)

83. BATTLE OFF BLOCK ISLAND—Navy's first major sea engagement. Following instructions to proceed to Rhode Island, Hopkins sailed from Bahamas. On April 4th, squadron met a small British convoy off Block Island, R.I.; captured a haul of rum. Good grog, but it inspired groggy gunnery when squadron encountered H.M. brig *Glasgow*. Lone Briton thrashed *Alfred* and *Cabot*, then escaped. With 20 dead, bad hangover, squadron limped into New London to face criticism and official censure. (lower right)

ROBERT Hopkins, Esqr.
Commodore of the AMERICAN Sea Forces

The intrepid Lt. Hall at Nassau

84. DISCIPLINE FOR AMERICAN NAVY. Written by John Adams for Continental Service, this little book was issued to Hopkins' squadron. Based on existing regulations in Royal Navy, Adams' "Regs" were strict. As Revolutionary New Englanders were strait-laced moralists, blasphemy in Navy drew heavier punishment than some offenses considered criminal today. But severity that may seem excessive today was tempered by democratic justice. If "Regs" bore down heavily on seamen, Continental officers were not spared. Congress demanded a show of naval leadership. Accordingly, Commander-in-Chief Hopkins was censured for not attacking foe at Norfolk—a side mission. Hopkins was also scolded for the Block Island fiasco. When the buck was passed to Abraham Whipple, that worthy requested court-martial, and got it—Navy's first. Whipple was exonerated, but Captain Hazard of sloop *Providence* was dismissed from Continental service. (left)

85. RED COATS EVACUATE BOSTON (Gen. Howe in action). British war moves throughout the Revolution were seldom clever or even sensible. Witness evacuation of Boston, carried out on March 17, 1776. True, Washington had scraped up some cannon and a pinch of powder. Early in March the Revolutionary Army advanced to Dorchester Heights overlooking city's waterfront. But the Redcoat Army and Fleet stood as giants occupying Lilliput. However, General Howe (succeeding Gage in top command) suddenly lost heart. Bag and baggage, he withdrew Redcoat forces and sailed for Halifax. And so New England's most important city was presented to Washington on a platter. Yankees held Boston for war's duration.

Brig Lexington

86. SEA BATTLE OF LEXINGTON (John Barry in action). Awarded captaincy of makeshift 16-gun brig *Lexington*, Barry sailed from Philadelphia looking for bear. On April 7, 1776, he came upon British 8-gun sloop *Edward* in lower Delaware. "She engaged us near two glasses (one hour).... We shattered her in a terrible manner as you will see." Marine Committee saw, and made Barry captain of frigate *Effingham*, then building at Philadelphia.

87. PHILADELPHIA BLOCKADE (Joshua Barney in action).

In May 1776, H.M. frigates *Roebuck* (44 guns) and *Liverpool* (28) sailed up the Delaware to block shipping to Revolutionary capital. When *Roebuck* blundered aground in mid-river, Lt. J. Barney of Continental Navy stepped in. Commandeering a Penn State row-galley, he dealt *Roebuck* a thumping cannonade. Next day the two Britishers meekly sailed away. Barney vs. *'Buck*. (above)

88. REDCOATS RIDDLED AT CHARLESTON (Fort Moultrie in action).

In June 1776 King's military experts decided to invade the American South. General Sir Henry Clinton's Redcoat Army was transported to Charleston, S.C., by fleet under Admiral Sir Peter Parker, R.N. Attacking on June 28, invaders struck a palmetto fort full of sharpshooters and Colonel Wm. Moultrie. By nightfall British were full of holes; Parker's flagship was junk; frigate *Actaeon* afire. End of Carolina invasion. (above)

89. BATTLE OF FORT MOULTRIE—"Sketches on spot by Lt. Henry Gray of 2nd (Moultrie's) Regt."

An eyewitness view of British naval assault on Moultrie and the consequences. The consequences being Redcoat defeat and subsequent retirement from Charleston arena. Lower picture shows H.M. frigate *Actaeon* briskly burning, and boat under Lt. Milligan triumphantly returning to fort with *Actaeon's* colors. Fed up with South, Sir Peter and Sir Henry limped north to New York. (above and below)

ergeant Jasper
escuing American
ag at Charleston

90. NEW YORK HARBOR, 1776— key to British grand strategy devised by Lord George Germain. Since Howe Bros. were clear of Boston, why not send 'em from Halifax to take New York Town? Then move 'em up the Hudson to Albany! Meantime, bring army down from Quebec. When two invasion forces meet—presto!— New England is cut off from American map. (But Germain's map did not show Washington marching from Boston to foil such a move. Nor did it show American warships convoying Yankee troops, New London to Long Island. Nor Paul Jones in sloop *Providence* carrying Army scouts of vanguard across Long Island Sound.)

Drive for
LOBSTERBACK

"BEHOLD THE CERBERUS,
the Atlantic plough!
Her precious cargo
Burgoyne, Clinton, Howe!
Bow, wow, wow!"

91. NAMED FOR THREE-HEADED DOG which guarded gates of Hades, H.M. frigate *Cerberus* inspired doggerel from British liberals who deplored chastisement of American Colonies. At Boston *Cerberus* was closely watched by Yankees (who kept eye on King's ships in manner shown in fine Lynd Ward illustration). Sent to guard New York back door in Long Island Sound, *Cerberus* needed three heads. Sloop *Providence* (Paul Jones) ran rings around bull-dog frigate, whose bark proved worse than her bite. Hence today, off New London—a buoy named "Cerberus."

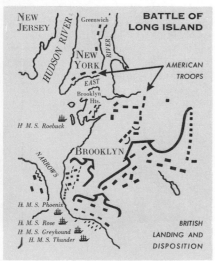

Plan of the Battle of Long Island

92. FORCED MARCH (Washington in action). On Long Island, Washington assembled what was probably the largest army he ever commanded—20,000 to 25,000. Contemptuous Tories called it a "rabble in arms." It was hindered more than helped by the 71 cannon delivered to Washington's camp by Hopkins' squadron. Few Yankees had know-how with heavy artillery, and the big guns proved white elephants. Had Howes been astute, they would have cornered Washington on disadvantageous Long Island. (at right)

New York

A M P H I B I A N ★ ★

93. NEW YORK CAMPAIGN (Howe Bros. in action). On June 30, 1776, Lord Howe and Sir William entered New York Bay with armada of 500 ships, 34,000 Redcoats. Washington glumly noted "the amazing advantage the enemy derives from command of the water." Then, New York virtually in grasp, the Howes dillydallied. Lord Howe anchored off Staten Island. Sir William studied Manhattan by telescope. While the Brothers stalled Washington dug in on Brooklyn Heights. Howes yawned.

94. BATTLE OF LONG ISLAND. Brooklyn Heights was poor position. For if Howes sailed up East River, Washington would be cut off on Long Island. However, Sir William finally landed invaders on Long Island below Brooklyn. After furious battle (August 27th) Washington got his troops over river to Manhattan, then retreated north to Harlem. (at left)

95. HESSIANS INVADE NEW JERSEY. November '76, Washington crossed Hudson to Jersey. After him went Cornwallis' Redcoats and German Hessians (shown climbing Hudson Palisades in sketch by British officer). Hesse Army was rented to George III for $550,000 a year, plus $55 for each man killed, $12 apiece for wounded. Washington saw that King paid bonus. At Trenton, N.J., Xmas night, Americans knocked Hessians for a row of andirons. (below)

96. ACTION AT SPUYTEN DUYVIL. Slow to follow up Brooklyn victory, Howes occupied New York in September '76. After riots, looting and fire ravaged the city, Redcoats drove northward. Washington retreated to White Plains, where he fought losing battle, then fell back into the Hudson Valley. British warships probed up Hudson to the old Dutch port of Spuyten Duyvil just a short

97. REDCOATS AT ANCHOR—"Original sketch by an English Officer on board Adm'l Howe's fleet." And picture of British strategy in winter of 1776-77. Despite Trenton setback, the Howes relaxed. Admiral Richard moored his 87 warships in New York Bay, whilst General Sir William dallied ashore with pretty mistress, Mrs. Loring. At ease, gentlemen, the war can wait. Type of strategy which evoked satirical verses in which "Loring" was rhymed with "snoring." Meantime, Revolution went on.

Residence of Gen. Howe
The Beekman Mansion

distance above the present site of George Washington Bridge. Spuyten Duyvil's guns spat so violently that Lord Howe's naval vanguard was stopped. But this British push up the Hudson River frightened Revolutionaries at Poughkeepsie into destroying unfinished American frigates *Congress* and *Montgomery*. It was a sorry setback for the Continental Navy. Two frigates sacrificed for nothing.

98. PRISON SHIP "OLD JERSEY"—spur to Paul Jones. In this wormy hulk moored in Wallabout Bay, Brooklyn, Yankee war-prisoners were packed like sardines in a poisonous can. Hundreds, many of them sailors, perished of madness and starvation. Prison camps of both sides were atrocious. But cruelty to captive seamen spurred Jones' raids on Nova Scotia and England. "Justly indignant at the barbarous treatment [they] suffered, I resolved to make the greatest efforts to succor them."

The Old Sugar House, Liberty Street,
N. Y., used as a prison by the British

Starring

FOR THE
CONTINENTAL Navy

99. WAR-SLOOP *PROVIDENCE* AT SEA (Paul Jones in action). After ferrying Washington's army to Long Island, Commander-in-Chief Hopkins led Continental Squadron to Providence, R.I., for repairs. In June 1776 *Andrew Doria*, under adept Nicholas Biddle, snared two transports laden with Royal Highlanders. *Columbus* and *Cabot* also made brave sorties. Then in August, Paul Jones with sloop *Providence* staged a lone-wolf raid off Nova Scotia. After a brush with H.M. frigate *Solebay* and long race to elude frigate *Milford*, Jones' sloop returned to Newport, R.I., in October with 16 valuable prizes! (above)

100. PAUL JONES' COMMISSION AS CAPTAIN (October 10, 1776). Belatedly promoted, Jones hoped for a frigate command. Meantime, eager to repeat Canadian foray, he proposed a daring raid to release American prisoners from Cape Breton coal mines. For expedition he was given leaky *Alfred* and new brig *Hampden*, latter under captaincy of Hoysted Hacker, a politician friend of Esek Hopkins. In bungle at outset, Hacker ran brig on reef at Newport. To Jones' dismay, Hopkins insisted Hacker go on with venture in sloop *Providence*. Swallowing indignation, Captain Jones once more set out. (at left)

In CONGRESS.

The DELEGATES of the UNITED STATES of New Hampshire, Massachusetts-Bay, Rhode Island, Connecticut, New York, New Jersey, Pennsylvania, Delaware, Maryland, Virginia, North-Carolina, South-Carolina, and Georgia, TO

John Paul Jones, Esquire,

WE, reposing especial Trust and Confidence in your Patriotism, Valour, Conduct, and Fidelity, DO, by these Presents, constitute and appoint you to be *Captain* ~~of the armed~~ ~~called the~~ ~~Navy~~ in the Service of the United States of North-America, fitted out for the Defence of American Liberty, and for repelling every hostile Invasion thereof. You are therefore carefully and diligently to discharge the Duty of *Captain* by doing and performing all manner of Things thereunto belonging. And we do strictly charge and require all Officers, Marines and Seamen under your Command, to be obedient to your Orders as *Captain* And you are to observe and follow such Orders and Directions from Time to Time as you shall receive from this or a future Congress of the United States, or Committee of Congress for that Purpose appointed, or Commander in Chief for the Time being of the Navy of the United States, or any other your superior Officer, according to the Rules and Discipline of War, the Usage of the Sea, and the Instructions herewith given you, in Pursuance of the Trust reposed in you. This Commission to continue in Force until revoked by this or a future Congress.

DATED at *Philadelphia October 10th 1776.*

By Order of the CONGRESS.
John Hancock PRESIDENT.

ATTEST *Cha Thomson secy*

101. *ALFRED* AND *PROVIDENCE* TRAP *MELLISH*. Soon after capture of big transport off Cape Breton, *Providence* (Capt. Hacker) fled home, leaving *Alfred* (Paul Jones) holding bag. Eluding old enemy *Milford*, Jones got *Alfred* and prizes to Boston by skin of his teeth. (above)

102. PROVIDENCE BLOCKADE. On Jan. 1, '77, H.M.S. *Diamond* ran aground off Warwick. Attacking with sloop *Providence*, Hopkins stranded himself on sand bar. *Diamond* escaped. "The Navy," Paul Jones wrote, "would be far better off without a head than with a bad one." (below)

103. NAVAL LEADER, 1777. Fighting figure (modern sculpting by Niehaus) could have been posed by Jones in Boston when he decided to visit Congress with complaints. En route, he penned constructive criticism that set leadership scale still standard measure in U. S. N. (right)

104. NAVY MAN WITH MIGHTY PEN. In wake of Breton exploit, Jones learned he was low on Navy's seniority list. Boiling, he sent hot letters to Congressmen protesting what seemed to him gross favoritism. Manly, awarded new frigate *Hancock*, Jones described as "despicable character." Saltonstall, also promoted, was "sleepy gentleman." Hopkins had "neither zeal nor talent." Declaring himself "citizen of the world" fighting for "rights of mankind," Jones said that he could yield seniority "only to persons of superior ability or merit."

106. ROBERT MORRIS—astute Marine Committeeman who took Jones' case to Congress. Dubbed "financier of the Revolution," this English-born Philadelphian appreciated value of competent leadership. Early in 1777, Hopkins was suspended; later he was dismissed from service. (Commander-in-Chief rank was never revived in Navy.) And Paul Jones was promised a frigate. (left)

Marine on poop-deck of Alfred

105. "I have sat on a Court Martial where the President of the court could not read the orders that appointed him, and a Captain of Marines had to make his mark in signing a report. As long as you have such characters for officers the Navy will never rise above contempt. . . . It is by no means enough that an officer should be a capable mariner. He should be as well a gentleman of liberal education, refined manners, punctilious courtesy, and the nicest sense of personal honor. When a commander has by tact, patience, justice, and firmness, each exercised in its proper turn, produced such an impression upon those under his orders in a ship, he has only to await the appearance of his enemy's topsails upon the horizon." J. P. J.

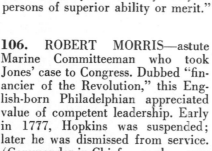

General Benedict Arnold

107. PIONEER DEFENDER OF LAKE CHAMPLAIN—schooner *Royal Savage*. After failure of Canada invasion in winter of 1775-76, General Benedict Arnold led shoestring army in escape south to Lake Champlain. At lakehead he found *Royal Savage*, captured from British by frontier captain, Jacobus Wynkoop. Commandeering this vessel, Arnold set up base at Crown Point near Ticonderoga. There he constructed a flotilla (three schooners, four galleys, eight gundalows); then sailed up lake to Valcour Island to meet British. Contemporary drawing shows *Savage* flying "Jack and Stripes"—perhaps earliest picture of this Revolutionary flag—defiant on Champlain.

Naval Battle in
CHAMPLAIN

108. BATTLE OF VALCOUR ISLAND (October 11, 1776). Containing 25 warcraft led by 18-gun sloop *Inflexible*, enemy flotilla under Capt. Thos. Pringle sloughed slam into Arnold's off Valcour. With toothpick for a club, Arnold waged tremendous fight to stop British on strategic lake. Odds were too long. As delineated by one of British officers, picture 111.

109. GEORGE III AS "MAN IN THE MOON"—from tract pub. London, 1776. Through lunar telescope King eyes mixed-up world—British army and fleet busy with America while England lies exposed to French fleet and Gallic cock crows lustily. With sea power diluted by transatlantic war, Britain had reason to fear pro-Yankee France. (at right)

Washington,
Lake Champlain
Galley, 1776

Left, view of the battle of
Lake Champlain in the year 1776

the Wilderness
C A M P A I G N

110. BATTLE FOR LAKE CHAMPLAIN—from watercolor painted on locale by British officer. As enemy flotilla closed in, Arnold's boats unleashed a fusillade that riddled schooner *Carleton*. The enemy "continued a very hot fire with round & grape Shot," Arnold reported. American flotilla "suffered much for want of Seamen & gunners." *Royal Savage* ran aground. Schooners *Congress* and *Washington* were lacerated. "The *New York* lost all her officers except her Captain. The *Philada.* was sunk." Arnold himself aimed gun on *Congress*. All-day slugging match cost Yankees dear: "killed & wounded ... about 60."

A VIEW OF THE NEW ENGLAND ARM'D VESSELS, IN VALCURE BAY ON LAKE CHAMPLAIN, 11 OCTOBER, 1776

1—Royal Savage—8 Six Pounders and 4 4 pounders—Burnt 11 Octr. 2—Revenge*—Eight Guns 4 & 3 pounders. 3—Enterprise*—10 4 poundrs. 4—Lee Cutter—One 12, One 9 & 4 4 prs—Taken 13 ctr. 5—Trumble*—One 18, One 12, two 9, & Six Six prs with Swivels &c. 6—Washington mounted same as Trumble taken 13 October. 7—Congress Armed as do—Burnt 15th Octr. 8—Philadelphia— 12. & 2. 9 prs Burnt 15 Octr. 9—New York♀ do Arm'd. 10—Jersey♀ do—taken 12 Octr. 11—Connecticut♀ Burnt 13 Octr. 12—Providence♀—Sunk 12 Octr in a Squall. 13—New Haven♀— urnt 13 Octr. 14—Spitfire♀ Burnt Do. 15—Boston♀ Sunk 11 Octr.

N B the Liberty Schooner & a Row Galley at Tyconderoga with those Mark'd * were taken or Destroy'd in 1777, those Mark'd ♀ Carried same Number & weight of Metal as the Philadelphia— e Above Vessels were Command'd by Benedict Arnold.

A VIEW OF HIS MAJESTY'S ARMED VESSELS ON LAKE CHAMPLAIN OCTOBER 11, 1776

1—Carleton—14 Six pounders (Lt. Dacres). 2—Inflexible—18 twelve pounders (Lt. Shank). 3—Maria—16 six pounders (Lt. Stark). 4—Convert—5 nine pounders (Lt. Longcroft). 5—Thundere -6 twenty-four pounders; 18 twelve pounders (Lt. Scott). 6—A Long Boats. 7—Gun Boats. 8—Valcure Island—

N B there were three Longboats with 2 two pounders on Sliders, 17 Gun boats, having one Gun—from Six to 24 pounders. Commander Captn Thos Pringle of the Royal Navy—Sir Guy Carleton wa n board the Maria in Both Actions.

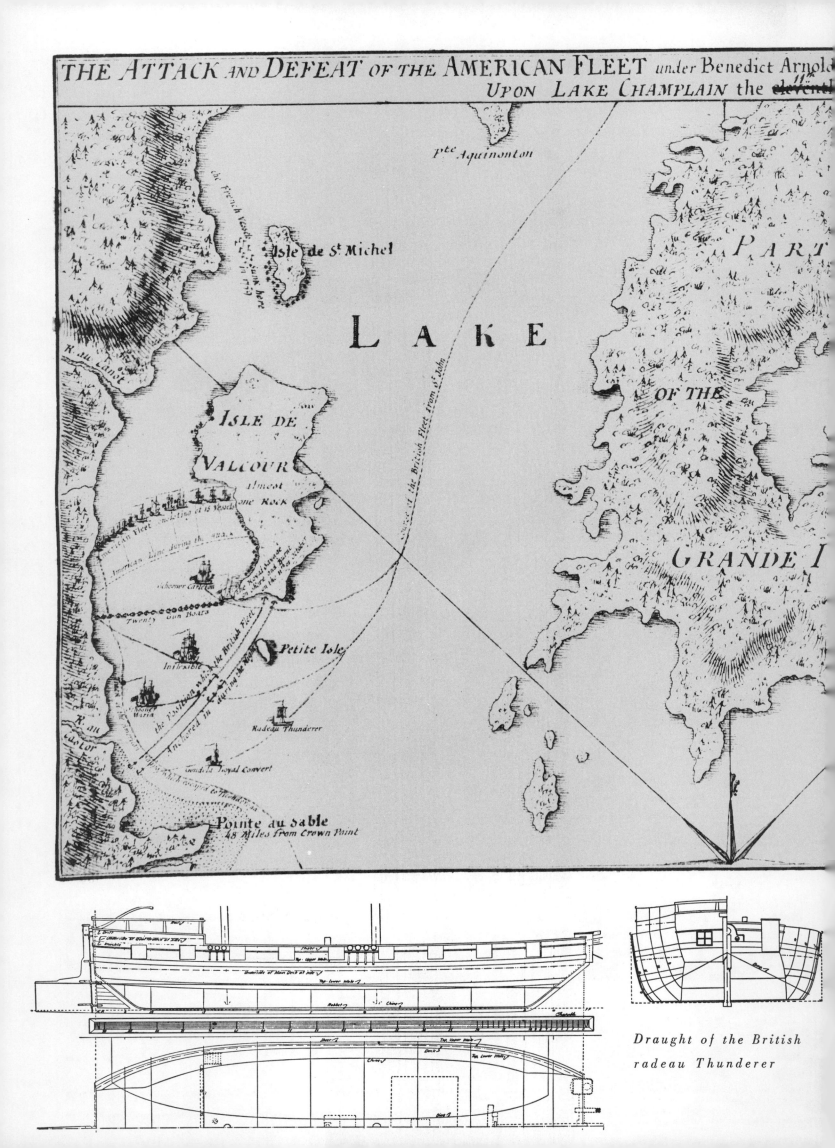

THE ATTACK AND DEFEAT OF THE AMERICAN FLEET under Benedict Arnold
UPON LAKE CHAMPLAIN the eleventh

pte Aquinonton

Isle de St Michel

LAKE

ISLE DE

VALCOUR almost one Rock

Schooner Carleton

Twenty Gun Boats

Inflexible

Petite Isle

Radeau Thunderer

Gondola Royal Convert

Pointe du Sable
48 Miles from Crown Point

PART

OF THE

GRANDE I

Draught of the British radeau Thunderer

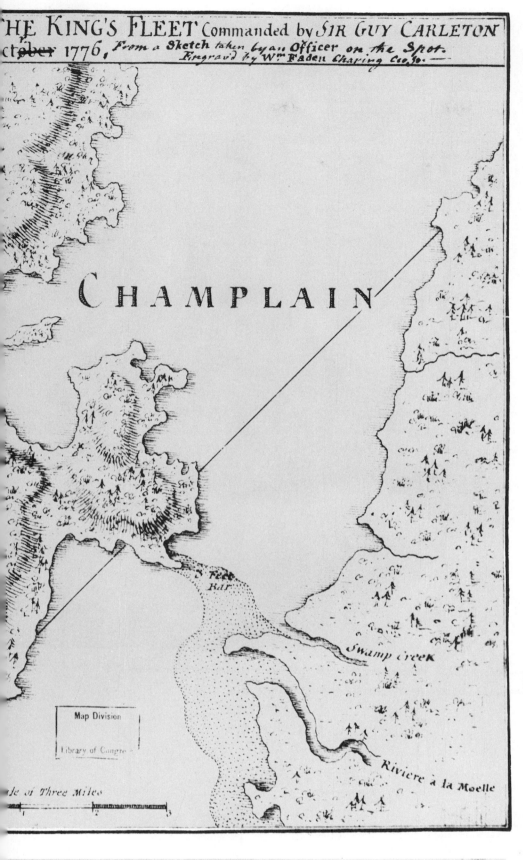

THE KING'S FLEET Commanded by SIR GUY CARLETON October 1776. *From a Sketch taken by an Officer on the Spot. Engraved by W. Faden Charing Cross.*

CHAMPLAIN

3 Feet Bar

Swamp Creek

Riviere à la Moelle

Map Division
Library of Congress

Scale of Three Miles

111. CHART: BATTLE OF VALCOUR BAY. Arnold was up against something when his motley frontier sailors faced sophisticates who could draw like this. And the enemy ships were as good as their charts. But Commodore Pringle's meticulous training proved his undoing. Unwilling to move until last knot was inspected, he delayed up Richelieu River until October, giving Arnold time to reach Valcour Is. below Plattsburg and take defensive position shown. Sir Guy Carleton's army and accompanying naval invasion forces now had autumn to beat as well as Arnold. Arnold lost on lake, but gave autumn time to muster winter against invaders.

Plan of the gundalow Philadelphia as taken off the relic raised from Lake Champlain in 1935, showing probable appearance in Arnold's action.

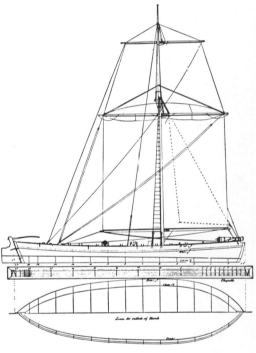

112. CHAMPLAIN CLIMAX—defeat that spelled victory. With five craft lost, Arnold's force dodged away during night; raced south down lake. Overtaken near Crown Point, Arnold made last stand, then scuttled boats, escaped ashore with survivors. However, damaged British flotilla had to put back to Canada for repairs. Northern New York invasion was thus postponed, giving Americans chance to stiffen Adirondack front. Champlain battle was called "strife of pygmies for prize of a continent." But Arnold's pygmies fought like giants. Prize was ultimately won by American sharpshooters at Saratoga.

113. CARON DE BEAUMARCHAIS—friend of the Revolution. Paris boudoir musician, poet and satirist, author of *Barber of Seville*, secret agent who recovered for King Louis the lively diary of Marie Antoinette, this extraordinary individual met American spy Arthur Lee in London. Devoted to Liberty, Beaumarchais promptly volunteered to give his aid to the Revolutionaries. He privately organized fake French-Spanish export firm which shipped million-dollar cargo (munitions and guns) to Dutch West Indies for eventual transhipment from St. Eustatius to Philadelphia.

Guns via
CONTINENTAL
Navy

114. LOGISTICS LIFELINE, 1777. From island of St. Eustatius in West Indies to Philadelphia, Pa., flowed life-blood of American war effort in third year of Revolution. Shipped by "Hortalez et Cie," (Beaumarchais in Paris), guns and war gear went from Europe to West Indies as "civilian goods." From Caribbean the "goods" were carried north by American Navy. Among vessels assigned to this hazardous haul were sloops *Reprisal, Hornet, Independence* and *Sachem*, schooner *Wasp*, and brigs *Lexington* and *Andrew Doria*. Running gantlet of British warships all the way from Delaware to West Indies and back, these spunky little naval vessels brought home hundreds of tons of war supplies, courtesy "Hortalez et Cie." (right, U.S. privateer)

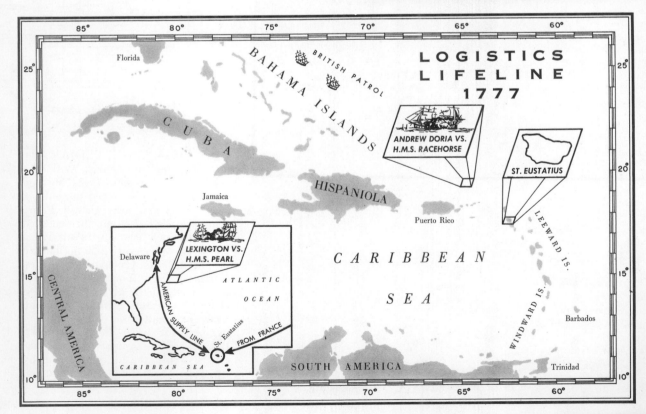

LOGISTICS LIFELINE 1777

ANDREW DORIA VS. H.M.S. RACEHORSE

LEXINGTON VS. H.M.S. PEARL

ST. EUSTATIUS

Privatee

Wasp

115. *LEXINGTON* CAPTURED BY H.M. FRIGATE *PEARLE*. Given horse sense, British would have stationed squadron off St. Eustatius instead of trying to patrol entire Gulf Stream. Even so they made West Indies run perilous. Among first ships on haul, brig *Lexington* (Captain Wm. Hallock) was caught off Delaware in December '76, homeward bound with munitions. Facing big frigate, little brig surrendered. When British prize crew came aboard, however, some amiable (and shrewd) Yankee announced that the little ship carried rum as well as guns. *Pearle's* people promptly got slugged with toddy—then with belaying pins. With captors made captive, *Lexington* men recaptured brig and sailed her safely into Baltimore! Records fail to detail H.M. Admiralty's comments on *Pearle*.

116. *ANDREW DORIA* CAPTURES *RACEHORSE*. From Providence to West Indies sailed veteran *Doria* (Captain Isaiah Robinson) in spring of 1777. After loading munitions cargo, she headed home at best speed. Which was too fast for H.M. war-sloop *Racehorse* (12 guns) encountered off Puerto Rico. In two-hour running battle, the *Horse* was badly beaten. *Doria* led her to Philadelphia where she was taken into Continental stable. Thanks to Continental Navy and Beaumarchais (who devoted his entire fortune to the effort), Americans were equipped with the weapons that won Battle of Saratoga. (at right)

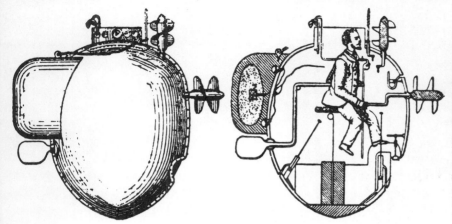

117. *MARINE TURTLE* (or *Maine Torpedo*)—amazing Revolutionary invention. Undersea boats went back to Jonah. But it remained for David Bushnell, genius of Saybrook, Conn., to create world's first combat submarine. "The famous Water Machine from Connecticutt is every Day expected in Camp," Samuel Osgood wrote from Roxbury to John Adams. "I wish it might succeed and [enemy] ships be blown up." After work at Yale in 1774, Bushnell built one-man sub driven by hand-cranked "water screws." Clam-shaped hull was oak coated with tar. Water ballast was let in for submergence; vessel surfaced when ballast was pumped out. *Turtle* had 30-minutes air supply.

R E V O L U T I O N A R Y
Submarine

118. WORLD'S FIRST SUBMARINE ATTACK—*Turtle* in action. New York Harbor. September night in '76. British had not yet seized Manhattan when Bushnell arrived with Water Machine to attack enemy fleet. Gen. Putnam's staff watching, *Turtle* set out from the Battery. Volunteer operator: Sgt. Ezra Lee of Lyme,

Conn., who drove sub down bay "by vigorous cranking." Reaching Howe's flagship *Eagle*, Lee tried to attach bomb to frigate's hull. He was unsuccessful, however; ship's copper bottom foiled his attempt. Enemy guards chased sub. But *Turtle* escaped. And bomb later exploded, scaring *Eagle* and her squadron galley-west. (below)

119. TORPEDO STRIKE!—Bushnell scores. Bereft of *Turtle* but not of ideas, Bushnell devised "water bomb" to be drifted against frigate *Cerberus* blockading New London in '77. Guard schooner spied bomb, hauled it in—fatal catch! Bomb blew up schooner, sent *Cerberus* running seaward in panic, tail in legs. (above)

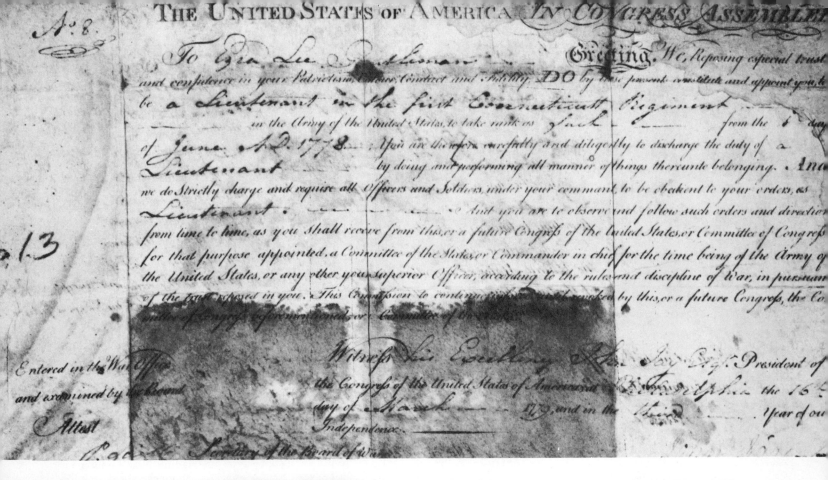

120. CONTINENTAL COMMISSION AWARDED EZRA LEE, the world's first combat submariner. Note Army promotion for exploit that was ignored by Navy. After her epic attack on *Eagle*, *Turtle* made other tries. She was finally sunk when shore guns demolished the tender carrying her up Hudson River.

COMMERCE RAIDERS

121. HANDWRITING ON BRITAIN'S WALL—battle report from Lambert Wickes. Crack skipper assigned to take Benj. Franklin to France. Wickes ran for Europe with 16-gun sloop *Reprisal* in autumn of '76. After landing America's No. 1 diplomat, he took *Reprisal* on first American raid in English waters (January 1777); snared five ships. Britons denounced French for aiding "pirate." French rebuked Franklin—with a wink.

L'Orient February 28, 1777

Gentlemen,

I wrote at my departure from Nantz which I hope came safe to hand & now imbrace this opportunity of informing you of the success of my last cruze. We captured five sail, none of which will be very valueable. I brought them all safe in here. One of them Swailon Packet from Falmouth bound to Lisbon in ballast engaged 45 minutes before she struck. We had one man kill'd & my first Lieut. had his left arm blow'd off by our own gunny. Lieut. of Marines was slightly wounded in the wrist, but they are both in a fair way to recover. The coming into any French ports with prizes is attended with so many difficulties that I have wrote to Doctor Franklin desiring him to send me home & am in hopes he will do so as soon as possible. Soon after my arrival I received an order from the Judge of the Admiralty Court to depart in twenty four hours with all my prizes. I however found means to evade those orders and got soon the matter settled with the Judge. In eight days after I received an order from the Intendant of this port to depart in 24 hours with all my prizes and not to presume to enter into any other French port under pain of being seized he further inform'd me, if I offered to cruize on this coast, that a French frigate would be dispatch'd to take me. If those threats were all to be put in execution, my situation would be truely deplorable as I am informed there is now several Brittish ships of warr cruizing for me. Those orders from the French Ministry I look on as fenness and only given to save appearances and gain time, as they are not yet quite ready for a warr, but I think it will certainly take place in May or June. It was with much difficulty I could evade the last positive order from the Ministry given me by the Intendant. I then beged leave to heave the ship down as she was very leaky. He told me it was not in his power to grant me liberty. I then told him the prizes were all dispatch'd & if he chose to send the reprisal out he must put hand on board, as me & my officers and men were determined not to proceed in her, in the present condition & desired him to send carpenters and caulkers on board to survey her. This he consented to. When they return'd they told him they thought it highly necessary to heave her down. He then told me he could not grant me liberty unless those officers would sign a certificate that they thought the ship would be in imminent danger if sent out without repairing. This they could not do as they had not been on board long enough to know how much water she made in a hour. They came on board the next day on a second survey, when they remained 4 hours on board, and on their return signed a satisfactory certificate. The Intendant then granted me liberty to come into port and heave down as our prizes is all gone. I am in hopes my troubles are nearly at an end. I sold the packett for 16,000 Livers clear of all losses, reclaimations or other demands after striping her of every thing that was valuable. I shall refer you to Thomas Morris, Esq. for the particulars concerning the other prizes as he transacted that business personally. I rec'd a letter this day from the Honbles. Doctor Franklin & Silas Dean informing me of those orders by the Ministry at Paris but think they are only to stop the clamour of the Brittish Ambasadore & says they hope I shall be able to stay longer than the time limmitted. When I first arrived I wrote to your Honble. Commissioners at Paris informing them of the number of prisoners taken & as there had lately been two American private ships of warr taken I thought it a good opportunity to negotiate an exchange of prisoners. In their answer they say they will imeadiately apply to Lord Stormant for an exchange but did not think it could be done without orders from the Brittish Court. I was permitted to keep them on board 7 days after my arrival & then obliged to discharge them & take the Intendants certificate for their discharge, from Gentlemen

Your most obedt. humble servt.
Lambt Wickes

P.S. Inclosed you have an exact list
of the prizes & cargoes

Facsimile of Lambert Wicke's letter

122. *REPRISAL* DODGES H.M.S. *BURFORD*. Accompanied by brig *Lexington* (Captain Henry Johnson) and cutter *Dolphin*, *Reprisal* raided Irish Sea in Spring of '77. Eighteen ships were snatched right out of British Lion's den. Returning to France, *Reprisal* was chased by 74-gun *Burford*; foxy Wickes made hairbreadth escape. An English journal roared: "The coasts of England have been insulted by the Yankees!" (at left)

123. LOSS OF *LEXINGTON*—first American warship captured overseas. While *Reprisal* was repaired at St.-Malo, *Lexington* staged lone-wolf raid in Channel. On September 17, 1777, she fell in with H.M.S. *Alert*—a little 10-gun cutter that looked easy. But *Alert's* shooting was deadly. After two-hour duel *Lexington* ran out of ammunition. Guns empty, Captain Johnson could only run. Overhauled, he had to surrender. (below)

AUGUSTATUS KUNINGAM

124. GUSTAVUS CONYNGHAM— sea raider who lived a saga. Sailing to France on supply ship *Charming Betty* in spring of '77, this Philadelphia sea dog was given naval commission and 10-gun raider *Suprise*. All he needed to begin a career which won him fame in Paris as "*Le Terreur des Anglais*." (Portrait at left)

125. END OF *REPRISAL*. In September '77 Wickes sailed boldly around Ireland, snatching prizes galore. Then headed home for America. Foes were eluded, but North Atlantic storm was not. Off Grand Banks, late autumn, valiant *Reprisal* foundered in wild seas. Only the cook survived to tell tale of raider's end. (at right)

126. TAKEN BY *SURPRISE*—British mail boat falls to Conyngham's lugger. Contemporary Dutch print illustrates Conyngham's first raid in English Channel. As though daring to intercept King's packet were not enough, Conyngham landed on Isle of Guernsey where he "had the impudence . . . to carry off the Lieutenant with the Garrison Adjutant, who were shooting rabbits for their diversion." So London press howled as Conyngham sailed to Dunkirk with prizes. Imprisoned in Dunkirk at demand of British Crown, he was allowed to escape; equipped by friends with speedy 14-gun cutter *Revenge*. (at right)

128. SABOTAGE IN ENGLAND—saboteur James Hill, hired by Silas Deane, fires Navy Yard, Portsmouth. Newgate report: "During a residence in America, Hill imbibed destructive principles." Captured, he was tried before Lord Sandwich (March 1777) and hanged "in sight of the ruins he occasioned." An old woodcut. (above)

127. *REVENGE* IN THE ENGLISH CHANNEL (Conyngham in action). "She is the fastest sailer known," a British spy reported, "and I do fear she will be a sore trouble." She was. In European waters she seized 60 British vessels. Early in '79 Conyngham returned to America, champion lone-wolf commerce raider. (above)

129. "CAP'N CUNINGHAM" IN BRITISH EYES. In April '79, *Revenge*, off America, was caught by H.M. frigate *Galatea*. Conyngham was shipped in chains to England. There, with 50 companions, he tunneled out of Old Mill Prison. British portrait doubtless reflected Admiralty's eyes, not Conyngham's. (right)

CAP.ᴺ CUNINGHAM.

130. AMERICAN FRIGATE *HANCOCK*—one of the best, and destined to be worsted. Masterpiece by Jonathan Greenleaf and Cross Brothers of Newburyport, Mass., *Hancock* was perhaps finest early-American frigate—a 750-ton 32-gunner, about 136½ feet long, with 35½-foot beam, 11-foot depth of hold. Among first of new Revolutionary warships on ocean, she sailed from Boston with light frigate *Boston* in May 1777; headed north to raid off Nova Scotia. Unfortunately, raid would demonstrate, once again, that ships are no better than their crews, crews seldom better than their captains. (Painting by noted marine artist G. C. Wales.)

DESIGN FOR Defeat

131. *HANCOCK* AND *BOSTON* TRAP H.M.S. *FOX*. After dodging H.M. ship-of-line *Somerset*, speedy American frigates reached Nova Scotian waters late in May. An unhappy team. For arrogant Captain John Manly of *Hancock*, commanding as senior officer, had been bickering from outset with *Boston's* Captain Hector McNeill. On morning of June 7th quarrelsome pair were lucky enough to bag frigate

Fox, a brand new 28-gunner which came frisking over the horizon. But an acrid wrangle ensued over disposition of prize. And when McNeill, fearing British search patrols, wanted to head southward into safer waters, officious Manly insisted on cruise northward to Halifax. He "pulled rank" and they sailed to Halifax—smack into arms of enemy squadron led by expert Sir George Collier. Fatal encounter. (below)

132. *HANCOCK* AND *BOSTON* VS. *RAINBOW* AND *FLORA*. Surprised by Sir Geo. Collier's squadron off Halifax (July 6, 1777) Yankee ships became separated in battle. H.M. frigate *Flora* recaptured *Fox*. H.M. frigate *Rainbow* and brig *Victor* boxed *Hancock*. *Boston* discreetly escaped. (above)

133. LOSS OF AMERICAN FRIGATE *HANCOCK*. With foremast amputated, deck afire, *Hancock* surrendered to *Rainbow*. Mc-Neill of *Boston* was court-martialed for quitting fray; Manly censured for losing *Hancock*. (Renamed *Iris*, she served in Royal Navy's fleet for war's duration.) (below)

Philadelphia
NAVY IN TIGHT

134. SURPRISE DRIVE ON REVOLUTIONARY CAPITAL was launched by Howes in summer of '77. Sailing from New York, British forces were soon driving up Delaware River. Where (as shown on historic chart) invasion fleet was halted by river obstructions and batteries of Fort Mifflin. (above)

135. BATTLE IN DELAWARE RIVER (October 22, 1777). Trying to pass Fort Mifflin, H.M. ship-of-line *Augusta*, frigates *Roebuck* and *Liverpool*, sloops *Pearl*, *Merlin* and *Vigilant* were shot up by Fort and Penn State row-galleys. (Battle scene done on locale by Lt. W. Elliot, R.N.) (Picture below)

136. LOSS OF AMERICAN FRIGATE *DELAWARE*. Just completed in yard above Philadelphia, light frigate *Delaware* was trapped by invasion. On Sept. 7, 1777, Captain Charles Alexander tried to run her downstream. Instead, she ran aground off city waterfront; and Redcoats had her. (right)

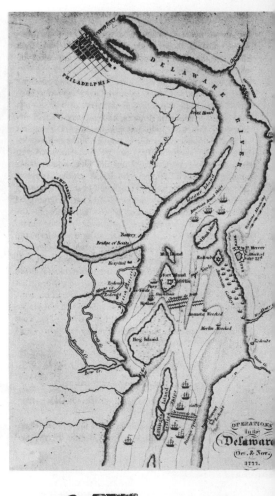

137. BATTLE IN DELAWARE RIVER —a German view. Action is incorrectly dated; fancy fort pure fiction. But hot scrimmage is no misconception. In action big flagship *Augusta* caught fire and blew up. Sloop *Merlin*, forced aground, was set ablaze. Lord Howe was finding Quaker City tough. (Listening to war report, Indians wear expressions which seem to say, "Civilization! We won't stay here!")

138. LOSS OF AMERICAN WARSHIP *ANDREW DORIA*. Trapped upstream near Philadelphia were naval vessels *Doria, Surprise, Repulse, Champion, Fly* and *Racehorse*. When Ft. Mifflin finally fell, all were burned to prevent capture. Also scuttled were incompleted American frigates *Washington* and *Effingham*. End of a Continental Navy squadron. (at left)

Campaign
CORNER

139. "BATTLE OF THE KEGS"—Bushnell's last try. Idea: float a batch of hairtriggered powder kegs down Delaware River to blast enemy ships. World's first mines! Late autumn of '77, this ingenious idea was tried. Kegs failed (sluggish current; faulty triggers; bad luck). So Bushnell himself was blasted; ridiculed so venomously he quit American camp and crept into retirement. Sample of ridicule:

'Twas early day as poets say,
Just as the sun was rising,
A soldier stood on a log of wood
And saw a sight surprising.

As in amaze he stood to gaze,
The truth can't be denied, sir,
He spied a score of kegs or more,
Come floating down the tide, sir.

Now up and down throughout the town
Most frantic scenes were acted,
And some ran here and some ran there
Like men almost distracted.

"Therefore prepare for bloody war
These kegs must all be routed,
Or surely we despised shall be,
And British courage doubted!"

The cannon roar from shore to shore,
The small arms loud do rattle,
Since time began, I'm sure no man,
E'er saw so strange a battle.

140. HOWES SLEEP IN PHILLY— British jibe at war situation, winter of 1777-78. While Bros. snooze, flagship *Eagle* rots on riverbank and Yankee steals horn from symbolic cow of commerce milked by Dutch, French and Spanish allies. Howes were much berated for Philadelphia move which left Gen. Burgoyne (who'd expected them up Hudson) out on fatal Adirondacks limb. Defeat of his army at Saratoga kept Americans in the war.

GREAT
ENCOURAGEMENT
FOR
SEAMEN.

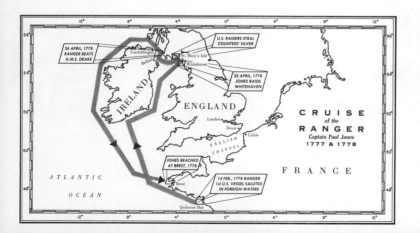

ALL GENTLEMEN SEAMEN and able-bodied LANDSMEN who have a Mind to diftinguifh themfelves in the GLORIOUS CAUSE of their COUNTRY, and make their Fortunes, an Opportunity now offers on board the Ship RANGER, of Twenty Guns, (for FRANCE) now laying in PORTSMOUTH, in the State of NEW-HAMPSHIRE, commanded by JOHN PAUL JONES Efq; let them repair to the Ship's Rendezvous in PORTSMOUTH, or at the Sign of Commodore MANLEY, in SALEM, where they will be kindly entertained, and receive the greateft Encouragement.---The Ship RANGER, in the Opinion of every Perfon who has feen her is looked upon to be one of the beft Cruizers in AMERICA.---She will be always able to Fight her Guns under a moft excellent Cover; and no Veffel yet built was ever calculated for failing fafter, and making good Weather.

Any GENTLEMEN VOLUNTEERS who have a Mind to take an agreable Voyage in this pleafant Seafon of the Year, may, by entering on board the above Ship RANGER, meet with every Civility they can poffibly expect, and for a further Encouragement depend on the firft Opportunity being embraced to reward each one agreable to his Merit.

All reafonable Travelling Expences will be allowed, and the Advance-Money be paid on their Appearance on Board.

IN CONGRESS, MARCH 29, 1777.

RESOLVED,

THAT the MARINE COMMITTEE be authorifed to advance to every able Seaman, that enters into the CONTINENTAL SERVICE, any Sum not exceeding FORTY DOLLARS, and to every ordinary Seaman or Landfman, any Sum not exceeding TWENTY DOLLARS, to be deducted from their future Prize-Money.

By Order of CONGRESS,

JOHN-HANCOCK, PRESIDENT.

DANVERS: Printed by E. RUSSELL, at the Houfe late the Bell-Tavern.

141. EARLIEST AMERICAN NAVAL RECRUITING POSTER—volunteers wanted for Revolutionary war-sloop *Ranger* readying to sail from Portsmouth, N.H., under Captain John Paul Jones. Replacing ship's original captain (one John Roach, who had been found "a person of doubtful character"), Jones raced to Portsmouth to take command of the new 18-gun sloop in the spring of 1777. Sailors were extremely scarce, but Jones soon signed 100 hands. Perhaps persuasive poster helped.

142. STARS AND STRIPES FOR *RANGER*. On June 14, 1777, Congress adopted American flag which legend associates with Betsy Ross. Legend adds that ladies of Portsmouth, lacking bunting, presented Paul Jones with a flag "quilted from cloth ravished from their virgin petticoats." More authentic are quotes from Jones on raising new flag over *Ranger*. "That flag and I are twins born in the same hour. . . . So long as we can float, we shall float together." Sailing for France on November 1, '77, *Ranger* was first warship to fly the Stars and Stripes.

CRUISE OF THE
Ranger

143. FIRST SALUTE TO AMERICAN FLAG BY FOREIGN POWER. Racing to France with *Ranger*, Jones carried word of Saratoga—ace news for Franklin's diplomatic hand in Paris. Entering Quiberon Bay, February 14, 1778, Jones found French fleet in roadstead. As *Ranger* sailed in at sunset, colors flying, French let go with "nine guns"—official recognition of American Republic. Britain handed France an ultimatum for this gesture. French smiled, *"C'est la guerre."* And America gained life-saving ally in war, while Britain now faced the threat of Channel invasion.

144. *RANGER* ATTACKS WHITEHAVEN. Determined to raid Britain, Jones sailed *Ranger* straight to England in April 1778; led landing party in assault on Whitehaven, night of 22nd. Fort guns were spiked, wharves burnt, Admiralty left in tumult, England in uproar. (at right)

145. AFFAIR OF COUNTESS'S SILVER. Top speed, Jones raided St. Mary's Isle, bent on seizing Earl of Selkirk for prisoner exchange. Finding Earl absent, Jones' sailors seized Lady Selkirk's silver plate. Although Jones returned loot, British leaders yelled "piracy." (at left)

146. "POINT YOUR GUNS!"—U.S.S. *RANGER* vs. H.M.S. *DRAKE*. After St. Mary's raid, Jones boldly approached Belfast, Ireland. Morning of April 24, 1777, *Ranger* was off Carrickfergus Harbor, brazen as brass. Jones was planning raid on port when he sighted bigger game—H. M. war-sloop *Drake* coming out of harbor. Evidently alerted by news from Whitehaven, the British warship sent out a smallboat to investigate *Ranger*. Jones seized the visiting officer; prepared for showdown. Then: "Alarm smokes appeared on both sides of the channel." As enemy came on, *Ranger's* crew went surly, a drunken quartermaster defied orders, Jones found himself confronted by insubordinate officers who wanted no part of battle with *Drake*. Later he reported "open mutiny." "I ran every chance of being killed or thrown overboard." Somehow Jones quelled his temper and his crew's; drove the men to battle stations. As *Ranger* waited on flat sea, *Drake* worked out slowly, bucking adverse afternoon tide. "This obliged me to run down several times," Jones logged the maneuvers, ". . . and to lay with courses up and main topsail to the mast." At length *Drake* weathered the point and

came within hailing distance. "*Drake* hoisted English colors, *Ranger* the American stars. The enemy hailed demanding what ship it was. I directed the master to answer, 'The American Continental ship *Ranger*; that we waited for them and desired that they would come over; the sun was now a little more than an hour from setting, and it was therefore time to begin.' The *Drake* being astern of *Ranger*, I ordered the helm up and gave her the first broadside. *Ranger* ran across the bows of *Drake*." As portrayed in splendid illustration, *Ranger* crosses *Drake's* bow. She is cleared for action with hammocks stowed in hammock rails; the hatches covered "to prevent anyone from deserting his post by escaping into lower compartments"; the Marines drawn up on foc's'le, quarterdeck (shown) and poop. Working with "crows and handspikes," *Ranger's* gunners are pointing her starboard 6-pounders at target. In foreground (right) powder monkeys kneel on deck, waiting to pass cartridges. Master at arms shouts orders through speaking trumpet while Captain John Paul Jones (at shrouds) awaits moment to open fire. This is zero hour. "Time to begin."

147. *RANGER* TAKES H.M.S. *DRAKE*. Twenty guns to oppose *Ranger's* 18, *Drake* was the bigger warship, carried twice as many men as *Ranger*. But in hour's battle, described by Jones as "warm and obstinate," *Ranger* shot *Drake* to rubbish. At climax *Drake's* Captain George Burdon was killed by musket ball. With "sails and rigging entirely cut to pieces ... hull very much galled" *Drake* surrendered—a dead duck. First major British warship taken captive by Americans, *Drake* was placed under *Ranger's* First Lieutenant, Thomas Simpson, who almost lost her through insubordinate move to sail

her across Channel on own hook. Jones finally reached Brest with prize to find himself toast of France—and beached by American Commissioners! British charges of "piracy" stuck. According to quaint naval laws of day, a warship might legitimately bombard some town and kill grannies and children, but never loot a Countess! Jones paid his men out of pocket for Selkirk silver, and had it returned. But diplomatic tangle continued, nevertheless; so did the row with slippery Lieutenant Simpson. These were brabbles which beclouded a great exploit—the snatch of a British warship from the majestic Lion's mouth.

148. FIGUREHEAD OF H.M. WARSHIP *DRAKE*. Superb specimen of Georgian wood carving, this likeness of Sir Francis Drake may have adorned the man-of-war captured by Paul Jones. Unfortunately origin of figurehead (now on display at Mystic Seaport, Marine Museum, Mystic, Conn.) remains undetermined. There were several *Drakes* in early Royal

Navy, but the fame of the vessel vanquished by *Ranger* suggests that its illustrious head was thus preserved. Captive *Drake* was laid up at Brest. Eventually Lt. Simpson (through political wire-pulling) gained command of *Ranger*. And John Paul Jones, certainly the greatest sea warrior of Revolution, found himself beached in France, no ship for almost a year.

Chapter II

THE REVOLUTION
(Continued)

149. REVOLUTION IN THE RED —cash "not worth a Continental." When issued in New York early in '76 this bill passed for about 25¢. By Jan. '78 it was so worthless its signer, patroon banker Roosevelt, became Tory. Yankee commerce ruined, war effort was going bankrupt. However, American Navy helped to keep patriot fires burning. Example: Conyngham's prizes financed American diplomatic service abroad for two years. Transport *Mellish* (captured by Paul Jones) literally provided Continental Army with uniforms. And during fateful winter of Valley Forge, John Rathburne with sloop *Providence* (and guts) won jackpot for Revolutionists.

150. FISHERMAN CATCHES ISLAND (John Peck Rathburne in action). "All the English need have done," Alexander Hamilton recalled, "was blockade our ports with 25 frigates and 10 ships of the line. Thank God they did nothing of the sort." While H.M. admirals hibernated at New York, Newport and Philadelphia, Captain Rathburne (ex-New Bedford fisherman) took sloop *Providence* down Gulf Stream to raid convoys. Winter convoys being scarce, he de-

cided to raid Bahamas. Rigging sloppy, guns masked, old *Providence* sailed in as tramp; caught island of New Providence by surprise. With lone sloop Rathburne accomplished more than Esek Hopkins with a squadron. Bagged were local fort, seven ships and 16-gun privateer.

151. YANKEES STEAL A BASE (January 1778). *Providence* caught Fort Nassau napping. Sailing for Charleston two days later, raiders carried off 1600 bbls. of powder, five captive vessels, tons of supplies and 30 released prisoners. A bonanza for Revolutionary treasury! But Rathburne, for amazing exploit, was paid off in paper "not worth a Continental." Staunchly he remained in uniform. His crew preferred privateering.

REVOLUTIONARY
Privateers

152. *OLIVER CROMWELL* VS. H.M.S. *BEAVER*. Big money-winners of Revolution were civilian-owned privateers. Example: Capt. Timothy Boardman's *Cromwell*. Bane of British

shipping, she even captured H.M. 20-gun sloop *Adm. Keppel*. In August '77, she was snared by *Beaver* (action pictured). For nailing Connecticut raider, *Beaver's* Captain James Jones

was given command of H.M. frigate *Penelope*—token of King's respect for Yankee privateers. (In 1782 *Penelope* vanished without trace in West Indies. A victim of some free-lance raider?)

153. PRIVATEER *ST. JAMES* IN ACTION. In 1776 some 143 Yankee privateers went to sea. Royal Navy halved the number by '77. But raiders made smashing comeback with tougher vessels. For instance, privateer *Pilgrim* (Capt. Johnathan Hara-den), captor of Quebec fur cargo worth $90,000. And 20-gunner *St. James*, another bonanza-winner, shown beating off a frigate in mid-Atlantic. Mark the name of *St. James* skipper —Captain Thomas Truxtun. Privateering also was Stephen Decatur, Sr.

154. PRIVATEER *THORN* IN ACTION. Conqueror of H.M. sloops *Gov. Tyron*, *Erskin* and *Sparlin*, 16-gun *Thorn* was poison to Royal Navy. Yankee privateers bagged 16 warships, 2,980 cargomen during Revolution. Net prize haul: $50,000,000.

THE SEASON OF Disaster

155. BEAT TO QUARTERS!—death rattle of Continental warship *Alfred*. To Europe in fall of '77 went Navy's No. 1 flagship accompanied by new frigate *Raleigh*—a sorry team. *Alfred's* Captain Elisha Hinman was a fighter. *Raleigh's* Captain Thomas Thompson (senior officer) was not. So they missed chance to bag big West India convoy in Atlantic. En route home from France (March '78) they encountered H.M. sloops *Ariadne* and *Ceres* off African coast. Thompson fled with *Raleigh* leaving *Alfred* battling to her doom.

156. AMERICAN FRIGATE *RANDOLPH*—warship ill-starred. As new frigates were considered political plums by Congressmen, captaincies usually went to wire-pullers. Typical was award of *Raleigh* to Thomas Thompson, an ex-slave shipper who impressed Paul Jones as "more fit to be a ship's carpenter than a captain." Thompson's subsequent court-martial (for leaving *Alfred* in lurch) failed to save Navy's No. 1 flagship—first major loss of 1778. Second major loss—*Randolph*—was even harder blow. Earliest of new American-made frigates to sea, this 32-gunner from Philadelphia yard of Wharton and Humphreys had stellar skipper in Nicholas Biddle—one of few good Congressional appointments. But a jinx sat on ship. On maiden voyage in spring of '77 she snapped a mast off Hatteras. When British Tars in crew staged mutiny, Biddle put it down with fairness that won him cheers from all hands; got lame ship into port. That autumn she crossed Atlantic only to be ordered home by nervous diplomats—futile mission. Then from Charleston she set out on West Indies cruise—which was fated to be her last.

157. LOSS OF AMERICAN FRIGATE *RANDOLPH*. Accompanied by four vessels of South Carolina State Navy (18-gun ship *General Moultrie* and war-brigs *Notre Dame, Polly* and *Fair American*), *Randolph* sailed for West Indies in February 1778. They caught one prize among the islands; then disaster struck. Off Barbados, morning of March 17th, a ship of-the-line loomed suddenly out of mist. H.M.S. *Yarmouth* (64 guns) was on top of *Randolph* before Biddle could maneuver his surprised squadron. In ensuing melee, *General Moultrie* fired into *Randolph* by mistake; *Yarmouth* dealt her another devastating broadside. Wounded, Biddle valiantly directed battle from a chair. As reported by a Carolina captain, the *Randolph* treated the *Yarmouth* "so roughly that the British ship lost her bowsprit and topmasts, being otherwise greatly shattered." Then a shot struck *Randolph's* magazine. With one volcanic blast the American frigate, Biddle and crew were gone. A sole survivor was picked up. Battle ended with ship's loss.

158. LOSS OF AMERICAN WAR-SLOOP *COLUMBUS*. *Alfred* taken. *Randolph* gone. Frigate *Effingham* abandoned up the Delaware (thanks to political meddling) after industrious John Barry salvaged her. March 1778 was a wicked month for the Continental Navy. Nor was it over. One of Continental vessels blockaded in Narragansett Bay, sloop *Columbus* was ordered to run the gantlet at first chance. Unhappily she was put under captaincy of Hoysted Hacker, whose naval record was already an anthology of errors. Sailing out of Narragansett late that March, he held *Columbus* so close inshore that she piled up on Point Judith. All hands escaped the wreck. And somehow Hoysted Hacker again escaped court-martial which should have hoisted him out of service. But exeunt *Columbus*.

159. LOSS OF AMERICAN FRIGATE *VIRGINIA*. Political plum awarded Maryland squire James Nicholson, 28-gun frigate *Virginia* was built by Geo. Welles of Baltimore. Starting maiden cruise on last day in March '78, Nicholson slammed the ship hard aground on shoal near Annapolis first night out. When H.M.S. *Emerald* and *Conqueror* sailed up at dawn, Nicholson went overside so fast he forgot his pants. First Lt. Joshua Barney bravely tried to defend ship. But *Virginia* crew mutinied and British captured a sitting duck. Whereupon Nicholson returned under flag of truce to request his trousers. Ridiculous attempt to save face (or pants) could not save *Virginia*— fourth American warship lost March '78.

160. *RALEIGH* ON FINAL CRUISE. After inglorious Thompson episode, *Raleigh* command went to John Barry, orphaned captain of defunct *Effingham*. Delighted, Barry spent summer of '78 in Boston readying *Raleigh* (at the left). Sailing on September 25th, she was met by foes first noon out—H.M.S. *Experiment* (50 guns) and war-sloop *Unicorn* (22). Barry ran for it, racing north. For two days *Raleigh* held the lead, then enemy overhauled. Boxed in, Maine coast looming ahead, Barry turned to fight. When *Unicorn* closed in, *Raleigh's* guns hit her hard. Then *Experiment* stepped in.

161. LOSS OF AMERICAN FRIGATE *RALEIGH*. Back to wall against Maine coast, *Raleigh* battled *Experiment* and *Unicorn* for nine hours. No Thompson or Nicholson, Barry had his crew fighting with every fist they could muster. But *Raleigh's* 32 guns were no match for enemy's 72. With ship shot to shambles, Barry rammed her on the beach, escaped into forest with most of crew. Salvaged, *Raleigh* sailed for Royal Navy until 1783—better ship than *Virginia,* sold out after two years.

ENTER NAVAL
Allies

162. *VIVE* BENJAMIN FRANKLIN! And Beaumarchais, Paul Jones, Marquis de Lafayette—other champions of democracy who won ear of Foreign Minister Vergennes. Also Yankees who won Battle of Saratoga, final argument that convinced French Court. Stepping in as America's ally in February 1778, France expanded the Revolution into global conflict. Backboned by 80 ships-of-line, French Navy embroiled British from West Indies to India. Then France induced Spain to fight: 60 more battleships against Britain. Holland, too, waded in on Yankee side. In summer of '78 the first French forces reached America.

163. ADMIRAL-GENERAL COUNT D'ESTAING—commander of first French expeditionary force dispatched to United States. Trained army officer, his appointment to fleet command typified Court influence in Royal French Navy which restricted high rank to nobility, aptitudes notwithstanding. Weeks elapsed while d'Estaing assembled naval forces at Toulon. Yet mere threat of French attack compelled British to revise war plans. While alarmed Admiralty in London girded Home Fleet for Channel defense, King's generals decided to abandon Philadelphia. In hotfoot retreat to New York, Redcoat forces were ambushed by Continentals near Freehold, N.J. In ensuing Battle of Monmouth, treacherous conduct of American General Charles Lee cost Washington chance to destroy British army under General Clinton (successor to boudoir-bound General Howe). Thus Monmouth, Washington's last major battle in North, was indecisive—British army and naval forces successfully retired to Manhattan. Clinton would clutch New York until war's end. But British withdrawal from Philadelphia stands as classic example of long-range influence of sea power on land operations. Although far over the horizon, d'Estaing's fleet had Redcoats on the run. French Navy turned the war tide.

CHARLES-HENRI,
COMTE D'ESTAING,
Chevalier des Ordres du Roi,
Lieutenant Genl. de ses Armées
Vice-Amiral de France,
Né le 24 Novembre 1729.

164. FRENCH OFF DELAWARE (July 8, 1778). D'Estaing's fleet included ships-of-line *Languedoc* (flagship), *Marseillaise, Provence, Tonnant, Sagittaire, Guerrière, Fantasque, César, Protecteur, Vaillant, Zélé, Hector*. Plus frigates *Chimère, L'Engageante, Aimable, Alcméne*. They are shown at mouth of the Delaware chasing H.M. frigate *Mermaid* to shore. (Drawing by Pierre Ozanne, naval constructor in d'Estaing's fleet.)

165. FRENCH OFF STATEN ISLAND. From Delaware, d'Estaing headed for New York; maneuvered off Staten Island as shown in Ozanne panorama. There he might have attacked British squadron (background). But American pilots refused to take deep-draft French warships into shallow channel beyond Staten. After conference with George Washington, d'Estaing set course for Rhode Island to aid Newport drive.

166. FRENCH AT NEWPORT—*à bas les Anglais!* D'Estaing's fleet arrived off Newport, July 29th. Trapped in Narragansett, British frigates *Juno, Flora* and *Cerberus*, sloop *Kingfisher*, corvette *Falcon* and a 40-gun troopship were sunk or burned to prevent capture. In Newport Harbor (extreme right) Hessians scuttled a dozen transports. At one stroke French erased more warships than American Navy had downed in two years.

167. BATTLE OFF RHODE ISLAND (August 12-13, 1778) occurred when Lord Howe arrived below Narragansett with British New York squadron to attack French. In wild tempest (recalled for years by Rhode Islanders as "great French storm") d'Estaing sailed out of Newport to lock horns with foe. Howe deftly outmaneuvered d'Estaing; in combat with H.M.S. *Iris, César* lost 70 killed, 100 wounded; British few.

168. D'ESTAING'S FLAGSHIP DISMASTED. Lamed by storm-damage, *Languedoc* was overhauled by H.M.S. *Renown,* cut down to a stump as shown. With flagship, two other vessels crippled, d'Estaing's fleet limped back to Point Judith, R.I. British won first big sea battle off U. S. coast; crushed allied drive to retake Newport.

169. FRENCH LEAVE NEWPORT. Word from Lafayette that a British armada would soon arrive alarmed d'Estaing, who headed for Boston. (Ozanne panorama shows French in Nantasket Roads; flagship *Languedoc* receiving new masts from battleship *Protecteur*.) When Admiral Sir John Byron reached Newport with fresh English squadron, French were gone. Lord Howe returned to England to protest mismanaged war in America.

170. FRENCH ON WAY TO BOSTON—in for boos and brickbats. D'Estaing's defensive move to Boston roused storm of American reproach. Retreating from untenable Rhode Island front, Gen. Sullivan declared America could win without allies. French were derided by Yankee provincials as "atheists" and "frogeaters." In Boston d'Estaing was challenged to duel; a French officer was killed in street brawl. Rum diplomacy.

171. FRENCH QUIT BOSTON. Humiliated by local bigotry, d'Estaing ordered fleet's departure. Painting by Monlenard shows French ship-of-line embarking smallboat—a farewell gesture illustrative of adieu to inhospitable New England. Leaving Boston late in 1778, d'Estaing sailed for West Indies. Mortified, Washington did his best to hush incident, repair diplomatic breach. But French withdrawal enabled British to tighten hold on Newport, reinforce New York, seize Penobscot beachhead in Maine, and mount major drive against American South. What price small-town intolerance! But Paris remained liberal.

172. AMERICAN FRIGATE *ALLIANCE*—rushed on diplomatic mission. Only 36-gunner constructed for Continental Navy, she was 151-footer with 36-foot beam, 12½ depth of hold; built in 1778 by the Hacketts of Salisburyport, Mass. Captained by ex-French naval officer, Pierre Landais, *Alliance* sailed from Boston for France in January '79, bearing Lafayette on special mission to smooth over the embarrassing d'Estaing affair.

173. BATTLE FOR SAVANNAH. Although d'Estaing left New England to cook its own codfish, he drew Byron's squadron to West Indies; dealt him a thrashing off Grenada. In October 1779, d'Estaing's fleet joined American forces in effort to drive enemy from Savannah, Ga. Allies lost this campaign and d'Estaing was ordered home under cloud. Few Americans realized that his fleet diverted British naval strength at a crucial hour for American Navy. One who did realize it was Paul Jones.

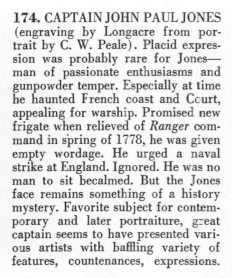

174. CAPTAIN JOHN PAUL JONES (engraving by Longacre from portrait by C. W. Peale). Placid expression was probably rare for Jones—man of passionate enthusiasms and gunpowder temper. Especially at time he haunted French coast and Court, appealing for warship. Promised new frigate when relieved of *Ranger* command in spring of 1778, he was given empty wordage. He urged a naval strike at England. Ignored. He was no man to sit becalmed. But the Jones face remains something of a history mystery. Favorite subject for contemporary and later portraiture, great captain seems to have presented various artists with baffling variety of features, countenances, expressions.

175. SKEPTICAL PAUL JONES— as he may have looked when American Commissioners in Paris gave him words instead of warship. While Franklin supported him, others ensnared him in political intrigues. So French-built frigates *Deane* and *Queen of France* went to other captains. Hopes for Dutch-built frigate *Indienne* went glimmering. (Below portrait "drawn from life by T. M. Moreau the Younger" was published in Parish after Jones' ultimate triumph with *Bonhomme Richard*. Congressmen who ignored Jones might well have heeded portrait's caption by Molière. "Such men rarely present themselves, and when Heaven gives them to us we must profit by it.")

176. STRANGE PAUL JONES— engraving by J. Chapman (1796). Portrait reflects British propaganda which advertised Jones as West Indies pirate. But Jones had other than British detractors. Jealous Commissioner Arthur Lee—Edward Bancroft (traitor-spy in Franklin's entourage)—these and other Americans in Paris maligned him; cost him captaincy of French and Dutch-built frigates; had him beached for months.

177. DOLDRUMS AT L'ORIENT— where Jones was stranded. Captain without ship, Jones paced water front in frustration; wrote importuning letters to French Court. To Rochefoucauld he declared he had been led "from great to little and little to less." To a friend: "*Were I to curse the man I hate, attendance and dependence be his fate.*" Then at L'Orient dockyard old Indiaman *Duc de Duras* went up for auction. Jones saw a chance!

178. VERSAILLES—where even Franklin failed to cut knot for Jones. Yet answer lay in Poor Richard's Almanack: "If you wish business done expeditiously, do it yourself." According to story, Jones read "Richard's" advice; determined to visit Louis XVI, himself. Timing may be exaggeration, but tale has it Jones obtained *Duras* option from French King within 24 hours of debut at Versailles. So aged vessel was procured for Jones at auction in 1779. Already she'd been condemned as unseaworthy. But Jones turned ratty decrepit cargoman into famous warship.

179. FRIGATE *BONHOMME RICHARD* —warship out of rummage. Vessel was 900-tonner, about 152 feet long with 40-foot beam, 19 depth of hold—fat and slow. Jones himself remodeled her, installed new decks, streamlined her hull to increase speed. For armament she was given twenty-eight 12-pounders for gun deck; eight 9-pounders for poop and forecastle; six heavy 18-pounders for hold aft —rusty museum-pieces from French Navy arsenal. She was ready in late spring of '79. Mongrel soon to be champion. (above)

180. MODEL OF *BONHOMME RICHARD*—as she looked when ready for war cruise. She was named after Franklin's "Good Richard." Crew was not so good. Some 250 hands, ship's company was amalgam of 79 Americans (exchanged prisoners), 77 Britishers, 30 Portuguese, and rabble of Malay lascars and homeless sailors of fortune. Himself a sailor of fortune, Jones had no objection to beachcombers; worked hard to sign them on. French Government offered 137 trained Marines. Among American element Jones was delighted to find Lieutenant Richard Dale who had served in Continental Navy on board the *Lexington*.

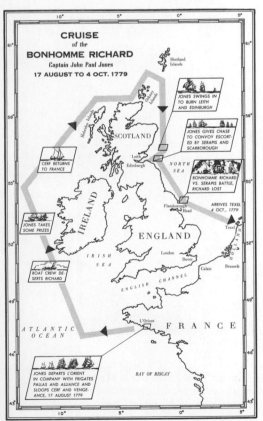

181. SOMBRE JOHN PAUL JONES— contemporary bust by French sculptor Houdon (considered excellent likeness by critics of day). Perhaps Captain wore this look on quarter-deck of *Bonhomme Richard* when at last she stood seaward from L'Orient. Assigned to sail with *Richard* were French frigate *Pallas*, sloops *Cerf* and *Vengeance* and American frigate *Alliance*. Jones was told these warships were to operate independently. Commodore without authority, he recognized dangerous setup, but refused to back down. "I resolved to expose myself to every peril." Including unruly consorts.

182. CRUISE OF THE *BONHOMME RICHARD*. Sailing from L'Orient, August 14, 1779, Jones led squadron on foray around British Isles. They took several prizes off Ireland. Then a boat's crew from *Richard* deserted; war-sloop *Cerf* abandoned cruise to return to France. Jones resolutely swung depleted squadron around Scotland determined to burn Leith or Edinburgh in reprisal for "burnings in America." Plan frustrated by bickering captains, he moved to ambush Baltic convoy due to arrive soon. (left)

Admiral's Day Cabin and swinging bunk, British Ship-of-the-line

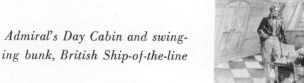

183. *BONHOMME RICHARD* INTERCEPTS H.M.S. *SERAPIS* (contemporary print issued at Paris by M. Guérin). Scene: off Flamborough Head. Date: September 23, 1779. "He who surprises well must conquer," Jones had written. His appearance off east coast of England certainly surprised British Baltic convoy under guard of brand new 50-gun frigate *Serapis* (at left) and 20-gun war-sloop *Countess of Scarborough*. As frightened merchantmen scurried to take cover, Jones maneuvered *Richard* to attack the *Serapis*. Latter's Captain Richard Pearson eagerly cleared for action as slow stranger made solitary approach. For Jones was unsupported by his supposed consorts. "I was obliged to run every risk and [attack] with the *Bonhomme Richard* alone." Ships reached gun-range about 7:00 P.M. After formal hails, mutual broadsides opened duel.

Model of the Richard in battle trim

184. *BONHOMME RICHARD* VERSUS *SERAPIS* (engraved by R. Collier from drawing by Hamilton). By masterful seamanship, Jones gained weather gauge. Advantage was canceled by horrible explosion in *Richard's* bowels when two of ancient 18-pounders burst at first broadside. With lower deck gutted, she staggered into battle afire and bleeding.

185. *RICHARD* RAKES *SERAPIS*. Painting by I. Butterworth portrays early maneuver in frigate battle, *Richard* managing a rake at close quarters. Unable to outsail Briton, Jones set teeth in resolve to outfight him. According to record, ships at right (presumably French *Pallas* and H.M.S. *Countess of Scarborough*) were not embattled during this gambit. However, Jones' ship came under fire of *Countess*, whose broadsides butchered most of French Marines on *Richard's* poop. Jones fought on. (at right)

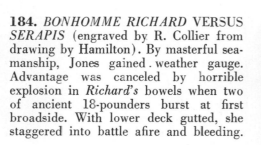

Early wood-cut of Jones

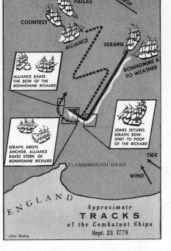

188. *RICHARD* AND *SERAPIS* IN DEATH GRIP (pirated picture). A "mirror copy" of Paton painting, this reproduction by Virtue, Emmins & Co. of New York puts reverse English on original. As exact maneuvers of *Richard-Serapis* fight were lost in confusion of controversial testimony, artists pictured battle according to predilection. Accurate illustration would show *Richard* caught between two fires—broadsides from *Serapis* and rakes from *Alliance*. As engagement roared on in moonlight, French frigate *Pallas* (Capt. Dennis Cottineau) stepped in with sloop *Ven-*

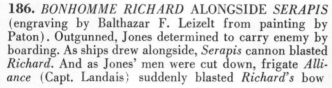

186. *BONHOMME RICHARD* ALONGSIDE *SERAPIS* (engraving by Balthazar F. Leizelt from painting by Paton). Outgunned, Jones determined to carry enemy by boarding. As ships drew alongside, *Serapis* cannon blasted *Richard*. And as Jones' men were cut down, frigate *Alliance* (Capt. Landais) suddenly blasted *Richard's* bow

187. *RICHARD* AND *SERAPIS* IN DEATH GRIP (contemporary painting by Sir Richard Paton). Somehow Jones' men succeeded in fastening line to *Serapis'* jib boom. Vessels were locked bow to stern, as shown, for rest of battle. Point-blank broadsides from heavy British 18-pounders sent cannonballs hurtling through *Richard*. Night sky and sea were tinted by red breath of the guns.

189. JOHN PAUL JONES ON QUARTER-DECK at height of *Richard-Serapis* battle. With ship shot to shambles, guns uprooted, decks guttering blood, Jones fought on. "I had only two 9-pounders on the quarter-deck that were not silenced." Ordering another 9-pounder hoisted topside, he himself took charge of the battery. (Engraved portrait by Carl Guttenberg after drawing by C. J. Notté)

190. BATTLE CLIMAX—Jones fells *Richard's* Master Gunner. Believing Jones and Lieutenant Dale had been killed, Master Gunner raced to poop deck; tried to haul down *Richard's* colors. Hearing cry for quarter, Jones yanked two pistols from belt; hurled them at man's head to knock him flat at foot of gangway ladder.

geance to hold *Countess of Scarborough* at bay. But *Alliance*, weaving in and out in series of crazy maneuvers, fired indiscriminate broadsides which ripped into *Richard* as well as *Serapis*. Had Pierre Landais gone mad? To Jones, attack from *Alliance* must have seemed diabolic nightmare. Struck by "friend" and foe, *Richard* was reduced to flaming junk. One is left to imagine the gun-roar, the oaths, the screaming, the crash of spars, the smell of burning tar and canvas. Jones reported his decks "mangled beyond . . . description."

191. "I HAVE NOT YET BEGUN TO FIGHT!" (From Dwight Franklin miniature group in Naval Academy Museum). As cry for quarter echoes through bedlam, *Serapis'* captain hails Jones. "Do you surrender?" trumpets Pearson, "do you strike?" Indomitable, Paul Jones bellows answer of the fighter who refuses defeat.

193. END OF *RICHARD-SERAPIS* BATTLE (contemporary painting by Lieut. Wm. Elliot, R.N.). A floating charnel of death and fire, *Richard* seemed on point of foundering when *Alliance* reappeared in smoke; in final gesture of madness, Landais dealt Jones' ship another terrible broadside. Still Jones fought on. A shot felled *Serapis'* mainmast. A grenade crashed into her magazine. Explosions disemboweled British frigate, left her gun deck an inferno. In dramatic reversal, *Serapis* was bested by a mortally wounded foe. (above)

192. *RICHARD* BLASTS *SERAPIS* (illustration by J. O. Davidson). In midst of battle some 200 British prisoners broke out of *Richard's* half-flooded hold. Somehow Jones and Lt. Dale drove these wild men to the pumps. Combat raged on.

Dropping grenades from the spars

194. "BOARDERS AWAY" (A Chappel version of the *Serapis* capture). Lt. Dale led cutlass-hands storming *Serapis'* deck. A brief scrimmage, and it was over. In 3½-hour cannon-match each ship had suffered some 300 casualties. Dale found Englishmen roasted at their guns. "Many stood with only the collars of their shirts upon their bodies." Historians would glorify this battle. But Paul Jones wrote: "Humanity cannot but recoil from the prospect of such finished horror. . . ."

195. PAUL JONES CALLS FOR BOARDERS (contemporary engraving by Augustus Robin of New York). Blasts turned *Serapis* into death ship. Appalled by carnage, Captain Pearson struck his colors. Signal went unnoticed as Jones assembled crew for final cutlass rush.

196. PAUL JONES BIDDING FAREWELL TO *BONHOMME RICHARD* (painting by Percy Moran). Two days after battle, fire-gutted *Richard* went under in heavy seas. With survivors on *Serapis*, Jones led his raider group on stormy run to North Sea, playing hide-and-seek with ships of British Home Fleet. Then he headed for the Texel, Holland.

197. COMMODORE PAUL JONES (idiotic British conception). Note battle incorrectly dated. Uniforms are fanciful, as are Jones' curly sideburns. And "Lieut. Grub," publicized as Jones' nephew, is gross fiction. Another propaganda story had Jones fiendishly torturing a man.

198. BRITISH PORTRAIT OF JONES (as "drawn from life" by Thos. Macklin). "Paul Jones resembles a Jack-O'-Lantern," one journal cried. "Hey! Presto! Like Mungo in the farce. Mungo here, Mungo there, and Mungo everywhere!" Obviously Jones did not pose for Mr. Macklin.

Shooting Lieut. Grub for endeavouring to Lower the American Flag to the Seraphis, Captn. Pearson of Flamborough Head, Septr. 1779.

199. PIRATE PAUL JONES (another propaganda picture). London society had been engrossed with the murder of Admiral Lord Sandwich's mistress by the Rev. James Hackman. But now Jones was season's sensation, featured as bloodthirsty picaroon and "renegade pirate."

200. BUCCANEER PAUL JONES (more misrepresentation). When Jones' group reached Holland with prizes *Serapis* and *Scarborough* (Oct. 4, 1779), British raged at Dutch for harboring "pirate." From Texel, Jones wrote bitter denials, pointing to naval record. But the smear stuck for years, as witness inane "Mr. Goff" burlesque of Jones as bearded freebooter. (Poster published London, 1832.)

201. RARE DUTCH PAUL JONES—as he was sketched by unidentified artist (possibly Simon Folcke) in Amsterdam theater. When he appeared on street, Dutch crowds roared song, *"Hie Komt Paul Jones Aan!"* British fury grew.

202. RARE FRENCH PAUL JONES—from frontispiece of *Memoirs de Paul Jones* published in Paris in 1798.

203. H.M.S. *ALARM*—type of frigate sent to blockade Jones at Texel. "For God's sake get to sea!" Lord Sandwich wrote one captain. "If you can take Paul Jones you will be as high in public estimation as if you had beat the combined fleets!" Sandwich was later denounced for sending against Jones only "a few frigates" and 64-gun battleship *Jupiter*.

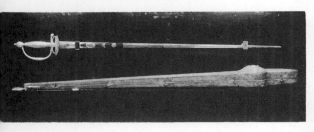

204. "LE FAMEUX COMMODOR PAUL JONES." ·(Rare print published in France shortly after *Bonhomme Richard* exploit.) France assured Jones haven if he could elude enemy off Holland. As Dutch were not yet in war, he was forced to leave neutral Texel and run blockade. Captaining frigate *Alliance*, he sailed out (Dec. 27, 1779); raced down Channel in plain view of British squadron; escaped into seascape off Brittany. After brief cruise off Spain, he sailed into L'Orient as hero. To French. Scheming Americans beached him!

205. PAUL JONES' GOLD SWORD. Paris roared welcome. King of France presented him with golden sword, Order of Military Merit, rank of Chevalier. Queen invited him to Opera. A Freemason, Jones was embraced by city's highest Masonic Lodge—the lodge of Voltaire and Franklin. But insidious clique (Arthur Lee and Bancroft) rigged his removal from *Alliance*. Only American-built frigate ever captained by John Paul Jones was returned to command of Pierre Landais, evil crackpot who almost sank the *Richard!*

206. VAGUE PAUL JONES (portrait never finished). Painted in America, this "Jones" seems strangely devoid of character. He was to remain almost featureless to contemporary American public. Promised command of new *America* (only ship-of-line built in America during Revolution), Jones winged home on French sloop *Ariel*. During voyage, he met and bested H.M. light frigate *Triumph*. Philadelphia cheered his arrival (Feb. 1781). Then Congress shelved a resolution to award him a medal. Service jealousies showed their hand. Promised laurels faded.

207. ROMANTIC PAUL JONES (bust from De Biron collection). Sensitive features of this sculpting suggest the Jones who won heart of La Belle France in Paris salon and Versailles garden. The Duchess of Chartes; Madame Tellisson; Dumas' daughter; "Madame XXXX"; Countess de Nicolson—Jones could conquer more than a *Serapis*. Abigail Adams (good New England housewife) saw him in Paris and described him as "an abigail" (lady's maid). But Jones was no simpering dandy or cheap philanderer. Only a poet could pen to the Countess Vendahl:

The loveliest form, the fairest face,
The brightest eye, the gentlest mind,
And every virtue, charm and grace
Should be to endless fame consigned.

Portrait Dims

208. COMIC PAUL JONES (early American absurdity). One of rarest "Joneses" in existence is this clownish portrait endowing him with silly sidewhiskers and Uncle Sam pants. Long after his heroic service, Jones was subject of invidious characterization by detractors. That Pecksniff

American historians belittled Jones throughout entire Victorian era is not surprising in light of the little awarded him by his American contemporaries. From Philadelphia he hurried to Portsmouth to take command of *America*. Fate and fatuous politicians deprived him of battleship.

209. 74-GUN "LINER" *AMERICA* —ship which never came in for Paul Jones. Constructed at Portsmouth, N.H., by John Langdon, she was 1,982-tonner, 182½ feet long, with 50½ beam, 23 depth of hold. Jones rushed vessel's completion; raised funds for project; squelched British plan to sabotage ship; made extensive changes in her design. Fate robbed him of cherished command. When storm wrecked 74-gun *Magnifique* at Boston, Congress awarded magnificent new *America* to France.

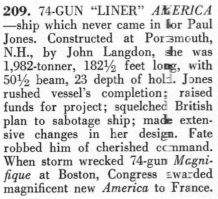

210. SAD PAUL JONES (painting on vellum by unknown contemporary artist). "When the *America* was taken from me, I was deprived of my tenth command," wrote captain who had won great battle on Britain's doorstep while political pets at home lost American warships wholesale. After transfer of battleship *America* to French, no man-of-war remained for Jones. With French, Spanish and Dutch fleets now fighting British, Yankee sailors were on sidelines. Facing anchor in remnant American Navy, Jones sailed to West Indies in 1783 as observer with French fleet under de Vaudreuil. His last cruise as American in Continental uniform.

211. MINIATURE OF PAUL JONES (memento by Countess de Lowendahl). After war, Jones returned to France to collect prize monies due *Ranger* and *Richard* crews. Old romances were renewed (as miniature suggests). Heart also on American service, he appealed for Government mission. Finally Jefferson, new Minister to France, sponsored him for a minor U. S. mission to Denmark.

*"The Celebrated Paul Jones"
Contemporary print;
artist unknown, probably British.*

*Best known portrait of Jones,
is this painting by Cecelia Beaux.*

*Paul Jones at sea; litho—crayon drawing
by Fred Freeman (used on the jacket) is
reconstructed from the
De Biron bust (text #204)
and the Moreau engraving (text #175)*

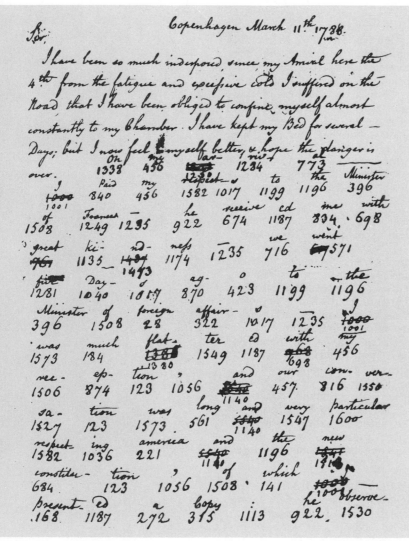

212. CODE LETTER FROM PAUL JONES TO JEFFERSON—dispatched from Copenhagen, March 1788. War was five years over when Jones visited Denmark as American diplomatic agent. Draft of letter to Jefferson (preserved in Masonic Library, Boston) displays simple code favored by Jones who used dictionary with words numbered at random for secret cipher. (Recipient employed a similarly coded dictionary to de-cipher message.) Democratic Danes welcomed Jones. But as mission was only temporary, he again faced "beach." In Paris the money due his sailors sank in sea of litigation. At home he was victim of smear campaign launched by James Nicholson. Weary of political intrigues, Paul Jones finally accepted Admiral's commission in Russian Navy; went to Muscovy to fight for what he believed Democratic Cause—Russia vs. Turkey.

213. OLDER PAUL JONES (modern portrait by Henri Toussaint). This might have been the Jones who returned to France from Russia after winning great Battle of the Liman against the Turks. A Jones disillusioned by vicious Empress Catherine, by palace scandals, by cruel Count Potemkin. Betrayed, ill, facing poverty, he found Paris in throes of French Revolution. There, forlorn, he died in obscurity, July 18, 1792.

214. DEATH'S HEAD OF JOHN PAUL JONES—inquest and some doubt. Over century passed before Paul Jones received deserved recognition by United States. In 1905 belated search was made for Jones' grave. Clues led to old Protestant Cemetery in forgotten corner of Paris. There, mummified body was found in nameless lead coffin. Careful autopsy and study convinced investigators, and "hero's remains" were transferred to Annapolis. But absence of uniform or medals in coffin left a ghost of doubt hovering. Again the Jones countenance blurs.

215. CAPTAIN JOHN PAUL JONES. Full face of Houdon sculpting is considered best likeness of best naval officer of Revolutionary War. The only American naval captain who never lost a battle or a ship, never faced court of inquiry, never free-lanced for prize money—his stature towers, monumental, above the other captains of American Revolution.

C O N T I N E N T A L
Navy Twilight

216. AMERICAN FRIGATE *WARREN* AND SQUADRON IN ACTION. Last of Continental Navy's original 32-gunners, *Warren* was built at Providence (1777) by Sylvester Bowers. John B. Hopkins (Esek's son) was made captain. He got her to Europe early in '78. Back with *Ranger* and *Queen of France*. They caught enemy sloop and seven cargomen off Virginia. Then Hopkins was suspended from Navy for smelly prize-money deal. *Warren* went to worse fate, turned over to Dudley Saltonstall for Penobscot Expedition.

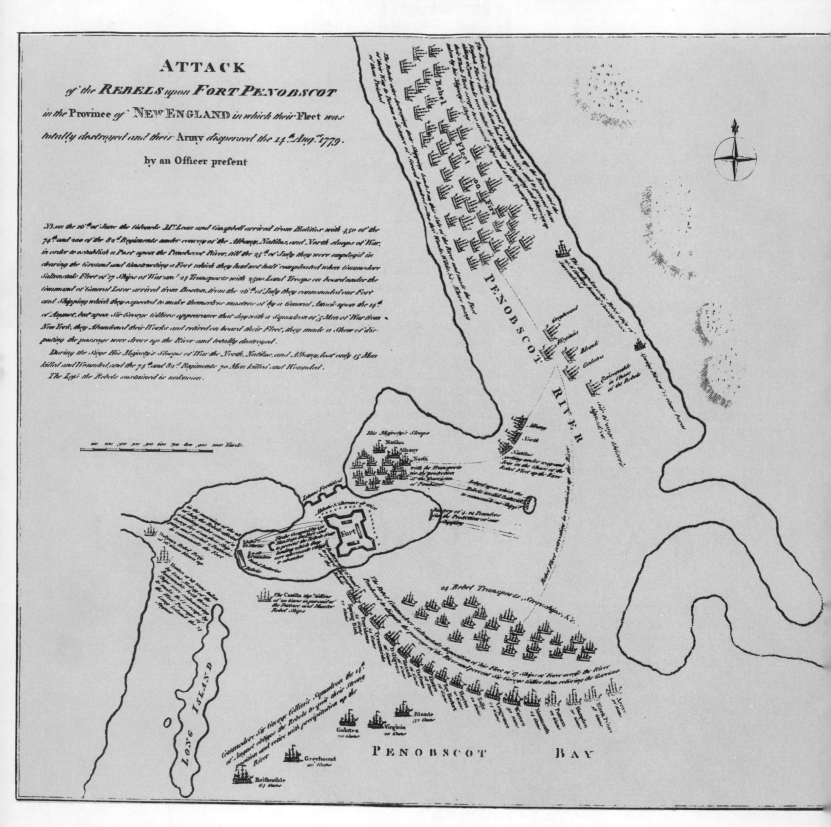

ATTACK

of the REBELS *upon* FORT PENOBSCOT

in the Province *of* NEW ENGLAND *in which their Fleet was*

totally destroyed and their Army dispersed the 14th Augst 1779.

by an Officer present

217. CHART OF PENOBSCOT EXPEDITION—worst defeat in American history. Determined to oust British invasion force from strategic base at mouth of Penobscot on Maine coast, Yankees assembled fleet which sailed from Boston, mid-July 1779. Largest seagoing force organized by Americans during Revolution, expedition contained frigate *Warren* (Saltonstall), war-brig *Providence* (Hacker), war-brig *Diligent* (Moses Brown), three Massachusetts naval brigs, one New Hampshire naval brig, 12 privateers and 22 transports laden with 3,000 troops. Army forces were under General Solomon Lovell and Colonel Paul Revere of "midnight ride" fame. Unfortunately, expedition was under leadership of naval officer characterized by Paul Jones as "sleepy gentleman." Note Hoysted Hacker (another Jones aversion) second in command. When fleet reached Penobscot, Commodore Saltonstall staged fatal demonstration of somnambulism. British fort with small garrison and little transport flotilla, guarded by three 20-gun sloops, was there for taking. But Saltonstall anchored American armada as shown on chart. General Lovell urged all-out attack. Saltonstall stalled. Two weeks drifted by. Delay gave British chance to dispatch alarm; mid-August brought H.M.S. *Raisonable* over horizon. At sight of enemy ship-of-line, Saltonstall fled up Penobscot River. Leading American armada "up the creek."

Brig of War Lowering a Boat

218. LOSS OF AMERICAN ARMADA IN PENOBSCOT. Pursued by Sir George Collier with H.M.S. *Raisonable*, plus frigates *Greyhound, Galatea, Virginia* and *Blonde* (which followed over horizon), Saltonstall's armada fled up Penobscot River. Five British ships chasing 41 American! Although American guns outnumbered enemy four to one, only a few shots were fired by *Warren* and consorts. Caught in shallow channel, Yankee vessels jammed together like helpless salmon. With cannonballs splashing astern, Saltonstall gave up; ran fleet ashore; set fire to vessels, and galloped inland. While frigate *Warren* and fleet went up in bonfire, British rushed in and captured some 500 Yanks. "Sleepy gentleman's" ultimate court-martial could not restore lost American armada. Nor could subsequent American censorship erase facts. It might (and did) delete them from American history books, but it could not prevent British publication of battle chart drawn by officer who witnessed Penobscot fiasco. Only word from Europe—news of Paul Jones' victory over *Serapis*—salvaged contemporary American Navy's prestige.

219. CRUISE OF WHIPPLE'S SQUADRON. At time Jones was readying *Richard* in France, Abraham Whipple led squadron from Boston on war cruise. With "Informal Commodore" were Bowers-built 28-gun frigate *Providence* (flagship), French-built *Queen of France*

220. LOSS OF WHIPPLE'S SQUADRON. Reinforced by frigate *Boston*, Whipple's group was sent south to bolster Charleston against new invasion threat. February 1780. Down came fleet of Admiral Arbuthnot with Red Coat army. Caught in Charleston Harbor, Whipple's four warships faced seven British. When H.M.S. *Renown, Roebuck* and *Romulus* pushed past Fort Moultrie, Whipple surprisingly surrendered. Exeunt frigates *Providence, Queen of France, Boston* and sloop *Ranger*. Another squadron gone!

221. PAROLE FOR CAPTURED YANKEE CAPTAIN—Revolutionary Navy at low ebb. Three frigates and famous sloop gone at one swipe! Whipple and Rathburne tethered to paroles of

(under bold John Rathburne), and sloop *Ranger* (sour Thomas Simpson). Out in Atlantic (July '79) they sighted big Jamaica convoy guarded by a 74-gun "liner." Whipple hesitated. But when Rathburne's ship pitched in, others took cue; snatched prizes for million-dollar haul!

type given *Boston's* Capt. Tucker (below). Charleston disaster left American Navy all but sunk. So was Revolutionary War effort—Washington bogged in Jersey; British storming through South. At sea, American frigates *Deane, Confederacy, Alliance* alone remained to show Stars and Stripes. But naval help was coming.

I The Subscriber *Samuel Tucker, Commander of the Continental Ship of War Boston* do hereby acknowledge myself a Prisoner of War to His Majesty, and most solemnly and strictly bind myself by all the full, implicit and extensive Faith and Meaning of a Parole of Honour, which I hereby give to His Excellency Vice-Admiral ARBUTHNOT; and that I will not directly, or indirectly, either by Word or Deed, take any further Part in the Dispute between Great-Britain and the British Colonies in North-America, until regularly exchanged for an Officer of equal Rank in His Majesty's Service.

May 28 1780   *Sam Tucker*

Loss of Whipple's Squadron

222. ROCHAMBEAU REACHES AMER-ICA—contemporary British view. Only expert diplomacy of Washington and Lafayette induced French Gov't to send expedition to States after d' Estaing fiasco. Carrying crack army of General Rochambeau, fleet under Admiral de Ternay set sail in May 1780. French armada included ships-of-line *Duc de Bourgogne* (flagship: 80 guns), *Neptune* (74), *Conquérant* (74), *Provence* (64), *Eveillé* (64), *Jason* (64), *Ardent* (64); 30-gun frigates *Surveillant*, *Amazone* and *Gentille*; cutter *Guêpe* and hospital ship *Fantasque*. After brush with British squadron off Bermuda, French reached Newport, R.I., in July.

French Turn The Tide

General Count Rochambeau, leader of French expedition to America in 1780

223. ROCHAMBEAU'S ARMY LANDING AT NEWPORT—contemporary German view. Illustration from Sprengle's *Allgemeines-historiches Taschenbuch* (pub. Berlin 1784) conveys something of French army *élan*. Although 1,000 on shipboard were down with fever, Rochambeau landed 5,500 with gorgeous pageantry novel to bleak New Englanders. Making determined effort to assuage local prejudice, French introduced Americans to brass bands, *coquetels* (cocktails) and ice cream. Rhode Islanders obligingly swallowed this frivolity. (below at right)

224. H.M.S. *LONDON*—pawn in Newport stalemate. Arbuthnot's flagship, she led British squadron pellmell to Rhode Island to blockade French fleet. Reinforced by second squadron under Sir Thos. Graves, Arbuthnot's force included one 90-gun ship-of-line, six 74-gunners and four smaller battleships. Held at Bay in Narragansett, de Ternay's fleet enjoyed the Newport season, while General Clinton, raging at this new French threat, assembled army forces in Manhattan for a Rhode Island drive. Washington put a stop to Clinton's intentions by threatening a flank attack from Hudson Highlands. So war in America drifted to stalemate in summer of 1780. Then—foul blow! After military conference with Rochambeau (at Hartford, Conn., Sept. 20th), Washington went to West Point on Hudson to inspect that important fortress. There he learned stunning news. General Benedict Arnold, West Point commander, had just gone over to the enemy! Arnold—a traitor! (left)

225. SPY IS CAUGHT—hanging of Arnold's accomplice. Bitterness, greed, ambition and hatred of French motivated Arnold's plan to sell out Hudson River defenses to British—$100,000 if he succeeded; $50,000 in event of failure. Plot fizzled when American guerillas intercepted British Major André near Tarrytown; found West Point map in spy's stocking. Cat out of bag, Arnold fled, leaving unfortunate major to go hang. So ended Arnold's scheme to open upper New York to the invasion he once fought so brilliantly to stymie on Lake Champlain.

226. TRAITOR ESCAPES—Benedict Arnold boarding H.M.S. *Vulture*. By warship he was whisked down Hudson to New York where English generals (contrary to story he was ostracized) welcomed him open-armed. Commissioned brigadier in British Army (1781) he led Redcoat forces on ravaging raid in Virginia. He also led invaders into home-state Connecticut; smashed Groton defenses; burned New London. Natives, who saw wagonload of wounded New Londoners deliberately pitched down a hill, thought *Vulture* appropriate name for his ship.

227. TOMB OF ADMIRAL DE TERNAY—only Allied admiral to die in America. Victim of uncongenial Newport winter, de Ternay succumbed to fever on December 15, 1780. According to early

American historian, "The admiral was buried with great pomp. Newport had never witnessed such a cortège. The troops were all under arms; the sailors bore the coffin on their shoulders to the cemetery in Trinity Episcopal churchyard. At the grave nine Catholic priests chanted the

services. . . . Even the Tory Gazette of Rivington honored his memory, announcing his death as of 'an officer of distinguished reputation . . . a real ornament of the elegant nation from whom he was derived.' " At de Ternay's demise, command passed to Admiral Destouches.

228. SIGNATURES OF FRENCH ADMIRALS IN AMERICA. An imposing autograph to display of sea power. General Washington met many of these French naval leaders in March 1781 when he visited Newport to confer with Admiral Destouches on flagship *Duc de Bourgogne*. Officers discussed French plan to sail from

Rhode Island to Chesapeake area to support Lafayette in campaign against Benedict Arnold. Destouches departed on March 8th with expeditionary force which included seven ships-of-line, a frigate division and H.M.S. *Romulus* (recently captured from British). French sailed at time British blockade was storm-damaged.

229. BATTLE OFF CHESAPEAKE CAPES. Fleet engagement roared off Maryland on morning of March 16, 1781, when Arbuthnot's squadron, pursuing Destouches, overhauled French about 60 miles from Chesapeake Bay. Naval antagonists were evenly matched: 560 French guns against 562 British. Fighting furiously, Destouches' "liners" battered Arbuthnot's van division, but took severe mauling in return. Although French won sea battle, British gained strategic advantage by escaping through fog to defensible anchorage inside Chesapeake, while Destouches headed French fleet back to Newport to repair battle damage. Both sides were dissatisfied by outcome. For failure to reach Virginia, Destouches was pensioned off; replaced by Admiral de Barras. For defeat at sea, Arbuthnot was replaced by Admiral Thomas Graves.

230. ADMIRAL DE GRASSE—more help on way. Spurred by advices of American envoys Colonel Laurens and Tom Paine (dispatched by Washington to France, special delivery of frigate *Alliance* and John Barry) French assembled third fleet for strike at British in America. Offensively-minded, de Grasse with 26 ships of the line sailed for Caribbean (March 1781) in deceptive gambit aimed at ultimate Chesapeake area denouement.

231. FLAGSHIP OF ADMIRAL DE GRASSE. Reaching West Indies, de Grasse, in ship-of-line *Ville de Paris* (model shown) led his fleet from Martinique to Haiti. Critics carped because he avoided British Caribbean force under Hood. But Haiti move was right step—toward Yorktown, Va.

232. GENERAL LORD CORNWALLIS—big game for American-French trap. Moving northward through Georgia and the Carolinas, Cornwallis with invasion force was hounded by hard-hitting troops of Nathaneal Greene. Came order from Clinton to head for Yorktown, Va., where Lordship's weary army could be supplied by sea. When Cornwallis marched out on Yorktown peninsula (August 1781) Washington and Rochambeau closed in. Frigate *Concorde* was rushed south to fetch de Grasse.

233. YORKTOWN BATTLE (American chart). As de Grasse entered Chesapeake Bay, allied armies pounded Redcoats in Yorktown village. Sunk by artillery fire were H.M. frigates *Guadeloupe*, *Fowey*, *Charon*, and war-sloop *Bonetta*. As shown.

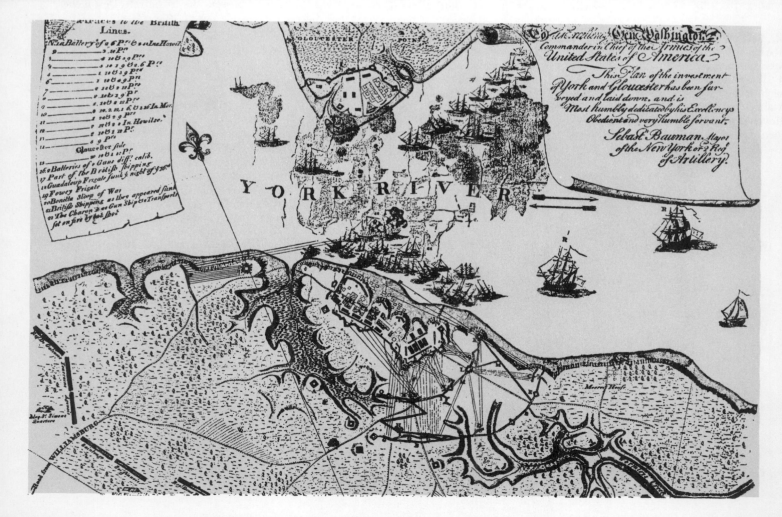

234. BRITISH AT YORKTOWN. Copy of contemporary French watercolor shows vessels sunk off beachhead by Redcoats. Fighting desperately to hold Yorktown peninsula, Cornwallis awaited naval relief from New York. Meantime, de Grasse was rushing northward from Haiti, pursued by Hood. Hood's copper-bottomed ships were the faster; sailed right by de Grasse (without seeing him) and on to New York. De Grasse tacked into mouth of Chesapeake; cooked Cornwallis' goose.

235. BATTLE OF VIRGINIA CAPES (Yorktown climax). Belatedly fleet of Adm. Graves (reinforced by Hood) arrived at mouth of Chesapeake. In showdown (begun Sept. 5, 1781) de Grasse's fleet drove British far out to sea. According to one authority, de Grasse's naval victory was "infinitely more important than Waterloo." For it secured Yorktown.

236. CORNWALLIS SURRENDERS TO WASHINGTON (October 17, 1781). Cornered at Yorktown by allied armies, sea escape cut off by French fleet, Cornwallis caved in. Last major land battle of Revolution, Yorktown sealed ultimate American victory. War drifted to end at sea.

237. IMPERIAL CLIMAX—Rodney versus de Grasse in West Indies. Returning to Caribbean after Yorktown triumph, de Grasse mustered forces at Martinique for strike at British Jamaica. Admiral Lord Rodney sailed out to stop French. In thunderous engagement off island of Dominica (April 12, 1782), Rodney defeated French-Spanish fleet under de Grasse. Battle saved Jamaica; ruined French naval prestige; gave Rodney chance to puff like a peacock. But Royal Navy was still in hot water. Involved in sea war with French, Spanish, and Dutch —forced out of Baltic by Scandinavians and Russians friendly to American Cause —plagued by Yankee privateers—British were weary. Upshot: peace proposals.

238. CRUISE OF FRIGATE *ALLI- ANCE*. By year of Yorktown, Continental warships roamed as Lilliputians in seas occupied by Titans. Shelving Captain Pierre Landais, who was now considered mad (in confirmation of Paul Jones' experienced opinion), burly John Barry took *Alliance* on important mission to Europe. On the return voyage (May 1781) he captured British privateer *Mars* and war-sloops *Trepassy* and *Atalanta.*

LAST OF THE
Continental

239. *ALLIANCE* VERSUS *ATALANTA* AND *TREPASSY*. During wicked four-hour battle off Nova Scotia, Barry, severely wounded, dealt with mutiny in crew (ragtag of British prisoners and American jailbirds), and knocked stuffing out of two British war-sloops. Both *Atalanta* (16 guns) and *Trepassy* (14) struck flag. En route to Boston *Atalanta* was recaptured (while under command of Barry's First Lieutenant, Hoysted Hacker!). Barry, of course, reached home base with *Trepassy* and *Mars.*

240. LOSS OF AMERICAN FRIGATE *CONFEDERACY*. Built by Jedidiah Willets, Norwich, Conn. A 320-gunner; 971 tons; about 155 feet long, with 37 beam, $12\frac{1}{4}$ depth of hold. Disabled by gale on shakedown in '78. Laid up until April 1781. Then down to West Indies (under Capt. Seth Harding) in squadron led by *Deane* (Commo. Sam'l Nicholson). North-bound, blown astray in storm off Delaware. Fell in with H.M.S. *Orpheus* and *Roebuck*. Ended up in Royal Navy as H.M.S. *Confederate.*

241. LOSS OF AMERICAN WAR-SLOOP *SARATOGA*. New 20-gunner built at Philadelphia. With Nicholson squadron to Caribbean. Captured three H.M. war-brigs and big Indiaman *Charming Molly*. Placing prize crew under Lt. Joshua Barney on board *Molly*, Captain John Young sailed off with *Saratoga*—into storm that fouled *Confederacy*. And oblivion. No one ever saw her again. British battleship recaptured *Molly*.

242. LOSS OF MASSACHUSETTS FRIGATE *PROTECTOR*. Little state navies aided Continental throughout Revolution. Among best of state warships was 26-gun *Protector*, shown blasting British privateer *Adm. Duff* (36 guns) in June 1779. In 1781 *Protector* was taken. By two frigates.

Navy

243. LOSS OF AMERICAN FRIGATE *TRUMBULL*. Last of 13 original Yankee frigates, 28-gun *Trumbull* was built by John Cotton at Chatham, Conn. Jinxed at launching, she could not cross mud-bar; was stuck in shallows for months. Finally to sea in 1780, she sailed under Captain James Nicholson (loser of *Virginia*). He recovered some face by winning fiery fracas with 36-gun British privateer *Watt* in Long Island Sound (May 1780). But *Trumbull*, mauled in action, was laid up for another year. Then, escorting convoy in August 1781, she was intercepted off Delaware by H.M. frigate *Iris* (ex-*Hancock*) and sloop *Gen. Monk*. Fighting night battle in storm, *Trumbull* was battered into surrender. Her loss left American Navy with two vessels—frigates *Alliance* and *Deane*. Almost total extinction.

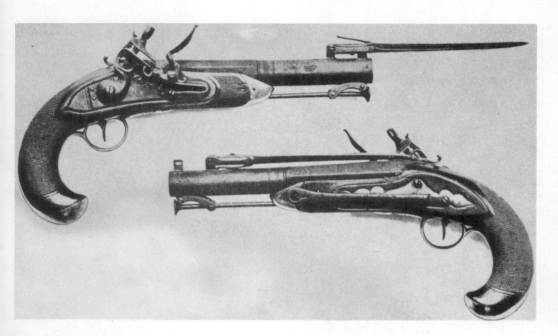

244. BOARDING PISTOLS WITH BAYONETS — cloak-and-dagger weapons of Joshua Barney. He needed them. Captured on board *Charming Molly* (after *Saratoga* vanished), he was recognized as parole violator; sent to England in irons; dungeoned in Plymouth's Old Mill. London friends aided over-the-wall escape and "underground" passage to Netherlands. Many English liberals helped Revolutionary movement—early proof Democracy's bonds are stronger than the iron manacles of Despotism.

Curtain Calls

245. "REAPPEARANCE OF JOSHUA BARNEY." Coming to America on Yankee privateer *Cicero*, redoubtable Barney was soon again at sea, skipper of Penn. State cruiser *Hyder Ally* (named for India nabob at that time fighting British). With this 16-gunner Barney captured H.M. sloop *Gen. Monk* in Delaware Bay, snatching surprised *Monk* from under wing of big frigate *Quebec*. Taken in April 1782, *Monk* was inducted into American Navy as *George Washington*. Barney captained her until peace terminated his Continental career.

John Barry

246. FINALE BY JOHN BARRY. March 1783. *Alliance* escorting ship laden with money cargo, Cuba to States. Off Havana, convoy is sighted by H.M. frigates *Alarm* and *Sybil*, plus war-sloop *Tobago*. Barry holds *Alliance* between gold-ship and enemies. Just as shooting starts, a large French warship tops horizon. As Britons flee, *Alliance* pounds *Sybil* with last American volley.

247. TREATY OF PARIS—title and signature pages of compact ending Revolutionary War. Signed September 3, 1783. But to all American purposes the war had been over a year. Yorktown broke the back of Britain's effort to quell the Revolution. And Americans would forever be indebted to French fleet that broke the British back at Yorktown. As Washington had foreseen, sea power settled the issue. By 1782 the Royal Navy, fighting from Halifax to Calcutta, was swamped. Even as Rodney smashed de Grasse in the Caribbean (clinching Britain's hold on area that produced one quarter of Empire's trade), a French fleet under brilliant Admiral Suffren smashed the Royal Navy off India. Against titanic panorama of global maritime war, the little American Navy—reduced to two frigates and a sloop—faded out. But its work was done. It had provided guns for Saratoga, cash for Philadelphia, powder for Valley Forge. It had met John Adams' demand for an ounce of naval effort that would compel enemy to expend pounds of power. Goodly contribution to victory that left Americans at liberty to build a Republic dedicated to equal justice and the democratic Rights of Man.

L'Envoy

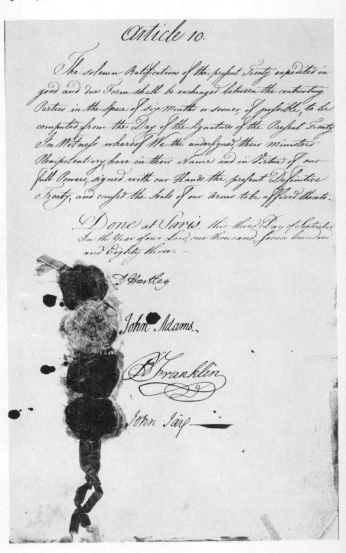

End of the Continental Navy

248. TOMB OF THE UNKNOWN SAILOR. Modern Defense Department estimates 342 battle deaths in Revolutionary Navy. Probably inaccurate figure. (*Randolph* went down all hands but one; *Raleigh*, *Alfred*, *Richard* suffered heavy casualties). No record reveals exact number of Revolutionary sailors killed; figure should include privateersmen. The ocean guards the identity of many who died in the War of Independence.

249. HAIL TO THE CHIEF! Celebration honors Washington. While leader of Revolutionary Army receives deserved acclaim, symbolic picture has appropriate naval background. But American Navy at Revolution's end was little more than a symbol. Of 19 Continental frigates, but two survived—*Alliance* and *Hague* (ex-*Deane*; her name changed after dubious conduct of Silas Deane brought him into disrepute). Not one of 13 original Yankee frigates, not a Yankee war-sloop had escaped obliteration or capture. To balance combat losses: two British war-sloops, a couple of brigs, one frigate (*Serapis*) captured. But Stars and Stripes were on sea at end. Navy would sail on.

250. TOMB OF JOHN PAUL JONES—in crypt of chapel, United States Naval Academy. From Revolution's crucible came the supreme lesson—good navy depends on good leadership. Hopkins, Nicholson, Simpson, Manly, Thompson, Saltonstall, Hacker—one after another fell the phonies commissioned through Congressional pull. Barry, Biddle, Whipple, Hinman, Barney—the fighters stood up. Four great sea warriors emerged. All were "mustangs." Wickes, the Maryland lobsterman; sailor-of-fortune Conyngham; fisherman Rathburne, so modest (and probably illiterate) that his name is almost lost to history; and, finally, the incomparable John Paul Jones.

251. POSTSCRIPT, J. P. J. ****
Enshrined at Naval Academy: the memory (if not the mortal dust) of Jones. For Navy, at least, his features —those of inspired and dedicated leadership—gradually came clear. Nation was not so ready with recognition. For example: Farragut was awarded $56,000 for taking New Orleans and Mobile. For commanding a squadron of steel cruisers that smashed up a handful of wooden gunboats at Manila, Dewey was lionized, given a lavish mansion. John Paul Jones never received penny of pay for seven years spent in service of Amer-

ica. Continental Congress did present him a vote of thanks—which cost taxpayers nothing. And in 1947 (two years after World War II) Congress posthumously awarded Captain John Paul Jones the Medal of Honor.

Chapter III

LAUNCHING THE U.S. NAVY

THE FOUNDER

252. FIRST COMMANDER-IN-CHIEF of the United States Navy—President John Adams. Foster father of the American Navy during Revolutionary War and sponsor of a national navy while two-term Vice President under Washington, doughty Mr. Adams, elected President in 1796, launched the Federal Navy of the United States. In May 1798 the Navy Department was organized at his behest. Spurred by Adams, the newborn Navy sailed from the cradle in 1798; stood seaward to do combat with the warships of a hostile France. Founder, guiding genius, first Commander-in-Chief, John Adams would always be revered in American History for his leading part in creation of the U.S.N. He would be remembered, too, as champion proponent of Freedom of the Seas. Some of history's saltiest observations on naval service and sea power bear his signature. On history's page, indelible.

"Neither nature nor art has partitioned the sea into empires, kingdoms, republics or states. . . . Let Mahomet, or the Pope, or Great Britain say what they will, mankind will act the part of slaves and cowards if they suffer any nation to usurp dominion over the ocean or any portion of it. Neither the Mediterranean, the Baltic, the four seas, or the North Sea are the peculiar property of any nation. A naval power is the natural defense of the United States. Our seacoasts, from their great extent, are more easily annoyed and more easily defended by a naval force than any other. With all the materials our country abounds; in skill our naval architects are equal to any; and commanders and seamen will not be found wanting." Signed: John Adams.

Flags on the Sea
COMMERCE AND CORSAIRS

253. AMERICAN MERCHANT SLOOP *EXPERIMENT* —Pacific pioneer. One of first Yankee traders to reach Asia, this little 85½-ton North River sloop, sailing from New York in December 1785, made first direct run from United States to China—a voyage of four months, 12 days. She was skippered by former Revolutionary privateersman, Stewart Dean; manned by crew of 15 men and boys. Profitably trading load of ginseng for cargo of tea and silk, she touched off a lively business with Canton that boomed American shipping revival. Such vessels as *Experiment* pioneered everywhere. But trouble loomed. "If we mean to have a commerce," wrote the American Minister to Spain in 1793, "we must have a naval force to defend it." Trade wars threatened. So did pirates.

254. BARBARY CORSAIR—menace of the Mediterranean. Flying the green "Turk's Head" of Mohammed, such craft lay in wait for American shipping east of the Pillars of Hercules. "Corsair" means "cruiser," and as such was colloquially applied to European and even American warships in the early days. But to Americans the word became synonymous with the sea raiders of the Barbary States—Morocco, Algiers, Tunis, Tripoli. Either kidnap and ransom or tribute and "protection money"— long before Columbus, the North-African powers had fixed a racketeer's clutch on Mediterranean ship traffic.

255. FRENCH WARSHIPS OF 1779. While the guillotine lopped heads in Paris, French Navy men in need of fleet reinforcements lopped topmasts and upper decks from over-age ships of the line; converted big vessels into type of frigate called *razée*—"the beshaven." After diplomatic break with United States in 1796, French Directory issued series of decrees which gave American shipping a close shave. Then at war with Britain, France claimed right to seize all neutral vessels England-bound or found carrying British goods. Within a year some 316 American merchantmen were taken prize by raiders flying the tricolor. Situation stimulated building of first U.S. naval vessels—men-of-war as large as, and sharper than, the French *razées*. War with France loomed.

Navy Down the Ways

256. NAVAL BUILDING, 1797. Rare engraving published in 1800 by W. Birch & Son of Philadelphia portrays construction of early U.S. warship—probably frigate *Philadelphia*, which was built at Philadelphia. War Department chartered the shipyards for the six frigates authorized by Congress in 1794. To invigorate American industry, War Secretary distributed construction contracts to yards in widely separated areas —Boston, Portsmouth, New York, Philadelphia, Baltimore, Norfolk. Ordnance contracts went to various foundries; timber contracts to southern lumbermen. Like today's naval vessel, the U.S. Navy's first warships contained materials from all parts of the country.

257. INSIDE "OLD IRONSIDES"—how they built the *Constitution*. One of the oldest naval photographs in existence, this camera view shows interior of *Constitution's* hull while frigate is under construction. Actually, vessel was being reconstructed when this picture was taken in 1857. She was, however, rebuilt on dimensions as fixed by Barry, Truxtun and Dale. Shipwright work, tools and timbering shown are much as they were when *Constitution* was born in her 1797 Boston cradle. Original cost: $302,718.

258. JOSHUA HUMPHREYS was the naval constructor nonpareil. Recognized by George Washington as a master craftsman, this Navy-minded Philadelphia Quaker obtained contract to design the nation's new warships by recommending speed and firepower that would make them "superior to any European frigate, and if others be in company, our frigates can always lead ahead and never be obliged to go into action but on their own terms." He proposed to achieve this end by designing a vessel which combined the bulk of French *razée* with the celerity of Baltimore clipper, giving her 24-pounder batteries (caliber previously carried only by line-of-battle ships). In effect, a pocket-sized ship of the line with scantlings equal to a 74-gunner's and armament heavier than that of any rival frigate afloat. Critics averred such ship could not support heavyweight armament. But, backbone of newborn U. S. Navy, the "Humphreys frigate" lived up to championship promise. Greatest of champions was U.S.S. *Constitution*, completed in 1798. (Model at right.)

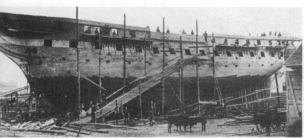

Old Ironsides at Portsmouth, May 1858

259. SAIL PLAN OF U.S.S. *CON-STITUTION*—design for a champion. She was 1,576-tonner, 175 feet in length, with 43½-foot beam, 14¼-foot depth of hold. From deck to truck, her mainmast towered 180 feet. Her hull was braced by novel trussing of Humphreys' pattern, calculated

to withstand unusual stresses imposed by many yards of canvas and clipper lines. Live oak scantlings, 22 inches thick at waterline, were calculated to bounce any cannonballs thrown by a foreign frigate. Design was drawn to order by Philadelphia draftsman William Doughty. Model made *c.* 1812.

261. CROSS SECTION, *CONSTI-TUTION'S* GUN AND SPAR DECK (below). In common with frigate type, she carried long guns on main (gun) deck, stubby carronades on spar deck. Rated 44-gunner, she was designed to mount over 50 guns. Her original main battery consisted of thirty 24-pounders. Secondary battery contained twenty-two 12-pounder carronades. Under ideal conditions her long 24's could puncture 22-inch oak hull at 1,000 yards—firepower that was disastrous to 13-inch British frigate-hulls of fir or pine at close range.

260. U.S.S. *CONSTITUTION*—Navy's greatest warship. "The *Constitution* employs my thoughts and my dreams," wrote John Adams as she neared completion. And when at last she stood seaward on July 23, 1798:

"The *Constitution* took the advantage of a brisk breeze and went out of the harbor and out of sight this forenoon, making a beautiful and noble figure amidst the joy and good wishes of thousands." A champion under way.

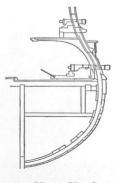

Boston Navy Yard, 1916

*United States in the Delaware
soon after launching, May 1779*

262. U. S. FRIGATE *UNITED STATES*—sister ship of *Constitution*. Early painting shows her presumably moored in the Delaware soon after launching at Philadelphia, May 1797. Launching was not so gala as flag display suggests, for frigate tore her bottom sliding down the ways. "Old Waggon" to her crew, she failed to equal *Constitution's* fast 13½ knots. But in years to come she would prove too fast for all foes except Time. Barnacled by 62 years of service, she would expire in the Norfolk debacle of 1861. She sailed on maiden cruise in 1798.

263. U. S. FRIGATE *CONSTELLATION*—stellar performer in first war fought by U.S. Navy. Rating 36 guns (standard for cruisers of her day), she was a conventionalized version of Humphreys' frigate, so ordered by a cautious Congress, uneasy at designer's innovations. Lighter than *Constitution* and *United States*, she was 1,278-tonner; length 164 feet; beam 40½; depth of hold 13½. Carried twenty-eight 18-pounders and twenty 12-pounder carronades. But (as shown in 19th-century photograph) she retained *razée*-clipper characteristics of Humphreys' design. And when she took to the water at Baltimore in September 1797, she embarked on a career second only to *Constitution's* in drama and duration. Fastest frigate of all—14 knots.

*Constellation under
partial sail, no date*

Anchors Aweigh!

NAVAL WAR WITH FRANCE

264. BENJAMIN STODDERT—FIRST SECRETARY OF THE NAVY. Chosen to head new Navy Department created by President John Adams, this patriotic merchant of Georgetown on the Potomac entered office on the eve of serious international situation. At outset his intelligence became apparent in a rare humility and rarer willingness to ask advice. "It was unfortunate that in conferring the appointment of the Secretary of the Navy upon me, the President could not also confer the knowledge necessary. . . . I wish you would give me such Observations as may direct me better in the future." With that approach, Stoddert energized the naval effort into one that accomplished much with little. As nation drifted into sea-war, Navy possessed but three frigates to pit against warships of France. Obtaining their men, munitions, and supplies, Stoddert sent them out to gain historic victory. At stake: American commerce on the Atlantic.

265. CHARLES MAURICE DE TALLEYRAND-PÉRIGORD—villain of the piece. Former Bishop of Autun, Talleyrand sided with antimonarchists during French Revolution; became Republican diplomat; then, suspected of anti-Jacobin sympathies, fled to America in 1794 to engage in land speculation. Returning to France after fall of Robespierre, he became Minister of Foreign Affairs under French Directory. After issuing decrees intended to stifle American commerce, he engineered "X Y Z Affair"—an attempt to extract tribute from U.S. Government, which American envoy Pinckney answered with flat, "No, no! Not a sixpence!" or stronger words to that effect. Weary of seizures of Yankee merchantmen, Congress (May 28, 1798) sanctioned capture of French warships in American waters. From John Adams to U.S. Navy went the word: "You are hereby authorized, instructed and directed to subdue, seize and take any armed vessels of the French Republic." This meant war!

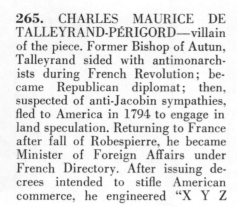

266. COMMODORE THOMAS TRUXTUN — Commanding Officer who cut the pattern for leadership in the U.S.N. Privateersman during Revolution, he was skipper of China trader when threat of sea-war with France brought him into naval service. Another Paul Jones, this salty Long Islander was self-educated, adventurous, a dashing "macaroni" and lady-killer, and a born sailor. Author of a book on rigging and a manual on celestial navigation, he was intellectually head and shoulders above other frigate captains of 1798—John Barry who captained *United States*, and Samuel Nicholson of *Constitution*. Dispatched to raid French naval bases in West Indies, Barry and Nicholson accomplished little. Truxtun, on similar mission with *Constellation*, fought lion's share of the war. "A most minute Attention to Duty is the making of a good Officer. . . ."

267. NAVY MAN OF 1798. Demanding the best, President John Adams got them by establishing monthly pay-rate of $15 to $17 and found—almost double the wages paid merchant sailors, and better than pay of skilled workmen ashore. Volunteers were permitted to examine ships and quarters before signing on. All hands were promised (and received) finest rations afloat. Enlistments were for the cruise; prize money an added inducement. Rugged discipline was in store for the American Tar, but his lot was tops compared with that of British Jack or French Frère Jacques.

268. *CONSTELLATION* READYING TO SAIL—19th-century photograph *left* showing how she may have looked when she prepared to stand out of Baltimore on her maiden war cruise. Typical of Truxtun's leadership were introductory letters he wrote to the officers, warrants, and petty officers of ship's crew. To his First Lieutenant: ". . . I wish you prosperity and honor, the Source of which is attention to duty, fondness for the ship and the general and particular Interest of the Service. . . . It is the duty of everyone and more particularly Officers, to support the Constitution and the Government under which we derive our commissions . . . an Officer . . . Shou'd be Civil and polite to everyone. . . . He is never to lose sight of that humanity and Care that is due to those who may . . . stand in the need of his assistance. . . . The United States must have a Navy or Cease to be a Commercial Nation . . ." Brains on quarterdeck.

269. CORVETTE *DELAWARE* IN ACTION. First capture of naval war with France occurred on July 7, 1798, when U.S.S. *Delaware* (20 guns) bagged French privateer *La Croyable* off Egg Harbor, New Jersey. Picture *right* is from painting on a punch bowl presented to Captain Stephen Decatur, Sr., skipper of *Delaware*. *Croyable* was renamed *Retaliation*. But French did the retaliating. Under Lt. Wm. Bainbridge, vessel was recaptured in autumn by frigates *Insurgente* and *Volontaire*.

Placing Topmast Rigging

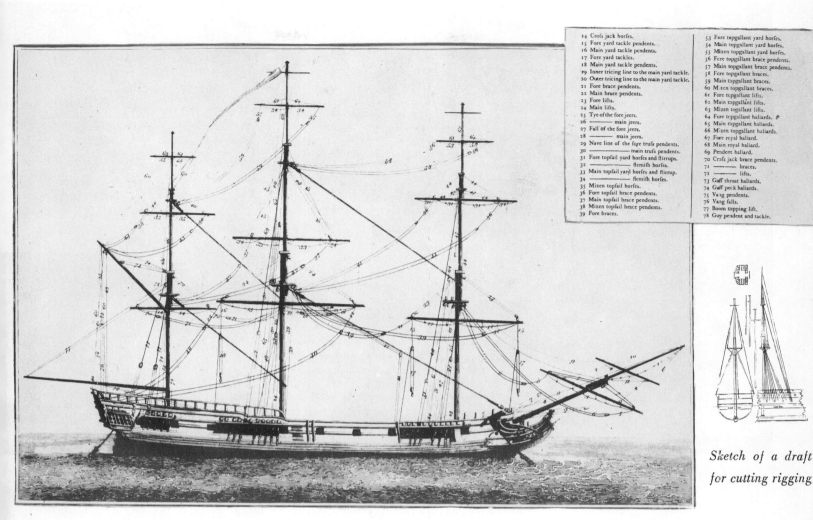

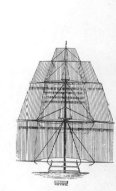

Sketch of a draft

for cutting rigging

270. TRAINING MANUAL, 18TH CENTURY. Two pages from Steel's "The Elements and Practice of Rigging and Seamanship," published 1789. This was one of the first books on seamanship available for use in the American Navy. Truxtun's book on celestial navigation was another best seller in service. So was Moore's "Practical Navigator," published in America in 1799. Revised in 1802 by Nathan'l Bowditch of Salem, book became famed "Bowditch's."

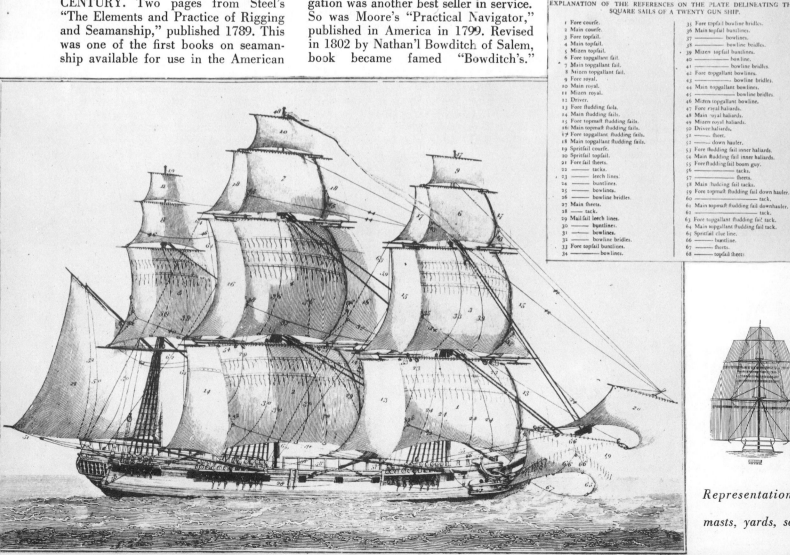

Representation of

masts, yards, sails

272. FRENCH FRIGATE *VENGEANCE*—wrecked by U.S.S. *Constellation*. Promoted to Commodore after first war cruise, Truxtun returned to West Indies with small U.S. squadron. Off French base at Guadeloupe, *Constellation* caught *La Vengeance*, 52-gunner. Ensued a five-hour slugging match. *Constellation* made Port Royal, Jamaica, with 25 dead, 14 wounded. *Vengeance*, a total wreck, had twice as many casualties.

271. *CONSTELLATION* CAPTURES FRENCH FRIGATE *INSURGENTE*—February 5, 1799. Sighting enemy cruiser off Nevis in West Indies, Truxtun's ship overhauled through squall that carried away the Frenchman's maintop. In ensuing battle, the French 36-gunner fired at *Constellation's* rigging to no avail, then closed in to grapple. Maneuvering ahead, Truxtun gained raking position. After half-hour engagement, *Insurgente* struck. American casualties:. two dead, two wounded. French: 29 dead, 71 wounded. *Insurgente*, taken into U. S. Navy, foundered in 1800.

273. U. S. WAR SCHOONER *EXPERIMENT* IN ACTION. Launched after war's outbreak were two light 12-gunners built on Baltimore-clipper lines—*Enterprise* and *Experiment*. Both sailed into boiling West Indies waters. Escorting merchant convoy off Haiti on New Year's Day, 1800, *Experiment* (Captain Maley) fought ferocious battle against picaroons who attacked her while she lay becalmed (as shown in famous drawing by Capt. William Bainbridge Hoff). In subsequent cruise, *Experiment* captured two French privateers and (by mistake) one British armed schooner.

274. AMERICAN PRIVATEER *RAMBLER*—typical Yankee raider of French War period. She flies a flag which was in use from about 1790 to 1810. The 15 stars indicate date, 1792-1796. Privateers of this kidney gave French merchantmen a rough run for the money in West Indies.

275. U. S. LIGHT FRIGATE *BOSTON*—conqueror of *Berceau*. During war emergency, patriotic citizens advanced money for construction of two 36-gun frigates, four light frigates, three war-sloops. Outstanding among "donated" vessels was 28-gun *Boston*, built by James K. Hackett of New Hampshire. Under Captain Little, she took 20-gun *Deux Anges*; on October 12, 1800, in last battle of war captured 24-gun corvette *Berceau*.

WAR WITH FRANCE

Historians called it the "Quasi-War with France"—quasi meaning "pseudo," or "simulated." A hairsplitting qualification, applied because Congress did not declare war and fighting was limited to American waters. But there was nothing pseudo to the forces afloat. No "quasi" dying to the sailors killed in conflict which cost Navy more battle-deaths than the wars with Mexico and Spain. Nothing simulated to Napoleon who, coming to power in 1799, decided loss of 85 French war vessels was over costly, and so bade Tallyrand devise a treaty satisfactory to U. S. "Quasi" was no word for the U. S. Navy's first war. It was *Constellation*'s war. Truxtun's war. Under Captain Sam Nicholson, *Constitution* fared poorly—leadership failure indicated by report which characterized captain as "good seaman probably ... but his noise & vanity is disgusting to the sailors." *United States*, under John Barry, accomplished little. When he mishandled ship during gale, rigging was saved by First Lieutenant James Barron, who won swift promotion for initiative. But Navy learned. And nation came out ahead with cost of naval effort, $6,000,000; value of trade protected, $220,000,000.

John Barry's Signal Book used by U.S. Fleet in the War with France

The Tripolitan

276. THE BARBARY STATES. Backwash of medieval Moslem world, Morocco, Algiers, Tunis, and Tripoli were Mediterranean ulcers that had long needed lancing. Ruled by evil assortment of sultans, deys, bashaws, and beys (some of whom were renegade Christians from Europe's underworld), Barbary States existed almost solely on piracy and "protection" rackets. Banded together, the European maritime powers could easily have wiped out these North-African racketeers. But Europeans appeased, even abetted the Barbary pirates. Referring to American ships in Mediterranean, Britain's Lord Sheffield wrote in 1783, "it will not be of interest of any of the great maritime powers to protect them from the Barbary States. If they know their interests, they will not encourage the Americans to be carriers. That the

Barbary States are advantageous to the maritime powers is obvious. . . . The Americans cannot protect themselves . . . they cannot pretend to a Navy." Two years later Jefferson wrote concerning Barbary: "The question is, whether peace or war will be cheapest. . . . The low opinion they entertain of our power cannot fail to involve us in a naval war." Embroiled with France, the young U. S. could not risk Mediterranean war. But in 1800 William Eaton, American consul at Tunis, wrote of the local ruler, "Can anyone believe that this elevated brute has seven kingdoms, two Republics, and a continent tributary to him, when his whole naval force is not equal to two line-of-battle ships?"

In May 1801 Tripoli called the turn by suddenly declaring war on United States. The U. S. reciprocated

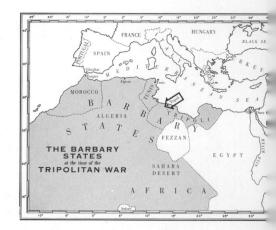

Scene of Naval Operations in the Mediterranean

Schooner Enterprise paying tribute to Trip

277. "TRIBUTE" FOR TRIPOLITANS was paid in cannonballs by U.S.S. *Enterprise* on August 1, 1801, when little war schooner, on blockade duty off enemy coast, encountered 14-gun corsair. Commanding *Enterprise*, Lieutenant Andrew Sterett reported engagement to Commodore Richard Dale: "Sir, I have the honor to inform you that . . . I fell in with a Tripolitan ship of war called the *Tripoli*, commanded by Rais Mahomet Rous. An action commenced within pistol shot, which continued three hours incessantly. She then struck her colors . . . having 30 men killed and 30 wounded. . . . We have not a man wounded, and we have sustained no material damage."

278. COMMODORE EDWARD PREBLE. Maine man. Noted for exploits as lieutenant in Revolutionary Navy. Fifteen years' experience as merchant skipper. Lieutenant on board *Constitution* during French war. Frosty-eyed. Ramrod stiff. And exactly the officer for squadron command after Dale dawdled on blockade duty, Commodore R. V. Morris muddled similar Mediterranean mission, and Truxtun resigned from service after squabble over rank. Determined to tighten slack with vigorous offensive, Preble sailed for Tripoli in 1803 with frigates *Constitution*, *Philadelphia*, and *John Adams*, brigs *Syren* and *Argus*, schooners *Nautilus*, *Vixen*, and fisty *Enterprise*.

War

279. *PHILADELPHIA* ON THE ROCKS! Proceeding ahead of Preble's squadron, frigate under Captain William Bainbridge snared Moroccan corsair *Mirboka* off Tangier. *Philadelphia* and *Vixen* then sailed on to Tripoli to establish preliminary blockade. Unlucky Bainbridge! On October 31, 1803, *Philadelphia* ran hard aground on an uncharted reef near Tripoli Harbor and Tripolitan gunboats closed in to get her. (above)

280. *PHILADELPHIA* CAPTURED! Despite crew's frantic efforts to back sails, pump ballast, and jettison guns to lighten ship, frigate could not be budged. In desperation Bainbridge ordered her foremast chopped away, but the stranded vessel was trapped. On ebbing tide, ship assumed steep list; gunners could not bring cannon to bear on attackers. Bainbridge had to surrender new *Philadelphia* with 22 officers and 315 men.

281. LIEUTENANT STEPHEN DECATUR—"firebrand of the Navy." One of two brothers reared in naval service by elder Stephen Decatur, he captained *Enterprise* in Preble's squadron. To be renowned for patriotic aphorism, "My country, right or wrong . . ." he gained early repute as a duelist and leader of daring exploits. He was first to volunteer when Preble, after stormy winter on Tripoli blockade, called for raiding party to enter enemy harbor and destroy captive *Philadelphia*. Choosing 83 volunteers from little *Enterprise* and flagship *Constitution*, Decatur packed all hands into disguised native ketch and sailed into Tripoli Harbor on night of February 16, 1804.

282. DESTRUCTION OF FRIGATE *PHILADELPHIA*. With crew secreted below decks, Decatur's ketch (aptly named *Intrepid*) approached captive ship. Sleepy Tripolitans allowed ketch to moor alongside. Then cutlass-swinging Americans boarded the frigate, planted explosives, and were off in 20 minutes. As *Intrepid* fled *Philadelphia* horrendously blew up.

283. LIFE-AND-DEATH SCRIMMAGE —dramatic moment in career of Decatur. During attack previously described, Decatur's brother, James, was treacherously slain by Tripolitan "Goliath" who had feigned surrender. Raging, Decatur chased and boarded the guilty enemy vessel. Pictures show combat in which Decatur was saved from Arabs by brave seaman.

284. BOMBARDMENT OF TRIPOLI— August 28, 1804. As illustrated by early N. Currier lithograph, Preble's squadron dealt enemy stronghold a lusty late-summer lambasting. *Constitution's* heavy gunnery silenced enemy batteries. Down came minarets and towers of bashaw's castle. Down also came ransom price for *Philadelphia's* captain and crew. To his bitter disappointment, Preble was ordered home by U. S. Government in September. With trouble brewing on Atlantic, peace with Tripoli was grudgingly negotiated in 1805. Final settlement came later. (left)

Another version of the Decatur vs. giant incident

285. PREBLE'S SQUADRON ATTACKING TRIPOLITAN FLEET—August 3, 1804. During spring and summer of year, Americans blockaded Tripoli Harbor and plastered enemy forts with intermittent bombardment —some 50 heavy guns against 115. Painting by Michele Corne illustrates general action against enemy stronghold. But attack proved indecisive.

286. COMMANDER-IN-CHIEF OF U. S. ARMY AND NAVY (1801-1809)—President Thomas Jefferson. Although described as pacifist, Jefferson went on record as pro-Navy. "Naval force can never undermine our liberties," he wrote. He felt, however, that Britain could not be met by agricultural America on the high seas; he wanted foreign trade cut, Britain boycotted, the seaboard guarded by gunboat flotillas.

287. "JEFFERSONIAN GUNBOAT" —too small a boy for man-size job. While Jefferson received public blame for inefficient gunboat fleet, such craft as the above (typical gunboat specimen) were recommended by Navy's Captain Thomas Tingey and by Army's General James Wilkinson. As Superintendent of Washington Navy Yard, Tingey temporized. Wilkinson was to face dismissal for "deals" with Spain and England. Average gunboat was a 50-footer mounting a single gun and manned by a crew of 25. Between 1806-1807 Congress authorized construction of some 238 gunboats.

288. *LEOPARD* CLAWS *CHESAPEAKE*. On June 22, 1807, U. S. frigate *Chesapeake* (Captain James Barron) was stopped off Virginia Capes by H. M. 50-gun frigate *Leopard*. Unready for action, *Chesapeake* was forced to lie to. When Barron refused to submit to search for "deserters," *Leopard*'s captain unleashed fire which mangled *Chesapeake*'s deck, killed or wounded 21 men.

289. THE PRESS GANG—demonstration of the "shanghai gesture." As evil conditions in the King's service slowed volunteering, and continuous warfare left H. M. Fleet chronically shorthanded, Royal Navy was empowered to seize English merchant seamen for naval duty. To crew-hungry British officers, any mariner who spoke English was potential Briton. So many a nasal-voiced Yankee was grabbed in the King's dragnet. In short, kidnaped.

British Recruiting, 1810

290. *PRESIDENT* CUTS NOTCH IN *LITTLE BELT*. After flogging two of victims through the fleet and hanging one (an unmistakable Yankee) at Halifax, British returned two *Chesapeake* men with icy apology. Outraged Americans demanded retaliation. In May 1811, H. M. frigate *Guerrière* stopped U. S. bomb-brig *Spitfire*; grabbed American sailor for "desertion." Provoked to action, U. S. Government ordered U.S.S. *President* out of Norfolk with instructions to locate *Guerrière* and recover shanghaied seaman. Sailing under Captain John Rodgers, American frigate put out, bone in teeth. Off Jersey Coast on night of 16th she overhauled British stranger. When Rodgers hailed, Britisher answered with cannon shot. Instantly *President* unleashed a broadside that struck home like a thunderbolt. Away with 31 casualties went H. M. war-sloop *Little Belt*—America's answer to Britain's arrogance. Incident raised storm of protest from London. But with over 2,000 American seamen struggling in British grip, U. S. Government wasn't impressed.

291. HERCULES ON HIGH SEAS—Figurehead of U.S.S. *Constitution*. Original figurehead, another Hercules, was work of skilled Boston woodcarver, Simeon Skillin. Splintered at Tripoli in 1803, first Hercules was replaced by figure of Neptune. Above model (at present in Marine Museum of the City of New York) decorated *Constitution* at later date in her career. Symbol of strength, allegorical figure stood for American sea power that, in 1812, proved no myth. Emerging as victor from French and Tripolitan Wars, U.S. Navy sailed into Second War for Independence as force to be reckoned with. Day came when *Constitution* proved truly Herculean.

292. NAVAL HEROES OF THE UNITED STATES —early American lithograph. This and similar prints were popular American parlor pinups in day of wooden ships, iron men. By end of 19th century's first decade, fledgling Navy was fast becoming sea eagle—small but full of fight. Sailing in Truxtun's wake, Commodore Preble had heightened the standard for future officership. In subsequent war with Britain, "Preble's Boys" carried on with verve and valiance that left service a remarkable example of value of inspiring leadership. Perhaps more than any contemporary officer, Preble was responsible for sea victories won by young American Republic in 1812 conflict with dowager Queen of the Seas.

Chapter IV

THE WAR OF 1812

INTRODUCTION

The United States Army did not win a single major battle. A grandiose war plan to invade Canada collapsed under an immense weight of headquarters stupidity and ineptitude. Militia Generals Jacob Brown and Andrew (Old Hickory) Jackson scored singular triumphs. William Henry Harrison, a retired captain, led a frontier force to victory. Militia General John Stricker put up a stiff defense at Baltimore. But the regular Army under professional leadership floundered in a misery of futility as one U. S. general after another proved a straw man. General Wm. Hull botched the opening offensive; lost Detroit and the Northwest frontier. Court-martialed. Old General Henry Dearborn muddled an ill-conceived Montreal campaign, made an ineffectual strike at York (Toronto), and bogged down on the Niagara front. Relieved of command. General Alexander Smyth flopped at Niagara. Dismissed. General James Winchester was captured at Raisin River, his forces massacred. General Zebulon Pike and 320 Americans were killed to no purpose at York. At Stoney Creek an American force of 2,000 was routed by 700 Canadians, and U. S. Generals William Winder and John Chandler were ignominiously captured. Near Montreal, General John P. Boyd with army of 2,000 was scrambled by a British force of 800. General Wade Hampton waded into dismal defeat on the Chateauguay. Inept Winder, recovered in a prisoner exchange, boggled the defense of Washington, and British seized the nation's capital. General John Armstrong, Secretary of War, was dismissed for intriguing against the President. Finally Major General James Wilkinson (by odd coincidence born in Maryland town named Benedict) was tried for conduct so unsavory that official whitewash failed to clear his name of treachery. Winfield Scott blamed officers for "sloth, ignorance and intemperance." Whatever, the Army's performance was the worst in its national history.

Only the little U. S. Navy stood up in the War of 1812. Jack facing Giant, it could not knock out the mighty sea forces of Great Britain. But on ocean and lake it hit those forces hard enough to save the nation's day.

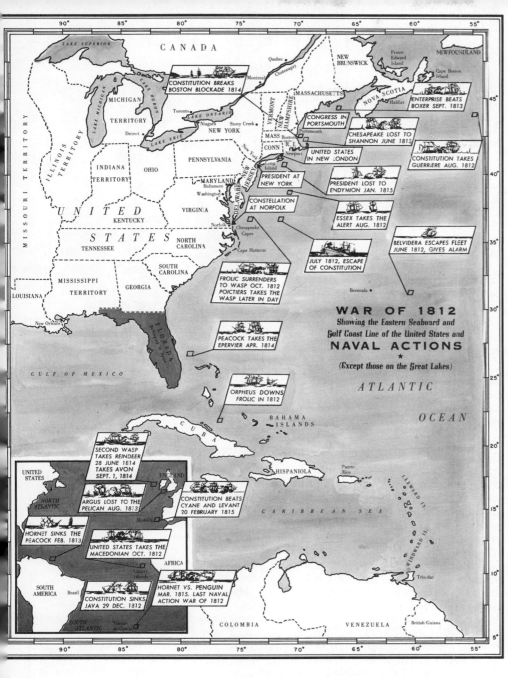

WAR OF 1812
Showing the Eastern Seaboard and
Gulf Coast Line of the United States and
NAVAL ACTIONS
★
(Except those on the Great Lakes)

293. THE WAR OF 1812 was a trade war fought between commercial rivals. John Bull, Ltd., versus Brother Jonathan. A great import-export firm and a small up-coming merchant arguing the market for rum and molasses, fish and furs, pots and pans. . . . There was a great deal of talk about Freedom of the Seas, by which Americans meant the right to ship to foreign ports and back without interference from Britain. Actually British trade restrictions were harder for Yankees to swallow than impressment. Britain backed down on both counts before the war began. But with American shipping business expanding leaps and bounds (and both sides in a temper) a clash was inevitable. . . . Trade war meant naval war— commerce raiding, coast defense, blockades, merchant convoys. So U. S. declared war with fantastic audacity. Only 18 warships to pit against Royal Navy with over 800! Eighteen warships to defend waters from Maine to Mexico and keep the Flag flying on the Seven Seas! As in no other war did U. S. Navy's survival depend on seamanship, marksmanship, leadership—and luck. Odds: over 40 to 1.

294. "M-DAY, 1812." Published 60 years later, this whimsical cartoon lampoons the Americans who were mustered by 1812 call to arms. Record suggests that U. S. Army of 1812 was poorest in nation's history. Cream of the crop volunteered for service in the miniature Navy, or sailed in lucrative and lusty local privateers.

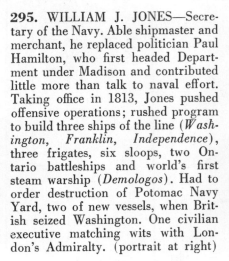

295. WILLIAM J. JONES—Secretary of the Navy. Able shipmaster and merchant, he replaced politician Paul Hamilton, who first headed Department under Madison and contributed little more than talk to naval effort. Taking office in 1813, Jones pushed offensive operations; rushed program to build three ships of the line (*Washington, Franklin, Independence*), three frigates, six sloops, two Ontario battleships and world's first steam warship (*Demologos*). Had to order destruction of Potomac Navy Yard, two of new vessels, when British seized Washington. One civilian executive matching wits with London's Admiralty. (portrait at right)

296. COMMANDER-IN-CHIEF of United States Army and Navy during War of 1812—President James Madison. Virginia lawyer, political philosopher, framer of the Constitution. An honest civilian misled by large talk from small generals with big heads. But when urged to immobilize Navy, he listened instead to Captains Bainbridge and Charles Stewart; agreed to offensive on sea. And he promoted naval activity for frontier lakes.

The

297. COMMODORE JOHN RODGERS. Veteran of French and Tripolitan Wars. Nemesis of H.M.S. *Little Belt*. Senior sea warrior of the Navy. Commanding New York squadron at war's outbreak, Rodgers led ships to sea within an hour of the news, resolved to evade delaying orders and strike an immediate blow. Misfortune dogged him from the start. Forced to rely on seamanship, marksmanship and leadership (luck go hang!), he kept his squadron above water in an ocean of enemies. Off Ireland he tricked a British skipper into taking him for English. "We're hunting Rodgers," the Briton confided. "An odd fish! And he's devilish hard to catch." They never did catch this'n.

298. COMMODORE WILLIAM BAINBRIDGE—also winner without benefit of luck. On leave as merchant skipper in St. Petersburg, Russia, at time of *Little Belt* clash, Bainbridge hotfooted to Finland for fast ship home to report for naval duty. Home, he was stunned to hear that America's coasts were to be protected by Tingey's toothpick gunboats; Navy's seven frigates were to be anchored, dismasted, and used as harbor batteries. In company with Captain Charles Stewart, Bainbridge visited capital; argued against an inert coast defense (we can meet the foe at sea); urged Madison to let Navy fight. Unluckiest of officers (captured in French War; taken with *Philadelphia* off Tripoli; accidentally injured in Finland), he, like Rodgers, would receive one break in battle—a broken leg. Like Rodgers he would win out, despite bad breaks. (portrait at left)

299. COMMODORE DAVID PORTER—officer who won an ocean. Boston born. Salt-water bred. Truxtun-trained. Postgraduate of the Preble school. But officer by virtue of ability rather than by seniority. Gentleman by inclination rather than by virtue of epaulets. "Strict, but never swore at his men." "Crews were best cutlass-and-gun hands in Navy." Independent thinker with horizon-wide imagination. Could write good prose. Draw fair sketch. Foster-father little Davey Farragut. Raise seagoing sons of his own. Of such material was "Logan" Porter, commander of light frigate *Essex* during war of 1812. Sea warrior who won Freedom of Pacific for U. S. commerce. (below)

300. ADMIRAL SIR JOHN BORLASE WARREN, R.N., commander of British Fleet on American station. Typical British admiral of 1812. Resting on his mental oars. Prepared to fight yesterday's war today. Dismayed to discover that American frigates weren't flukes, he soon was forced to appeal for reinforcements, "lest Trade be inevitably ruined." Badgered by setbacks on the sea, he favored bullheaded countermeasures to punish American shores. His blockade methods were more effective than his shore bombardments. He was replaced in 1814 by Vice Admiral Cochrane—bully who made mistake of attacking New Orleans. (at left)

Leaders

301. CAPTAIN JAMES R. DACRES, R.N., commander of H.M. frigate *Guerrière*. Proud, princely, product of his Byronic class and time, Dacres typified British warship captain of 1812. With perhaps extra pinch of ability thrown in. Arrogant as "Copenhagen" Jackson, he issued reckless challenges; once offered to bet a hat his ship could thrash any American frigate in "a few minutes tête-à-tête." He could never understand how a homespun skipper like Hull won hats.

302. REAR ADMIRAL SIR THOMAS MASTERMAN HARDY, R.N.—leader of naval force sent to harry New England coast. Officer (Nelson's flag captain at Trafalgar). And gentleman (unlike fellow-admiral, Cockburn, he conducted relatively punctilious campaign). Cleverly bottled Decatur at New London in 1813. Considered undersea warfare off Groton a breach of etiquette. Utterly frustrated in effort to teach manners to Conn. Yankees. (below)

303. CAPTAIN PHILIP B. V. BROKE, R.N. An innovator in the Royal Navy. One of those who tried to practice as well as preach Nelson's teachings. However, such Broke innovations as daily gun drill shocked stuffed-shirt Admiralty no end. Preferring maxims to marksmanship, they shipped him to Halifax—suitable Siberia for a crank who wasted King's powder. But when Broke's frigate *Shannon* met U.S.S. *Chesapeake* the powder proved unwasted. A Briton who refused to lean on luck.

304. CAPTAIN JAMES LAWRENCE —veteran of wars with France and Tripoli; commander of U. S. sloop *Hornet* at outbreak of War of 1812. Described as a "colossal figure" with muscles to match, Lawrence towered on the quarterdeck, an animated monument. He would earn early renown by conquering H.M. war-brig *Peacock*. And would win undying fame by losing his life in battle with H.M.S. *Shannon*—drama in which Navy lost a perishable frigate, but gained for itself an enduring slogan.

305. CAPTAIN ISAAC HULL —Connecticut Yankee in no king's court. Old mariner. Vet of '79 and Tripoli. Consummate sailor. Canny tactician. Captaining *Constitution* in 1812, he would dodge enemy fleet as fox eludes hounds. Then turn like tiger and tear a Britannic water buffalo to pieces. Rated by experts "above any single ship captain of the war," he showed the stuff which kept U. S. Navy going against longest odds in its history.

306. CAPTAIN JACOB JONES. Another "Preble Boy." Entered naval service as an oldster of 31, after dabbling in medicine and law. Made up for lost time on board *United States* during French War; paced nimble youngsters thereafter. Master-Commandant of U. S. war-sloop *Wasp*, come 1812, this Marylander was young enough to handle gunnery in way which would make name of Jones anathema to Georgian England.

307. COMMODORE OLIVER HAZARD PERRY—officer who won Great Lake. Strange infant in Navy's cradle. Rhode Islander reared in U.S.N., but preferred dilettante study of theatricals to texts on gunnery and navigation. Assigned to gunboat squadron at Newport when war approached, he refused minor role; demanded a leading part in war drama. He got it. Madison sent him to stage where he could star as "Hero of Erie."

308. DOWN TO THE SEA IN SHIPS they flocked in droves—swashbuckling deck hands, salty mariners, cabin boys, apprentices, shellbacks and lads as green as starboard lights. Enlistments in those days were for the cruise, thus 1812 Navy fared far better than Army in matter of recruits. Prize money, too, had considerable appeal. Barefoot Jack before the mast lived a rough, tough, tarry life, but not so rough as his Royal Navy counterpart. A Captain Porter might promise 36 lashes for the first man put on report (and keep the promise). But a Porter would (and did) first forgive new hands for accidental offenses committed. Tyrannical Bligh of odious *Bounty* fame was made Rear Admiral in contemporary British service. There were no Blighs in the U.S.N. of 1812. Jack's discipline was leavened with democracy. He touched a forelock to authority on deck, but ashore he was as good as the next American. As early illustration suggests. (picture at right, above)

THE SAILOR'S FAREWELL
Dear Nancy, dispel all thy bosom's alarms.
I fear not the storms on the main;
Not long on the ocean I part from thy charms
Till I meet thy embraces again.

The Men

309. BRITISH TARS OF 1812. Akin to their American cousins. But lacking Yankee spirit of independence which made for nimble mind and enthusiastic fist. Driven rather than led. Prisoners on board their own ships. Victims of same impressment program which had outraged American lads, Tom o'London and Bob o'Liverpool hardly knew what they were fighting for. Good sailors, though. And brave as any. As shown below in sketch by Cruikshank—typical flogging on board British warship of period. Evidently the Tar trussed to the grating (customary fashion) has been unjustly condemned. Heroic shipmate steps in to take lashing.

GREAT BRITAIN

310. U. S. FRIGATE *CONSTELLA-TION* (early photo). Throughout War of 1812 she was bottled at Norfolk by blockaders. Sister of 38-gunners *Congress* and *Chesapeake*, she survives today. (Other U. S. frigates of 1812: *President*, *Constitution*, *United States* (44's) and *Essex* (32).

311. U. S. FRIGATE *PRESIDENT*. Flagship of Commodore Rodgers at beginning of War of 1812, she is shown off Marseilles on Mediterranean cruise. Sister of 44-gunners *Constitution* and *United States*, she was unluckiest; destined to be last American warship taken by British.

Warships

poop and forecastle of conventiona. British war-sloop, they horrified U. S. Navy conservatives (e.g. Thomas Tingey). Then, sailing into action, they horrified Royal Navy. (U. S. Navy's only war-sloops at outbreak of 1812 conflict. But more on way.)

313. U.S. WAR-BRIG *ARGUS*. Built at Boston in 1803; 16-gunner; largest of type in Navy. Other U. S. war-brigs in 1812 Navy: *Syren* (16 guns); *Rattlesnake* (14); *Enterprise* (12); *Nautilus* (12); *Vixen* (12); *Viper* (10). Only one survived war.

312. U.S. WAR-SLOOP *WASP*—18-gunner nonpareil. Twin sister of war-sloop *Hornet*, she was built in 1806 on original design of Philadelphian Josiah Fox, onetime Humphreys-partner. Genius in own right, Fox endowed *Wasp* and *Hornet* with Baltimore clipper lines, steep-raked bow and stern, and ship rig. Lacking

314. *SUMMARY*. In addition to ships enumerated, 1812 Navy contained ex-light frigate *John Adams* (28 guns), classed as corvette, and older *Adams* (28 guns), out of commission. Total: 18 ocean-going warships. Seven frigates (*Constellation* eliminated) to fight Britain's 116. Not a ship of the line to fight 230. But Navy had guts!

 U N I T E D   S T A T E S

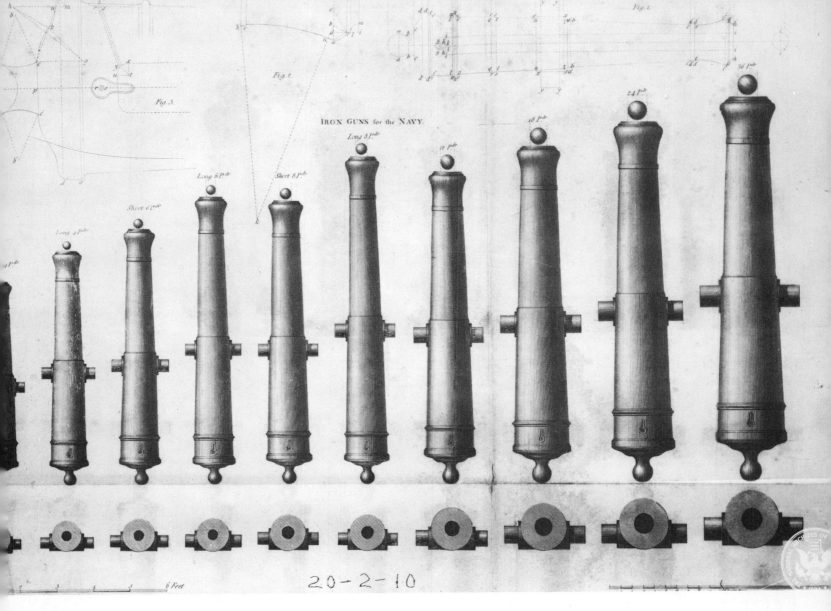

IRON GUNS for the NAVY

20-2-10

and Weapons

315. U. S. NAVAL GUNS, 1812 PERIOD. Similar to cannon of Revolutionary design were the American-forged pieces of 1812. Guns are cast-iron, muzzle-loaded smoothbores, length of barrel varying from 18.4 to 20.6 times diameter of cannonball. Standard on American warships was the so-called "medium gun"—the 24-pounder—main battery weapon carried by *Constitution* and other U. S. frigates. Best naval guns of 1812 (Perry's opinion) were forged in Georgetown on the Potomac. Arsenal in Philadelphia sent munitions.

316. CARRONADE (1800 DESIGN). Produced by British late in 18th century, the close-range carronade was common in American Navy by 1812. Era saw few innovations in naval ordnance, but there was some experimenting with gun sights and pivot mounts. Some gun mounts, like one shown, traveled on rollers in arc of metal track. The 32-pounder carronade—in effect a sawed-off cannon —packed a smashing punch, murderous for ship close aboard. Good secondary weapon in heavy frigates of *United States* class. Not so good in ship of *Essex* class, too small to fight close-quarters duel with average frigate. On display at Mystic Seaport Museum, Mystic, Conn., weapon in photo may have been on *Constitution*.

317 "LONG TOM" GUN OF 1812. Such cannon as the above, mounted on broadside carriage, were main weapons of American privateers. Shooting at British, they proved most accurate weapons of their day. To train "Long Tom," crew shifted weapon on skids by means of hand-spikes. As with other naval guns, wedges were adjusted under breech to gain either high or low elevation.

A COMPLETE LIST OF THE A

Showing the Name, Number of Guns, Commander's name, and Station of each

Names.	*Guns.*	*Commanders.*	*Present Station.*	*Names.*	*Guns.*	*Commanders.*	*Present Station.*	*Names.*	*Guns.*	*Commanders.*	*Present Station.*
Adams,	32	C. Morris,	Near Alexandria Vir.	Comet,*	14	Lt. Boyle,	Chesapeake Bay.	John Adams,	20	—— ——	New-York
Alert, b.	18	J. Renshaw,	New-York	*D. of Gloucester, b*	12	—— ——	Sacket's Harbour,	Isaac Hull,	10	Lt. Newcomb,	Massachusetts Bay
Argus,	18	Lt. Allen,	On a cruise	Despatch,	—	Lt. Page,	Norfolk	Julia,	2	Lt. Trant,	Lake Ontario
Adeline,	—	—— ——	Chesapeake Bay	Essex,	32	D. Porter	On a cruise	Louisiania,	20	—— ——	——
Asp,	—	Lt. Smith,	Lake Ontario	Enterprize,	14	Lt. Blakely,	Eastern coast	Lady of the Lake,	3	—— ——	Lake Ontario
Ætna, bomb				Elizabeth,	2	—— ——	Lake Ontario	*Macedonian, b.*	38	J. Jones,	New-London
Analostan,	—	Smith,	Cartel Service	Fair American	4	Lt. Chauncey,	Ditto	Madison,	28	I. Chauncey,	Lake Ontario
Boston,	32	—— ——	Washington, repairing	Ferret,	—	Lt. Crawley,	Southern coast	Mary, bomb,		—— ——	Ditto
Constitution,	44	C. Stewart,	Boston, do.	Gen. Pike,	32	A. Sinclair,	Sacket's Harbour,	New-York,	36	—— ——	Washington, repairi
Constellation	36	C. Gordon,	Norfolk.	Growler,	5	Lt. Mix,	Lake Ontario	Neptune,	—	Lt. Jones,	To Russia
Congress,	36	J. Smith,	On a cruise,	Gov. Tompkins	6	Lt. Brown,	Ditto	Nonsuch,	13	Lt. Mork,	Southern coast
Carolina,	14	—— ——	Southern coast.	Hornet,	18	Lt. Biddle,	New-London	Oneida,	18	Lt. Woolsey	Lake Ontario
Conquest,	8	Lt. Pettigrew,	Lake Ontario.	Hamilton,	9	Lt. M'Pherson,	Lake Ontario	Ontario	1	Lt. Stephens,	Ditto

STEELE'S List of the Royal Navy o

N. B. The Ships in Italic were taken from the enemy; and the letters after each denote the power from whom taken;

74 *Abercrombie, f.* W. C. Fabie
74 Aboukir.
74 Achilles, A. P. Holles
74 Ajax, Sir R. Lawrie, bt.
74 Alfred, J. S. Horton.
74 America, J. Rowley.
74 Armada, G. Grant.
74 Asia, A. Shippard.
74 Assistance, Com. R. Mends.
64 Africa, Rr-Adm. H. Sawyer, capt. J. Bastard.
64 Ardent, G. Bell.
64 *Argonaut, f.* (Hos. Ship) Lt. J. James.
50 Adamant, V. Ad. W. A. Otway, capt. M. Buckle
50 Antelope, Ad. Sir J. T. Duckworth, K. B. Capt.
44 Argo, C. Quinton.
40 Acasta, A. R. Kerr
38 *Africaine, f.* Hon. E. Rodney
38 *Alcmene, f.* E. L. Graham
38 *Andromache, b.* G. Tobin
38 *Amelia, f.* Hon. F. P. Irby
38 Apollo
38 Arethusa
38 *Armide, f.* F. Temple
36 Aigle, Sir J. Louis, bt.
36 Astrea, C. M. Schomberg
32 Æolus, Ld. J. Townsend
32 Aquilon, W. Bowles
20 Acorn, G. M. Bligh
18 *Achates, f.* I. Davies
18 Ablicore, H. T. Davies
18 Amaranth, G. Pringle
18 Apelles, C. Robb
18 Arab, J. Wilson
18 Arachne, C. H. Watson
18 Ariel, D. Ross
18 Atalante, F. Hickey
16 Abundance, J. Oake
16 *Acteon, f.* B. C. Cator
16 Alonzo, J. Bayley
16 Avenger, U. Johnstone
14 Acute, Lt. J. A. Morrell
14 Agressor, Lt. J. Watson
14 *Antelope, s.* Lt. D. Boyd
12 Arrow, Lt. Scriven
10 Adonis, Lt. D. Buchan
10 Alban, Lt. W. S. Key
10 Algerine, Lt T Greensword
10 Alphan, Lt Jones
8 Ætna (Bb)
98 Barfleur, Sir E. Berry, bt.
98 Boyne, Rr-Adm. Sir H. B. Neale, bt capt. C. Jones
80 *Brave, f.* (PS) Lt H. Raye
74 *Bahama, s.* (PS) Lt J. Milne
74 Barham, J. W. Spranger
74 Bedford, J. Walker
74 Bellerophon, Rr-Adm J. Ferrier, capt. J. Halstead
74 Bellona, Rr-Adm G. J. Hope, capt. G. M'Kinley
74 Berwic, E. Brace
74 Blake, E. Codrington
74 Bombay, N. Thompson
74 Brunswic, (PS) lt J H Sparkes
74 Bulwark, Rr-adm C. P. Durham, capt. J. A. Worth
64 *Bienfaifant, f.* (PS) Lt W. H. Boyce
64 Bristol, E. Wyndham
50 *Batavier, b.* (HS) Lt. T. D. Birchall
38 Bacchante, W. Hoste
38 *Belle Poule, f.* G. Harris
38 Briton, Sir T. Staines kt
36 Belvidera, B. Byron
36 *Brune, f.*
32 Bucephalus, W. J. Lye
18 Banterer, C. Ward
18 Baraconta
18 Beagle, J. Smith
18 Blossom, I. B. Rowley
18 *Bonne Citoyenne, f.* G. Green
18 Briseis, L. Ross
18 Brisk, E. Bounsher

16 Badger, J. L. Manley
16 Bustard, C. A. Strong
14 Basilisk, Lt G. French
14 *Brevdageren, d.* Lt T. P. Devon
14 Bruizer, Lt W. Price
10 Britomart, W. B. Hunt
8 Ballahou, Lt N. King
120 Caledonia, J. Coghlan
80 *Christian, VII d.* H. L. Ball
74 Canada, (PS) Lt W. B. Watts
74 Centaur, J. C. White
74 Chatham, Rr-adm M. H. Scot capt. R. Mansel
74 Clarence, H. Vansittart
74 Colossus, T. Alexander
74 Conquestador, Lord W Stuart
74 Cornwal, J. Broughton
74 Courageux, P. Wilkinson
74 Cressy, C. Dashwood
74 Cumberland, T. Baker
64 *Caton, f.* (HS) Lt. W. Brett
64 Crown, (PS) Lt W. Wickham
50 Centurion, (RS)
36 *Chesapeake, a*
38 Ceylon
38 Crescent, J. Quilliam
38 *Clorinde, f.* T. Briggs
36 Curacoa, J. Tower
32 Castor, C. Dilkes
32 Cerberus, T. Garth
32 Ceres, (RS) Lt E. Leigh
32 Circe, E. Woolcombe
32 Cleopatra, J. Pechell
32 Cornelia, W. F. Owen
32 Comus, M. Smith
22 Cossack, W. King
22 Crocodile, W. Elliot
20 Comet, G. W. Blaney
20 Cyane, T. Forrest
18 Calypso
18 Castilian, D. Braimer
18 Cephalus, E. Flyn
18 Charybdis, J. Clephane
18 Cherub, T. T. Tucker
18 Childers, J. Bedford
18 Clio, W. Farrington
18 Colibri, J. Thomson
18 Columbine, R. H. Maddle
18 Crane, J. Stuart
18 *Cretan, f.* C. F. Payne
18 Crocus, A. Adderly
18 Cruiser, T. R. Toker
18 Curlew, M. Head
18 Cygnet, R. Russel
18 Calliope, J. M'Kerlie
16 Charger, J. Askew
16 *Corso, s.* lt. G. Taylor
16 Cormorant
14 Censor, lt. M. R. Lucas
14 Centinel, lt. W. King
14 Cheerly, H. F. Pogson
14 Conquest, lt. W. Boswell
14 Constant, lt. J. Stokes
14 Cracker, lt. M. Fitton
12 Confounder, lt. J. Valobra
10 Cadmus, T. Fife
10 Chantieleer, R. Spear
10 Cheerful, lt. J. Smith
10 Cherokee, W. Ramage
10 Cordelia, T. F. Kennedy
4 Cuttle, lt. W. Paterson
74 *Dannemark, d.* H E R Baker
74 Defiance, R. Raggett
74 Dragon, Rr-adm. Sir F. Laforey, bt capt T. Forrest
74 Duncan, R. Lambert
64 Diadem, J. Pechell,
64 Dictator, J. Hanwell
50 Diomede, E H Fabian
44 Dolphin, A. Black
38 Doris
38 Dromedary, S. P. Pritchard
36 *Doedalus, f.* M. Maxwell
36 *Desiree, f.* A. Farquhar
63 Dryad, E. Galwey
32 Druid, F. Stanfell
22 Daphne, P. Pipon

18 Dauntless, D. Barber
18 Demarara, W. H. Smith
18 Derwent, G. M. Sutton
18 Dotterell, W. W. Daniel
16 Diligence
16 Drake, G. Grant
14 Daring, lt. W. R. Pascoe
14 Desperate, L. W. Jenkins
14 Dexterous, lt. N. Tomlinson
14 *Diligente, f.* E. Ives
12 Dapper, lt. H. Harford
12 Decuoverts, lt. R. Williams
12 Defender, lt. M'Cannadey
12 Depford, (tend.) lt. J. Debenham
10 Decoy, lt. J. Pearse
10 Dart, lt. Allen
10 Dominica, R. Hockings
10 Dwarf, lt. S. Gordon
8 Devastation, (Bb) T Alexander
74 Eagle, C. Rowley
74 Edinburgh, R. Rolles
74 Egmont, J. Bingham
74 Elizabeth, E. L. Gower
74 Elephant, C. J. Austen
64 Europe, (PS) lt. W. Styles
44 Experiment, (RS) lt. J. Slade
36 Euryalus, G. H. L. Dundas
28 Enterprise, (RS) lt. C Barker
18 Echo, T. Perceval
18 Eclair, J. Bellamy
18 Eclipse, H. Lynne
18 Egeria, L. Hole
18 *Electra, f.* W. Gregory
18 *Emulous, a* W. H. Mulcaster
18 Enchantress, (GS and PS) lt. J. Pasley
18 Erebus, H. J. Lyford
18 Espoir, R. Milford
18 Espiegle, J. Taylor
14 Earnest, lt. R. Templer
14 Escort, lt. G. V. Crosbie
12 Elizabeth, E. F. Dwyer
12 Evertion, lt. Murray
10 *Entrepenrnte, f.*
6 *Ems, d.*
80 Foudroyant, R. T. Hancock
74 Fame, W. Bathurst
74 *Firme, s.* (PS) Lt. H. Boyce
74 *Fyon, d.* (PS.) Lt. E. N. Greensword
38 *Freya, d.* W. J. Scott
38 *Furieuse, f.* W. Mounsey
36 Fortunee, G. F. Seymour
36 *Franchise, f.* R. Buck
36 *Fredericksiein, d.* D F. Beaufort
32 Fox, D. Paterson
22 *Fylla, d.* H. Prescott
20 Favorite, R. Forbes
20 Fawn, T. Fellowes
18 *Fantome, f.* J. Lawrence
18 Ferret, A. Halliday
18 Forester, A. Kennedy
18 Frolic
16 Foxhound, J. Parish
14 Fancy, Lt A. Sinclair
14 Fearless, Lt C. Basden
14 Flamer, Lt T. England
14 Forward, Lt R. Bankes
14 Furious, Lt J. Mundell
12 Fairy, E. Grey
12 Fervent, Lt G. Stewart
8 Furnace, (Bb)
4 Fierce
98 Glory, (PS) Lt R. Tyle
74 Ganges, Lt F. J. Leroux
74 Genereux, Lt J. Allen
74 Glocester, R. Williams
74 Guilford, (PS.) Lt J. Crouch
50 Glatton, R. G. Peacock
50 Grampus, R. Barrie
44 Gladiator, R. Adm. W. Hargood, capt. C. Hewett
44 Gorgon, (HS.) R. Adm. F. Plokmore, capt Malnwaring
36 Galatea, W. Losack

38 *Guerriere* f.* capt J R Dacres
3 Glenmore, (RS.)
22 Garland, T. Huskinson
20 *Ganymede, f.* J. B. Purvis
18 Goree, H. D. Byng
18 Goshawk, Hon W. Napier
18 *Guadalope, f.* A. Stowe
16 Gannet, J. Porteous
14 Gallant, Lt. W. Crow
14 Growler, Lt. H. Anderson
10 Goldfinch, E. Waller
6 Green Linnet
4 Gleaner, T. Trickey
110 Hibernia, V Ad. Sir E. Pellew bt. 1st capt. Rr-Adm. J. Pellew, 2nd capt. C. S. Smith
74 Hannibal, Sir M. Seymore bt.
74 Hector, (PS.) Lt. A Lighterness
50 Hindostan, D. Weir
38 Horatio, Lord G. Stuart
38 Hussar, J. C. Crawford
36 *Hamadryad, s.* E. Chethem
36 Havannah, Hon. C. Cadogan
36 *Helder,* B. J. Serrell
36 Hotspur, Hon. J. Percy
32 Hyperion, W. P. Cumby
20 Hermes, P. Browne
24 Hyæna, (SS.) J. Foxton
18 Harpy, B. N. Hoar
18 Hasty, J. Dickinson
18 Hazard, J. Cooksley
18 Hecate, Hon. H. J. Peachy
18 Helena, H. Montresor
18 Herald, G. Jackson
18 Hesper, H Collier
18 Hyacinth, W. Hamilton
16 Helicon, H. Hopkins
16 Hound, J. Black
14 Haughty, Lt J Harvey
12 Hearty, Lt J Rose
10 Hope, Lt E. W. Garrett
8 Holly, Lt (SS) Treacher
4 Herring, Lieut. J. Murray
98 Impregnable, Adm. W. Young capt E. Griffiths, capt G. C. M'Kenzie
78 *Impetueux, f.* V. Adm. G. Martin, capt C. Inglis
74 Illustrious, V. Adm. Sir S. Hood, bt K. B. capt. W. H. Webley
74 *Implacable,* I. R. Watson
74 Invincible, C. Adam
74 Irresistable, (PS) R. Mansell
38 *Imperieuse, s.* Hon H. Duncan
38 *Junon, f.* J. Saunders
36 †Java, H. Lambert
36 Inconstant, E. W. C. Owen
36 Iphigenia, L. Burtis
32 Jason, hon. J. W. King
18 Jalouse, A. Lave
18 Indian, H. Jane
6 Imogen, W. Stevens
14 *Insolent, f* E. Brazier
12 Intelligent, lt. N. Tucker
10 Jasper, H. Jenkinson
18 Juniper, lt N. Vassall
74 Kent, T. Rogers
74 *Kron, Princen, d.* T. Osmer
74 *Kron Pincessen, d.* lt. T. Burdwood
18 Kangaroo, J. Lloyd
18 Kingfisher, E. Tritton
16 Kite, B. Crispin
74 La Hogue, hon. T. B. Capel
74 Leviathan, P. Campbell
64 *Leyden, b.* J. Davie
64 Lyon, Rr-Ad hon R. Stopford, capt. hon. G. Douglas

* Captured on the 19th of August 1812, by the United States' frigate Constitution, Captain Hull, and destroyed.

† Captured by the United States' frigate Constitution, Captain Bainbridge, and destroyed.

50 Leopard, W. H. Dillon
38 Lavinia, G. Digby
38 Leonidas, A. I. Griffiths
38 *Loire, f.* T. Brown
36 Latona, hon R. Rodney
36 Leda, G. Sayer
28 *Lille Belte, d*
24 Laurestinus, T. Graham
18 Lightning, B. C. Doyle
16 Leveret, Sir G. W. Willes, K.
14 Liberty, lt. G. Guise
14 Linnet, lt. J. Treacy
14 Locust, lt. R. Fair
10 Lynx,
10 Lyra, lt. R. Bloye
80 *Malta f.* Rr-Ad B. Hallowell capt. S. H. Inglefield
74 Magnificient J. Hayes
74 *Marengo, f.* lt. H. Squire
74 Marlborough, Rr-Adm. G. Cockburn, capt. B. Ross
74 Mars, H. Raper
74 Milford, Rr-Adm T. F. Freemantle, cap. J. D. Markland
74 Minden, A. Skene
74 Montaque, Rr-Adm M. Dixon, capt M. H. Dixon
74 Mulgrave, T. J. Maling
64 Monmouth, Rr-Adm T. Folsy, capt W. Nowell
50 Malabar, (SS.) F. Bradshaw
38 Macedonian,* J. S. Carden
38 *Melpomene, f* G. Falcon
36 Magicienne, Hon. W. Gordon
36 Maidstone, G. Burdett
36 Malacca, W. Butterfield
36 Melampus
36 Menelaus, Sir P. Parker, bt.
36 *Modeste, f.* Hon. Elliot
32 Medusa, hon. P. D. Bouverie
36 Mermaid, D. Dunn
32 Minerva, R. Hawkins
28 Mercury, C. Milward
20 Minstrel, J. S. Peyton
18 Metor, (Bb.) P. Fisher
18 Minorca, R. Wormeley
18 Morgiana, C. Scott
18 Moselle, H. Litchfield
18 Mosquito, J. Tomkinson
18 Mutine, N. De Courcy
16 Magnet, F. M. Maurice
16 Merope
16 Maria, lt. Blight
14 Manly, E. Collier
14 Mariner, lt. J. Russell
14 Martial, lt. C. T. Leavers
14 *Morne Fortune, f.* lt. J. Steele
14 Muros, J. Aberdour
10 Mullet, lt. Evans
8 Misletoe, lt. Williams
4 Mackarel, lt. T. H. Hughes
74 Namur, Rr-adm Sir T. Williams, kt capt C J Austen
74 *Norge, d.* J S Rainier
74 Northumberland, H Hotham
64 *Nassau, d.* lt. W Field
38 *Niemen, f.* S Pym
38 *Niobe, f.* W J Montague
38 Nisus, P Beaver
38 Nymphe, F P Epworth
36 *Nymphen, d.* J Hancock
32 Narcissus, J R Lumley
32 Nereus, P Heywood
32 Niger, (P & HS) lt. Todman
28 Nemesis, Hon J A Maude
20 North Star, T. Coe
18 Nautilus, P. Dench
18 Nimrod, F. Mitchell
16 Nancy, lt. J A Kilwick
16 Nightingale, C. Nixon
14 Netley, lt. G. Green,
14 Nonpareil, lt. J C Sherwin
98 Ocean, R Plampin

* Captured by the United States' frigate *United States*, Com. Decatur—The Macedonian now belongs to the American Navy.

74 Orion, Sir A C Dickson bt
36 *Oiseau, f.* lt. W Needham
36 Orlando, J Clavell
36 Orpheus, H Pigot
36 Owen Glendower, B Hodgso
18 Osprey
16 Oberon, J Murray
16 Orestes, W R Smith
10 Onyx, lt. C Squire
10 Olympia, lt. W Witzdeyer
10 Opossum, T. Wolridge
10 Ortenza, lt. E Blaquier
98 Prince of Wales, J E Dougle
74 *Pegase, f.* (PS) lt. G. Dececerdoux
74 Pembroke, J. Brisbane
74 Plantagenet, R Lloyd
74 *Pompee, f.* Sir J. A Wood k
74 Poietiers, Sir J P Beresford k
74 *Princess Caroline d.* H Downman
74 *Princess Sophia, d.* lt. Bligh
74 *Puissant, f.* B W Page
64 *Prince Frederic,* Rr-adm I Buller, bt capt J S Grove
64 *Prothee, f.* (PS) lt. T Bird
50 Panther, (PS) lt. J Harrison
40 *Prevoyante, f,* (SS)
38 *Pomone, f,* F W Fane
38 *President, f.* S Warren
36 Phœbe, J Hillyar
36 Phœnix, J. Bowen
36 *Pique, f.* Hon. A Maitland
36 Pyramus, J W D Dundas
28 *Princess, b.* (GS) J Galloway
24 Porcupine, R. Elliot
18 *Papillion,* J Hay
18 Partridge, J M Adye
18 *Peacock, W. Peake
18 Pelorus, J P Rowley
18 Peruvian, A F Westropp
18 Persian, C Bartram
18 Pheasant, J. Palmer
18 Philomel, G H Guion
18 Pilot, I T Nicolas
18 Plover, C Campbell
18 Podargus, W Robillard
18 Port Mahon, F W Burgoyne
18 Procris, J Norton
18 Prospero, J H Godby
18 Pylades, J Wemyes
16 Paulina, W Percival
16 Peteral
16 *Phipps, d.* T Wells
16 *Pickle, f.* lt. W Figg
16 Porpoise, T Stokes
14 Partian, J H Garetty
14 Piercer, lt. J Kneeshaw
14 Pincher, lt. S Burgess
14 Portia, H Thompson
14 Protector, lt. G Mitchener
12 Plumper, lt. J Bray
10 Patriot, lt. W Hutchinson
10 *Paz, s.* lt. P Dumaressy
10 Pigmy, lt. E Moore
10 Pioneer, lt. Morris
98 Queen, Lord Colville
4 Quail, lt. J Osborn
110 Royal George
110 Royal Sovereign, J Bissetc
80 Royal William, (GS) Adm Sir R Bickerton, bt capt Fowler
74 Ramilies, Sir T Hardy, bt
74 Repulse, R H Moubray
74 Revenge, Sir J Gore, kt
74 Rodney, G D King
74 Royal Oak, Rr-adm. Lord A Beauclerc, capt T Shortland
64 Raisonable, E S Clay
64 Ruby Com. A F Evans
44 Regulus, J Tailour
38 Resistance, P L Rosenhagen
38 *Revolutionaire, f.* T E Woolcombe

* Captured by United States sloop of war Hornet, Capt. Lawrence, and destroyed.

AMERICAN NAVY,
Vessel, to July 1, 1813---Including those on the Lakes.

Names.	Guns.	Commanders.	Present Station.
President,	44	Com. Rodgers,	On a cruise
President,	12	M·Donnough,	Lake Champlain
Petapsco,*	12	Mortimer,	Chesapeake
Perseverance	—	Dill,	Cartel service
Pert,	3	Lt. Adams,	Lake Ontario
Raven,	8		ditto.
Revenge,*	16	West.	Chesapeake
Syren,	14	Lt. Bainbridge,	Eastern coast
Scourge,	8	Lt. Osgood,	Lake Ontario
Spitfire, bomb,			
Scorpion,	6	Lt. Kennedy,	Chesapeake
Troup,	18		Southern coast
Viper,	12	Gadsden	

Names.	Guns.	Commanders.	Present Station.
United States,	44	S. Decatur,	New-London.
Vengeance, bomb,			
Vesuvius, bomb,			

Besides the above, there are a number of revenue cutters, and about 178 gun boats; a few of which are on the lakes—also, two block vessels in the Delaware.

Building—A seventy-four at Portsmouth, (N. H.) and another at Charlestown, (Mass.) besides frigates and smaller ships in different ports.

Two sloops of war have lately been launched on Lake Erie.

* Vessels marked thus are hired by the United States.

Great Britain, for 1813.

signifying American, b Batavian, d. Danish, f. French, and s. Spanish.

38 Roto, d. P Somerville
56 Rhin, f. C Malcosm
56 Romulus, G W H Knight
18 Racehorse, J De Rippe
48 Racoon, W Black
48 Raleigh, G W Hooper
46 Recruit, H F Senhouse
48 Redwing, E A King
18 Reindeer
48 Rifleman, J Pearce
18 Ringdove, W Dowers
48 Rosamond, D Campbell
48 Rosario, W Henderson
48 Rose, T Mansell
18 Rover, I Finley
6 Ranger, G Acklon
6 Rapid, W Mather
6 Rattler, A Gordon
6 Raven, G G Lennock
6 Redpole, A Fraser
6 Reynard, H Stewart
44 Redbreast, lt. Sir G Keith, bt
44 Richmond, E O Shaugnessy
44 Rinaldo, Sir W G Parker b
42 Reball, lt C Jones
0 Resolute, lt J W Greene
0 Ruodian, G Moubray
8 Rolla, S Clark
12 St. Salvador del munda, s. (GS) V Adm Sir R Calder, bt capt J Nash
12 San Josef, s. Adm Ld Keith, K B & K C capt G Malcolm, capt S Jackson
0 Sussex, (HS) lt. W Cockeraft
0 San Nicolas, s. (PS) lt. J R Mould
4 San Antonio, (PS) lt. Squire
4 San Domaso, s. (PS) lt. T Thompson
4 San Domingo, Rt Hon Sir J B Warren, bt and K B capt C Gill
4 San Ildefonso, s. (SS) lt. F Harley
4 San Juan, s. (RS) Com G V Penrose
4 San Ysidro, s. (PS) lt. G J Deceourdoux
4 Sceptre, T Harvey
4 Scipion, f. H Heathcote
4 Stirling-Castle, J Brenton
4 Suffolk, (PS) lt A Gilmour
4 Sultan, J West
4 Superb, Hon C Paget
4 Swiftsure, E S Dickson
4 Sampson, (PS) J Steventon
4 Standard, Hon C E Fleming
4 Stately, W Stewart
4 Serapis, W Lloyd
48 Salsette, H Hope
48 Shannon, P B V Broke
58 Sir Francis Drake
58 Spartan, E P Brenton
58 Statira, H Stockpole
58 Surprise, Sir T Cochrane, bt
58 Surveillante, f. E Tucker
58 Sybille, f. C Upton
58 Semiramis, Rr-Adm C Tyle, capt C Richardson
56 Stag, P Hornby
52 Solebay, V Adm R Murray, capt R Curry
52 Success, T Barelay
20 Sabrina, A R M·Kenzie
18 Sabine, E Wrottesley
18 Sambrang. b. J Drury
18 Sapphire, H Haynes
18 Sappho. H O'Gready
18 Scorpion, R Giles
18 Scout, A R Sharpe
18 Scylla, C M·Donald
18 Sea Lark, J Warrand
18 Sake
18 Sophie, N Lockyer
18 Sparrow-hawk, J Pringle
18 Spitfire, J Ellis

18 Stork, R L Coulson
18 Surinam, b S E Watt
18 Swallow, E R Sibly
18 Sylph, W. Evans
16 Savage, W Bissell
16 Shark, (RS, R Gore
16 Sheldrake, J Gifford
16 Sparrow, J N Taylor
16 Spy, R Anderson
16 Stromboli, (Bb)
16 Swaggerer, lt. G J Evelyn
16 Swift, W Moubray
16 Seahorse,
16 Sea-Flower,
14 Sharpshooter, lt. G Goldie
44 Snap, G R Sartorius
14 Snipe, lt. C Champion
14 Spider, f. F G Willock
14 Sprightly, lt. J Petet
14 Starling, lt. C F Napier
14 Staunch, lt. H Craig
14 Steady, lt. G Green
14 Strenuous, lt. J Nugent
12 Sylvia, lt. R Palk
10 Sharpedon, T Parker
10 Shearwater, W R Smith
10 Somers, lt. G Dickens
10 Surly, lt. R Welch
8 Subtle, d. lt. C Brown
74 Thesens, W Prowse
74 Tigre, f. J Holliday
74 Tremendous, V Adm·sir W Smith, knt capt Campbell
74 Triumph,
64 Trident, (GS.) Rr-Adm J Laugharne, capt R B Vincent
50 Trusty, (PS.) lt J Coxwell
58 Tenedos, H Parker
58 Theban, S T Dighby
36 Trent, V Adm E Thornbrough, capt T Young
36 Tribune, G Reynolds
32 Thames, C Napier
28 Thisbe, Rr-Adm sir C Hamilton, bt capt T. Disk
20 Talbot S Swaine
20 Tartarus. J Pasco
20 Termagant,
20 Thais, E Scobell
20 Tortoise, T Cook
18 Thracian, J Carter
18 Trincomaleo, A Renny
18 Tweed, T E Symonds
16 Thorn, G Cranston
16 Tisiphone, W Lowe
16 Tuscan, G M Jones
14 Teaser
14 Thrasher, lt J Dornford
12 Tigress, lt W Carnaigie
20 Thistle, J K Whyte
10 Tickler, lt S Hopkinson
10 Tyrian, A Baldwin
8 Thunder, (Bb) W O Pell
8 Trial, lt T Sproule
110 Ville de Paris, G Bariton
100 Victory, V Adm sir J Saumarez, bt capt Dumaresq
98 Union
74 Valiant, R D Oliver
74 Venerable, D Milne
74 Vengeance, (PS) lt J. Edwards
74 Vengeur, T Dundas
74 Victorious, J Talbot
74 Vigo, Rr-Adm J A Morris. capt H M Omanuey
64 Veteran, lt H M Marshall
64 Vigilant, (PS) lt W Somerville
44 Ulysses, Rr-Adm W Brown, capt W. Fothergill
40 Unite, f. E Chamberlayne
38 Volontaire, f. hon G G Waldegrave
38 Undaunted, R Thomas
36 Venus, d. K M'Kenzie
32 Unicorn, G B Salt

28 Vestal, S Decker
22 Volage, D H Mackay
18 Vautour, P Lawless
18 Volcano, (Bb) J Griffiths
16 Vulture, H Baugh
16 Utile, lt W Gilchrist
14 Vixen, lt M Wright
14 Urgent, lt P Rigby
12 Variable, lt R B Yates
12 Virago, lt W R A Pettman
10 Vesta, lt G G Miall
10 Venturer, f. lt T Younger
6 Violet, lt J B Pettet
84 Waldemaar, d. lt P Despourrine
74 Warspite, hon H Blackwood
44 Woolwich, (SS) R Turner
32 Wilbelmina, B G Norton
30 Wanderer, F Newcombe
18 Weasel, J. W. Andrew
18 Wolverene, C. Kerr
16 Wasp, a
16 Wizard, F Moreshby
14 Wrangler, lt J C. Crawford
13 Watchful, lt G. Foz
10 Woodlark
74 York, A. W. Schomberg
74 Zealous, T. Boys
18 Zenobia B Foley
16 Zephyr, T C Hichens

KING'S SHIPS IN ORDINARY.

80 Alexander, f
74 Albion
74 Aclide (SR)
74 Anson
74 Arve Princen d.
74 Atlas
74 Audacious
50 Aikmaar, b.
44 Adventure (RS)
44 Assurance (RS)
38 Active
38 Alceste, f
38 Acbur
38 Amazon
38 Ambuscade, f
32 Amiable, f
32 Amphion
32 Amsterdam f
28 Alligator,
20 Ariadne,
20 Aurora,
18 Asp,
18 Avon,
14 Attentive,
14 Archer,
14 Belleisle, f.
64 Belliquex,
18 Brakel, b
58 Boadicea,
38 Bourbonaise, f
38 Braave, b
24 Blanche, f
12 Buffalo,
12 Bull-Dog, (Bb)
80 Cæsar,
80 Canopus,
74 Campdownb b
74 Captain,
64 Carnatic,
74 Conqueror,
74 Culloden,
64 Cambrain,
38 Carriere f (RS)
38 Clyde,
16 Cubas, s.
56 Caroline,
36 Cliffonee,
28 Carysfort,

28 Cyclops,
24 Champion,
20 Camilla,
18 Combattant,
16 Coquettee,
16 Curieuse, f
98 Dreadnought
94 Devonshire,
74 Donnegal, f
74 Dublin,
64 Delft, b
64 Dordrecht, b
50 Drochterland, b
38 Diana,
36 Dedaigneuse f
28 Dido, (PS)
18 Dasher,
18 Delight, f
16 Driver,
12 Discovery,
74 Edgar,
74 Excellent,
50 Europa,
40 Egiptienne, f
40 Endymion,
36 Emerald,
24 Eurydice,
18 Elven, d
18 Euderen, d.
14 Eling,
14 Epervier, f
6 Express,
98 Formidable,
74 Fortitude,
38 Fisgard, f
38 Fama, s
36 F-edericks-waarn, f
18 Falcon,
80 Gibraltar, f
74 Goliah,
74 Grafton,
64 Gylikheid, d
64 Guylderland, d (RS)
18 Gluckstadt, d
16 Galgo,
64 Haerlem, d
38 Har-Fruen d
18 Hydra,
82 Hebe,

32 Heroine,
18 Halifax,
18 Hureyac f
18 Hornet,
14 Hardy,
12 Havoc,
12 Hecla, (Bb)
64 Inflexible,
64 Intrepid,
74 Justitia, d
24 Jamaica, f.
17 Juba
14 Jaseur,
64 Lancaster,
50 Leander,
28 Lapwing,
28 Ligura, s.
16 Leucadia,
18 Lynx,
4 Landrail,
74 Maida, f
74 Majestic,
74 Monarch,
74 Mont Blanc, f
40 Magnanime,
38 Milan, f
16 Merlin,
16 Megæra, (FS)
16 Musette, f
98 Neptune,
38 Nereide, f
18 Ned Elven. d
16 Nearque, f
74 Odin, d
10 Ornen, d
98 Prince,
98 Prince George
74 Princess of Orange, b
64 Polyphemus,
54 Prudent,
38 Piedmontaise f
38 Pearlen, d
38 Phaeton,
36 Penelope,
16 Perseverance,
32 Pearl,
28 Pegasus, (RS)
22 Perseus,
20 Poulette, f
22 Prompte, f
18 Perte, f
18 Pluto,
16 Prometheus,
10 Pilchard,
110 Q. Charlotte,
32 Quebec,
74 Renown,

74 Resolution,
74 Rippon,
74 Rivoli, f
74 Robust,
18 Roman, f
16 Rattlesnake,
12 Rapide, f
80 Sans Pareil, f
74 Saturn,
74 Scarborough,
74 Skield, d
74 Spartiate
74 Spencer,
74 Syreen, d
64 St Albens,
35 Santa Dorothea
35 Santa Margaretta, s,
36 St Fiorenzo,
36 Scine, f
28 Sagesse, f
24 Squirrel,
18 St Pierce,
18 Swan,
16 Scourge,
16 Seagull,
16 Speedy,
16 Superieure, f
10 Swinger,
12 Sulphur, (Bb)
98 Temeraire,
80 Tonnant, f
74 Terrible,
74 Tree Cronen, d
74 Thunderer,
50 Tilbury,
50 Tromp, b
50 Texel,
38 Thetis,
36 Thalia,
35 Topaze, f
32 Terpsichore,
32 Tourterelle,
32 Triton,
10 Terror, [Bb]
10 Transit,
64 Utretcht, d
64 Vanguard,
40 Vlikter, b
16 Vimeria, f
0 Vesuvius (Bb)
98 Windsor Castle,
64 Wassenzar b
32 Winchelsea,
16 Wellington,
64 Zeeland, b
12 Zebra (Bb)

SHIPS BUILDING IN DIFFERENT PLACES.

74 Agincourt,
36 Anacreon,
120 Britannia,
74 Benbow,
74 Black Prince,
74 Blenheim,
74 Boscawen,
36 Barossa,
18 Bacchus,
80 Cambridge,
74 Cornwallis,
56 Creole,
74 Defence,
36 Diamond,
18 Despatch,
38 Forte,
18 Fly,
18 Grasshopper,
100 Howe,
74 Hawke,
74 Hercules,
74 Hero,
18 Heron,
74 Indus,
50 Isis,
50 Jupiter,
98 London
18 Lively,
46 Lacedemonian,
36 Lyffey,
74 Medway,
74 Minotaur,
18 Myrmidon,
120 Nelson,
38 Naiad,
100 Princess Charlotte,
74 Pitt,
74 Powerful,
36 Pallas,
36 Parana,
22 Perseus,
74 Redoubtable,
74 Rochfort,
74 Russell,
50 Romney,
120 St Vincent,
74 Sandwich,
50 Salisbury,
38 Scamander,
38 Sirius,
18 Satellite,
98 Trafalgar,
80 Talavera,
36 Tartar,
74 Vindictive,
18 Wolf,

318. MAMMOTH AND MITE—defiant Yankee poster displaying disparity between Royal Navy and American of 1812. In design similar to those of 1776, British warships of 1812 were bigger; packed more firepower. Ships-of-line in *Caledonia* class, built in 1808, were 2600-ton three-deckers toting 120 guns—largest in R.N. until 1839. Reflecting Nelson influence, British warships had shed superfluous gilt. Vessels were now painted black with yellow band marking gun ports; had red gun decks (to absorb bloodstain). Very Nelsonian. Britain's men-of-war were powerfully reinforced by Nelsonian "hearts of oak" reputation. But Nelson himself was gone (1805: Trafalgar). So were colleagues Hyde Parker and Cuthbert Collingwood. The great Jervis was in his dotage. Leading H.M. fleets against America, Admirals Warren, Sawyer, Cockburn, Cochrane, Hardy and Griffith were no Nelsons. However, genius was hardly necessary for R.N. of 1812. A whale has but to yawn and it catches fish.

John Bull taking a lunch.

ESCAPE OF THE BELVIDERE, *Commanded by the Late ADM.ˡ Rᵗ BYRON C.B. from the* AMERICAN SQUADRON.

319. ESCAPE OF H.M.S. *BELVI-DERA*. Sailing from New York, night of June 21, 1812, Commodore Rodgers raced into Atlantic with U.S.S. *President, United States, Congress, Hornet* and *Argus*. Target: Jamaica convoy, England-bound with silver cargo. On 23rd Americans sighted frigate *Belvidera*, mistook her for convoy escort, and chased. *Belvidera* was in bag when a *President* chase gun exploded, killing 16 men and dealing Rodgers a broken leg. As shown in English painting, quarry escaped. So did the bonanza convoy.

320. U. S. LIGHT FRIGATE *ESSEX* TAKES H.M. WAR-SLOOP *ALERT*. Soon after Rodgers sailed, *Essex* (left behind for repairs) breezed out of New York under command of David Porter. Sighting enemy sail on morning of August 3rd, Porter masked his ship's guns and played merchantman. *Alert* took the bait. When she raced up with cheering crew to snatch the prize, *Essex* surprised her with a broadside that left 16-gun sloop all acockbill. First Royal Navy vessel taken by Americans in War of 1812.

Opening

Africa   CONSTITUTION   Shannon   Æolus   Guerriere   Belvidera

Entered according to Act of Congress Nov. 25, 1813 by A. Bowen

Constitution's Escape from the British Squadron after a chase of sixty hours

321. U. S. FRIGATE *CONSTITU-TION* CHASED BY BRITISH SQUADRON. After lucky escape from Rodgers, H.M.S. *Belvidera* rushed war alarm to Halifax where Admiral Sawyer, base commander, promptly dispatched energetic Broke with squadron to New York area. Thus U.S.S. *Constitution* (Master Commandant Hull), en route to New York, was waylaid on July 17th off Jersey Coast. *Constitution* ran. Britons chased. Wind died. Ships crawled, inching through dead calm by means of smallboat tow and kedgings (as shown in contemporary print). Slowly H.M. "liner" *Africa* and frigates *Shannon, Guerrière, Belvidera* and *Aeolus* closed in. Just as their jaws opened to snap—! Even spry Philip Broke could not catch old Isaac Hull.

Guns

322. *CONSTITUTION* OUT-SMARTS BRITISH SQUADRON. Each time the enemy closed in *Constitution* dodged out of the box. Employing every device available, Hull kept American frigate just beyond gun-range of pursuers for three grueling days. Making most of light breezes on the 19th, he gained a little lead, deftly picking up smallboats on the run. That evening, sighting clouds, Hull deliberately misled enemy by furling sail as though anticipating a squall. When British followed suit, Hull spread canvas at top speed, sent *Constitution* sprinting through rainy gusts; next morning had her safe over the horizon. Time and again in War of 1812 British would be baffled by similar combination of superb seamanship and Yankee ingenuity. As for *Constitution*, this was merely a shakedown preamble.

Constitution

323. *CONSTITUTION* MEETS *GUERRIÈRE* (August 19, 1812). Returning from bold cruise in Canadian waters, Hull's frigate encountered Captain Dacres' about 750 miles out of Boston. Eager for battle, both captains closed for combat. Cagey Hull let *Guerrière* open long-range fire. *Constitution* yawed to prevent rakes, then closed to 50 yards to deliver stunning broadside that almost wrecked *Guerrière* (and Dacres' ego) first blast. As shown in famous painting by T. Birch, A.C.S.A.

324. *CONSTITUTION* HULLS *GUERRIÈRE*. Dragging mizzenmast overside, the British frigate reeled. Luffing under her bows, *Constitution* rocked her with savage fire, Yankee gunners shouting, "Hull her! Hull her!" Hull hulled her. *Guerrière's* bowsprit snagged in *Constitution's* rigging. Both Dacres and Hull called for boarders. As cutlass clashed on cutlass, the ships wrenched apart and *Guerrière* wallowed in mortal hurt, green seas pouring into her vitals. Contemporary French view. (at left)

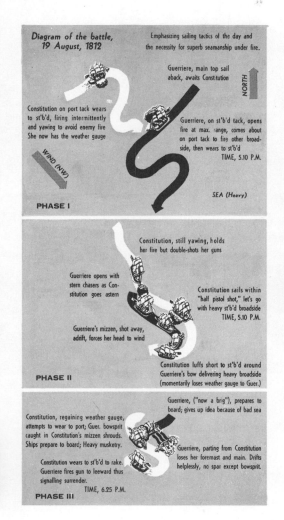

Diagram of the battle, 19 August, 1812 — Emphasizing sailing tactics of the day and the necessity for superb seamanship under fire.

PHASE I

Guerriere, main top sail aback, awaits Constitution

NORTH

Constitution on port tack wears to st'b'd, firing intermittently and yawing to avoid enemy fire She now has the weather gauge

Guerriere, on st'b'd tack, opens fire at max. range, comes about on port tack to fire other broadside, then wears to st'b'd TIME, 5.10 P.M.

WIND (NW)

SEA (Heavy)

PHASE II

Constitution, still yawing, holds her fire but double-shots her guns

Guerriere opens with stern chasers as Constitution goes astern

Constitution sails within "half pistol shot," let's go with heavy st'b'd broadside TIME, 5.10 P.M.

Guerriere's mizzen, shot away, adrift, forces her head to wind

Constitution luffs short to st'b'd around Guerriere's bow delivering heavy broadside (momentarily loses weather gauge to Guer.)

PHASE III

Guerriere, ("now a brig"), prepares to board; gives up idea because of bad sea

Constitution, regaining weather gauge, attempts to wear to port; Guer. bowsprit caught in Constitution's mizzen shrouds. Ships prepare to board; Heavy musketry.

Guerriere, parting from Constitution loses her foremast and main. Drifts helplessly, no spar except bowsprit.

Constitution wears to st'b'd to rake. Guerriere fires gun to leeward thus signalling surrender. TIME, 6.25 P.M.

325. *CONSTITUTION* FLAYS *GUERRIÈRE*. As frigates separated, a *Constitution* broadside chopped down *Guerrière's* foremast. Then Briton's mainmast crashed, and she drifted helplessly, strewing the sea with flotsam and corpses. When Hull closed in for another rake, Dacres abjectly surrendered. London stated he was captured by a ship-of-line.

v s . G u e r r i e r e

326. *CONSTITUTION* CAPTURES *GUERRIÈRE*. Early lithograph is too placid; *Guerrière* was a rolling hulk when Dacres struck flag. In 55-minute battle Britisher was smashed beyond salvage, with 78 casualties. *Constitution* was barely hurt with 14. In losing frigate, Royal Navy also lost face, suffering first major defeat in 14 years. Tonic for American morale.

327. BOWSPRIT SEEN FROM THE BULWARKS—as *Constitution's* sailors saw it. Men at these guns saw plump Captain Hull order open fire with an exuberant leap in the air that burst his britches. Later saw him decline Dacres' sword with chuckle, "But I'll trouble you, sir, for that hat." Later saw Boston cheering "Old Ironsides." (below: photo circa 1900)

Celebration Hulls Victory

328. *WASP* TAKES *FROLIC* (October 18, 1812). Battle banged off Chesapeake Capes when Jacob Jones' *Wasp* ambushed a convoy, and escort brig *Frolic* opened fire. In gun duel *Frolic* fired on "up wave," whereas Jones ordered *Wasp's* on "down dip." When *Frolic* gave up, gutted by plunging shots, only four living men stood her deck. Shortly afterward, *Wasp* herself was captured. It took H.M.S. *Poictiers*—a 74-gun battleship—to do it. *Frolic* was beyond salvage.

329. *UNITED STATES* MEETS *MACEDONIAN* (October 25, 1812). Lone-wolf cruises were game that autumn. Hence frigate *United States* roaming alone off the Canary Islands. Along comes H.M.S. *Macedonian*, crack frigate under Captain Sam'l Carden. Noted "sundowner" and ruthless flogger, Carden mistook *United States* for light frigate *Essex*. By time he realized error, he himself was in for a flogging. By "Old Waggon" and Stephen Decatur. (picture at right)

330. *UNITED STATES* CAPTURES *MACEDONIAN* (below). Steady under easy canvas, Decatur evaded Carden's rushing tactics; lambasted Briton with long-range fire that reduced her to shambles. Two hours of playing whipping boy, and Carden surrendered. British casualties 104; American, 12. To Decatur, Carden whined, "What will they do to me?" "Old Waggon" hauled him and his ship to Newport. "A national disgrace," roared the London *Times*. "In the name of God, what was done?"

Flush of

331. BLOOD AFTER THUNDER— scene on board *Macedonian*. "It was like a tremendous thunderstorm," a sailor wrote. "There were torrents of blood. Cries rang through the *Macedonian*. I saw a man named Aldrich torn open; he was thrown overboard. [Our part of] the ship was called 'slaughter house.' " Nelson's red paint could not conceal blood spilled here.

Victory

332. *CONSTITUTION* MEETS *JAVA* (December 29, 1812). Replacing Isaac Hull (given command of Portsmouth Navy Yard), Commodore Bainbridge took *Constitution* and *Hornet* on cruise to South Atlantic. Leaving *Hornet* to blockade a British sloop at Bahia, he sailed off Brazil looking for bear. He found fine specimen in H.M. frigate *Java*, ex-French, superb sailer, under expert Henry Lambert. Early in combat distinguished by mutual skill, an American shot felled H.M.S. *Java's* mizzenmast.

333. *CONSTITUTION* DOWNS *JAVA*. With galling fire, "Old Ironsides" raked *Java's* deck. Return fire from *Java* smashed *Constitution's* steering wheel with blast that drove copper bolt into Bainbridge's thigh. Crippled, the Commodore hung on as cannonade roared and *Java* rammed her bowsprit over *Constitution's* quarter. When British tars tried to board, *Java's* captain was slain by Marine snipers in *Constitution's* maintop. *Java* men fell back. Warships separated. Briton's mainmast crashed. And she surrendered with 122 men down to *Constitution's* 34. After sinking abandoned hulk, Bainbridge headed "Ironsides" to Boston, victor despite long adversity. Wailed the London *Pilot*, ". . . a third British frigate has struck her flag to an American. This is an occurrence that calls for most serious reflection. . . ."

334. *HORNET* DOWNS *PEACOCK* (February 24, 1813). Driven away from Bahia by enemy battleship, sloop *Hornet* cruised northward around hump of Brazil. Off British Guiana, she met crack H.M. brig *Peacock*. Proud bird's 20 guns were no match for *Hornet's* heavy 18. Nor was *Peacock's* skipper a match for strapping James Lawrence. Two *Hornet* broadsides were enough. Carrying dead skipper, nine British tars and two Americans of rescue party, riddled *Peacock* sank shortly after action. London morale sank deeper.

*Wounded but
Victorious*

335. CHAMPION OF 1812. *Constitution.* (From early woodcut made of oak taken from one of her knees.) Lord Lansdowne to Parliament: "If anyone were asked about the services of our own navy he would have some difficulty answering." But in 1813!

336. AMERICAN CARTOON OF 1812—(above) U.S.N. at work on J. Bull. Box score as of Jan. 1813: 3 H.M. frigates, 3 sloops downed to loss of one U. S. sloop, 3 small brigs. Old Tom Jefferson to John Adams: "I congratulate you on our Navy."

337. BRITISH CARTOON OF 1812 —by Cruikshank. Cahoots with Devil and Napoleon, President Madison is shown in bad company. (War evoked a spate of vitriolic cartoons and verse. British propaganda of 1812 featured U. S. Army defeats; avoided Navy.

*Bainbridge on
the Constitution*

Prayer before battle

338. *CHESAPEAKE* VERSUS *SHANNON* (June 1, 1813). Promoted to frigate command, big James Lawrence of *Hornet* fame took over *Chesapeake* at Boston. Blockading harbor was H.M. frigate *Shannon* captained by P. B. V. Broke, who sent Lawrence formal combat challenge. "Only by repeated triumphs can your little navy console your country for loss of trade." Lawrence took *Chesapeake* seaward to fight it out. Rash move for ship with an untried crew. Aware he might be out-maneuvered, Lawrence rushed straight at enemy.

Lion Strikes Back

339. *SHANNON* BOARDS *CHESAPEAKE*. *Shannon's* opening broadsides hit hard. As *Chesapeake* wallowed, badly hurt, the Britons, led by Broke, swarmed aboard. During wild scrimmage, Lawrence fell, fatally wounded, shot through the lungs.

340. "DON'T GIVE UP THE SHIP!" gasped Lawrence when carried below. Appeal destined to become Navy's watchword. Unhappily it went unheard on *Chesapeake's* deck where 32 of her men were cut down in 15-minute cutlass fight. Down came flag.

ORDER.

Officers of the Navy of the United States.
Masonic Societies.
Clergy.

CAPTAINS.		CAPTAINS.
HULL,		STEWART,
BAINBRIDGE,		BLAKELY,
CREIGHTON,		PARKER.

LIEUTENANTS.		LIEUTENANTS.
BALLARD,		WILKINSON,
&		
HOFFMAN,		NICHOLSON,
REILLY,		NORRIS,

Relatives.

Capt. CROWNINSHIELD, and ten Masters of ships, who accompanied him in the Flag.

341. FOR WHOM THE BELLS TOLLED—Lawrence funeral procession. (From "An Account of the Funeral Honors Bestowed on the Remains of Capt. Lawrence and Lieut. Ludlow," pub. Boston, 1813.) Under flag of truce, seven Salem skippers sailed to Halifax to bring dead heroes home. From famous ·India Wharf, cortege paced through Salem to cemetery while bells tolled "melancholy knell." Pallbearer roster of Navy greats. But in *Chesapeake's* wake came recrimination. Even as Navy eulogized Lawrence, angry Department court-martialed Lt. W. S. Cox for "deserting post under fire." (Ancient history? In 1952 the Navy cleared Cox's name on descendant's claim that he acted under orders to carry wounded Captain Lawrence below decks at critical moment.)

Shannon and Chesapeake enter Halifax.

A VIEW OF THE GALLANT ACTION
...ESTY'S FRIGATE THE SHANNON AND THE CHESAPEAKE AMERICAN FRIGATE.

342. "TARS OF OLD ENGLAND TRIUMPHANT." (Engraving published London, July 1813; artist unidentified.) Clearly expresses British jubilation at capture of U. S. warship after year of staggering naval defeats. Also expresses violence of combat which cost *Chesapeake* 145 casualties to *Shannon's* 72. Both frigates were 38-gunners. But Lawrence and men were new-formed crew; Broke and company had team-worked for seven years. *Shannon's* Tars triumphed because they were best trained hands in Royal Navy. Also among best led.

BRITISH VALOUR and YANKEE BOASTING or, Shannon versus Chesapeake.

343. "BRITISH VALOR AND YANKEE BOASTING, or *Shannon* vs. *Chesapeake*"—contemporary jape in London *Town Talk* by English caricaturist Cruikshank. Artist neglects to show Captain Broke taking a skull-slash from Lieutenant George Budd, U.S.N. (a blow that incapacitated Broke for rest of life). Fierce resistance by *Chesapeake* men robbed battle of humor. Ship was butcher-shop when they finally surrendered.

344. "YOU MAY KISS MY TAFF-RAIL!" jeers English cartoon published by Thos. Tegg of Cheapside six months after *Shannon* victory. By summer of 1813 British blockaders ranged from Long Island to New Orleans. The *Columbian Centinel* mourned "shipping rotting at the docks; grass on the wharves." U. S. commerce was expiring. "Torpedo" (below) refers to American effort to break blockade with mine warfare. An effort that worried the British.

The YANKEY TORPEDO.

345. *ARGUS* FALLS TO *PELICAN* —August 13, 1813. Another hard jolt to Navy was loss of *Argus* after plucky 20-gun brig had carried new Ambassador to France, then captured 20 British merchantmen as raider in Irish Sea. Unfortunately *Argus* took one ship too many, seizing vessel loaded with liquor. Certainly brig's crew was entitled to celebrate. But as usual, rum-and-seawater formula proved fatal. After dodging a pack of British frigates, *Argus* blundered into H.M. brig *Pelican* (20 guns). In battle, Master Commandant Wm. Allen was mortally stricken, his gunners hit everything but the target. *Pelican* quickly swallowed *Argus*.

Point Counter Point

346. *ENTERPRISE* KNOCKS OUT *BOXER* (September 5, 1813). Sailing from Portsmouth on autumn cruise, American brig (converted schooner) *Enterprise* encountered brand new British war-brig *Boxer* off coast of Maine. The two 14-gunners promptly engaged in ferocious slugging bout. *Boxer's* Captain Blyth was killed. Yankee skipper, Lieutenant Wm. Burrows, fell. On *Enterprise* quarterdeck, Lieutenant E. R. McCall continued battle (his first) like a veteran. *Boxer* aimed high. *Enterprise* shot low. Body blows dealt Briton were her undoing. Commenting on *Boxer's* defeat and capture, the London *Times* wailed, "The fact seems to be clearly established that the Americans have superior mode of firing."

347. *BOXER* A LOWLY MERCHANTMAN. In Portland cemetery her captain was ceremoniously buried beside *Enterprise's* Captain Burrows. Ship was ruined for naval service. Her sternboard and figurehead survive in famous Mystic Museum.

348. AMERICAN JIBE AT BRITAIN—an 1813 cartoon illustrating defeat of *Boxer*. But Americans could do little crowing in 1813. British blockade held U. S. shipping locked in from Maine to Mexico. Desperate Yankees now tried undersea warfare.

rehead of H.M.S. *Boxer*.

aboard of H.M.S. *Boxer*.

Stop, Stop Stop Brother Jonathan, or I shall fall with the loss of blood— I thought to have been too heavy for you— But I must acknowledge your superior skill— Two blows to my one!— And so well directed too! Mercy mercy on me, how does this happen!!!

Ha-ah Johnny! you thought yourself a *Boxer* did you!— I'll let you know we are an *Enterprizing* Nation and ready to meet you with equal force any day.

W. Charles del et Sculp

A BOXING MATCH, or Another Bloody Nose for JOHN BULL.

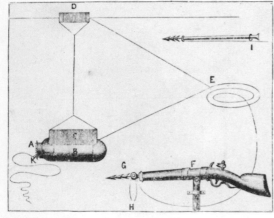

FULTON'S TORPEDO. Inventor's drawing shows harpoon gun (F) for firing harpoon (G) into bow of enemy vessel. Attached to harpoon, line (H) uncoils (E) and pulls float (D) and torpedo-bomb (B) into prow of target ship. Bomb is exploded by clockwork timer (A) set to accommodate attack.

Undersea
WAR OF

349. FIRST SUBMARINE *NAUTILUS*—too radical for Navy. Twenty years after Bushnell. Robert Fulton of Philadelphia. Portrait painter, gunsmith, man with idea for submarine. Cold-shouldered in America, he goes to Paris for backing. Result: *Nautilus,* built in 1801—undersea boat 21 feet long, 7 in diameter, copper-hulled; her portrait (above) by artist himself. As shown, she sailed on surface. Submerged, she went by hand-driven screw. And she worked. In the Seine. Off Brest. But Napoleon, engrossed with Josephine and land warfare, lost interest. So Fulton tried England. He interested Prime Minister Pitt. But horrified

Admiral Jervis, who called Pitt "a fool to encourage a mode of war which we do not want." Fulton returned to States; tried Congress; won appropriation of $5,000 for undersea experiments. Navy scoffed (in 1810) when he failed to torpedo target-ship *Argus* (thanks to Commodore Rodgers, protecting vessel with belt of netting). But (in 1812) Americans remained to pray. Undersea mines; torpedoes fired by gun; Navy's first torpedo boat; submarine *Mute*—these and world's first steam warship!—all by Mr. Robert Fulton.

MAP
of
New London
and its vicinity
Exhibiting the situation of the
Harbour. Forts. Frigates.
&c.

Engraved & Printed by A. Doolittle New Haven Aug.t 25.th 1813

Warfare

1 8 1 2 ★ ★

350. NEW LONDON BLOCKADE —target for 1813 submarine. Late in May 1813, Commodore Stephen Decatur ran New York blockade with *United States, Macedonian* and *Hornet.* Only to run into bigger block off Block Island. Pursued by Admiral Sir Thomas Hardy, Decatur retired topspeed to New London, where Hardy proceeded to lock him in with frigates *Ramillies, Orpheus, Endymion* and *Statira*—as shown on chart (above) published August 1813 at New Haven. Excerpt from Connecticut newspaper (summer of 1813):

"A gentleman of Norwich has invented a diving boat, which by means of paddles he can propel under water. . . . He has been three times under the bottom of *Ramillies* off New London. . . . So great is the alarm and fear on board the *Ramillies* that Commodore Hardy keeps his ships under way at all times." With Hardy threatening harsh reprisal for undersea attacks, U. S. Navy officially deplored torpedo warfare—hypocrisy which caused David Porter to comment that Navy "preferred the more chivalric method of mowing down crews with grape and canister." Who was the Norwich hero? Some say a Mr. Mix. Hardy suspected Fulton.

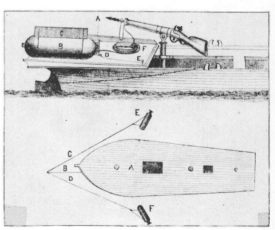

FULTON'S TORPEDO-BOAT. Inventor's drawing shows harpoon gun mounted in stern of skiff. When harpoon is fired, torpedo-bomb (B) is cast overside. As boat races off, torpedo may strike either bow of advancing ship (lower diagram). Torpedo timer was made in New York.

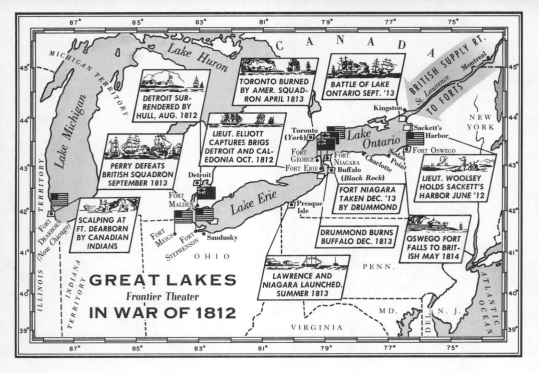

GREAT LAKES
Frontier Theater
IN WAR OF 1812

351. FRONTIER THEATER IN WAR OF 1812—the Great Lakes. Scenery: woods and water, pioneer towns and log stockades. But beachheads of enormous importance. At stake the United States–Canadian border—upper and lower Canada, upper New York State, northern Pennsylvania, Ohio, Michigan Territory, the entire American Northwest. Yet on this vital stage the opening war drama verged on military burlesque. In repeat performance of Revolutionary War strategy, U. S. Army forces attempted to invade Canada and were thrown back by British who then tried to invade United States. The American invasion effort was a farce. It was promoted by a Congress dizzy with war hysteria. Roared John C. Calhoun (a leading "War Hawk" in the House): "I believe that in four weeks time the whole of upper Canada and a part of lower Canada will be in our power." Four weeks! It took Major General James Wilkinson, U.S.A., six months to travel from New Orleans to Great Lakes front—a junket which led Winfield Scott to remark that the General must have journeyed "on his hands and knees." Meantime, General Wm. Hull, invading Canada from Detroit, retreated in frantic panic; surrendered Detroit (August 1812) without a shot. Isolated, Fort Dearborn was scalped by Canadian Indians; and Michigan, Lake Erie and vast American Northwest lay wide open to enemy. Autumnal American drives on Niagara and Montreal floundered into fiasco. Happily, Governor General Sir George Prevost, in charge of British forces in Canada, proved as inept as his adversaries. Neither British nor American war chiefs seemed aware of fact that keys to the Great Lakes Theater were the lakes themselves—natural highways for the transport of troops and war supplies. At Kingston, junction of St. Lawrence River and Lake Ontario, the British had built a small naval base. Some 60 miles distant the U.S.N. had pioneered a naval station at Sackets Harbor. Opposing strategy seems obvious. Seizure of Kingston would plug the St. Lawrence, give Americans immediate control of Lake Ontario, and thus deprive British of their supply line to Niagara and points West. Conversely, seizure of Sackets would place Ontario in Britain's palm. But American war planners consistently bypassed Kingston. For his part, General Prevost muffed a chance to capture Sackets when it was defended by one lone war-brig. Eventually Captain Sir James Yeo, R.N., arrived at Kingston with 36 officers, 450 men. But he was ordered to maintain a strict defensive on Lake Ontario. Also on defensive was Commodore Isaac Chauncey, U.S.N., sent from New York Navy Yard to take command at Sackets. So naval affairs on Ontario drifted into a doldrum stalemate. Smash hit of the Great Lakes theater would be staged on Erie. By Oliver H. Perry.

Drama on the

★ ★ ★ O N T A R I O

352. COMMODORE ISAAC CHAUNCEY—in over-all command of American lake forces. Considered lofty strategist, this Tripoli veteran proved better on base than on battle line. Arriving at Sackets Harbor in autumn of 1812, he launched program to outbuild British lake fleet based at Kingston. Under his direction two large corvettes were constructed, seven schooners armed, keels laid for two huge battleships. With long-range foresight he projected naval base at Presque Isle on Lake Erie. But on quarterdeck his foresight developed astigmatism. "Never despise your enemy," he wrote wisely. Then went on to over- admire Yeo. Avoiding Kingston, he favored strike at York (Toronto)— easy mark but hardly worth the powder. After crossing lake and burning York (April 1813), Chauncey's forces sailed on westward to attack in Niagara area. Meantime, British forces under Prevost and Yeo sailed from Kingston for second strike at Sackets. Only heroic stand by militia under Quaker general, Jacob Brown, saved Chauncey's Ontario base from capture. When Brown, transferred to Niagara front, later appealed for naval assistance, Chauncey sulked on paper, "I shall not be diverted by any sinister attempt to render me subordinate to the Army." Picayune idea.

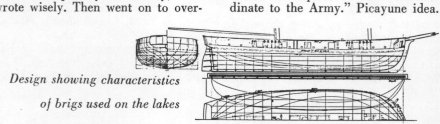

Design showing characteristics of brigs used on the lakes

353. BATTLE OF LAKE ONTARIO —contemporary view. After drubbing at Sackets Harbor, the enemy raided several lake ports in reprisal for assault on York. In June 1813, British forces looted village of Charlotte (near Rochester, N.Y.), then hit Sodus Point where they burned a few houses and the local hotel. Returning hell-for-canvas to Sackets, Chauncey's squadron fought some futile skirmishes with Yeo's. If action pictured (September 1813) resembles yacht race rather than battle, the artist was not inaccurate. Chauncey himself described his favorite tactic as "edging away." And Yeo was indisposed to argue. Few shots were fired in these regattas. In May 1814 the British suddenly struck Oswego, grabbed fort and pillaged town—then sailed away. Battle for Ontario ended in a building race, the Canadians launching a giant warship at Kingston to offset the 100-gun *New Orleans* looming up at Sackets. A fist-shaking finale to a conflict decided on Erie.

Great Lakes
S T A L E M A T E

354. LIEUTENANT MELANCTHON WOOLSEY—Lake Ontario defender. Stationed at Sackets Harbor with little 16-gun brig *Oneida* (sole American warship on Ontario at war's outbreak), Woolsey contrived to hold strategic base against British assault in June 1812. Mooring *Oneida* in harbor neck at Sackets, he landed her offside guns to use as shore battery. Gunners ashore joined those on *Oneida* in lambasting Sir George Prevost's attack force which included a 22-gun corvette, two war-sloops, three armed schooners. Scourged by blistering cross fire, British limped back to Canadian base at Kingston. Saving of Sackets Harbor was U. S. Navy's sharpest performance on Ontario. Once burnt, foe went shy.

355. CAPTURE OF H.M. BRIGS *DETROIT* AND *CALEDONIA* AT FORT ERIE. After General Hull's surrender of Detroit, British invasion forces massed at western end of Lake Erie for drive into Ohio. While American frontiersmen under General Wm. Henry Harrison girded for showdown, American naval forces under Lieutenant Jesse D. Elliott prepared to defend eastern end of the lake. In good beginning, Elliott readied a small squadron at Black Rock (Buffalo). And on night of October 7, 1812, his sailors surprised and captured H.M.S. *Detroit* and *Caledonia* anchored off Fort Erie. Carrying $200,000 fur cargo, *Caledonia* made rich prize. Then, with furs, Elliott went into winter hibernation. So Erie command passed in following spring to Master Commandant

Oliver Hazard Perry, who reported from Rhode Island with 150 Narragansett seamen and a head full of dramatic ideas. Chief idea: to rush the building of a squadron at Presque Isle and blow British naval forces off Lake Erie. Sizable project to launch from a beach on the edge of wilderness. But it did not faze Perry. The timber was there for ships. And so was master shipwright Noah Brown, genius who could have built the Ark five times faster than his scriptural namesake. But everything from anchors to cordage had to come overland from 'way back East. Gear from New York, guns from Georgetown, yet they got there. Brown and Perry did the rest. And behold, brigs *Lawrence* and *Niagara*, 500-tonners, 20 cannon each. Warships where there'd been woods, water, thin air!

356. POWDER FOR COMMODORE PERRY—overland logistics line. Perry's naval guns were rushed from Georgetown Foundry on Potomac (from cannon-maker who promised to build church if Perry won battle: hence, Foundry Methodist Church in Georgetown). Munitions were rushed to inland base at Pittsburgh by Conestoga wagon whose drivers boasted "Philadelphia to Pittsburgh in twenty days!" Photographed 100 years after gallop with Perry's munitions: one of old powder wagons.

Erie

357. PERRY ON BOARD WARBRIG *LAWRENCE*. (Left: rare woodcut portraying Perry with a beard!) By summer of 1813, Perry's vessels were launched. In addition to 20-gun brigs *Lawrence* and *Niagara*, Perry's squadron contained *Caledonia* (3 guns), six 1-gun schooners and sloop *Ariel* (4 guns). Ready to meet British squadron on Lake Erie.

358. BATTLE OF LAKE ERIE (September 10, 1813) exploded after Perry led his squadron to western end of lake, answering call for help from hard pressed General Harrison. Cutting British supply line between Canada and Sandusky front, Perry invited attack by enemy squadron under Commodore Robert Barclay, R.N., tough Trafalgar veteran. Barclay's squadron included new corvette *Detroit* (14 guns), sloop *Queen Charlotte* (17), brigs *Lady Prevost* (13) and *Hunter* (10) and two small craft. Leading Americans into battle near Put-in-Bay, flagship *Lawrence* (below, right) was hard hit by flagship *Detroit* (left) and the *Charlotte*.

359. BATTLE FLAG OF U.S.S. *LAWRENCE*. With characteristic dramatic instinct, Perry flew flag displaying the last words of Captain Lawrence. But desperate battle signals from Perry were somehow ignored by Lt. Jesse Elliott, captain of *Niagara*, who held his ship at distance while Perry's vessel was bashed into pulp by enemy *Queen Charlotte*.

Campaign

360. PERRY ABANDONS SHIP. With over half the crew down and all but one gun disabled, Perry ordered *Lawrence* abandoned. Overside in smallboat, he directed survivors to pull for *Niagara* lurking on the sidelines. With him Perry took his famous motto flag, but the national ensign was not lowered on board *Lawrence* until he reached *Niagara*.

361. PERRY TRANSFERS TO *NIAGARA*—contemporary lithograph depicts crucial episode. Believing Perry had given up, British on *Queen Charlotte* sent up gusty cheer. Then, noting direction of Commodore's boat, *Charlotte*'s gunners fired furiously at the craft. Perry's men got him through. Most of sailors in American squadron were raw recruits, among them a company of Negroes promised freedom if they served in Navy. Trained or no, they performed better service than Lieutenant Elliott, whose dubious conduct in battle was never satisfactorily explained. Reaching *Niagara*, Perry ordered Elliott to leave ship and bring up dilatory schooners while he himself took command of *Niagara*.

A page from Perry's signal book show-

ing where to fly flags and their meaning.

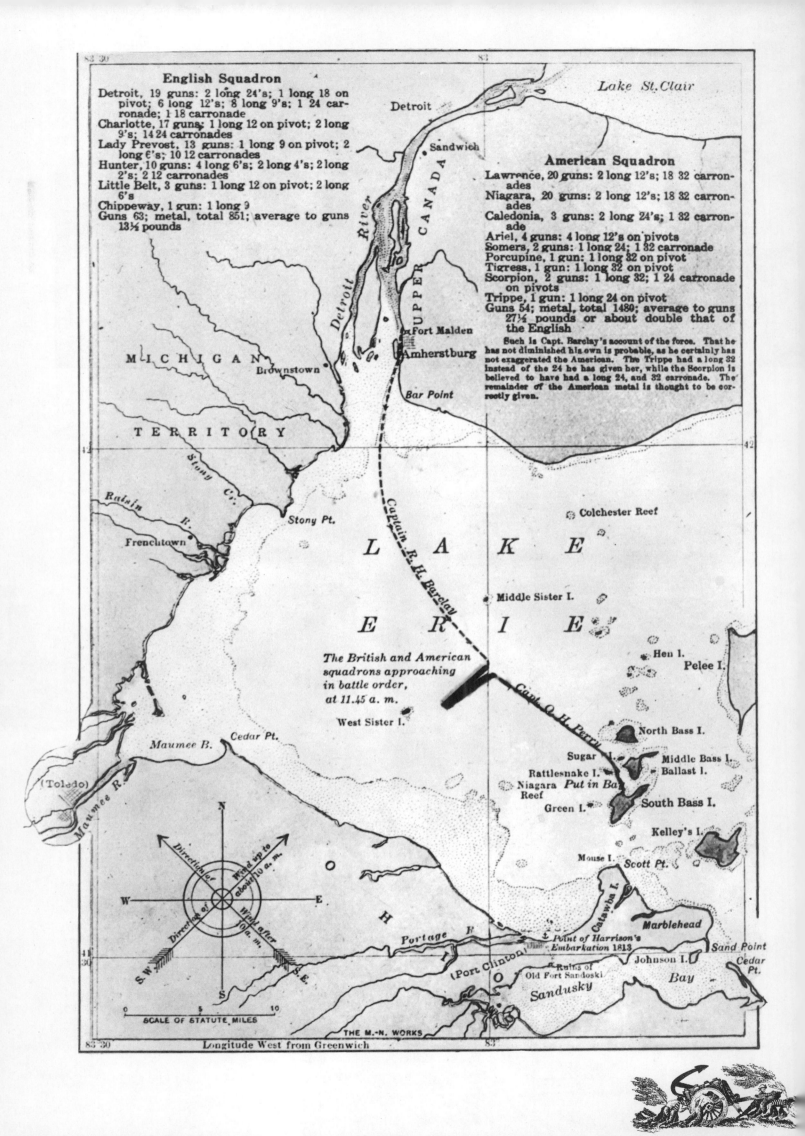

English Squadron

Detroit, 19 guns: 2 long 24's; 1 long 18 on pivot; 6 long 12's; 8 long 9's; 1 24 carronade; 1 18 carronade
Charlotte, 17 guns: 1 long 12 on pivot; 2 long 9's; 14 24 carronades
Lady Prevost, 13 guns: 1 long 9 on pivot; 2 long 6's; 10 12 carronades
Hunter, 10 guns: 4 long 6's; 2 long 4's; 2 long 2's; 2 12 carronades
Little Belt, 3 guns: 1 long 12 on pivot; 2 long 6's
Chippeway, 1 gun: 1 long 9
Guns 63; metal, total 851; average to guns 13½ pounds

American Squadron

Lawrence, 20 guns: 2 long 12's; 18 32 carronades
Niagara, 20 guns: 2 long 12's; 18 32 carronades
Caledonia, 3 guns: 2 long 24's; 1 32 carronade
Ariel, 4 guns: 4 long 12's on pivots
Somers, 2 guns: 1 long 24; 1 32 carronade
Porcupine, 1 gun: 1 long 32 on pivot
Tigress, 1 gun: 1 long 32 on pivot
Scorpion, 2 guns: 1 long 32; 1 24 carronade on pivots
Trippe, 1 gun: 1 long 24 on pivot
Guns 54; metal, total 1480; average to guns 27½ pounds or about double that of the English

Such is Capt. Barclay's account of the force. That he has not diminished his own is probable, as he certainly has not exaggerated the American. The Trippe had a long 32 instead of the 24 he has given her, while the Scorpion is believed to have had a long 24, and 32 carronade. The remainder of the American metal is thought to be correctly given.

Lake St. Clair

Detroit

Sandwich

UPPER CANADA

Detroit River

Fort Malden
Amherstburg

Bar Point

MICHIGAN

Brownstown

TERRITORY

Stony Cr.

Raisin R.

Stony Pt.

Frenchtown

Colchester Reef

L A K E

E R I E

Middle Sister I.

Captain R. H. Barclay

Capt. O. H. Perry

The British and American squadrons approaching in battle order, at 11.45 a. m.

West Sister I.

Hen I.
Pelee I.

North Bass I.

Sugar I.
Rattlesnake I.
Niagara Reef
Green I.

Middle Bass I.
Ballast I.
Put in Bay
South Bass I.

Cedar Pt.

Maumee B.

(Toledo)

Maumee R.

Kelley's I.

Mouse I.
Scott Pt.

Catawba I.

Marblehead

O
H
I
O

Point of Harrison's Embarkation 1813

Portage R.

(Port Clinton)

Ruins of Old Fort Sandoski

Sandusky

Johnson I.

Bay

Sand Point
Cedar Pt.

Direction of Wind up to about 10 a. m.
Direction of Wind after 10 a. m.

N
W — E
S

S.W.
S.E.

0   5   10
SCALE OF STATUTE MILES

THE M.-N. WORKS

PERRY'S VICTORY ON LAKE ERIE.

362. *NIAGARA* LEADS U. S. SQUADRON TO VICTORY. With fresh ship and Elliott's schooners, Perry headed squarely for enemy. Early N. Currier lithograph carries caption: "This plate represents the position of the two Fleets at the moment when the *Niagara* is pushing through the enemy's line and pouring her thunder upon them. . . ." Melee. Tornado of cannon balls. Blizzard of bullets from Kentucky marksmen in American rigging. British line broke.

Commodore Barclay, one-armed since Trafalgar, fell with remaining arm shattered. Down came Royal flag. (Three-hour carnage toll: British, 41 dead, 94 wounded; American, 27 dead, 96 wounded.) Perry sent Gen. Harrison dramatic dispatch: "We have met the enemy, and they are ours." But more. Beaten on Erie, British lost hold on Detroit. Harrison soon flung them back into Canada. And entire American Northwest was "ours." Saved by man who could act.

We have met the enemy and they are ours. Two Ships, two Brigs one Schooner & one Sloop.

Yours, with great respect and esteem

O H Perry.

363. FROM PERRY TO GENERAL HARRISON (above copy in Perry's handwriting). Laconic dispatch reported one of most decisive battles in naval history. American victory on Erie caused British Prime Minister Castlereagh to propose peace conference to Madison. And the great Wellington told British cabinet to pigeonhole imperial plans in regard to conquering American Ohio territory.

364. BARGAIN SALE—12 years later. Lake Erie victory was one of most economical in history of warfare. Ohio, Michigan, Illinois and points west won by nine little vessels, 532 men and an enthusiast with a flare for theatricals. Its combined tonnage less than that of a modern destroyer, Perry's bantam squadron had performed like a battle fleet. The cost to taxpayers? Almost nothing.

ERIE GAZETTE

THURSDAY, JUNE 9, 1825.

Notice.

WILL be sold at Public Auction, on Monday the 8th day of August next, at the United States Navy Yard, Erie, Pa. a large quantity of

Public Property;

among which are about 50 ANCHORS, from Four to Twenty hundred weight;— the standing rigging of the brigs Niagara, Lawrence, & Queen Charlotte, nearly new. A large number of SAILS, fit for merchant vessels; Forty-six thousand weight of iron knee rigger; a large quantity of Blocks, of various kinds, from 6 to 20 inch; about 30 IRON CANNON and CANNON-ADES, from 6 to 18 pounders; a large quantity of Shot, of various sizes; six thousand pounds of damaged powder; considerable quantity of Slop Clothing, &c.— The variety of articles are too numerous to be recited. Persons wishing to purchase, by calling on the week previous to the sale, shall be furnished with a complete list of all the articles to be sold, and shall have an opportunity of inspecting and examining the quality, &c. A credit of six months will be given on all sums over Fifty Dollars, by giving bond with good security.— Sale to commence at 12 o'clock, and to continue by adjournment, from day to day, as long as necessary.

By order of the Board of Navy Commissioners,

GEORGE BUDD,
Commanding Naval Officer.
U. S. Navy Yard, Erie, Pa.
June 9, 1825.—ts.

☞ The Editors of the *Patriot, Journal*, and *Emporium*, Buffalo, and *Gazette*, Black Rock, will publish the above 8 weeks and forward their accounts to this office for payment.

Notice.

WILL be exposed to sale, at Public Auction, on Tuesday the 12th day of July next, at 12 o'clock, at the U. S. Navy Yard, Erie, Pa. the following United States vessels, to wit: The Brigs

Lawrence, Niagara, Queen Charlotte and Detroit;

to be sold as they now lie, sunk or otherwise, in the bay of Presque Isle; the purchaser or purchasers to give bond with security, to remove the said Vessels within the space of six months from the time of sale, if they in any degree obstruct the navigation. A credit of six months will be given upon one half of the purchase money, and a credit of nine months upon the residue thereof, the purchaser or purchasers offering unexceptionable security to ensure payment at the maturity of the bonds.

GEORGE BUDD,
Commanding Naval Officer.
U. S. Naval Station, Erie, Pa.
May 26, 1825 —ts

365. CONTEMPORARY CARTOON OF GEO. III AND HIS QUEEN. With reference to Erie victory, this lusty jibe gave Americans a hearty laugh. Note: fermented pear juice, a laxative, was called "perry."

Queen Charlotte and Johnny Bull get their dose of Perry

366. BACKLASH AT BUFFALO (December 30, 1813). Harrison and Perry could not do everything. Left to defense of General Wilkinson, Buffalo area at east end of Erie was wide open when British General Drummond struck on Christmas Eve. After grabbing Fort Niagara (where sentinels were snoozing) British burned Buffalo, razed Black Rock. Aside from unhappy New Year for local settlers—especially women scalped by Drummond's Indians— Buffalo raid was military stroke of little consequence. War's storm center shifted to eastern seaboard and Champlain while gun-thunder rolled in from Atlantic—and far Pacific.

Odyssey of the

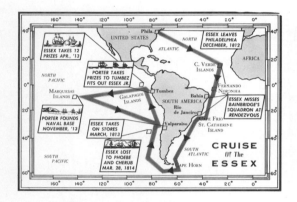

367. CRUISE OF THE *ESSEX*— Pacific raider extraordinary. Sailing from Philadelphia in December 1812, light frigate *Essex* headed for South Atlantic to join Bainbridge's squadron. Missing Bainbridge at Bahia rendezvous, Captain David Porter took vessel southward around Horn to harry British whalers in Pacific Ocean. After replenishing stores at Valparaiso, Chile, in March 1813, *Essex* stalked British whaling fleet in Galapagos Islands. As shown at left.

David Porter's frigate Essex with prizes in the Galapagos.

368. COMMERCE RAIDER IN GALAPAGOS, frigate *Essex* dealt British whaling industry ruinous blows. Armed British whalers had driven American rivals from area when *Essex* arrived on scene in April 1813. *Essex* soon captured 12 vessels —half of enemy whaling fleet. The best was refitted as cruiser *Essex Junior*. She is shown with *Essex* evading H.M.S. *Saturn* (not in picture). Porter's pocket squadron chased British whalers from East Pacific.

369. AWAY TO THE FAR MARQUESAS sailed Porter upon hearing British warship squadron was hunting him near Galapagos. Voyaging 3,000 miles to little-known Pacific islands, Porter put in at Nukahiva (October 1813). He founded Madisonville (at left) —first American overseas naval base. Leaving Marine Lt. John Gamble and 29 Navy men in Marquesas with four prize ships, Porter sailed for Valparaiso with *Essex* and *Junior*. (Sketch by Porter.)

370. *ESSEX* VS. *PHOEBE* AND *CHERUB* (March 28, 1814). Entering Valparaiso harbor, *Essex* and *Junior* were immediately blockaded by H.M. frigate *Phoebe* and warsloop *Cherub* under Captain J. M. Hillyar, R.N. Facing 56 heavy guns, Porter's ships were outmatched. While rival captains glowered across neutral water, crews traded broadsides of shouted doggerel.* Unfortunately hostilities could not be resolved by butchering the King's English. Fearing blockade reinforcement, Porter attempted escape with *Essex* during a gale. Tempest carried away her maintop, and she was caught. Now the cannon shouted.

Essex

371. END OF U.S.S. *ESSEX*. *Phoebe* off her stern, *Cherub* on her bow, *Essex* was boxed against grim Point of Angels foreshore. Ensued two hours of mayhem—one of worst slaughters of 1812 War. An American survivor was 12-year-old Midshipman Davey Farragut, captured with his pet pig "Murphy." Vividly he recalled the carnage. "I was standing near the captain when a shot came [aboard], killing four men and scattering the brains of one over both of us." *Essex* was a charnel with 89 dead, 66 wounded, when "Logan" surrendered. British lost 5 killed.

372. SEQUEL TO SOUTH SEAS MUTINY. While *Essex* lay bleeding at Valparaiso, mutiny festered in far-off Marquesas. Escaping with loyal sailors in ship with odd name of U.S.S. *Sir Andrew Hammond*, Marine Lt. Gamble and three "mids" eventually reached the Sandwich Isles (Hawaii). Unluckily, H.M.S. *Cherub* arrived on scene. And Americans (more Crusoe-like than those in picture) were captured. But U. S. marked Hawaii for future reference.

373. EPIC EPILOGUE. En route to Halifax with *Essex* survivors in captive *Junior*, Porter escaped in cockboat as convoy sailed past Long Island. New York treated doughty "Logan" to ovation. Although his career became mired in a sour service squabble, Commodore Porter was to hold enduring rank in history as leader of war cruise unmatched in naval annals. While Britannia regained control of Atlantic, David Porter won freedom of Pacific. (right)

374. U.S.S. *PEACOCK* TAKES H.M.S. *ÉPERVIER* (April 27, 1814). One of three new American 22-gun sloops commissioned early in 1814, *Peacock* (named after Britisher sunk by *Hornet*) sailed out of New York as though invisible to blockaders. Heading for South Atlantic, she encountered H.M. brig *Épervier* (18 guns) off Florida. Crackshooting ship under Lewis Warrington handily captured British brig. Prize laden with £25,000 gold bullion was whisked through blockade into Savannah, after which proud *Peacock* staged raid in Bay of Biscay. A naval exploit calculated to evoke another burst of Yankee rodomontade. (at left)

375. SECOND *WASP* IN ACTION —"Boarders Away!" in English Channel. Last of three new American war-sloops to get to sea, *Wasp* was not destined to be least. "The *Peacock* has spread her plumage to the winds, and the *Frolic* is taking her revels on the ocean, but the *Wasp* I fear will remain a dull drone." So wrote Master Commandant Johnston Blakely, his ship under blockade at Portsmouth while her sisters roamed free. Then a late April gale, and *Wasp* was out, too fast for His Majesty's patrols. Proud as *Peacock* and luckier than

Frolic (whose revel was summarily terminated in Cuban waters by chance meeting with H.M. frigate *Orpheus*), *Wasp* flew across the Atlantic. Raiding England's waters in June 1814, Blakely's sloop snatched 14 prizes before Admiralty woke up. For a stunner, *Wasp* slaughtered H.M. war-brig *Reindeer* on King's doorstep. (See next page) Typical of sloop, brig and schooner actions of this war is the painting at right by John Clymer, showing marine sharpshooters and boarders engaged in a "single-ships" encounter.

Flashes and

376. *WASP* DOWNS *AVON* (September 1, 1814). By mid-August half of Home Fleet was hunting *Wasp*. H.M. war-brig *Avon* had misfortune to find quarry. Wash drawing at left shows *Wasp* and *Avon* in battle that ended *Avon*. Three weeks later, *Wasp* appeared off Madeira; snared a brace of British merchantmen in those waters. Then, heading for South Atlantic, she vanished with all hands —dead silence after blue lightning.

T h u n d e r h e a d s

377. "OLD IRONSIDES" OUT AGAIN. Slipping out of Boston, *Constitution* conducted three-month war cruise early in 1814. After her return to Boston, British clamped tight blockade on eastern seaboard. At Norfolk, *Constellation* was locked. *United States* was bottled at New London; *President* at New York; *Congress* at Portsmouth. With all U. S. frigates thus manacled, Britain launched offensive aimed to win war.

378. *FLASHBACK!* Portsmouth boys meet the boys from Plymouth! The sloop *Wasp* with a crew of 173 men (average age 23 years—almost all hands New Englanders), encountered the British brig *Reindeer* on the 28th of June, 1814. *Wasp's* crew had been hard-trained by Master-Commandant Johnston Blakely, who had drilled the crew of the *Enterprise* before the Boxer *affair*. *Reindeer's* men, called the pride of Plymouth, were equally experienced and well disciplined, commanded by the able Captain William Manners. With breezes light enough for an even-keel duel, the two ships maneuvered from early morning till 1:15 when Blakely called his crew to quarters. For two hours more, the ships stood; then Manners, to windward, engaged. Seeing the enemy would weather him, Blakely tacked, furled sail and waited while *Reindeer* came down on his port quarter. At 60 yards Manners opened with 12 lb. carronades; *Wasp*, whose guns would not bear, stood stoically under fire until Blakely, suddenly putting his helm alee, fired in succession all the guns of his broad-

© Fred Freeman 1956

side. Already wounded, Captain Manners put his bow against *Wasp's* quarter and started to lead his men to board. Two musket balls from *Wasp's* main top pierced his skull, killing him instantly. Now boarding party from *Wasp* surged aboard *Reindeer.* Grimy with powder smoke, gunners mates fought with every available weapon—with handspikes and belaying pins as well as pistols, pikes, knives and cutlasses. *Wasp's* broadside fire had been so heavy, the musketry of her Marines so accurate that most of the British officers were casualties, and fifty percent of the crew. *Reindeer,* cut to pieces in line with her ports (see left), surrendered in 19 minutes—with 25 dead, 42 wounded. Aboard *Wasp:* 5 dead, 21 wounded. *Wasp-Reindeer* engagement was one of the bloodiest cutlass fights of the war.

Boarding as tactic was recommended by naval doctrine of the time only for "single-ships" actions or against merchantmen. Frequently, boarding actions resulted from collision between men-of-war rather than from tactical intent.

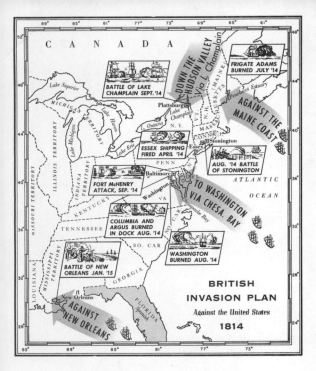

379. BRITISH INVASION PLAN. British grand strategy of 1814 called for drives (1) against Maine coast; (2) against Washington, D.C.; (3) into New York State via Lake Champlain; (4) against New Orleans. As of June 1814 this plan seemed highly feasible. U. S. Army was disintegrating; U. S. Navy blockaded; U. S. commerce on rocks. Politicians in New England were talking secession. While American morale was threadbare, London celebrated downfall of Napoleon. And Waterloo victory released Wellington's armies for campaigning in America. So! Forward the fleet of Admiral Alex. Cochrane, Chesapeake-bound with 10,000 vets.

380. KINDLING FOR PENOBSCOT BONFIRE—U.S. light frigate *Adams*. Led by Admirals Hardy and Griffith, British invasion forces struck Maine in July 1814. Caught up Penobscot, *Adams* (above) was burned by her crew. As local defenses collapsed, British Lion walked into Bangor, bit off large piece of Maine. But some of New England's coast was not so easy to chew. Lion would break teeth on rocky chunk of Connecticut granite.

British Invade
UNITED STATES

382. TOO MUCH IRON FOR SIR THOMAS. On August 9, 1814, Hardy struck Stonington, Conn.—town supposedly holding captive Mrs. James Stewart (wife of British consul) and harboring sheep run over from Block Is. Doubtless more interested in mutton than matron. Hardy hoped to replenish squadron's larder. With only three old cannon for defense, little port looked easy. But natives included a Capt. Holmes. Also (some say) Nathan'l Fanning, *Bonhomme Richard* veteran. So Hardy got some iron for his diet. From gun shown below.

381. VICTIM OF CONNECTICUT RAID—ship *Osage*. On April 8, 1814, H. M. warships anchored off Saybrook, Conn. Mission: shore raid on nearby Essex to destroy local shipping. About 240 men were landed under a Lt. Coutts who, according to news account, "had gained familiarity with locality by visiting it in disguise of a clam peddler." Raiders struck Essex at 4:00 A.M. "Flames from the burning vessels lighted up the country for miles around." Citizens went unmolested. And, "Through the mystic ties of Free Masonry, a vessel belonging to Judea Pratt of New York City was saved. Lt. Coutts ordered the vessel to be burned, but Mr. Pratt gave him the Masonic sign. . . . The troops were withdrawn." Unfortunately, Masonic bonds could not prevent destruction of some $160,000 worth of Essex shipping. Up in smoke went five merchant ships, eight sloops, four brigs, four schooners, "one pleasure boat." After war, Lt. Coutts described raid on Essex as "most unpleasant duty."

383. BATTLE OF STONINGTON—Britons at Bay. In forgotten epic of War of 1812, Connecticut Yankees gave Royal Navy a whaling. Aiming three old cannon against 140 naval guns, defenders slugged foe galley west. Fine modern painting by G. B. Mitchell (below) shows Hardy's frustrated squadron: frigate *Pactolus* and brig *Despatch* (in background); 74-gun "liner" *Ramilles* (right). Ships hurled 50 tons of metal at town while bomb-ketch *Terror* (center) flung "carcasses" filled with what polite historians called "fetid substances." (Yankees called them "stinkpots.") Americans smashed up several landing efforts, riddled *Pactolus* and *Despatch*. After 3-day battle, British limped off to Fisher's Island. Yankee losses: 1. British: about 100. (below)

Scene of the Battle

THE BATTLE OF STONINGTON

(Attributed to Philip Freneau, known as "Bard of the Revolution")

Four gallant ships from England came
Freighted deep with fire and flame
And other things we need not name,
To have a dash at Stonington.

Now safely moor'd, their work begun;
They thought to make the Yankees run,
And have a mighty deal of fun
In stealing sheep at Stonington. . . .

The Yankees to their fort repair'd,
And made as though they little cared,
For all that came—though very hard
The cannon played on Stonington.

The Ramilles began th' attack.
Despatch came forward—bold and black—
And none can tell what kept them back
From setting fire to Stonington.

The bombardiers with bomb and ball
Soon made a farmer's hayrick fall
And did a cow-house sadly maul
That stood a mile from Stonington.

They killed a goose, they killed a hen,
Three hogs they wounded in a pen.
They dashed away, and pray what then?
This was not taking Stonington!

The shells were thrown, the rockets flew,
But not a shell of all they threw
Though every house was in full view,
Could burn a house in Stonington.

To have their turn they thought but fair—
The Yankees brought two guns to bear,
And, sir, it would have made you stare,
This smoke of smoke at Stonington.

They bored Pactolus through and through,
And killed and wounded of her crew
So many, that she bade adieu
T'the gallant sons of Stonington.

The brig Despatch was hulled and torn—
So crippled, riddled, so forlorn,
No more she cast an eye of scorn
On the little fort of Stonington.

The Ramilles gave up th' affray,
And with her comrades sneaked away;
Such was the valor on that day
Of British tars at Stonington.

But some assert, on certain grounds,
(Besides the damage and the wounds),
It cost the King ten thousand pounds
To have a dash at Stonington.

384. STONINGTON BATTLE FLAG.
This gauzy banner was of stouter stuff than its look. Like 3-gun seaport, it contained too much iron for Sir Thomas Hardy. Stonington was mortifying defeat for Admiral who'd been Nelson's Flag Captain at Trafalgar. Easier target might have been Block Island—neutral during War of 1812.

BRITISH TAKE
Washington

385. AMERICA BLOCKADED.
South of New England the war went badly from the first. In December 1812, British declared Chesapeake and Delaware areas under blockade. Enter Rear Adm. Sir George Cockburn, arriving off Hampton Roads in February 1813 with fleet containing ships-of-line *Marlborough, Dragon, Poictiers, Victorious,* and frigates *Acasta, Junon, Statira, Maidstone, Belvidera, Narcissus, Lauristimus, Tartarus.* In June came Vice Admiral Warren with Halifax squadron led by ship-of-line *San Domingo.* Also add 74-gun *Sceptre, Plantagenet, Spencer* and *Bulwark,* plus frigates *Romulus, Fox, Nemesis, Superb, Nimrod, Bacchante, Tenedos, Spartan.* Against this armada stood frigate *Constellation* (blockaded at Norfolk). And Captain Tarbell with 15 toothpick gunboats in Elizabeth River. And Joshua Barney with another toothpick flotilla up Chesapeake. So U.S. foreign trade plunged from $108,000,000 (as of 1807) to $7,000,000 in 1813. So grocery prices soared out of sight in New York, Philadelphia, Charles-

ton. Schools closed for lack of tariff funds. Merchants went bankrupt. And London launched tough program to "render the war so onerous to them that they (the Americans) will come to terms." So Lewiston, Del., was bombarded. Raiders struck Havre de Grace and Fredericktown, Md. And Hampton was looted and raped in atrocious assault which left permanent

blotch on record of vicious Admiral Cockburn. Mourned the bard, Angus Umphraville:

She comes! the proud invader comes,
To waste our country, spoil our homes,
To lay our towns and cities low,
And bid our mothers' tears to flow,
Our wives lament, our orphans weep,
To seize the empire of the deep!

CAPTURE OF THE CITY OF WASHINGTON

386. INVADERS SEIZE WASHINGTON (August 24, 1814)—low ebb of American military effort. At Norfolk, British effort to capture *Constellation* was frustrated by Commodore Cassin and gunboaters under Captain Tarbell and Lieutenants Neale and Shubrick. Up Chesapeake, H.M.S. *Poictiers* was torpedo-blasted (probably by inventor Elijah Mix). So Lion roared. And in summer of 1814, Admiral Alexander Cochrane arrived up Chesapeake with 3,400 Wellington veterans. Troops under General Sir Robert Ross, amphibious force under Admiral Cockburn landed in Maryland for drive on U.S. capital. At Bladensburg, near Washington, invaders were met by raw militiamen (under General Winder) who fled at novel sight of Congreve signal rockets. Hero of day was Joshua Barney (who had served in French Navy during U.S. naval war with France!). After fighting delaying action on Chesapeake, Barney burned his gunboats up Patuxent River, raced to Bladensburg with 400 sailors and Marines. Twice his force repelled enemy charges. Then Barney fell wounded; was captured by British for last time in remarkable career. But U.S. sailors stood ground long enough to give President and Government officials chance to escape capital. While affrighted Congressmen (including former "War Hawks") fled, British stormed into Washington. Proclaimed retaliation for burning of York (Toronto), Washington rampage was intended to divert U.S. troops from frontier. Picture of British entering Washington is from contemporary volume of English history. (above)

Adm. Cockburn Burning and Plundering Havre de Grace

387. BURNING OF WASHINGTON (evening of August 24, 1814). At left, invaders are swarming over the Potomac dockyards; new 44-gun frigate U.S.S. *Columbia* goes up in flames. At lower right, British sailors cheer the destruction of new American warsloop *Argus*. Smoke pours from Senate House (1) and Treasury (m), and flames billow from "President's Palace" in background. While invaders sacked Washington, H.M. frigates *Seahorse* and *Euraylus* led three bombbrigs and rocket ship in attack on fortifications of Alexandria, across Potomac. After burning public buildings, British retired from capital. Commodore Rodgers with a few Navy hands fired some futile shots at British warships retiring down Potomac.

388. REAR ADMIRAL SIR GEO. COCKBURN, R.N.—burner of Washington. In company with General Ross and Wellington veterans, Cockburn stormed into U.S. capital with naval brigade and *Chasseurs Britanniques* —a sort of Foreign Legion composed of vagabonds, jailbirds and Spanish mercenaries. According to story, he entered "President's Palace" in time to enjoy dinner laid out for Madison. Evidence indicates he dickered with American highwayman Joseph Thompson Hare for kidnap and delivery of President—plot that fell through. His deliberate policy of rape and murder to chastise the Americans "for building forts and acting with so much rancor" aroused citizenry to fury. Cried the Boston *Gazette*, ". . . a savage monster. A disgrace to England." Even colleague officer Sir Charles James Napier deplored Cockburn for "bad employment of British troops. Very disgusting. At Hampton every horror was committed." London, however, promoted Cockburn to Sea Lord, awarded him honor of transporting Napoleon to St. Helena. (at left)

389. INVADER "PETRIFIED"—Captain Peter Parker, R.N.—only high-ranking enemy naval officer ever killed on American soil. While Cockburn scorched Washington, H.M. frigate *Menelaus* sailed up Chesapeake to create diversion below Baltimore. Observing he desired a "frolic with the Yankees," Captain Parker led forage party ashore on Kent Island (near present site of Chesapeake Bay bridge). When party blundered into a militia patrol, Parker was slain by blast of buckshot. His body, preserved in cask of Jamaica rum, was shipped to Halifax on board H.M.S. *Tonnant* (in company with remains of General Ross, riddled near Baltimore a few days later and similarly pickled). Considered "handsomest officer in Royal Navy," Parker was lamented as great loss, his death evoking an ode from Byron, the deceased's cousin.

His demise and embalming also evoked some American verses (probably by Philip Freneau) entitled "Peter Parker Petrified." Excerpts:

Secure as if they owned the land
Advanced this daring naval band
As if in days of peace.
Along the shore they proudly went
And often asked some friends in Kent
Where dwelt the fattest geese.

The British marched with loaded gun
To seize the geese that gabbling run
About the isle of Kent.
But what could hardly be believed,
Sir Peter was of life bereaved
Before he pitched his tent.

Some Kentish lad, to save the geese,
And make their noisy gobbling cease,
He took a deadly aim.
By Kentish hands, Sir Peter fell,
His men retreated with a yell
And lost both geese and game.

STAR SPANGLED BANNER

390. ATTACK ON FORT McHENRY (September 13-14, 1814). Collapse of American defenses at Washington encouraged British to drive on Baltimore, home port of many privateers. In campaign to take Baltimore, Cochrane sailed up Chesapeake with invasion fleet. He found harbor guarded by Fort McHenry with cannon largely manned by U.S. sailors. In ensuing bombardment (pictured by contemporary print) McHenry held out.

391. ORIGINAL STAR-SPANGLED BANNER—flag that flew at Fort McHenry. Cochrane's warships bombarded fort while British army of 6,000 attacked on landside flank. About 13,000 American regulars and militia defended ground. In fort two companies of "Sea Fencibles" and detachment of Barney's sailors reinforced garrison. "And the rocket's red glare, the bombs bursting in air, gave proof through the night that our flag was still there." Note 15 stars (one shot away) and 15 stripes—out of date for 1814. Banner was not yet national flag. McHenry made it so.

392. "THE STAR-SPANGLED BANNER" — original draft. Discussing prisoner exchange, Francis Scott Key witnessed bombardment from British vessel. Putting brave words to old tavern tune, he wrote immortal stanzas adopted century later as U.S. national anthem. Note phrase "clouds of the fight," later changed. Song thrilled Baltimore after the British withdrew.

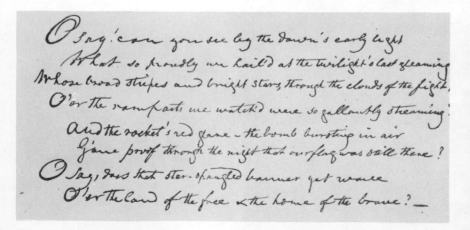

BATTLE OF
Lake Champlain

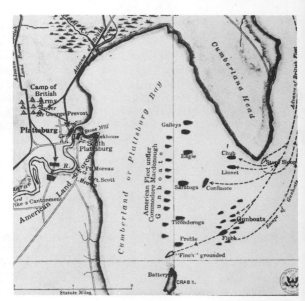

393. COMMODORE THOMAS MACDONOUGH—"Themistocles" of Lake Champlain. While Ross and Cockburn muddled in Maryland, Sir George Prevost led invasion force of 14,000 in drive on Plattsburg, N. Y. Object: open up Lake Champlain. But Prevost's naval squadron (16 vessels under Commo. George Downie) ran into this Preble Boy committed to defend strategic lake.

394. BATTLE OF PLATTSBURG BAY (September 11, 1814). Off Plattsburg, Macdonough squared away with flagship *Saratoga* (26 guns), brig *Eagle* (20), ex-steamer *Ticonderoga* (17), sloop *Preble* (7) and ten row-galleys. Belatedly Downie entered bay with flagship *Confiance* (37 guns), brig *Linnet* (16), sloops *Chubb* and *Finch* (11-gunners) and a dozen galleys. Bloody battle ensued.

395. *SARATOGA* SWINGS TO VICTORY. *Confiance's* first broadside set *Saratoga* afire, mangled 40 men. Americans hung on as battle seesawed, vessels reeled, Downie was slain by cannon shot, sloop *Finch* disabled. At crucial moment, Macdonough worked a system of "springs" (bow and stern anchors on tricky cable) to turn *Saratoga's* undamaged side toward enemy. Flogged by fresh broadsides, *Confiance* struck flag; her consorts followed suit. Champlain defeat sent Prevost retreating into Canada; saved New York frontier. (below: the climax)

Sam C. Reid

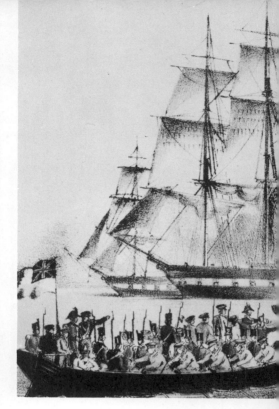

397. PRIVATEER *GEN'L ARM-STRONG* TAKES ON H.M. FLEET (September 25-26, 1814). Putting into Fayal, the Azores, 14-gun brig *General Armstrong* found herself bull's-eye in British fleet rendezvous when H.M. battleship *Plantagenet* (74 guns) arrived with frigate *Rota* and sloop *Carnation* to await H.M.S. *Thais* and *Calypso*—invasion force bound for New Orleans! Although in neutral port, New York privateer was ordered to surrender. Captain Sam Reid said "Never!" *Plantagenet's* barges attacked. *Armstrong's* Long Tom smashed them up. *Carnation* stepped in. She retired with maintop down, 15 dead. Every *Rota* officer was disabled as battle raged through night. Reid finally scuttled ship, escaped ashore with valiant crew. Scrap cost British 182 men; sent fleet to repair yards; delayed Delta drive.

396. AMERICAN PRIVATEERS TAKE BRITISH CARGOMAN—powerful influence on John Bull policy. Some 526 American ships registered as privateers in War of 1812; snared huge bag of 1,344 British merchantmen during conflict. Slow start gained momentum until Lloyd's of London was tolling for three lost ships per day average in 1814. (above)

398. PRIVATEER *GRAND TURK* (below)—ship-killer of Wiscasset, Maine. One of war's more voracious specimens, this 309-ton, 18-gun brig is seen easing into port of Marseille with cargo of loot. Perhaps war's richest privateer was *Yankee*, of Bris-

tol, R.I.—ship that came in with $3,000,000 bag of 40 prizes. Runners-up, *Scourge* and *Rattlesnake* (New Yorker and Philadelphian) teamworked to bag 45 prizes. *Chasseur, Lion, Neufchatel* of Baltimore—these and scores of other rampaging ocean

raiders caused Admiralty Secretary John Croker to demand naval escortage for all British merchantmen. But warship escorts failed to daunt U. S. privateers. As in Revolution, the freelances of 1812 sloughed British commerce. Losing money on war, English merchants favored peace.

The Privateers

New Orleans

CLIMAX

399. BATTLE OF NEW ORLEANS (January 8, 1815)—death rattle of British invasion effort. At Ghent peace had been signed in December 1814. Word failed to reach British in- vasion forces bound for New Orleans. Privateer *Armstrong* had left invad- ers out for blood. They got it. Enter- ing delta, the vanguard brushed aside Lake Borgne naval defenses under Commo. Dan Patterson and Lt. T. ap C. Jones. Then they met up with Andrew ("Old Hickory") Jackson and army of coonskin sharpshooters. Sneering at American "Dirty Shirts" Adm. Cochrane urged frontal attack. Down went 2,000 Britishers in the Mississippi mud. (Home went Gen. Sir Edward Packenham—another high-ranking corpse in a pickle bar- rel.) American losses: 13. (below)

BATTLE OF NEW ORLEANS AND DEATH OF MAJOR GENERAL PACKENHAM On the 8th of January 1815.

BRITISH VALOUR

CAPTURE OF THE UNITED STATES FRIGATE PRESIDENT COMMODORE DECATUR BY THE ENDYMION FRIGATE CAPTAIN HOPE
after an anxious chase of eighteen hours and a desperate fight of Two hours and a half, Jan.ʳ 15.1815.

American Force
60 Guns 440 Men

British Force
40 Guns 340 Men

HATRED OF SIN.

The Gallant Captain Hope
giving orders to his Crew—

Commodore Decatur ordering the
Anchors to be thrown Overboard

Holy Lord God! I love thy truth,
  Nor dare thy least commandment slight;
Yet pierc'd by sin, the serpents tooth
  I mourn the anguish & the bite.

But though the poison lurks within,
  Hope bids me still with patience wait
Till death shall set me free from sin,
  Free from the only thing I hate.

Had I a throne above the rest,
  Where angels and archangels dwell;
One sin unslain, within my breast,
  Would make that heaven as dark as hell.

The prisoner, sent to breathe fresh air,
  And bless'd with liberty again;
Would mourn were he condemn'd to wear
  One link of all his former chain.

But oh! no foe invades the bliss,
  When glory crowns the Christian's head,
One view of Jesus as he is,
  Will strike all sin for ever dead.

        Josiah John Shaw,
        June 26th, 18

Crippled state of the Enemys
ship at the close of the Action.

Commodore Decatur giving up
his sword to Captain Hope

Published by J. FAIRBURN, Jun.ʳ Fountain Court, Minories, sold also by Champant & Whitrow Jewry Street

400. U.S.S. *PRESIDENT* CAPTURED BY H.M.S. *ENDYMION* (January 14, 1815). Unaware of peace, Americans planned new naval offensive. Summoned to New York, Stephen Decatur was assigned frigate *President* for war cruise. Racing to sea in winter gale, she grounded outside Narrows. Thus lamed, she fell afoul H.M.S. *Majestic* (50 guns) and 38-gunners *Endymion, Pomone* and *Tenedos*. Decatur lost running battle off Long Island; *President* fell.

401. *CONSTITUTION* BATTLES *CYANE* AND *LEVANT* (February 20, 1815). Breaking out of Boston at Christmas, "Old Ironsides" led H.M. Halifax squadron a merry Atlantic chase. No peace news reached her captain, red-headed Charles Stewart. Nor did it reach H.M.S. *Cyane* and *Levant*, patrolling off Madeira. Intercepting *Constitution*, the two Britishers maneuvered to attack—54 guns against 44. Stewart accepted the odds. To enemy's sorrow. As shown below.

SEA POWER
Conclusion

402. *CONSTITUTION* TOWING CAPTIVE *CYANE*—homeward bound with prize. Striking while "Ironsides" was hot, Captain Stewart dealt sloop *Levant* a thrashing, then turned to flog frigate *Cyane* until she lowered flag. British recaptured *Levant*. But *Constitution* reached States with *Cyane*. Fact that peace was previously signed did not abbreviate "Old Ironsides'" record. Three frigates and war-sloop knockout left her all-time Navy champion. (right)

403. "HATRED OF SIN"—propaganda for young Britons. Published in London after War of 1812, the tabloid (left) was distributed as patriotic effusion to season's crop of English schoolboys. As shown, *Endymion's* victory over *President* was much publicized. The religious note seems oddly out of key with the martial theme. (From Irving S. Olds collection.)

HORRID MASSACRE
at
DARTMOOR PRISON ENGLAND.

Where the unarmed American Prisoners of War were wantonly fired upon by the guard, under the command of the Prison Turn-key, the blood thirsty SHORTLAND; Seven were killed, and about Fifty wounded, (several mortally,) without any provocation on the part of our unfortunate American Citizens!——"Blood has a voice to pierce the Skies!"

NOW war is o'er and peace is come to greet our happy land,
A tale, sad deed of wickedness, has lately come to hand,
A tragic story you shall hear, from Britain comes the news,
Of Yankee sailors there confin'd, and how they have been us'd,
Our hardy tars and seamen bold, a shameful, dire disgrace,
To British power and British rule, at Dartmoor was the place.
The tragic scene was acted o'er, and dreadful massacre,
By one sad fellow, SHORTLAND call'd, and all accounts agree
That he a ruthless tyrant was, most fell and savage plan,
And preconcerted sought the lives of unoffending men,
The 6th of April now last past, the evening of that day,
When pris'ners to their wards retir'd and quickly went their way,
To take their rest in calm content, well knowing of the peace,
And humble hope, and perfect trust they soon would be releas'd,
And to their country joyful come to wife and children dear,
To fathers, mothers, kindred friends, who'd shed full many a tear
For their mishap, by chance of war, from their embraces torn,
But joy had now began to dawn in prospect of return,
And cheerful was each youthful heart, and more experienc'd tar
As peace had now been quite confirm'd, and ended was the war.
In pleasing thoughts and grateful hopes another day had gone,
And patience now each sailor had, quite sure of his return,
But Shortland he the jailor was, and great advantage had
Instead of good bread he decreed, each prisoner should have had
And that full short one half a pound to every captive soul,
The wicked, vile and cheating knave, is prov'd a murderer foul,
Now hear the story true and plain, in journal fully given,
Correct reported from the press, exact from Dartmoor prison,
This gentle jailor, careful soul, one day to Plymouth went,
But orders gave before he went, what bread he would have sent,
To every prisoner in his charge, a pound (not one ounce more)
Though a pound and half each man receiv'd the very day before
As that was due by right and rule to prisoners young or old.
Confined there, his just due share, 'twas cheating to withhold,
One half a pound! remorseless and unfeeling man this jailor
sure must be,
From every prisoner to exact so large, so great a fee!
Nor he nor care nor feeling had, but feeling for himself,
And thus he meant his purse to fill by such ill gotten pelf,
The prisoners they in humble sort such treatment did refuse,
And thought it hard by one vile man to be so much abus'd.
And patiently till setting sun was closing in the day,
They waited for the usual food from prison did not stray,
But finding now their bread withheld, and was to them deny'd
They burst the door to ask their right, and to their keepers cry'd
The officers in garrison their murmurs thought were just,
And judg'd the jailor much to blame to abuse so great a trust,
The conduct of the keeper then they much did reprobate,
The day was sped, the men got bread, in evening tho' 'twas late
The next day Shortland being told what pass'd the day before,
When he at Plymouth absent was, away then from Dartmoor,
Resolv'd a vile and savage plan, inhuman and unjust,
To find pretence on unarm'd men, his bayonets for to thrust,
And soon he found a wicked way to find out a pretence,
That prisoners they would run away, or 'scape thro' wall or fence
A vile and weak pretence it was, the news if we have right,
Not to secure, but murder sure, the prisoners in his sight,
In malice and revenge, for what had pass'd some days before,
When he away at Plymouth was, and absent from Dartmoor.

In story now it does appear, correct and truly penn'd,
And you may judge, and see it plain, if you will well attend,
This artful, base, designing man the prisoners to annoy,
The alarm bell rung, the guard call'd out the prisoners to destroy
Forsooth! there was great fear to dread, he search'd and found
in well,
A hole was made for boy to creep and get again a ball,
Which oft was thrown by boys at play, their usual daily sport,
In pastime who at prison wall did every day resort,
And frequent would their balls bounce o'er into the prison yard
And frequent were these boys deny'd by surly, churlish guard,
To get again their balls for sport their pastime and their play,
And so their joy was ofttimes spoil'd and ended for the day,
The boys thus baulk'd, and being griev'd to lose their ball & play
Contriv'd to make a way to gain, and get their balls away,
The vigilance of Shortland when their creeping hole espied,
Oh! oh, said he this shall not be, and to the guard he cried,
'Come on, come on, ye Britons bold, the pris'ners are in arms,
And soon we must put down these dogs, to free us from alarms
The soldiers stood all in a maze as he gave the command,
And doubting of his curs'd design, they made a silent stand,
Then seizing from the hand of one, a musket he did take,
And cry'd of these damn'd yankees we'll a good example make,
'Fire! fire! my lads!' the murd'rer cried, the trigger then he drew
And swift as light'ning on the wing their deadly bullets flew,
The bleeding victims on their knees in vain for mercy plead,
The savage monster drunk with rage completes the horrid deed,
Legs, arms, and brains were scatter'd round, when this dire
scene war o'er,
And Dartmoor's helpless pris'ners lay immers'd in blood & gore,
One wounded sore in vain attempts to gain his prison door,
Alas, his life is almost spent he bleeds at every pore.
Shortland, the trembling victim soon with Argus-eyes espies,
While hellish malice clouds his face, wrath flashes from his eyes
Oh! spare my life,' the sailor cries, but ah! the weak appeal
Was made to hearts like flinty rocks, unmov'd as harden'd steel,
'Charge!' said the ruffian, at his word the bloody fiends advance
The purple fluid stains the ground, his swelling bosom pants,
Then straight his spirit soars away, to await his high award,
And leaves his hapless cause before his country and his God.
Sixty brave tars by Shortland's means lay weltering in their gore
High heaven itself had ne'er beheld such coward acts before,
Columbian's sons arouse! to arms! nor dread the tyrant's pow'r
The thunders roll, the light'nings flash, the clouds with tempest lour
Say to proud Briton's treach'rous slaves! ye tyrants of the main
Give us redress, let Shortland swing; or meet our swords again.
Old George beware! if you again the contest should renew,
We'll show you that the Yankee lads have better pluck than you
Revenge is sweet and on the book of heav'n now stands enroll'd
Your hellish deeds, your murd'rous acts, your bribery with your
gold,
Look to yourself, for should again the vengeful sword be drawn
The setting sun of England's pride should hail Columbia's dawn
The stripes and stars should proudly wave, and Neptune from
his car,
Would yield to us his tridents up to hurl the bolts of war!
Your haughty ensign by our tars from your tall masts be torn,
Your Red Coats dread to see True Blue, on swiftest pinions borne
So, for the present, 'fare ye well' your long lost fame regain,
And when we settle up accounts, we'll call on you again.

☞ Printed by Nathaniel Coverly, Jun. Milk-Street, Boston.

404. "THE DARTMOOR MASSACRE"—postwar hangover. Built in 1809 to hold Napoleonic War captives, England's Dartmoor Prison housed some 1,700 U. S. Navy men and privateersmen captured in War of 1812. On April 6, 1815, American prisoners rioted, protesting bad food and delayed release. Nervous commandant ordered guards to fire; seven Americans were killed, 60 wounded. Although British Government paid indemnity to families of men slain, shooting of unarmed P.O.W.'s raised tremendous storm in America. Contemporary reaction was expressed in characteristic verse. Above is mild sample of versifying.

405. *HORNET* SLAYS *PENGUIN* (March 23, 1815). Having run New York blockade in wake of *President*, U. S. war-sloops *Hornet* and *Peacock* set course to rendezvous at Tristan da Cunha in South Atlantic. Arriving ahead of time at remote islet, *Hornet* (Capt. James Biddle) encountered H.M. war-sloop *Penguin* (18 guns). Ensued a 22-minute cannon match in which *Penguin* was utterly butchered by superior American gunnery. (British losses: 14 killed, 28 wounded. American losses: one killed, 10 wounded.) Cruel for sailors who died in this carnage was fact that war had been formally ended three months before. After *Penguin's* hulk was burnt, *Hornet* joined *Peacock* in a run to Indian Ocean. On June 30, 1815, *Peacock* captured brig *Nautilus* off Java—last naval action of war. Last British ship taken by U. S.

406. PEACE TABLEAU, 1815—Minerva ("American wisdom") dictates peace terms which Mercury ("American commerce") hands to Britannia and Hercules ("American might") forces her to accept. A contemporary American fable. With commerce paralyzed, Treasury a poorhouse, Army a joke, and Navy blockaded, U. S. was in no position to force terms at end of War of 1812. But building of three 74-gun "liners," huge 100-gunner on Lake Ontario, and steam warship *Demologos* did add some muscle to figurative American Hercules of symbolic tableau. (right)

Peace of Ghent 1814.   and Triumph of America

Minerva, represents the wisdom of the United States. Mercury   on the other side, America passes in Triumph through
their commerce. Hercules their force. Minerva dictates the conditions   the Arch in her way to the temple of peace
of peace which Mercury presents to Britannia and Hercules forces   attended by Victory and followed by a numerous train
her to accept on the shield of America are the names of those   Trophies are seen and in the back ground are the
who signed the Treaty, on the obelisk those of the braves   ruins of the Capitol.

UNDER
THE PRESIDENCE
OF MADISSON
MONROE SECRETARY
OF STATE

407. PEACE CONFERENCE AT GHENT, FLANDERS—diplomatic draw which ended War of 1812. With most of war issues unsettled, it was strictly a "negotiated peace." Even signers shaking hands over treaty looked skeptical (Admiral Lord Gambier for Britain at l.; John Quincy Adams for U. S. at r.). However, with both sides willing to appease, the peace proved solid and long-lasting.

408. "PREBLE'S BOYS." Early N. Currier lithograph expresses high esteem awarded naval leaders of 1812 by postwar generation. Some 265 Navy men were slain in War of 1812.

Nation would long recall them and their captains as invincibles. If America failed to win war, "Preble's Boys" prevented loss of it. Built, led and manned by independent thinkers—nonconformists who could improvise, experiment, dare innovation—the American Navy bantam was able to slug it out with a stuffy shirt.

Chapter V

FROM SAIL TO STEAM

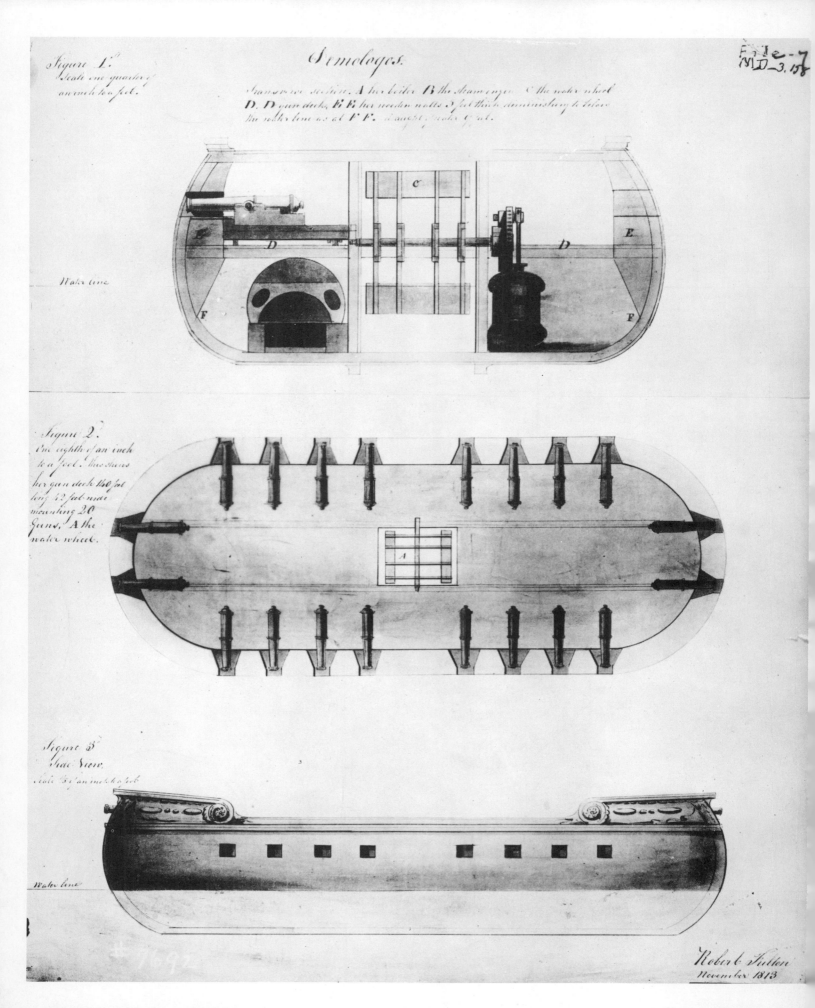

409. ORIGINAL PLAN DRAWING OF *DEMOLOGOS* by Robert Fulton. Commonly called "steam floating battery," 2,475-ton *Demologos* was one of most radical vessels ever built for U. S. Navy. Twin hulls were joined catamaran fashion by gun deck with batteries arranged as shown. The 16-foot paddle wheel was set in a channel-way amidships. Below water-line, engines and boilers were protected by timbering five feet thick. Vessel's length: 156 feet. Beam: 56. Draft: about 12.

Steam Cloud
ON THE HORIZON

410. ROBERT FULTON—American nautical genius who lifted the lid. He did not invent the steamboat—steamer experiments were begun as early as 1543. First marine engine patent was awarded English inventor Jonathan Hulls in 1736. Within two decades following Revolutionary War, ten more or less workable steam-driven boats were invented by American tinkers. But it was Fulton who turned the tide. After failure to interest Napoleon and British Admiralty in submarine warfare, New York engineer undertook building of steamer *Clermont* which chugged round the bend in 1807 to inaugurate wave of the future. Still, navies were slow to catch on (in 1812 official attitudes were expressed by scornful doggerel which began, "Jonathan Hulls with his paper skull . . ." However, Fulton won attention of alert Naval Secretary Wm. Jones. Result: a contract for warship *Demologos*.

411. LAUNCHING OF *DEMOLOGOS*—YARD OF ADAM AND NOAH BROWN. Fabulous as Fulton's steam battery were shipwrights who built her under inventor's supervision. Biblically-named Browns had worked miracles for Perry at Presque Isle. Working on *Demologos* in New York yard, they launched her in October 1814, four months after laying keel. Browns also built for Fulton the submarine *Mute*, whose record in history remains silent as her name. But "Voice of the People" raised clamor in naval circles. Armed with twenty 32-pounders and two undersea "submarine guns," *Demologos* had firepower to incinerate average enemy frigate. Spy reports endowed her with mechanical lances and hoses that threw streams of scalding water. Declaring dreadful vessel "outlawed," British started building steam warships.

412. *DEMOLOGOS* ON TRIAL RUN. The world's No. 1 steam warship chugged as a nonesuch down New York Bay. Under engine power she made 5 knots; might have gnawed her way through British blockade had War of 1812 continued. As it was, she gnawed through all

existing conceptions of naval tactics dependent on wind. But she was ahead of her time. Completed shortly after war's end, vessel was rechristened *Fulton* in honor of great inventor who died in 1815. After shakedown under Captain David Porter (who installed needless auxiliary sails), *Fulton* was immobilized as receiving ship in Brooklyn Navy Yard. There she was demolished by explosion and fire on June 4, 1829. Some said she was blown up by gunner's mate who'd been disrated and flogged the previous morning. Others thought careless powder stowage caused blast which killed 24 victims,

including Lt. S. M. Breckenridge and "a woman who happened to be on board at the time." For "Voice of the People" a grim valedictory. But she had already made steam-throated announcement of a revolution in naval warfare that would one day sweep from the ocean every last sailing sloop, frigate and ship-of-the-line.

413. TAYLOR'S "FLOATING EXPLOSIVE BATTERY." Following Fulton's lead, numerous naval inventors designed steam vessels of *Demologos* type. With more fire in imagination than under

boilers, John P. Taylor conceived of scene above. Despite eager experimenters, engineering got off to slow start in Navy. In 1815 work was suspended on second "steam frigate" at Baltimore, Fulton's

vessel proving too radical for conventional naval captains. Machinery replace canvas? Steam outdo the wind? Unthinkable in 1815 when Navy heads were concentrating on war with hostile Algiers.

Payment Deferred
WAR WITH ALGIERS

414. BARBARY PAYOFF was due when Dey of Algiers unleashed corsair fleet in 1807 to raid American shipping. Once conflict with Britain was concluded, Congress, at Madison's urging, declared war. Late in May 1815, U. S. squadron led by Stephen Decatur in new frigate *Guerrière*

sailed for the Mediterranean. In June, Algerine frigate *Mashuda,* flagship of Admiral Rais Hammida, was boxed by *Guerrière* and U. S. sloops *Ontario* and *Épervier. Mashuda* and *Hammida* were shot to rubbish in about 30 minutes. American losses were none. (at right)

415. DECATUR OFF ALGIERS—end of a Dey. Shortly after *Mashuda's* abolishment, *Decatur's* scouts trapped Algerine brig *Estedio.* Decatur then led squadron directly to Algiers. Confronted by naval cannon, Omar the Dey hastily released American captives, agreed to end ransom demands. Dey's capitulation (June 20, 1815) ended fifth war fought by American Navy. In April 1816, Omar tried to hedge on promises. So British-Dutch fleet blew evil city of Algiers to Gehenna.

Reorganization

OF THE YOUNG NAVY

416. BENJAMIN CROWNINSHIELD— Secretary of Navy during War with Algiers. Induced Congress to create Board to handle administrative detail. First Navy Board, composed of three senior captains, served until 1842. First Commissioners: Rodgers, Hall and Porter— acorn of future "Pentagon." In meantime, Navy lost several of its best leaders.

417. VICTIM OF YELLOW JACK was Oliver Hazard Perry, felled in 1819. Dispatched on diplomatic mission to South America, Perry procured first U. S. treaty signed with Venezuela. During return voyage he died on board U. S. schooner *Nonsuch*—stricken by dread fever that downed more Navy men than any war in nation's history up to World War II.

EXEUNT HEROES

418. VICTIM OF DUELING CODE was Stephen Decatur. Trouble was begun by Commander Jesse Elliott, who claimed Oliver Perry received undue credit for Lake Erie victory. Supporting Perry, Decatur became involved in controversy with Captain James Barron, who had been suspended from service after *Chesapeake-Leopard* affair. Blaming Decatur for court-martial, sorehead Barron challenged him in 1820. They met at Blandensburg. Barron shot to kill. Decatur was slain.

419. CAPTAIN JAMES BARRON— officer who killed Decatur. It was an act that tarnished Barron's career. With nation outraged at wholly needless tragedy, Navy took steps to outlaw infantile dueling code and homicidal face-savings.

420. TRUXTUN'S GRAVE—Christ Churchyard, Philadelphia. Denied a captain for his flagship in 1802, Truxtun resigned from service, sat out War of 1812. As journalist noted, "Navy lost one of its brightest ornaments." In 1816 Truxtun was elected Phila. sheriff. He died in 1822.

421. U. S. SHIP-OF-THE-LINE *WASHINGTON*. One of three 74-gun "liners" laid down during War of 1812, she sailed with Navy's first battleship squadron. Builders Hartt and Badger of Portsmouth, N. H. Completed October 1815. A 2,200-tonner, she was about 190 feet long, with 50-foot beam, 20-foot depth of hold. Armament: thirty long guns, thirty-three mediums, twenty carronades—all 32-pounders. Complement: 750 men. Sister ships were *Independence* and *Franklin*. Fourth 74-gunner on Navy roster was U.S.S. *Columbus*, laid down at Washington, D. C., in 1816—a 2,480-tonner, 192 feet long, with 52-foot beam, about 22 depth. Navy's four pioneer battleships proved erratic sailers, but performed memorable service. *Independence* remained in Navy until 1900. *Columbus* died in 1861, *Franklin* in 1853. Less durable *Washington* was through in 1843.

Navy Expanding
UNITED STATES SAILING

422. U. S. SHIP-OF-THE-LINE *OHIO* — considered Navy's finest "liner." Designed by Henry Eckford. First ship built at New York Naval Shipyard. Was begun in 1817; completed in 1821. Over-all length 208 feet, beam 53⅝. Variously armed with 86 to 102 guns, heaviest being 42-pounders. Magnificent sailer; Navy's favorite command. Her armament marked a return to mixed batteries, and her christening introduced American naval practice of naming battleships after states. *Ohio* remained in Navy's service until 1883. (right)

425. U. S. SHIP-OF-THE-LINE *DELAWARE* — another "finest." Doughty designed, she was laid down at Norfolk in 1817; launched in 1820. A 2,602-tonner; length 196¼ feet, beam 53, depth of hold about 21½. Variously armed with mixed batteries of long 42's, medium 32's and 42-pounder carronades. She is shown proving sea-keeping qualities in rip-roar gale in Gulf of Lyon. She was destined to die at her birthplace, blown up and scuttled, come 1861.

ginia and *New York* were never completed. *Alabama* was launched as storeship (renamed *New Hampshire*) in 1864. *Vermont* was the Navy's last wooden battleship. (below)

423. STRIKE IT UP FOR *NORTH CAROLINA*—sistership of *Delaware*. Another Doughty "liner," she was laid down at Philadelphia Navy Yard in 1818; launched in 1820. Like her classmates, she was rated 74-gunner; carried from 86 to 102 guns in mixed batteries. Complement: some 820 men. Considered the "show ship" of her day, she was popular flag vessel in Mediterranean; remained in service until 1867. Mazurka was published in her honor during Civil War.

424. U. S. SHIP-OF-THE-LINE *VERMONT*—Navy's last 74-gunner. Designed by Doughty for 1817 building program, she was laid down at Boston in 1818; not completed until 1845. Another hardy specimen, she remained in service until 1902. Three other 74-gunners were begun in 1818 —*Virginia* at Boston, *Alabama* at Portsmouth, *New York* at New York. Driblet appropriations kept them on the stocks until Time, Civil War and armor plate left them obsolete. *Vir-*

Under Canvas
FLEET, 1815 TO 1840

426. U. S. FRIGATE *BRANDY-WINE*—one of Navy's new 44-gunners. Laid down at Washington Navy Yard under Doughty's supervision, she was launched in 1825. Vessel of 1,708 tons; length 175 feet, beam 45, depth of hold about 14½. Cost: approximately $825,000. Armament: fifty 32-pounder long guns and carronades. Complement: 480. Popular in Navy's last sail-frigate flotilla, she starred in class which included U.S.S. *Potomac, Columbia, Cumberland, Raritan, Savannah, St. Lawrence, Sabine* and *Santee*. (picture at left)

427. U. S. WAR-SLOOP *ERIE*. Built by Thomas Kemp at Baltimore in 1813, she was redesigned, rebuilt by Doughty at New York Navy Yard; re-launched in 1821. As enlarged, she was 559-tonner, length about 122 feet, beam 32½, depth of hold about 15. Rated a 20-gunner, she was odd number in fleet of period which included new heavy 22-gun sloops *Boston, Concord, Natchez, Peacock, Ontario,* and new light 18-gunners *Fairfield, Falmouth, Lexington, St. Louis, Vandalia, Vincennes* and *Warren.* American sloops of 18- to 20-gun class were unlucky. *Concord* was wrecked off Africa. *Peacock* was lost off Oregon. *Boston* was wrecked in the West Indies. Famous *Hornet* went down off Tampico. Later sloops of same type, *Albany* and *Levant* foundered at sea. Heavy peacetime losses in the old canvas-back American Navy.

428. LAUNCHING OF U.S.S. *PENNSYLVANIA*— America's largest line-of-battle ship. Designed by Samuel Humphreys. Laid down at Philadelphia Navy Yard in 1822. Launched in 1837. Biggest sailing warship ever built for U. S. Navy, *Pennsylvania* was 3,104-tonner; length 210 feet, beam 56¾, depth of hold 24¼. Rating 120 guns, she was armed with sixteen 8-inch shell guns and one hundred and four 32-pounders. Intended as mighty coast-defense bulwark against potential blockade, vessel proved cranky sailer, hard to handle as a balky elephant. And year this canvas-backed pachyderm was completed, over 700 steamers were in American merchant service; Navy possessed one tiny 142-ton steamboat. But midget steamer could run rings around big white elephant —in a calm. At Norfolk in '61 "Pennsy" was cremated.

429. PRINCE METTERNICH OF AUSTRIA—mastermind behind Holy Alliance. Concocted by Czar of Russia, Emperor of Austria and King of Prussia, Holy Alliance was pledged to crush the spread of democracy. Italian democrats were squelched. Encouraging Spain's hopes of regaining lost American colonies, Alliance voted in 1823 to "engage mutually to put an end to representative government in Europe, and to prevent its being introduced in those countries where it is not yet known." President James Monroe countered with doctrine: "Hands off the Americas!"

430. U. S. SHIP-OF-THE-LINL *FRANKLIN* headed Pacific Squadron that dampened Czarist ambitions toward Oregon Territory. Previously claimed by British, American and Spanish, as well as Russian explorers, Territory which extended from Alaska to California became target for dispute in 1820's. After Monroe Doctrine announcement, presence of 74-gun *Franklin* on Callao station doubtless influenced Russian decision to abandon Oregon claims—a move concluded by peaceful treaty with U. S. in 1825. While Russia thus retired peacefully, other powers threatened.

NAVY SUPPORTS
Monroe Doctrine
SQUELCHING THE HOLY ALLIANCE

431. READY TO ENFORCE MONROE DOCTRINE were such vessels as U.S.S. *Ontario*—one of Navy's sloop flotilla. Britain proposed mutual British-American stand against Alliance powers, but Secretary of State John Quincy Adams advised Monroe to treat problem as all-American. In December 1823, Monroe announced Doctrine (as drawn up by Adams) in message to Congress. "The American continents . . . are henceforth not to be considered as subject for future colonization by any European power."

432. COMMODORE DALLAS TO VERA CRUZ (1838). Monroe Doctrine was primarily devised to check Spain's South American ambitions. But when French took Vera Cruz on hair-trigger pretext in 1838, Dallas and U.S. squadron arrived. Check!

433. INSIDE VIEW OF SAILING WARSHIP. Another glimpse of Old Navy from *Gleason's Pictorial*. Add smell of brine, tar, oakum, hemp, paint and pitch, rum and perspiration. (Captions are from the original text.)

THE HULL OF AN AMERICAN MAN-OF-WAR

1. *Sailors furling Sails*
2. *Poop on Quarter Deck*
3. *Bob-Stays*
4. *Figure Head*

5. *Sailors lowering a Cask*
6. *Surgical inspection*
7. *Captain's Cabin*
8. *Dining-Room*

9. *Cook's Galley*
10. *Midshipmen's Cabin*
11. *Sailors' Berths*
12. *Exercising the Guns*

★ ★ H e y d a y   o f   t h e

OPEN AMIDSHIPS, FROM STEM TO STERN

13. *Officer's Cabins*
14. *Dining-Room of Officers*
15. *Dressing a Wound*
16. *Musket exercise*

17. *Sailors' Mess Room*
18. *Mending Sails*
19. *Provision Room*
20. *Sick Bay or Hospital*

21. *Lowering a Boat*
22. *Sail and Cordage Room*
23. *The Prison*
24. *Shot Magazine*

25. *Spirit Room*
26. *Powder Magazine*
27. *Blocks, Pulleys, etc.*
28. *General Store-Room*
29. *Casks and Tanks*
30. *Dunnage*

Sailing Navy ★ ★ ★

434. WOODEN SHIP, IRON MEN. VIEWS FROM "ICONOGRAPHIC ENCYCLOPEDIA."

HANDS IN SACK. HAMMOCKS REMAINED IN NAVY UNTIL THE 1920'S.

OFFICERS IN OLD NAVY LOOK ALMOST MODERN—NOTE THE SWORDS.

QUARTERMASTERS AT HELM. IN DAY WHEN STEERING TOOK BRAWN.

GUN DECK OF FRIGATE. EVERYTHING SHIPSHAPE, BRISTOL FASHION.

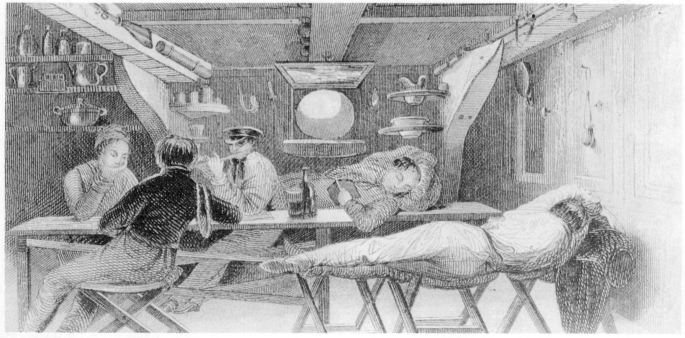

JUNIORS IN WARDROOM. POWDER HORN AND FLUTE TYPIFY PERIOD.

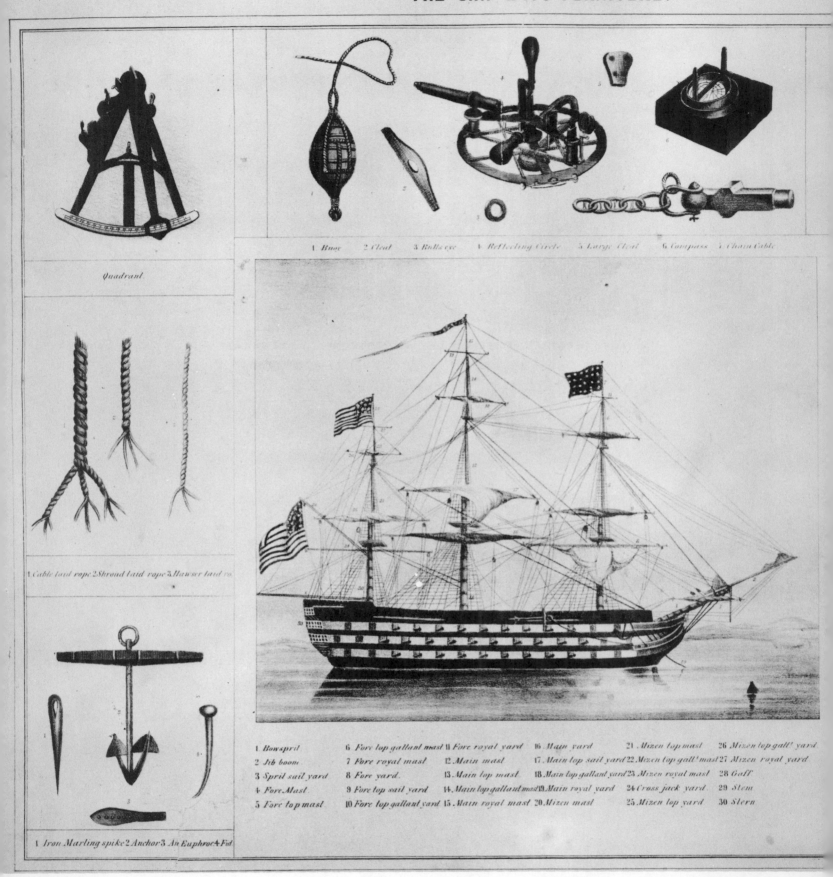

Quadrant.

1 Cable laid rope 2 Shroud laid rope 3 Hawser laid ro.

1 Iron Marling spike 2 Anchor 3 An Euphroe 4 Fid.

1 Buoy   2 Cleat   3 Bulls eye   4 Reflecting Circle   5 Large Cleat   6 Compass   7 Chain Cable

1 Bowsprit.	6 Fore top gallant mast.	11 Fore royal yard.	16 Main yard.	21 Mizen top mast.	26 Mizen top gall' yard.
2 Jib boom.	7 Fore royal mast.	12 Main mast.	17 Main top sail yard.	22 Mizen top gall' mast.	27 Mizen royal yard.
3 Spril sail yard.	8 Fore yard.	13 Main top mast.	18 Main top gallant yard.	23 Mizen royal mast.	28 Gaff.
4 Fore Mast.	9 Fore top sail yard.	14 Main top gallant mast.	19 Main royal yard.	24 Cross jack yard.	29 Stem.
5 Fore top mast.	10 Fore top gallant yard.	15 Main royal mast.	20 Mizen mast.	25 Mizen top yard.	30 Stern.

435. "THE SHIP AND ITS FUR-NITURE" — navigational and deck gear of late sailing Navy. Quaint poster published by American Sunday School Union of Philadelphia displays rigging plan, tackle and various tools indigenous to U.S.N. in heyday of sail. Marlinspike seamanship was at its height in this period when Navy's fleet was led by ships-of-the-line and Navy hands walked the capstan to "Blow the Man Down." Day would soon come when "marling" spike, euphroe and fid would be replaced by monkey wrench, oil can and mechanic's hammer. But Navy's sailing warships were sufficient for operations between 1816 and 1861.

The first propeller

made by John Fitch 1796

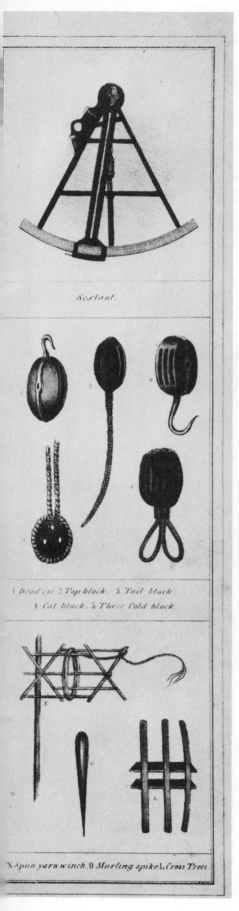

Sextant.

1 *Dead eye* 2 *Top block.* 3 *Tail block.*
4 *Cat block.* 5 *Three fold block.*

8 *Spun yarn winch.* 9 *Marling spike.* 10 *Cross Trees.*

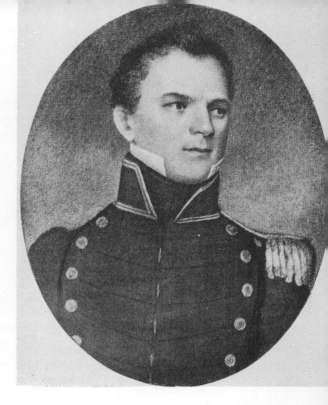

436. OUTSTANDING LINE OFFICER, HEYDAY OF SAIL—Lieutenant Hiram Paulding, U.S.N. A 16-year-old midshipman saved day for war-schooner *Ticonderoga* in Battle of Lake Champlain. When matches squibbed and a battery flubbed, nimble-witted Hiram Paulding fired the cannon by blazing at touch-holes with ready pistol. Brains displayed in War of 1812 put epaulet on Paulding's shoulder in period when average lieutenant was growing gray. The Algerian War. Service in West Indies pirate-hunting squadron. Pacific cruise to South Seas in *Dolphin*, pursuing mutineers in whaler *Globe*. Across the Andes 1,500 miles on horseback, carrying dispatches from Commodore Hull to General Bolivar. Adventures not untypical of time, but missions accomplished with acumen by no means common on contemporary quarter-decks. Crack navigator and seaman, courageous fighter, deft diplomat—Paulding owned unusual number of capacities, including ability to write literate prose. Gentleman as well as officer, he ran a happy as well as taut ship; led, rather than drove, his men. Then—at height of his career—tragedy. Aiding Central Americans, he arrested reckless soldier-of-fortune William Walker (1857). This act won gratitude of the Nicaraguans but incurred the enmity of U. S. President Buchanan, who venomously dismissed Paulding from naval service. Reinstated in 1861, he was forced to burn the ships he loved to save them from Confederate capture at Norfolk. But his intellectual reach could span the gap between sail and steam; at critical hour he sponsored building of Ericsson's ironclad *Monitor*. Lieutenant Hiram Paulding, U.S.N., had what it took to make Admiral and deserve the rank.

437. QUARTER-DECK KING IN HEYDAY OF SAIL—Captain John ("Mad Jack") Percival, U.S.N. Sometimes they called him "Roaring John." When he roared, they were liable to be too scared to call him anything. As a lad (in 1797) he'd been impressed on a British warship at Lisbon. Served two years in Royal Navy, unwilling hand in H.M.S. *Victory*. Legend had it that he sailed a lugger from Africa to Pernambuco, entire crew sick or dead of fever. Legend also that he could quell a mutiny by squinting an eye. No legend that he sailed down bay from Baltimore in a fishing smack (summer of 1813) and captured the tender of H.M.S. *Eagle*. He was sailing master of U. S. sloop *Peacock* when she punished H.M.S. *Épervier*. Skipper who took *Dolphin* to South Seas. Salt of the old school. King of the Quarter-deck. Humorous—irascible—blustery—unpredictable. Tyrant on Thursday; benevolent on Friday. Grog 'em and flog 'em. And keep an oak coffin in your cabin against Judgment Day. (But fill it with tea just for luck, and preach to it your own Sunday funeral sermons—no longbox is going to get Jack Percival!) It remained for the march of time to overtake "Roaring John." He would raise a storm in Hawaii by demanding repeal of local laws against prostitution. Would outlive the era of monarchial captaincy, smoothbore cannon and canvas. Steam was as uncongenial to him as diplomacy. But when a better stick-and-string sailor came over the horizon, "Mad Jack" Percival wanted to meet him. Preferably with a broadside from "Old Ironsides"—ship he commanded on cruise to China, 1843. Percival, sir! Cape Cod!

The first life-boat;

lined with cork over wood

was used at a wreck in 1817

438. BLUEJACKETS OF 1830's.
Bosn's Mate (at right) was probably
sketched from life by Sgt. E. C.
Young on board U.S.S. *Concord*.
Initials "G. B." stand for "George
Brown," who seems otherwise capable
of standing for himself. His pose is
somewhat more realistic than that of
"Fancy Jack" (below)—a popular
N. Currier lithograph in day of pretti-
fied portraits. Daughters in crinoline
doubtless sighed over this parlor
pin-up. Less tailoring and more tar
would have conveyed truer picture of
American man-o'-war's-man in heyday of canvas. Uniform appears fairly
authentic—varnished hat, jumper or
monkey jacket, broad-bottom trousers, pumps. American sailors of 1776
had no official uniform, but by 1830
costume shown was more or less enlisted standard. Wide-bottom trousers (in vernacular "canvas drawers") were easily rolled to knee for
deck work; could be quickly kicked
off in event of emergency swim. Black
neckerchief was originally worn as
sweatcloth (not, as is commonly supposed, in honor of "Nelson's death").
Salt of sailing days wore his hair in
pigtail doubled up ("clubbed") at
nape of neck, the pigtail tarred. Hence
nickname "Jack Tar," and sailor collar to protect jacket or jumper from
tar-stain. Tape on collar and cuffs
was originally decorative, as was hat
ribbon. And decoration could be
applied to individual taste. (Regulation stripes and hashmarks were not
authorized until 1866.) Stars on
collar were also purely decorative—
Jack liked to sew. By way of further
decoration, he might have stars tattooed on his hand, and stripes scarred
on his back. Jack was proud of both.

**439. SAILOR SPORTS IN HEY-
DAY OF SAIL**—dancing the fan-
dango at Port Mahon. Next to
"splicing the mainbrace" with a
dipper of grog, dancing was probably bluejacket's favorite pastime.
(Ladies first, without saying; reference is to pastime subject to proper
illustration.) Hornpipes were popular on deck; jigs, rigadoons, or anything which might be improvised for
"Possum Up a Gum Tree," went
ashore. With girls in every port, Navy
terpsichore was enthusiastically international. Favorite station was Port
Mahon in Mediterranean. There, Sgt.
E. C. Young, serving in U.S.S. *Concord*, painted this lively and heretofore unpublished, picture for ship's
Commanding Officer, M. C. Perry.
(From rare collection, Mystic Seaport Museum, Mystic, Connecticut.)

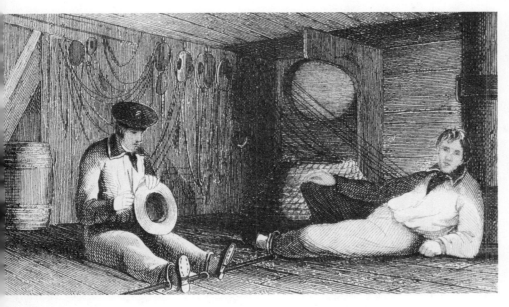

Wooden Ships and Men in Irons

440. LINE-CROSSING CEREMONY IN HEYDAY OF SAIL. One of earliest naval ceremonies (probably of religious origin), high jinks took place on man-of-war when she crossed the Equator. Victims ("pollywogs" crossing line first time) were initiated by veterans ("shellbacks"). Presided over by "King Neptune," high jinks included dousing victim. As illustrated, ceremonies could become rambunctious. But casualties on board were not entitled to Purple Heart. Nor even captain's sympathy.

441. NAVY BANDSMEN OF THE 1830's. Napoleon sponsored full-size military bands, favoring plenty of audible brass, pot-bellied drums and such compelling percussion instruments as the "Jingling Johnny"—a monster glockenspiel laden with cymbals, gongs, triangles and tin pans. American Navy bands, less ostentatiously equipped, were usually confined to shore station. Calbraith Perry seems to have acquired one for U.S.S. *Concord*. (Another painting by Sgt. E. C. Young, hitherto unpublished.)

UNIFORM OF THE BAND

U.S. SHIP CONCORD

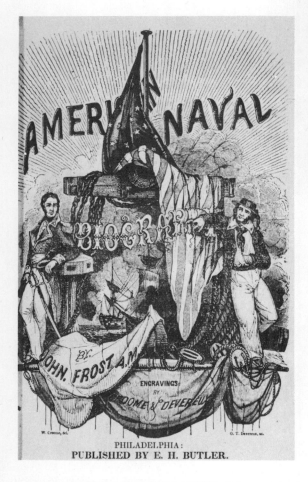

PHILADELPHIA:
PUBLISHED BY E. H. BUTLER.

442. PARLOR NAVY OF 1840's.
Frost's *American Naval Biography*:
Victorian fireside reading. Patriotic
sentiments for father, romantics for
the ladies and moral lessons for the
young. Not Jack Percival's Navy!

WILLIAM BAINBRIDGE.

ITTLE research
is necessary to find
the materials of this
commander's life.
It has already em-
ployed some of the
ablest pens in the
country; and de-
servedly, for among
the many who have
distinguished them-
selves in the youthful noon of the navy of our country, few have ranked higher than Commodore William
Bainbridge. By his own merit and exertion, he
raised himself from the rank of a common sailor, on
a merchantman, to the highest rank of the navy, and
in this responsible situation conducted himself in
such a manner as to win the approval of every candid
mind. The honour of his nation, the dignity of his
station, the respect due his own personal character,—
these were the interests he ever felt bound to support,
and it was the magnanimous maintenance of these
that procured him renown among his fellow-citizens.
WILLIAM BAINBRIDGE was born at Princeton,
New Jersey, May 7, 1774, being descended from

445. PAGE FROM FROST'S
AMERICAN NAVAL BIOGRAPHY.
Opening sentence of this sketch reveals more of book's character than
of Bainbridge's. Victorians neglected
John Paul Jones; preferred heroes
of 1812, the romantic "Golden Age."

443. JAMES FENIMORE COOPER
—celebrated novelist and naval historian. (From portrait painted at
time he was youthful midshipman.)
Quitting Navy to follow writing
career, Cooper became leading literary luminary of his day. In 1820's,
his Leather-Stocking Tales won phe-
nomenal success. His *History of the
Navy of the United States* (1839)
remained definitive until out-dated
by works of historian George Bancroft. One of few noted writers to
emerge from American Navy, Cooper
tended to color historical fact with
nationalistic bias. However, his pen
was less slanted than contemporary
quill of Commander Alexander Slidell
Mackenzie, U.S.N., whose biography
of "Hero of Erie" Cooper characterized as absurd. Five years in uniform
provided background for Cooper's
best-seller sea stories *The Pilot*
(1823) and *The Red Rover* (1827).

**444. FRONTISPIECE AND ILLUS-
TRATION FROM COOPER'S *RED
ROVER.*** Many a sea chest and ditty
bag in 1830 Navy contained this lusty
novel, bettered only by Dana's *Two
Years Before the Mast* and Melville's
*White Jacket, The World in a Man
of War*—sea classics by non-Navy men.

Sea Story

In memory of William Mulloy,
A native of Troy, State of New York,
A cooper on board the United States ship Delaware 74.
His adze becoming edgeless,
His staves worm-eaten,
His hoops consumed,
His flags expended, and
His bungs decayed,
He yielded up his trade with his life
On the twenty-ninth of April, 1829.

Although his skin's of dusky hue,
His heart was pure, his friendship true
His glass upon this earth is run,
He'll rise again in Kingdom Come.
His duty he performed with care
As captain's cook of Delaware.

Epitaphs on old tombstones at Port Mahon

446. FAKE NAVY HERO—Ned Buntline. Born Edward Z. C. Judson, he was also born liar, rabble rouser, publicity hound. Resigning midshipman's commission after brief service in U.S.N. during Seminole Wars, he embarked on dime novelist career under pen name "Buntline" (rope used in furling squaresail). In day when Royal Navy displayed intellectual caliber by distributing free copies of Dana's *Two Years Before the Mast* to British crews, American crews were devouring Buntline's "shilling shockers." Balderdash, blackmail and bigamy marked his career as fictioneer, yellow journalist, politician. Posing as symbol of Americanism, he started anti-England riots; organized the foolish Know-Nothing Party. He would best be remembered as sponsor of "Buffalo Bill" and the Wild West Show. But "Sailor Ned," as he liked to be called, was no naval hero. Publicity to contrary, his Navy career consisted of short hitches in *Constellation* and *Boston*; one minor skirmish in the

On the Health of Men,   *From the KEDGE ANCHOR.*

In port, in tropical climates, give the men a little coffee before they go to work in the morning.

The inconsiderate indulgence in new rum, has been one great means of increasing the numbers attacked with yellow fever.

Do not allow the men to lay about in night dews; and particularly not to wait about at wharfs.

Allow the men the use of fresh water whenever it can be spared, for washing clothes, and also for themselves.

Everglades. A figure symbolic of Johnsonian quip: "Patriotism is the last refuge of the finished scoundrel."

NAVY OF FICTION AND FACT

447. NAVY OF FACT. Brady's *Kedge-Anchor*, first published in 1847, was in its 10th edition 12 years later. (Frontispiece at right.) Forerunner of modern *Bluejacket's Manual*, book indicated skills and procedures actually needed. (Brady himself said, "You can learn it much better by practice than explanation.") Each ship was a city in itself—480 men in 170 feet of a heavy frigate—fitted for months of cruising without supply or repair, except what could be done independently at sea. Sea officer was concerned with endless detail of running delicate, powerful machine of wood, rope, acres of canvas. Men of these ships had to be tough, able, ready; range of skills required is amazing. *Kedge-Anchor*, the how-to-do book of the sailing navy, described naval doctrine for deck and sailing seamanship, ships organization and station bills; outlined simple tactics.

Old sailors, old battles —

THE

KEDGE-ANCHOR;

OR,

YOUNG SAILORS' ASSISTANT.

APPERTAINING TO THE PRACTICAL EVOLUTIONS OF MODERN SEAMANSHIP, RIGGING, KNOTTING, SPLICING, BLOCKS, PURCHASES, RUNNING-RIGGING, AND OTHER MISCELLANEOUS MATTERS, APPLICABLE TO SHIPS OF WAR AND OTHERS

Illustrated with Seventy Engravings.

ALSO,

TABLES OF RIGGING, SPARS, SAILS, BLOCKS, CANVASS, CORDAGE, CHAIN AND HEMP CABLES, HAWSERS, &c., &c. RELATIVE TO EVERY CLASS OF VESSELS.

BY WILLIAM BRADY, S. M., U.S.N.

SECOND EDITION.

IMPROVED AND ENLARGED, WITH ADDITIONAL MATTER, PLATES, AND TABLES.

NEW YORK:
PUBLISHED BY THE AUTHOR,
AND SOLD AT R. L. SHAW'S NAUTICAL STORE, NO. 222 WATER ST.
1847.

448 REALISM IN HEYDAY OF SAIL—four pages (below and facing) from Howe's *Life and Death on the Ocean*. Descriptions vividly portray general quarters drill and battle action as experienced on American sailing frigate. Also vividly portrayed are customs, manners and morals aboard U. S. Navy, 1830-1860—excerpts from the Rev. Charles Rockwell, Chaplain, U.S.N. Navy's first chaplain was William Balch, Congregational minister commissioned on October 30, 1799. Pioneer chaplains were usually amateur parsons who served for duration of cruise. In 1823, Navy Department ruled that naval chaplains must be ordained clergymen. Navy Chaplain's Corps of 1840 contained nine members. In 1842 Congress fixed number at 24, a figure unchanged until eve of World War I. In addition to religious duties, early chaplains were charged with education of midshipmen and junior officers—a chore almost as difficult as mixing piety with gunpowder. That Old Navy's "flock" stood in need of some "sky-piloting" is attested by the writings of Chaplain Rockwell. Needless to say, such realistic reporting was deplored by contemporary Navy heads and national leaders, then as today highly sensitive to public opinion. The trick is to impress American mothers by banning a *Moon Is Blue* (in 1840 *Lalla Rookh* was frowned upon) while censoring all reports of Sailor Boy's capers in far-away Hawaii, Panama or Puerto Rico. And if Jack had a girl in every port, he had little else to look forward to. Had Old Navy heads paid less attention to censorship, more to Rockwell's comments concerning officer morality, the *Somers* case (later in chapter) might never have made the grim headlines which came out, censorship despite.

Moderate weather.—Man the fore and main-tacks and sheets, attend the rigging—have hands on the lower yards to overhaul it—haul aboard—check the top bow-lines, weather lower lifts, and a little of the lee-main-brace—avast the sheets; get the tacks close down, and then haul aft the sheets—haul taut the main-brace, lifts, trusses, and bowlines.

Blowing fresh.—Man well the sheets, overhaul the leech-lines and lee-bunt-lines; ease down the lee-clew-garnet, slack top bowlines, lower lifts, and lee-main-braces, until the tacks are down; then haul aft the sheets, haul taut the lee-main-brace, weather lifts and bow-lines, and, if necessary, hook and haul taut the rolling-tackle, to ease the trusses.

Above and at right from "The Kedge Anchor"

MEN AND THINGS IN THE AMERICAN NAVY.

nailed, as a protection against the devil; and ship owners will rarely purchase a vessel which, by meeting with repeated accidents at sea, has proved to be unlucky.

Sailors have a peculiar superstition with regard to cats, especially black ones. Some years since, two men fell from the mast-head on board one of the ships in our navy, in a single day, of whom one was killed, and the other had his arm broken. Finding that one of the crew had killed a cat the night before, his shipmates regarded that as the cause of these accidents, and could not be appeased until the man was severely whipped; and then, as no one would mess with him, it was necessary to send him on shore. Clergymen have, in times past, been regarded as bringing ill luck to a ship on board which they sail, on the ground that the devil owes them a spite, and, as prince of the power of the air, strives, by means of tempests, to destroy them. This superstition may, however, have owed its origin to the story of Jonah, and the troubles which he brought upon his shipmates.

There are those who regard the playing of a death-march as a sure sign that some one on board is soon to die; and I have known a highly intelligent officer who would punish a man for such an act as soon as for a gross crime, on the ground, as he said, that he never knew it fail of being soon followed by a death. When lying in the bay of Gibraltar, during a violent storm, two of our massive anchors were broken, and we were driven rapidly out to sea. There was, at the time, on board, the body of one of the crew, lying in a coffin, with a view to his being buried on shore. Being compelled, however, to inclose him in his hammock, and bury him at sea, the carpenter was compelled to cut the coffin up into small pieces, and throw it overboard, because the men were superstitious and fearful as to its remaining on board.

The credulity of seamen as to ghosts and apparitions, good and bad signs, lucky and unlucky days, and the like, are owing, in part, to the peculiarly dangerous and exciting mode of life which they lead, to the many marvelous stories that are told in order to astonish the young and inexperienced, or to beguile the tedium of the night watches; but, more than all, to their being, from an early age, cut off from religious instruction. There are seamen who most religiously believe that when a man has been hung from the fore-yard-arm, two voices always reply when the man who is stationed there by night is hailed, one being that of him who has been hung; nor would the wealth of the world induce them to keep watch there.

That seamen have commonly much wit and humor, all know who have had intercourse with them. They have a great number of pithy expressions at ready command, and are very quick at repartee. This is owing to the fact that their mode of life is so peculiarly varied and exciting, that their minds act much more rapidly than those of most other men, as also to their being in such close and constant contact and collision with those around them, to which we may add the attention and applause secured by such as, by their ready wit, can aid in cheering the spirits of those around them, and thus relieve the monotony of a long and tedious voyage at sea. The craving for social excitement, on the part of seamen, leads them also to be very attentive hearers on the Sabbath, and few congregations on shore will follow a plain, but condensed and rapid, logical argument with so full an understanding of it as will a body of seamen on board our men-of-war. The wit and the songs of seamen are, for the most part, however, of a low, vulgar, and licentious cast.

This is the more to be regretted, as seamen are fond of the excitement of music, and, where a sailor has a fine voice, his songs are often called for, as well by officers as by the men.

As most seamen are, from an early age, cut off from kind parental restraint, and from moral and religious instruction, and exposed to the hardening and debasing influence of vice, it is not strange that, among other bad habits, they should form that of lying. Fear of punishment, too, leads them to resort to falsehood to conceal their guilt, when charged with it; nor dare they disclose the evil deeds of their shipmates, for fear of reproach and personal injury from them. Hence, most common sailors are inveterate liars, where their interest leads them to be so; nor is their word or oath, in such cases, regarded as of much value by those who know them well. One of our ship's boats, with ten or twelve rowers, had been ashore at a port where we were lying at anchor, and the midshipman who had charge of it, as is often done, had given the men a bottle of ardent spirits to drink, with a view to gain favor with them. As the men came on board, the officer of the deck saw that they had been drinking, and charged them with it. They all, to a man, stoutly denied the charge, and persevered in doing so, even after the officer of the boat had admitted before them that he had given them the spirits, and, in thus doing, had violated the rules of the ship. Events of this kind are of frequent occurrence on shipboard. It is, indeed, true that we hear much of the noble frankness of seamen, in freely confessing their faults, just as if there was some merit in it. The amount of it is, however, that such is the standard of morals to which they have conformed themselves, that they feel no guilt as to those things of which they so freely speak, but rather take pride in them.

Thieves are in very ill odor on shipboard, mainly because every one is exposed to suffer from them. When detected and brought up for punishment, the boatswain's mate always whips them with a relish. Still there is much thieving on board a man-of-war, and no small article of value is safe if exposed where it may be taken. Another prominent vice of seamen is selfishness. Many will, doubtless, be surprised at this statement. They have so often heard, in anniversary addresses and the like, that seamen are the most liberal, noble hearted and generous men in the world, that they really believe it to be true. But let us look, for a moment, at facts in the case. Seamen, on shipboard, are under such despotic rule, and are, in so many ways, checked and restrained, that they become peculiarly selfish and sensitive as to what they regard as their rights; and, where they dare to be so, are noisy and obstinate in defending them.

Much of the apparent liberality of seamen is shown when, from the influence of ardent spirits, they are hardly moral agents. I have known a seaman on shore, in a foreign port, buy a donkey with its load of fresh meat on the way to market, and, taking out his jack-knife, he cut up the meat, and divided it among the poor who thronged around him, and then, turning the donkey adrift, he went on his way. He was so drunk, however, that he hardly knew what he was doing. Money, too, has not the same value to a sailor, who has no one to provide for but himself, that it has to others. When a seaman gives three or five dollars to a disabled shipmate, the only difference it makes with him is that he has three or five dollars less in two or three hundred dollars of which to be robbed, when drunk, or otherwise defrauded of, at the end of his cruise. Sailors are often tired of the land before they have spent all their

SEAMANSHIP IN SAIL

SETTING TOPGALLANT SAILS BLOWING FRESH.

Point the yards to the wind, and loose the sails; sheet home first to leeward, and then to windward—having a hand to leeward to light the foot over the topmast stay; hoist away, trim the yards, and haul taut the bow-lines.

Note.—In setting topgallant sails over single-reefed topsails, see that the sheets are out square alike.

449. SAILING NAVY first relied on fast frigates like Continental *Hancock*. Later, Humphreys' *Constitution* showed what colonies could produce. Warship under sail had to be heavy—built to bear shot and stress of battle, hard sailing, tiered batteries of iron ordnance running length of ship—carried huge rig to get speed. Square rig with complication of yards and braces was needed to get full area, and helped in maneuvering. Tactically superior to fore-and-aft rig, warships under square sails could stop, turn, back down—maneuvers essential to tactics based on broadside firing. Speed and power were opposed requisites which navy resolved by building big ships, training superb crews; gunnery and expert handling won battles.

TO BACK AND FILL IN A TIDE-WAY.

This manœuvre is only executed when a ship is to proceed up or down a rapid river against the wind, which is supposed to be light, and may be done by two methods, viz., driving before the wind, or broadside to it. When the channel is broad enough, the latter method is preferable, as the ship will be more under the command of her helm.

MEN AND THINGS IN THE AMERICAN NAVY.

…ney, and are anxious to ship again. They feel much more at home …sit down on the deck, cut up their victuals with a jack-knife, and …nk their tea out of a quart-cup, than to conform to table usages on …re. The same is true also of their clothes; while the unrighteous …y in which they are fleeced by landlords and others, leads them to …gard those around them as a set of landsharks, and to hasten on ship-…rd for safety.

…We had on board our ship an old quarter-master, who had been to sea …m childhood. He said that once, after a long cruise, he was seven …ys on shore before he spent all his money, and that when he went to … rendezvous to ship again, they scolded at him for having been gone …long. On one occasion he was paid off at Pensacola, and finding it …ficult to get rid of his money, he hired a house for a month, with a …n servant, and a yellow girl for a housekeeper. Having staid a few …ys, and paid all his bills, he had sixty-five dollars left, and not knowing …w else to get rid of it, he had it all changed into silver half dollars, …en, going to a plantation near, he gave each negro one of these coins, …d then went and shipped for another cruise.

…Licentiousness, of the lowest and most debasing character, is the …bitual and easily besetting sin of most common seamen. That a …lor has a wife in every port he visits is an axiom in their creed and …ctice; and, so far are they from being ashamed of this fact, that they …l most resolutely argue in favor of this indulgence as right, on the …und that such is their course of life, that they cannot, like other men, …ll sustain the social and domestic relations, and perform the duties of … marriage connection. And this unblushing advocacy of the grossest …e, must, forsooth, be regarded as a specimen of the noble frankness … the sailor, of which we hear so much. Allurements to licentiousness … among the surest and most common means of enticing seamen into …se snares, which greedy and rapacious landlords so often spread for …m. When the agent of these landsharks visits a ship just returning …m a distant voyage, he excites the passions of his wretched dupes by …ering his services as a guide to her whose " house is the way to hell, …ding down to the chambers of death."

…In times past, it has been customary with our naval commanders, when …foreign ports, both of savage and of so-called civilized and Christian …tions, to permit hundreds of abandoned females to spend nights on …rd our national ships; thus converting them into floating brothels, and …eply disgracing the land from whence they came. The experiment …s tried on a limited scale by a base and profligate commander, on …rd two ships belonging to the station where we cruised; the one just …fore our arrival, and the other while we were lying in the same port. … decided, however, was the opposition of many of the officers to this …e profanation of our country's flag, that the evil was soon checked, …d did not spread to the other vessels in the squadron. So gross and …tal are most common seamen in this respect, that the most serious …ficulties which occur on board our national ships arise, from opposing …ir wishes for liberty to go on shore in foreign ports, mainly with a …w to gratify their lower passions and appetites.

…The known corruption, in principle and practice, of many of the …nger and some of the older officers in the navy, as to licentiousness, … a serious obstacle to efforts for the reformation of the common sea-…n. What good can be hoped for, in this respect, when the commander … a ship or squadron, when wintering in a foreign port, openly hires

MEN AND THINGS IN THE AMERICAN NAVY.

in forming their characters and directing their conduct, and in making them what they should, or what they should not be. I can, however, only glance, in closing, at a few peculiarities of the singular, unnatural, and highly artificial state of society, under the influence of which, as existing in our naval service, the minds and morals of our officers are shaped. Midshipmen ought, before receiving a warrant, to be closely examined as to their habits, moral character, and health. Many a reprobate and ungovernable son has, as a last resort, been placed in the navy with a view to subdue him, when, perhaps, his constitution has been impaired by vicious indulgence, or undermined by disease; and thus, physically weak and morally debased and depraved, has become a burden to the service, and a curse to all around him. Unable to endure the exposure and fatigue of duty, beneath the scorching sun, or chilling night-air, or drenching rain, or amid the howling tempest, he hangs upon the sick-list, and the duties he should do fall heavily upon others. Delicate boys, transferred, at a tender age, from the school-room, or luxurious parlor, to the steerage of a man-of-war, with its coarse fare and hard accommodations, its noise and riot, its loss of rest and fatiguing duty on deck, are full apt to wilt and wither, like the tender plant torn from its native earth and placed in harder and more ungenial soil. These causes, with youthful intemperance and licentiousness, have not only driven many from our navy, but have undermined or seriously injured the health and constitutions of large numbers still connected with it. I once heard a number of lieutenants give it as their united and deliberate opinion, that were there an invalid list formed in our navy, of those who were permanently diseased, it would embrace one half the officers of the grade of lieutenant and upward. Most of these, it is true, are engaged in active duty, but a little extra exposure to the weather, or over exertion, or undue indulgence of some of the animal appetites brings them upon the sick-list, and the burden of their duties rests severely on others.

The late increase of pay, in our navy, has a tendency to encourage and enable the younger officers to appear and dress like gentlemen. Compel a young man to live on coarse fare and dress poorly, to use his sheets for a table-cloth, to borrow clothes of his messmates and be meanly served, and you humble and degrade him, and greatly lessen his pride of character and self-respect. A man's conduct and language are affected not a little by the dress and style of living of himself and those around him. An increase of pay furnishes the means of an earlier and better settlement in married life than could otherwise be hoped for; and no one, who has not witnessed the fact referred to, can know how much is effected by a devoted and honorable attachment to a lovely and virtuous woman, in restraining from vice wild and reckless young men, when peculiarly exposed to temptation, and cut off from all moral and religious restraint.

I am happy to state, that there is an increasing number of officers in our navy, who, by their virtues and their moral and religious worth, are a credit to the service, and would grace any circle in which they might be placed. There are others, however, and sorry am I that it is so, who, though wearing swords and epaulets, and claiming to be gentlemen, are so in dress alone; their conduct and their language grossly belying their outward appearance and their vaunted claims to gentility. Some of this class are so lost to all sense of decency, that their common conversation at the mess-table and elsewhere, is most loathsome and offensive to every virtuous mind, and such, withal, as should forever exclude them

TO GET UNDER-WEIGH AND STAND BEFORE THE WIND.

Make all preparations for getting under-weigh, heave-in, and make sail as before. Lay the main and mizen topsails square aback; the fore one sharp aback, according to the side it is intended to cast—heave-in, cant her the right way with the helm before tripping, and as soon as the velocity of the stern-board is greater than that of the tide, shift the helm, grapple the buoy, run up the jib as soon as it will take, and haul aft the weather-sheet. While falling off, cat and fish the anchor; as she gathers head-way, shift the helm; when before the wind, right it—square the head yards, and brail up the jib—set topgallant sails, royals, and foresail—haul taut the lifts, trusses, backstay-falls, and if necessary, set the studding-sails.

IN GETTING UNDER-WEIGH, TO BACK ASTERN AND AVOID DANGER.

Make all preparations as before. If required to cast on the starboard tack, sheer her with the starboard helm; to bring the wind on the starboard bow, brace the yards aback, about half-way up with the larboard braces; haul out the spanker and keep the boom nearly amid-ships. Heave up briskly, grapple the buoy, and as soon as the anchor is up, put the helm hard a-weather to keep her to—cat and fish the anchor. Having made sufficient stern-board, shift the helm, brace the after yards, ease off the spanker sheet, and run up the jib. When full aft, brace up the head yards, and as she gathers headway, right the helm and make sail. To cast on the larboard tack, sheer her with the port helm, brace all sharp aback, and proceed as before.

GETTING UNDER-WEIGH IN A NARROW CHANNEL.

At anchor in a narrow channel, riding to a strong leeward tide, and blowing fresh; a ship astern, and also one on each quarter, so near that there is not room to wear, for casting; it is necessary to put to sea, and to do so a passage must be effected between the two ships. Make all preparations for getting under-weigh, and heave-in as described before. Loose the topsails; if riding by the star-board cable, give her a *rank sheer* with the starboard helm; set up the starboard back-stays, and bear aft the larboard ones; overhaul lifts and trusses; haul out the spanker, and get the boom over on the larboard quarter; lead along the main tack and sheet; run up the jib, and haul aft the weather sheet; "Heave round cheerily;" run the anchor up, grapple the buoy, and as soon as she fills, meet her with the helm; board the main tack to catch her; trim the jib and spanker sheets, set the foresail, and trim sharp; haul taut the bowlines; stand on as far as may be necessary.

Note.—A good deal of uncertainty attends this manœuvre; if there is room, it would be the best plan to lay the yards aback. It is confidently asserted by old experienced seamen, that the above method is perfectly practicable.

Everything having been previously prepared, heave in and make sail as before. Sheer her with a starboard helm; brace the head yards sharp up with the starboard braces, and counter brace the after ones; haul out the spanker, and get the boom on the larboard quarter; heave in, and up anchor; up jib as soon as it will take; and when the stern-board exceeds the velocity of the tide, shift the helm. When the after sails are full, trim the spanker, let flow the jib sheet, cat and fish the anchor, haul aft the jib sheet, brace round the head-yards, and make sail.

TO GET UNDER-WEIGH, AND STAND OUT ON A WIND.

Make all preparations—commence heaving in; loose jib and spanker; top up and bear over the boom on the right quarter, and the helm to the side which it is intended to cast; "heave up;" get the buoy; haul out on the spanker as soon as it will take. When the wind gets abeam, run up the jib, and meet her with the helm; cat and fish the anchor; loose, sheet home, and hoist the topsails, brace up, bring by and make sail.

DRIVING BEFORE THE WIND.

This is only done in a very narrow channel. Heave up the anchor, and get her before the wind, with just sail enough to keep her so. Suppose her under topsails, and as she drops with the tide, it becomes necessary for her to remain stationary, to allow a ship to pass her stern,—set topgallant-sails, and if required to shoot ahead, drop the foresail. If to avoid a rock, or ship astern, put the helm up or down—haul out the spanker—brace up, and haul aft the jib-sheet, as she comes too; shoot across until clear of danger, when put the helm up, brail up the spanker, shiver the after yards, and when before the wind, brail up the jib. If in standing across, she should get too near the shore—get her on the other tack, by wearing or box-hauling.

TO MAKE A FLYING MOOR.

Make all necessary preparations for coming-to; overhaul and bitt a double range of the weather cable, and bitt the lee one at the range to which she is to be moored. When approaching the anchorage, reduce sail to topsails, jib and spanker, if moderate, but if fresh, to jib and spanker only; when near the berth of the first anchor, luff-to, stream the buoy, and when the headway has nearly ceased, let go the weather anchor, up helm, stand on and veer away roundly, to prevent the range from checking her; when the full range is nearly out, hard down the helm, down jib, clew up the topsails, out spanker, and let her lay the range out taut; when taut, let go the lee anchor, *furl sails*, bring-to on the weather-cable, reeving away on the lee one, and heave into the moorings. Moor taut, to allow for veering; clap on service, and veer it; if hemp cable, square the yards, stop in the rigging, and clear up the decks.

TO CHASE TO WINDWARD.

To chase to windward, run upon the same course with the enemy, until he is brought perpendicularly to the same course; when tack and continue the second board, until he is again brought perpendicularly to the same course; always continue this manœuvre by tacking every time the chase is a-beam, on either board, and she will come in the shortest method by your superiority of sailing. Should the chase pass the point, when the chase bears a-beam, he must go about with all dispatch.

Note.—The chase goes about as soon as the chase is exactly a-beam, because at that time, the distance between them is the least possible upon the different boards they hold.

OBSERVATIONS FOR A SHIP TO WINDWARD, WHICH IS CHASED.

The weather ship will always be joined, since it is granted that she does not sail as well as the pursuer, it will be then to her advantage to keep constantly on the same tack, without losing time to heave about, for tacking cannot be so favorable to her as to her adversary, whose sailing is superior.

TO CHASE TO LEEWARD.

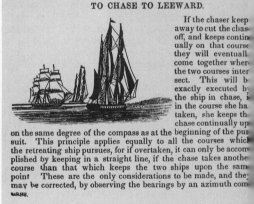

If the chaser keep away to cut the chase off, and keeps continually on that course they will eventually come together where the two courses intersect. This will be exactly executed by the ship in chase, if in the course she had taken, she keeps the chase continually up on the same degree of the compass as at the beginning of the pursuit. This principle applies equally to all the courses which the retreating ship pursues, for if overtaken, it can only be accomplished by keeping in a straight line, if the chase takes another course than that which keeps the two ships upon the same point. These are the only considerations to be made, and they may be corrected, by observing the bearings by an azimuth compass.

TO WINDWARD OF AN ENEMY, WITHIN PISTOL SHOT.—*The weather main rigging is shot away—both ships with main topsails to the mast.*

Up helm, fill away, and run the enemy on board, before she gets headway to prevent it.

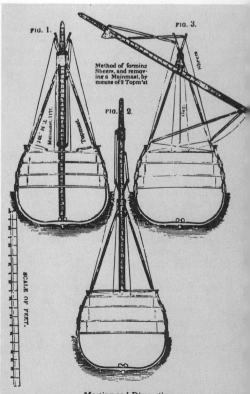

Masting and Dismasting.

Exhibit of the Navy Ration,

Showing the component parts for each day of the week, and the value at which they are to be computed, under the 2d, 4th and 5th Sections of the Act of Congress, " To establish and regulate the Navy Ration," approved 29th August, 1842.

Days of the Week.	Pounds.						Ounces.							Pints.	
	Beef.	Pork.	Flour.	Rice.	Raisins or dried fruits.	Pickles or Cranberries	Biscuit.	Sugar.	Tea. Coffee. Cocoa. Either.	Butter.	Cheese.	Beans.	Vinegar.	Spirits.	
Sunday		1			1		14	2	½			½		½
Monday	1						14	2	½	1				½
Tuesday		1	½				14	2	½					½
Wednesday				½	1		14	2	½		1			½
Thursday	1						14	2	½	1		½	2	½
Friday			½	½			14	2	½		1			½
Saturday		1			1		14	2	½			½		½
Weekly Quantity	4	3	1	1	½		98	14¼	7	4	3	1½		1½

VALUATION OF THE WEEKLY QUANTITY, &c.

3 pounds of Pork		7½ cents per pound,		22½ cents.
4 " Beef	6	"		24 "
1 " Flour	4	"		4 "
1 " Rice	3	"		3 "
½ " Raisins, &c.	13	"		6½ "
" Pickles, &c.	12½	"		6½ "
98 ounces of Bread	4	"		24½ "
14 " Sugar	8	"		7 "
7 " Tea	} of same val. 80	"		8½ "
" Coffee				
" Cocoa				
4 " Butter	23	"		5½ "
3 " Cheese	16	"		4 "
1½ pints of Beans	24	" gallon		4½ "
" Molasses	64	"		4 "
" Vinegar	20	"		1½ "
" Spirits	14	"		14 "

Averaging 20 cents per day, or weekly - - - - $1.40

The foregoing exhibit of the component parts, &c., of the Navy Ration, has been compiled in pursuance of the act of Congress, and will be strictly observed by commanders of vessels and by pursers, as a regulation of this Department, prescribing the daily issue of provisions, and the valuation at which they are to be commuted. All persons "attached to vessels for sea-service," are entitled individually to one ration per day.

Every commissioned or warrant-officer, of, or over, twenty-one years of age, may, at his option, commute the entire ration, or only the spirit portion of it: provided the commutation, in either case, be made for not less than three consecutive months. And every other person, of the above-named age, entitled to a ration, may commute the spirit component, under the limitation of time, unless sooner detached, or entitled to a discharge.

No officer or other person, under twenty-one years of age, shall be permitted to draw the spirit part of his ration. Its value in money, as estimated by the foregoing table, will be credited to him by the purser, and paid whenever the commander of the vessel, to which such officer or person may belong, shall direct.

The messes of a ship's crew may, with the sanction of the commanding officer, commute, daily or weekly, one or more entire rations, for not less than three months (unless sooner detached, or entitled to a discharge); the commutation to be paid by the purser, at such times as the said commanding officer shall deem fit.

Pursers having the delivery of rations, will make out and transmit, monthly and otherwise, by the earliest opportunities, to the Bureau of Provisions and Clothing of this Department, abstracts of provisions, agreeably to such forms as may be furnished to them from that bureau, approved by the Second Comptroller of the Treasury; their provision accounts, as heretofore, will be rendered to the Fourth Auditor's office.

A. P. UPSHUR, *Secretary of the Navy.*

A Table showing the Complement of Officers and Crew allowed to Vessels of each Class, U. S. N.

Rank or Ratings.	Ships of the Line. 3 DECKS.	2 DECKS 1st Class.	2d Class.	Razees.	Frigates. 32 Pounder.	24 Pounder.	18 Pounder.	Sloops. 32 Pounder.	24 Pounder.	16, 32 lb. Carronades.	Brigs.	Brigantines & Schooners.	Steamers. 1st Class.	2d Class.	3d Class.	Receiving Vessels. Ships of the Line.	Frigates.	Smaller.	PAY PER MONTH.	Remarks.
Captain	1	1	1	1	1 or 1		1												As regulated by law.	(a) To act as Watch Officers if necessary.
Commander	1	1	1	1				1	1	1	1	1	1	1					
Lieutenants	9	6	6	6	5	4	4	3	3	3	2	2	3	2		4			
Master	1	1	1	1	1	1	1	a1	a1	a1	a1	a1	1	1				
Surgeon	1	1	1	1	1	1	1	1	1	1	1	—	1	—				
Purser	1	1	1	1	1	1	1	1	1	1	1	1	1	1				
Chaplain*	1	1	1	1	1	1	1											
Professor of Mathematics	1	1	1	1	1	1	1											
Passed or other Assistant Surgeons	4	3	3	2	2	2	2	1	1	1	1 p'd	1 p'd	1 p'd	1				
Passed and other Midshipmen	21	18	18	12	12	12	12	8	7	6	3	3	7	5		4	6		
Boatswains	1	1	1	1	1	1	1	1	1	1	1	1	1	1				
Gunner	1	1	1	1	1	1	1	1	1	1	1	1	1	1				
Carpenter	1	1	1	1	1	1	1	1	1	1	1	1	1	1				
Sail-maker	1	1	1	1	1	1	1	1	1	1	1		1	1				
Clerk to Captain or Commanding Officer	1	1	1	1	1	1	1	1	1	1	1	1	1	1				
Clerk to Commander	1																	
Clerk to Purser	1	1	1	1	1	1	1	1	1	1	1	1	1	1					YEOMEN. $40 in Ships of the Line; 35 in Frigates; 25 in Sloops; 18 in smaller.
Yeoman	1	1	1	1	1	1	1	1	1	1	1	1	1	1				$18	
Armorer	1	1	1	1	1	1	1	1	1	1	1	1	1	1				19	ARMORER. $25 in Ships of the Line; 20 in Frigates; 15 Sloops.
Ship's Steward	1	1	1	1	1	1	1	1	1	1	1	1	1	1				19	
Master at Arms	1	1	1	1	1	1	1	1	1	1	1	1	1	1				19	
Boatswain's Mates	8	6	6	4	4	4	3	2	2	2		2	3	2				19	
Gunner's Mates	6	4	4	2	2	2	2	1	1	1	1	1	2	1				19	
Carpenter's Mates	4	3	3	2	2	2	2	1	1	1	1	1	1	1				$19	
Sail-maker's Mates	2	1	1	1	1	1	1	1	1	1								15	
Ship's Cook	1	1	1	1	1	1	1	1	1	1	1	1	1	1				18	
Coxswain	1	1	1	1	1	1	1	1	1	1	1	1	1	1				18	
Quarter-Masters	12	10	10	8	8	8	6	4	4	3	4	3	4	3	2			18	
Quarter-Gunners	24	18	18	12	12	10	8	4	4	4	2	2	4	2	2			18	
Captains of Forecastle	4	4	4	4	4	2	2	2	2	1	1	1						18	
Captains of Tops	8	8	8	6	6	6	4	2	2									15	
Captains of Afterguard	2	2	2	2	2	2	2	1	1	1	1							15	
Captains of Hold	2	2	2	1	1	1	1	1	1	1								15	
Cooper	1	1	1	1	1	1	1	1	1	1	1		1					15	
Painter	1	1	1	1	1	1	1	1	1	1								15	
Armorer's Mate	1	1	1	1	1	1	1	1	1	1			1					15	
Surgeon's Steward	3	3	3	2	2	2	2	1	1	1	1	1	1	1				18	
Ship's Corporal	3	3	3	2	2	2	2	1	1	1	1	1	1	1				15	
Master of Band	1	1	1	1	1	1	1											18	
Cabin Steward	1	1	1	1	1	1	1	1	1	1	1	1	1	1				15	
Cabin Cook	1	1	1	1	1	1	1	1	1	1	1	1	1	1				15	
Ward-room Steward	1	1	1	1	1	1	1	1	1	1	1	1	1	1				15	
Ward-room Cook	1	1	1	1	1	1	1	1	1	1	1	1	1	1				15	
Seamen	250	200	180	125	110	100	80	42	40	26	15	15	40	10	8			10	
Ordinary Seamen	250	200	180	125	110	100	80	42	40	26	15	15	40	10	8		20	10	
Landsmen and Boys	374	226	226	151	112	85	52	41	30	19	16	16	30	12			40	9	For landsmen, and $8 to $6 for boys.
Musicians, First Class	8	6	6	6	6	6	5											$12	
Musicians, Second Class	6	5	5	4	4	4	4											10	
Chief Engineer													1	1	1				
First Assistant Engineer													2	2	1				
Second Assistant Engineer													2	1	1				
Third Assistant Engineer													2	1	2				
Firemen													18	8	2				
Coal Heavers													18	4	1				
Total, excepting Marines	1025	754	714	500	430	380	300	181	161	121	80	79	209	85	50	106			By special order. By special order.

MARINES.

Captains	1	1	1			1									1				As regulated by law.
Lieutenants	2	2	2	1	1	1	1						2	1	3				
Sergeants	4	3	3	3	3	3	2	2	2	2			2	1	3				
Corporals	4	4	4	4	4	4	4	2	2	2			1	1	3				
Drummers	2	2	2	1	1	1	1	1	1	1			1		1				
Fifers	2	2	2	1	1	1	1	1	1	1			1		1				
Privates	60	52	52	40	40	40	40	20	20	20			20	12	31				
Total Marines	75	66	66	50	50	50	49	26	26	26			26	15	40				
Total complements	1100	820	780	550	480	430	349	210	190	150	80	79	235	100	50	146			

* Razees and Frigates having the Commander of a Squadron on board, are also entitled to a Chaplain.

A Table showing the Quantity of Provisions, Slop Clothing and Small Stores, for 200 men, for four months, in the U. S. Navy.

SMALL STORES.

Tobacco (plugs)	1,000	Pea-jackets (1 pair each)	100
Soap (bars)	800	Trowsers (1 pair each)	200
Mustard (bottles)	100	Duck Frocks (1 each)	200
Pepper (bottles)	100	Duck Trousers (2 pairs each)	400
Knives (1 each)	200	White Flannel Shirts (2 each)	400
Spoons (1 each)	200	Blue Flannel Shirts (2 each)	400
Fine Combs (1 each)	200	Drawers (2 pairs each)	400
Coarse Combs (1 each)	200	Hats (1 each)	200
Tin Pots (1 each)	200	Shoes (1 pair each)	200
Tin Pans (1 each)	200	Stockings (2 pairs each)	400
Scrubbing Brushes (1 each)	200	Black Handkerchiefs (1 each)	200
Ribbon (pieces)	100	Boots (1 pair each)	200
Tape (pieces)	100	PROVISIONS.	
Needles (papers)	100	Bread (pounds)	22,320
White Thread (pounds)	50	Beef (pounds)	14,652
Blue Thread (pounds)	50	Pork (pounds)	10,914
Thimbles (1 each)	200	Flour (pounds)	1,819
Beeswax (cakes)	100	Raisins (pounds)	910
Blacking (boxes)	200	Tea (pounds)	400
Scissors (1 pair each)	200	Sugar (pounds)	3,210
Shoe Brushes (1 pair each)	200	Rice (pounds)	3,636
Mittens (1 pair each)	200	Beans (pounds)	5,460
Cotton Handkerchiefs	50	Pickles (pounds)	1,819
		Vinegar (gallons)	228
SLOP CLOTHING.		Spirits (gallons)	750
Mattresses (1 each)	200		
Blankets (2 each)	400	*Allowing per centage for waste.*	

N. B.—All recruits, when received on board of receiving-ships of the U. S. Navy, are required to have an outfit in slop clothing, &c., of one blue cloth jacket, one pair of blue cloth trowsers, 2 duck frocks, one pair of duck trowsers, two blue flannel shirts, one pair of drawers, one hat, one pair of shoes, two pairs of stockings, one black silk handkerchief, two pounds of tobacco, two pounds of soap, one knife, one tin pot, pan and spoon; the greater part of which they have when transferred to vessels for sea-service. This being the case, there is no necessity for having the full amount, as above stated, in slops and small stores in the purser's department, for issue in the course of four months.

QUANTITY OF WATER FOR EACH CLASS.

Ships of the Line—Three Decks, 110,000 gallons; Two Decks—1st Class, 82,000 gals.; 2d Class, 78,000 gals.; *Razees,* 55,000 gals.; *Frigates*—32 Pounder, 48,000 gals.; 24 Pounder, 43,000 gals.; 18 Pounder, 34,900 gals.; *Sloops*—32 Pounder, 21,000 gals.; 24 Pounder, 19,000 gals.; Sixteen 32 lb. Carronades, 15,000 gals.; *Brigs,* 8,000 gals.; *Brigantines* and *Schooners* 7,900 gals.; *Steamers*—1st Class, 23,500 gals.; 2d Class, 10,000 gals.; 3d Class, 5,000 gals.; *Receiving Vessels*—Ships of the Line, 14,600 gals.

A Table showing the Size, Quantity, Quality and Number of Sails allowed to each Class of Vessels, U. S. N.

Names of Sails.	Ships of the Line. No. of Sails.	No. Canvas.	Size Rope. Head.	Foot.	Leech.	Hoist.	Razees. No. of Sails.	No. Canvas.	Size Rope. Head.	Foot.	Leech.	Hoist.	Frigates. FIRST CLASS. No. of Sails.	No. Canvas.	Size Rope. Head.	Foot.	Leech.	Hoist.	SECOND CLASS. No. of Sails.	No. Canvas.	Size Rope. Head.	Foot.	Leech.	Hoist.	Sloops. FIRST CLASS. No. of Sails.	No. Canvas.	Size Rope. Head.	Foot.	Leech.	Hoist.	SECOND CLASS. No. of Sails.	No. Canvas.	Size Rope. Head.	Foot.	Leech.	Hoist.
Fore Sails	2	1	3½	6	6	—	2	1	3	5½	5½	—	2	1	3	5½	5½	—	2	1	2½	5½	5½	—	2	2	2½	4½	4½	—	2	2	2½	4½	4½	—
Fore Top Sails	2	1	3½	6	4½	—	2	1	3	5½	4	—	2	1	3	5½	4½	—	2	1	2½	5½	4	—	2	2	2½	4½	4½	—	2	2	2½	4½	3½	—
Fore Top-gallant Sails	2	4	2	4	2½	—	2	4	2	3½	2½	—	2	5	2	3½	2½	—	2	5	2	3½	2½	—	2	6	1½	3	2½	—	2	6	1½	3	2½	—
Fore Royals	2	7	1½	2½	2	—	2	7	1½	2½	2	—	2	7	1½	2½	2	—	2	7	1½	2½	2	—	2	8	1½	2	1½	—	2	8	1½	2	1½	—
Main Sails	2	1	3½	6	6	—	2	2	3	5½	5½	—	2	1	3	5½	5½	—	2	2	2½	5½	5½	—	2	2	2½	4½	4½	—	2	2	2½	3½	3½	—
Main Top Sails	3	1	3½	6	4½	—	3	1	3	5½	4	—	3	1	3	5½	4½	—	3	1	2½	5½	4	—	2	2	2½	4½	4½	—	2	2	2½	4½	3½	—
Main Top-gallant Sails	2	4	2	4	2½	—	2	4	2	3½	2½	—	2	5	2	3½	2½	—	2	5	2	3½	2½	—	2	6	1½	3	2½	—	2	6	1½	3	2½	—
Main Royals	2	7	1½	2½	2	—	2	7	1½	2½	2	—	2	7	1½	2½	2	—	2	7	1½	2½	2	—	2	8	1½	2	1½	—	2	8	1½	2	1½	—
Mizen Top-sails	2	2	2½	5	4	—	2	2	2½	4½	3½	—	2	2	2½	4½	4	—	2	3	2½	4½	3½	—	3	3	2	4	3	—	2	3	2	3½	2½	—
Mizen Top-gallant Sails	2	5	1½	2½	2	—	2	5	1½	2½	2	—	2	6	1½	2½	2	—	2	6	1½	2½	2	—	2	7	1½	2½	1½	—	2	7	1½	2½	1½	—
Mizen Royals	2	7	1½	2½	1½	—	2	7	1½	2½	1½	—	2	8	1½	2	1½	—	2	8	1½	2	1½	—	2	8	1½	2	1½	—	2	8	1½	2	1½	—
Lower Studding-sail	2	6	2½	2½	—	—	2	6	2½	2½	—	—	2	6	2½	2½	—	—	2	6	2½	2½	—	—	2	7	2½	2½	—	—	2	7	2	2	—	—
Fore Top-mast Studding-sails	2	5	2	2½	—	—	2	5	2	2½	—	—	2	6	2	2½	—	—	2	6	2	2½	—	—	2	6	1½	2	—	—	2	6	1½	2	—	—
Fore Top-gallant Studding-sails	2	7	1½	2½	—	—	2	7	1½	2½	—	—	2	7	1½	2½	—	—	2	7	1½	2½	—	—	2	8	1	1½	—	—	2	8	1	1½	—	—
Main Top-mast Studding-sails	2	5	1½	2½	—	—	2	5	1½	2½	—	—	2	6	1½	2½	—	—	2	6	1½	2½	—	—	2	6	1½	2	—	—	2	6	1½	2	—	—
Main Top-gallant Studding-sails	2	7	1½	2½	—	—	2	7	1½	2½	—	—	2	7	1½	2½	—	—	2	7	1½	2½	—	—	2	8	1	1½	—	—	2	8	1	1½	—	—
Flying-Jibs	2	6	—	3½	—	3	2	6	—	3½	—	3	2	6	—	3	—	3	2	6	—	3	—	3	2	7	—	2½	—	3	2	7	—	2½	—	3
Standing-Jibs	2	3	—	3½	—	4	2	3	—	3½	—	4	2	3	—	3½	—	4	2	4	—	2½	—	4	2	4	—	2½	—	3	2	4	—	2½	—	3
Fore Try-sails	2	3	3½	2½	—	—	2	3	3½	2½	—	—	2	3	3½	2½	—	—	2	3	2½	2½	—	—	2	3	2½	2½	—	—	2	3	2½	2½	—	—
Main Try-sails	1	1	3½	2½	—	—	1	1	3½	2½	—	—	1	1	2½	2½	—	—	1	1	2½	2½	—	—	1	1	2½	2½	—	—	1	1	2½	2½	—	—
Storm Mizen	1	1	2	3	3	—	1	1	2	3	3	—	1	1	2	3	3	—	1	1	2	3	3	—												
Spankers	2	3	2½	4	3	3½	2	3	2½	4	3	3½	2	3	2½	4	3	3½	2	3	2½	4	3	3	2	4	2	3½	2½	3	2	4	2	3½	2½	3
Fore Storm Stay-sail	1	1	—	3½	4	4½	1	1	—	3½	4	4½																								
Main Storm Stay-sail	1	1	—	3½	4	4½	1	1	—	3½	4	4½																								
Miz. Storm Stay-sail	1	1	—	3	3	3½	1	1	—	3	3	3½																								
Fore Top-mast Stay-sails	2	1	—	3½	3½	3½																													

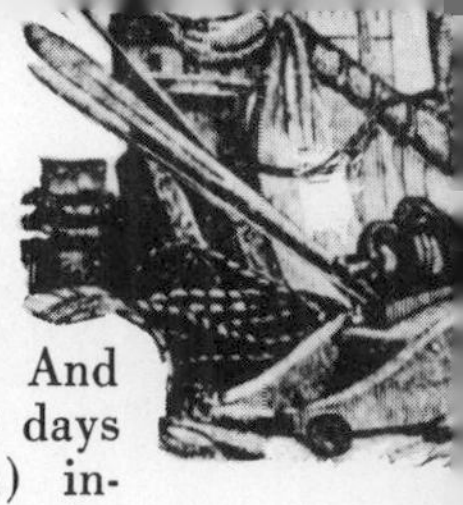

STATION BILL FOR FIRE, IN THE MERCHANT SERVICE.*

Coolness and steadiness in any misfortune by fire are essential to arrest it.

If a fire break out below, the hatchways should be immediately covered, to prevent a draught of air.

Ring the ship's bell to call the men to their stations.

MEN'S NAMES.	DUTIES.
A very steady man	To the helm.
The carpenter, and one man.	First, to cover hatchways with gratings and tarpaulins. Secondly, to rig pumps and lead hoses; and Thirdly, get the tools ready for cutting away, if required.
The chief mate, boatswain, and ship's cook.	To attend where the fire is, and pass water to it, &c.
A man of each watch or more.	To the pumps, and to draw water as for washing decks.
A boy.	To collect all the buckets to the part where the water is being drawn.
Remainder of starboard watch.	First duty to haul up courses, brail up trysails and spanker. Second duty, draw and pass water with the fire buckets; then for third duty see below.
Remainder of larboard watch.	First duty, to haul up courses, brail up trysails and spanker. Second duty, to soak small sails and bedding to throw over and smother the fire; then for third duty see below.
Cabin steward, and cabin boy.	If any powder or other combustibles are on board, to throw them overboard if possible, or drown them.
Second mate to direct fire hose, and the supply of water from deck.	If the fresh water is in tanks, turn the waste-valves† of two of them for a first supply for the pump, and then go to direct fire hose, &c.
The crew.	Third duties of the crew, the yard and stay-tackles to be got up ready for getting out boats.
The crew.	Fourth duties of the crew, if the fire appears to increase, out boats, and lower down the quarter boats; let them lay off in a string to windward, with a man and a boy as keepers, ready for the rest of the crew if required.
The captain	To attend at all the stations as he deems best.

If the ship cannot be saved, the passengers and crew are the first objects, with some fresh water and biscuit; a compass, quadrant and Bowditch. Unless there is sufficient time, and it can be done without endangering the sea-worthiness of the boats, nothing should be taken that is not essential to the mere preservation of life, and necessary for navigating the boats.

* This bill ought to be written out or printed, and hung up for every one's inspection.

† The mate ough to have the key of the valves of the water tanks in his own keeping.

451. EARLY STATION BILLS here shown were doctrine for warships—and in some cases merchantmen, too. (In their similarities to the modern, Navy hands will recognize forerunners of bills in use today.) Ship fires were particularly dangerous in wood-hull canvasback vessels. And ocean abandonments in sailing days (no radio; no aircraft search) invited slow death by thirst, sunstroke or starvation on Sahara seas. (Note: "fearnaught" of ship's carpenter was handy sheet of rough wool cloth.)

TAKING TO THE BOATS.

The captain should in his own mind, and by a private memorandum, station the passengers and crew to the boats on board, and likewise make the persons here specified be responsible for having the following articles put into the boats.

Captain.	Compass, Maury on Navigation, sextant, spy-glass, Nautical Almanac, pencils and writing paper, general chart, pocket watch, pair of compasses, &c.
First mate.	Oars, masts, sails, boat-hooks, bolt of canvass, boat's compass, Bowditch's chart, ensign.
Second mate.	Two or three bags of biscuits, some breakers of water, quadrant, pencils and writing paper half-gill measure, a musket, box of cartridges, and flints or caps.
Surgeon	Pocket instruments.
Carpenter.	Hammer, nails, sheet-lead, grease, fearnought, oakum, saw, chisel, turn-screw, cold chisel, a vial of sweet oil, any small iron rod.
Third mate, or boatswain.	Coil of inch rope, long reel, deep-sea reel, painted canvass, marling-spikes, spun-yarn, &c.
Sail maker.	Palm, needles, twine, fishing-lines, hooks, painted canvass, boat's awning.
Cook, and steward.	Tinder-box, flints and tinder, small box, lantern and candles, cheese, cabin biscuit, chocolate.
Each person.	A tin pot, a pocket knife, a change of flannels and stockings.

With a scarcity of food, savages attempt to lessen the cravings of hunger by tightening a belt around the waist; and by sucking a pebble they in some degree alleviate thirst. Chewing tobacco may also be serviceable under such circumstances. In such emergencies all must fare alike.

STATIONING THE CREW.

In dividing the crew into watches, care should be taken t the physical force is as equally distributed as possible, and t there be as many seamen, ordinary seamen, boys, and marin in one watch as in another.

Petty officers should be chosen from among the seamen, a those selected who have been long in the service, and h proved faithful. Forecastle men should be middle-aged seam with a few ordinary seamen and landsmen. Young active s men should be selected for topmen, also a few ordinary seam landsmen and boys. After-guard, a few elderly seamen, w ordinary seamen and landsmen. Waisters are chiefly landsm with a few ordinary seamen; in single-decked vessels, wh there are no waisters, more men should be stationed on the fo castle and in the after-guard, in proportion to the number of crew of the different classes of vessels. Idlers are excused fr keeping watch—they are officers' servants, cooks, &c., &c.

Divide each watch into first and second parts, and appoin captain to each part; number the men belonging to the fo castle, having all the larboard watch even, as two, four, six, the starboard odd; have the numbers painted on canvass, let each man sew it on his bag and hammock; having also greater distinction, the larboard painted red, and the starbo black. The men should be below alternately, so that when watch is below, there should be an equal number of the c watch on deck.

STATIONING THE CREW AT QUARTERS.

Captains of the guns should be chosen from among the men who have been long accustomed to them, steady, good sight, and quick motion. The largest and stoutest should be chosen to man the long guns, the others the car ades. The boarders should be stout men—the firemen and trimmers, active young men. Be particular to station the near where they are accustomed to do their duty as possibl order to prevent confusion. Let all the first part of the g crew be in one watch, and the second part in the other, so in the event of going to quarters in the night, the watch on can clear away the guns, while the watch below will clear a the hammocks.

To a twelve-pounder cannonade are stationed four men one boy. All the men stationed at the long guns of a do decked ship, should be armed with cutlasses, and called "bo ers"—the first of the gun's crew to be called second boarders, *vice versa*. They are only to be called on when require "board," or in a case of great emergency to "repel boarders," then every man will repair to the upper-deck, except the firen quarter-gunners, and powder boys, who will remain below to tect the ports, or to assist in extinguishing a fire.

All the men stationed at the cannonades should be boar and sail-trimmers. As boarders, the first part should be ar with pikes; the second part with small-arms, who are to repe boarders, but not to quit the ship.

In a single-decked ship, all the men stationed are board the first part to be armed with cutlasses, and the second pikes.

The battery being manned, distribute the rest of the cre follows:—have a quarter-master at the signals, when in a sq ron—topmen and marines in the tops, to repair damages, act as small-arm-men—a quarter-master and two men at th lieving tackles—men stationed at the passages, to pass full empty boxes; also others at the shot-lockers. Mastmen t the rigging clear—cook, and armorer at the galley—the car ter and his mates at the pumps and wings—the master-at-a and ship's corporal in the light-room—the gunner, his m quarter-gunners, and cooper, in the magazine, and the sur and assistants in the cock-pit.

BOATS AWAY!

DUTIES OF BOATS' CREWS.

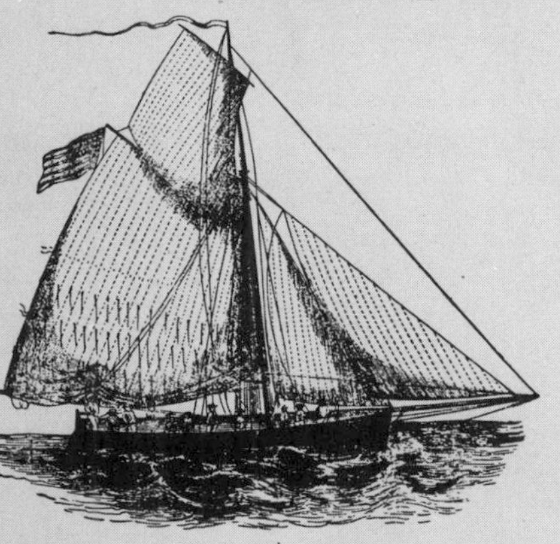

A SHIP OF WAR'S LAUNCH.

Nothing sooner indicates the order and discipline of a vessel of war, than the clean state and efficient condition of the boats, together with the personal appearance of their crews. In this particular, sufficient care is not always observed in the service; in well regulated ships, the coxswains are compelled to report to the senior lieutenant the state of their respective boats, and in the morning to ascertain from the officer of the boat, the manner he may require the crews to be dressed for the day &c., &c.

BOATS UNDER SAIL.

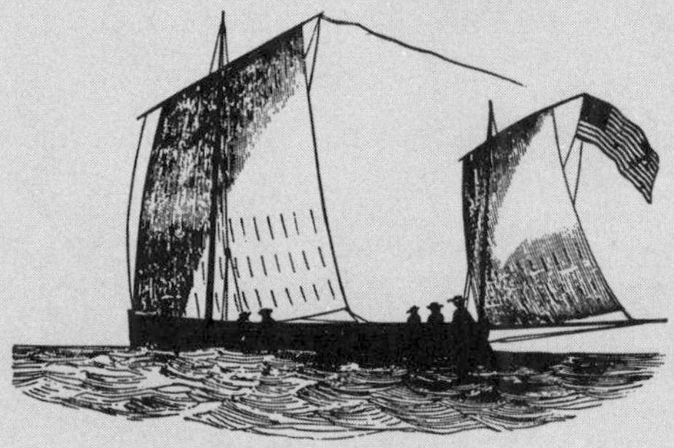

A SHIP OF WAR'S CUTTER.

Care should be taken that the halliards be coiled up clear for running, that the sheets be not belayed, and that the crew, in shortening sail to a squall, do not shift their seats, or, as is too common a custom, stand upon the thwarts to gather in the shaking sail; in lowering a lug, or lateen sail, haul down alone on the luff, (the fore-leech;) the after one better be left untouched.

Coxswains should also be cautioned of the danger of letting go the helm. This is often inadvertently done wrong—sometimes to secure the heel of the bumkin, or to get a pull of the main or mizen-sheet. By this thoughtless practice, boats are liable to fly up in the wind, the sails to be taken aback, be difficult to lower, and eventually to cant over and capsize to windward.

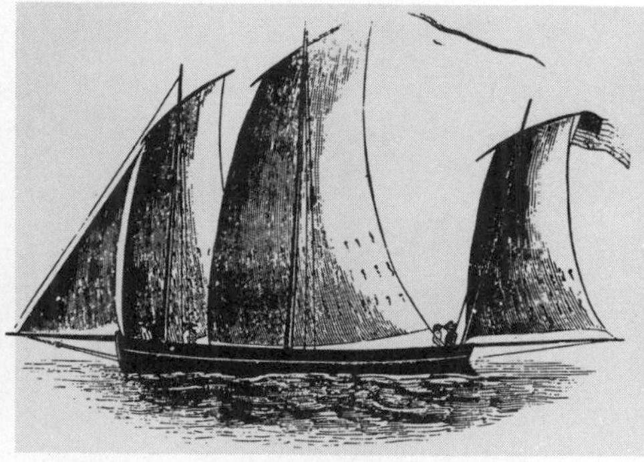

If a boat be crank, or if it be wished in working to windward to accelerate speed, all hands should sit down in the bottom of the boat. If in haste, working to windward, pull the weather oars.

A boat with only one sail, such as a lug, should never attempt beating to windward, except when necessary to give the crew a spell.

Let no one ever sit on the gunwale, but accustom the crew to sit in their places, and to make and shorten sail without stirring from their seats. Besides the due execution of this manœuvre, the safety of the boat is much implicated in the degree of attention paid to this rule.

In taking in a lug sail, lower the halliards and haul down on the weather-leach.

Note.—Keep boats out of the water as much as possible.

A MAN OVERBOARD, AT SEA.

If the ship be going free, and particularly if fast through water, it is recommended to bring-to with the head-yards a-ba for it is obvious if the main-yard be left square, the ship will longer coming-to, will shoot farther, increase the distance fr the man, and add materially to the delay of succor.

It will however require judgment, especially if blowing fr to be careful and right the helm in time, or the ship will fl too much, gain sternway, and risk the boat in lowering dow

The best authority recommends, that if possible, the s should not only be hove a-back when a man falls overboard, she ought to be brought around on the other tack; of co sail ought to be shortened in stays, and the main-yard k square. This implies the ship being on a wind, or from position of having the wind not above two points abaft the be

The great merit of such a method of proceeding, is, that if evolution succeeds, the ship when round will drift towards man, and although there may be some small risk in lower the boat in stays from the ship, having at one period sternw there will in fact be little time lost, if the boat be not lowe until the ship be well round, and the sternway at an end. Th is more mischief done generally, by lowering the boat too so than by waiting until the fittest moment arrives for doing coolly. It cannot be too often repeated, that almost the w depends upon the self-possession of the officer of the deck.

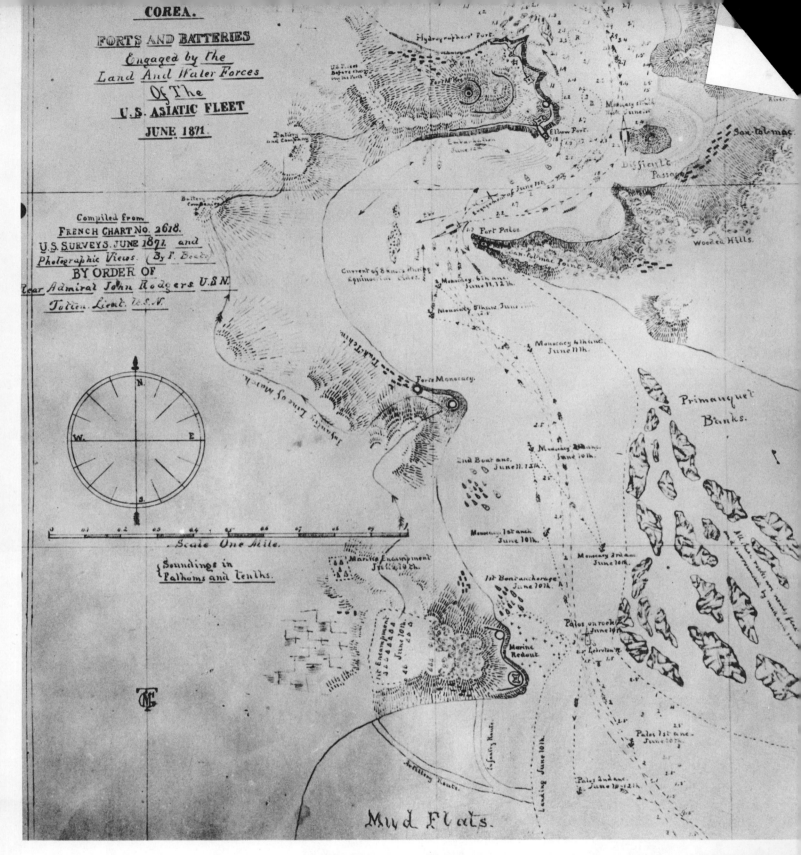

CORER.

FORTS AND BATTERIES
Engaged by the
Land And Water Forces
Of The
U.S. ASIATIC FLEET
JUNE 1871.

Compiled from
FRENCH CHART No. 2618.
U.S. SURVEYS. JUNE 1871. and
Photographic Views. By F. Boers.
BY ORDER OF
Rear Admiral John Rodgers U.S.N.
Totten Lieut. U.S.N.

Scale One Mile.

Soundings in
Fathoms and Tenths.

Mud Flats.

920. NAVAL CHART, SALEE
RIVER. Cause of conflict: Americans
charting river below Seoul in pioneer
effort to open "Hermit Kingdom" to
commerce. In Rodgers' squadron:
4 gunboats, steam frigate *Colorado*.

921. DIRECT HIT!—chastisement
for Korea. U.S. gunboats *Monocacy*
and *Palos* supported attack on river
forts. Remarkable photograph caught
this shell-hit on native Fort McKee.
Fort could only be taken by storm.

922. KILLED BY SHELL-HIT.
Armed with obsolete muskets and wooden coehorns, Koreans had little chance against American troops, big guns. Defending river citadel, native "Hermits" suffered heavy losses. Rodgers reported, "Only when the last man fell did the conflict end." (Korea photographs are from collection presented to President Grant.)

923. KOREAN OFFICIALS on board U.S.S. *Colorado*. After squadron entered Salee River they obdurately refused to deal with Admiral Rodgers and U.S. Minister, Mr. Low.

924. WOUNDED KOREANS on board gunboat *Monocacy*. Native "Hermits" fought to last man to hold McKee. Stubborn defense surprised Americans who wiped out garrison.

The Manner of an ENGAGEMENT

Excerpts from John Hamilton Moore's work Published in 1784

The Diſpoſition, which is the beſt calculated for the Operations of naval War, is formed by drawing up the Ships in a long File or Right Line, prolonged from the Keel of the hindmoſt to that of the foremaſt, and paſſing longitudinally through the Keels of all the the others from the Van to the Rear, ſo that they are, according to the Sea Phraſe, in the Wake of each other.

In this Line or Order of Battle, all the Ships of which it is compoſed are cloſe hauled upon the ſtarboard or larboard Tack, about 50 Fathoms diſtant from each other.

The Line cloſe hauled is peculiarly choſen as the Order of Battle, becauſe if the Fleet, which is to Windward, were arranged in any other Line, the Enemy might ſoon gain the Weather-gage of it; and even if he thinks it expedient to decline that Advantage, it will yet be in his Power to determine the Diſtance between the adverſe Fleet in an Engagement, and to compel the other to Action. The Fleet to Leeward being in a Line cloſed hauled, parallel to the Enemy, can more readily avail itſelf of the Change of the Wind, or of the Neglect of its Adverſary, by which it may, by a dextrous Management, get to Windward of him; or ſhould he fail in his Attempt he will nevertheleſs be enabled, by the favourable State of the Wind, to avoid coming to Action if the Enemy is greatly ſuperior, or to prevent him from eſcaping if he ſhould attempt it.

Beſides theſe Advantages, this Order of Battle is ſingularly convenient and proper in other Reſpects. The Sails of each Ship are diſpoſed in ſuch a Manner as to counteract each other, ſo that the Ships in general neither advance nor retreat during the Action.

The large Ships, being higher between Decks, are leſs incommoded with the Smoke, and their Cannon are managed with greater Facility.

The Fire-ſhips do not ſucceed ſo well againſt large Ships as the ſmaller ones; the Artillery will ſink them or oblige them ſooner to relinquiſh their Deſign, and they are eaſily towed away by the great Long-boats.

The Advantages of a Weather-line are generally, that it may approach the Enemy ſo as to determine the Time and Diſtance of Action. If it is more numerous than the Lee-line, it may eaſily appoint a Detachment to fall on the Van and Rear of the latter, and incloſe it between two Fires. It is little incommoded by the Fire or Smoke of the Cannon, and may diſpatch the Fire-ſhips, under Cover of the Smoke, upon the diſabled Ships of the Lee-line, or whereſoever they may occaſion Perplexity and Diſorder, by obliging the Enemy to break the Line and bear away.

The Weather-line has, nevertheleſs, its Defects, which ſometimes counterbalance the Advantages above recited. If the Sea is rough and the Wind boiſterous, it cannot readily fight with the Lower-deck Battery. it cannot decline the Action without the dangerous Expedient of forcing through the Enemy's Line; and, if it keeps the Wind, the Lee line may incloſe and totally deſtroy it,

The Line to Leeward has alſo its Advantages, which have occaſionally been preferred to thoſe of the Weather-line. The Ships of the former may uſe the Guns of their lower Decks without the Hazard of taking in much Water at the Ports in ſtormy Weather; whereas the Line to Windward dares not open them without the greateſt Danger. If the Lee-line, although more numerous, cannot ſo eaſily double upon the Van and Rear of the Enemy, and incloſe them between two Fires, it may nevertheleſs have Opportunities of tacking, and cutting off a Part of the Enemy's Rear, by obliging them to bear away or ſeparate from the reſt. The diſabled Ships to Leeward are much more readily removed from the Line than thoſe to Windward: without being obliged to tack and continue expoſed to the Enemy's Fire, they bear away and remain at a competent Diſtance from the Fleet in a State of Safety; finally, the Lee-line can with more Facility avoid the Action than its Adverſary, a Circumſtance which is extremely favourable to an inferior Squadron.

The Defects of the Lee-line, on the contrary, are, that it cannot decide the Time and Diſtance of the Battle, which may commence before it is ſufficiently formed, and it will perhaps be attacked by an Enemy, who bears away upon it in regular Order. The Fire and Smoke of the Weather-line are a greater Inconvenience to it, and it cannot eaſily break the Enemy's Line with its Fire-ſhips, which are very ſlowly and with great Difficulty conveyed to Windward.

It muſt be remarked, that the Admiral's Ships attentively preſerves her Station in the Center of the Line; for if the Commander in Chief ſhould give Way to the Caprice or Inattention of any of thoſe under his Direction, it would introduce an endleſs Diſorder into the Squadron.

In an Engagement, the Ships are generally brought to with the Main-top-ſails laid back, and their Fore-top-ſails full, for the Purpoſe of bearing away more readily when Occaſion requires.

The Preparation is begun by iſſuing the Order to clear the Ship for Action, which is repeated by the Boatſwain and his Mates at all the Hatchways, or Staircaſes, leading to the different Batteries. As the Management of the Artillery in a Veſſel of War requires a conſiderable Number of Men, it is evident that the Officers and Sailors muſt be reſtrained to a narrow Space in their uſual Habitations, in order to preſerve the internal Regularity of the Ship. Hence the Hammocks, or hanging Beds of the latter, are crouded together as cloſe as poſſible between the Decks, each of them being limitted to the Breadth of fourteen Inches. They are hung parallel to each other in Rows, ſtretching from one Side of the Ship to the other nearly throughout her whole Length, ſo as to admit of no Paſſage, but by ſtooping under them; as the Cannon therefore cannot be worked while the Hammocks are ſuſpended in this Situation, it becomes neceſſary to move them as quick as poſſible. By this Circumſtance a double Advantage is obtained; the Batteries of Cannon are immediately cleared of an Incumbrance, and the Hammocks are converted into a Sort of Parapet, to prevent the Execution of ſmall Shot on the Quarter-deck, Tops, and Forecaſtle. At the Summons of the Boatſwain, "Up all Hammocks," every Sailor repairs to his own, and, having ſtowed his Bedding properly, he cords it up firmly with a Laſhing, or Line, provided for that Purpoſe. He then carries it to the Quarter-deck, Poop, or Forecaſtle, or wherever it may be neceſſary. As each Side of the Quarter-deck and Poop is furniſhed with a double Net work, ſupported by Iron Cranes, fixed immediately above the Gunnel, or Top of the Ship's Side, the Hammocks thus corded are firmly ſtowed by the Quartermaſter between the two Parts of the Netting, ſo as to form an excellent Barrier; the Tops, Waiſt, or Forecaſtle, are then fenced in the ſame Manner.

Whilſt theſe Offices are performed below, the Boatſwain and his Mates are employed in ſecuring the Sail-yards to prevent them from tumbling down when the Ship is cannonaded, as ſhe might thereby be diſabled, and rendered incapable of Attack, Retreat, or Purſuit. The Yards are now likewiſe ſecured by ſtrong Chains, or Ropes, additional to thoſe by which they are uſually ſuſpended. The Boatſwain alſo provides the neceſſary Materials to repair the Rigging wherever it may be damaged by the Shot of the Enemy, and to ſupply whatever Parts of it may be entirely deſtroyed. The Carpenter and his Crew, in the mean while, prepare his Shot-plugs and Maul to cloſe up any dangerous Breach that may be made near the Surface of the Water, and provide the Iron-work neceſſary to refit the Chain Pumps, in caſe their Machinery ſhould be wounded in the Engagement.

The Gunner, with his Mate and Quarter-gunner, is buſied in examining the Cannon of the different Batteries, to ſee that their Charges are thoroughly dry and fit for Execution, to have every Thing ready for furniſhing the Great Guns and ſmall Arms with Powder as ſoon as the Action begins, and to keep a ſufficient Number of Cartridges continually filled to ſupply the Place of thoſe expended in Battle. The Maſter and his Mates are attentive to have the Sails properly trimmed according to the Situation of the Ship, and to reduce or multiply them, as occaſion requires, with all poſſible Expedition. The Lieutenant viſits the different Decks to ſee that they are effectually cleared of all Incumbrance, ſo that nothing may retard the Execution of the Artillery, and to enjoin the other Officers to Diligence and Alertneſs in making the neceſſary Diſpoſitions of the expected Engagement, ſo that every Thing may be in Readineſs at a Moment's Warning.

When the hoſtile Ships have approached each other to a competent Diſtance, the Drums beat to Arms, the Boatſwain and his Mates pipe all Hands to Quarters at every Hatchway. All the Perſons appointed to manage the great Guns immediately repair to their reſpective Stations. The Crows, Handſpikes, Rammers, Sponges, Powder-horns, Matches, and Train-tackles, are placed in Order by the Side of every Cannon. The Hatches are immediately laid to prevent any one from deſerting his Poſt by eſcaping into the lower Apartments. The Marines are drawn up in Rank and File on the Quarter-deck, Poop, and Forecaſtle.

The Combat uſually begins by a vigorous Cannonade, accompanied with the whole Efforts of the Swivel-guns and the ſmall Arms. The Method of firing in Platoons, or Vollies of Cannon at once, appears inconvenient in the Sea-ſervice, and perhaps ſhould never be attempted unleſs in the Battering of a Fortification. The Sides and Deck of the Ship, although ſufficiently ſtrong for all the Purpoſes of War, would be too much ſhaken by ſo violent an Exploſion and Recoil. The general Rule obſerved on this Occaſion throughout the Ship is to load, fire, and ſponge the Guns with all poſſible Expedition, yet without Confuſion or Precipitation. The Captain of each Gun is particularly enjoined to fire only when the Piece is properly directed to its Object, that the Shot may not be fruitleſsly expended. The Lieutenants, who command the different Batteries, traverſe the Deck to ſee that the Battle is proſecuted with Vivacity, and to exhort and animate the Men to their Duty. The Midſhipmen ſecond the Injunctions, and give the neceſſary Aſſiſtance, wherever it may be required, at the Guns committed to their Charge. The Gunner ſhould be particularly attentive that all the Artillery is ſufficiently ſupplied with Powder, and that the Cartridges are carefully conveyed along the Decks in covered Boxes. The Havock produced by the Continuation of this mutual Aſſault may be conjectured by the Reader's Imagination; battering, penetrating and ſplintering the Sides and Decks, ſhattering or diſmounting the Cannon, mangling or deſtroying the Rigging, cutting aſunder or carrying away the Maſts and Yards, piercing and tearing the Sails, ſo as to render them uſeleſs, and wounding, diſabling, or killing the Ship's Company.

When the adverſe Fleets approach each other, the Courſes are commonly hauled up in the Brails, and the Top-gallant-ſails and Stay-ſails furled. The Movement of each Ship is chiefly regulated by the Main and Fore-top-ſails and the Jib, the Mizen-top-ſail being reſerved to haſten or retard the Courſe of the Ship; and, in fine, by filling or backing, hoiſting or lowering it, to determine her Velocity.

Such is now the Practice of naval War, that the neceſſary Order of Battle, and the Fabric of our Ships, very ſeldom permit the Aſſault of Boarding, unleſs in ſingle Actions. No Captain ought therefore to abandon his Station in the Line under any Pretence whatſoever, unleſs his Ship is too much diſabled.

An Ambition to diſtinguiſh himſelf ſhould never ſeduce any Captain to break the Line, in order to atchieve any diſtant Enterprize, however the Proſpect may flatter him with Succeſs. He ought to wait the Signal of the Admiral, or his Commanding Officer; becauſe it is more eſſential to preſerve the Regularity of a cloſe Line, which conſtitutes the principal Force of the Fleet, than to proſecute a particular Action, which, although brilliant in itſelf, has ſeldom any material Conſequences, unleſs its Object is to ſeize a Flag-ſhip, and even this can only be juſtified by Succeſs.

If he conquers in Battle, he ought to proſecute his Victory as much as poſſible, ſeizing, burning, or deſtroying the Enemy's Ships. If he is defeated, he ſhould endeavour, by every Reſource his Experience can ſuggeſt, to ſave as many of his Fleet as poſſible, by employing his Tenders, &c. to take out the wounded and put freſh Men in their Places, by towing the diſabled Ships to a competent Diſtance, and by preventing the Execution of the Enemy's Fire-ſhips. In order to retreat with more Security, he may range his Fleet into the Form of a Half-Moon, placing himſelf in the Centre; by this Diſpoſition, the Enemy's Ships which attempt to fall upon his Rear, will at once expoſe themſelves to the Fire of the Admiral and his Seconds in a diſadvantageous Situation.

If his Fleet is too much extended by this Arrangement, the Wings or Quarters are eaſily cloſed, and the Half-moon rendered more complete, in the Midſt of which may be placed his Store-ſhips, Tenders, &c.

By what we have obſerved, the real Force or Superiority of a Fleet conſiſts leſs in Number of Veſſels and the Vivacity of the Action, than in good Order, Dexterity in working the Ships, Preſence of Mind and ſkilful Conduct in the Captains.

On Boarding

The Stratagem of Boarding is chiefly practiſed by Privateers upon Merchant-ſhips, who are not ſo well provided with Men, and rarely attempted in the Royal Navy; the Battle being generally decided in Men of War, by the vigorous Execution of a cloſe Cannonade.

An officer ſhould maturely conſider the Danger of boarding a Ship of War, before he attempts it, and be well aſſured that his Adverſary is weakly manned; for perhaps he wiſhes to be boarded, and if ſo, a great Slaughter will neceſſarily follow.

There is, perhaps, very little Prudence in boarding a Ship of equal Force, and when it is attempted it may be either to Windward or to Leeward, according to the comparitive Force or Situation of the Ships; if there be any Swell or Sea it may be more adviſeable to lay the Enemy aboard on the Lee-ſide, as the Water is there the ſmootheſt; beſides, if the Boarder is repulſed, in that Situation he may more eaſily withdraw his Men, and ſtand off from his Adverſary; but as the Weather-ſhip can generally fall to Leeward at any Time, it is perhaps more eligible to keep to Windward, by which ſhe will be enabled to rake her Antagoniſt, and fire the Broadſide into her Stern, as ſhe croſſes it in paſſing to Leeward, which will do great Execution amongſt her Men, by ſcouring the whole Length of the Deck.

Boarding may be performed in different Places of the Ship, according to the Circumſtances, Preparation, and Poſition of both the Aſſailants, having previouſly ſelected a Number of Men armed with Piſtols and Cutlaſſes, a Number of Powder-flakes or Flaſks, charged with Gunpowder, and fitted with a Fuſe, are alſo provided to be thrown upon the Enemy's Deck, immediately before the Aſſault. Beſides this, the Boarder is generally furniſhed with an earthen Shell, called a Stink-pot, which, on that Occaſion, is ſuſpended from his Yard-arms or Bowſprit-end. The Machine is alſo charged with Powder mixed with other inflammable and ſuffocating Materials, with a lighted Fuſe at the Aperture. Thus prepared for the Action, and having grappled his Adverſary, the Boarder diſplays his Signal to begin the Aſſault; the Fuſes of the Stink-pot and Powder-flaſks being lighted, they are immediately thrown upon the Deck of the Enemy, where they burſt and catch Fire, producing an intolerable Stench and Smoke, and filling the Deck with Tumult and Diſtraction; amidſt the Confuſion occaſioned by this infernal Apparatus, the Detachment provided ruſh aboard Sword in Hand, under Cover of this Smoke, on their Antagoniſt, who is in the ſame Predicament with a Citadel ſtormed by the Beſiegers, and generally overpowered, unleſs he is furniſhed with extraordinary Means of Defence, or equipped with Cloſe-quarters, to which he can retreat with ſome Probability of Safety.

Cloſe quarters are ſtrong Barriers of Wood, ſtretching acroſs a Merchant-ſhip in ſeveral Places. They are uſed as a Place of Retreat when a Ship is boarded by her Adverſary, and are therefore fitted with ſeveral ſmall Loop holes, through which to fire the ſmall Arms, whereby the Ship's Crew may defend themſelves and annoy the Enemy. They are likewiſe furniſhed with ſeveral ſmall Caiſſoons, called Powder-cheſts, which are fixed upon the Deck, and filled with Powder, old Nails, &c. and may be fired at any Time from the Cloſe-quarters upon the Boarders.

A Table Showing the Weight, Size and Length of Guns and Carriages, U. S. Navy.

SIZE OF GUNS.	WEIGHT OF GUN. (cwt. qrs. lbs.)	WEIGHT OF CARRIAGE. (cwt. qrs. lbs.)	LENGTH OF GUN. (ft. in.)	TOTAL. (cwt. qrs. lbs.)
2 Pounder, Long Gun,	70 0 0	–	9 1	
2 "	61 0 0	–	9 2	
2 "	51 0 0	8 2 0	8 4	59 2 0
2 "	60 0 0	–	9 2	
2 "	50 0 0	–	8 4	
2 "	42 2 0	8 1 0	8 2	50 3 0
2 "	61 2 0	9 1 0	9 2	70 3 0
2 "	41 0 0	–	8 0	
2 "	41 0 0	8 0 0	7 0	49 0 0
2 "	32 0 0	–	6 7	
2 "	51 0 0	–	9 0	
2 "	43 0 0	–	8 0	
4 " Long Medium,	49 0 0	6 3 0	9 4½	55 3 0
4 "	49 0 0	–	8 4½	
4 "	49 0 0	6 3 0	8 4	55 3 0
4 "	32 0 0	–	6 7	
8 "	38 0 0	5 2 0	8 0	43 2 0
8 "	40 0 0	5 2 0	9 2	45 2 0
8 "	36 0 0	–	7 7½	
2 "	23 0 0	4 3 0	6 8½	27 3 0
9 "	18 0 0	–	6 1	
9 "	18 0 0	3 3 0	5 11	21 3 0
2 inch Peace Maker,	150 0 0			
0 inch Shell Gun,	136 3 9			
8 " "	63 0 0	–	8 10	
8 " "	68 2 0	–	9 1	
8 " "	64 0 0	–	8 10	
8 " "	53 0 0	–	8 4	
CARRONADES.				
2 Pounder,	27 0 0	7 2 0	4 3	34 2 0
2 "	20 0 0	–	4 1	
2 "	21 0 0	–	4 2	
2 "	19 0 0	6 2 14	–	25 2 14
4 "	13 0 0	5 2 0	3 7	18 2 0
4 "	15 0 0	6 0 0	3 9	21 0 0

At left: Table from the "Kedge Anchor" (circa 1850)

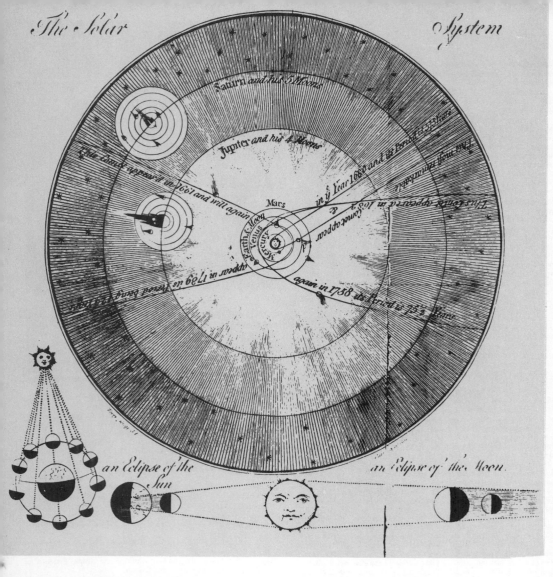

an Eclipse of the Sun.   *an Eclipse of the Moon.*

From John Hamilton Moore's, "Practical Navigator," 1784 London Edition

at the end of a line which was then hauled in to see how far ship had traveled from buoy, or "chip," in recorded time. By this "dead (deduced) reckoning," mariners found their way on trackless oceans.

Big problem was accurate determination of east-west position. European governments recognized this early. Spanish, French offered prizes in 16th and 17th centuries for solution. After failure of 1711 attack on Canada due to error "in the Logg," British set up Board of Longitude, offered £20,000 prize—finally won by chronometer that could keep a standard time at sea. Second aspect of problem was accurate charts.

American contribution to burgeoning art of navigation in early 19th century was mainly theoretical. American navigators used foreign charts, even in own waters. English were greatest mappers. Great age of exploration ended with Cook in late 18th century, was followed by age of worldwide detailed surveys, such as that of *Beagle* in 1831-36, which produced 82 new Admiralty charts (—and passenger Charles Darwin's theory of evolution). Practice of U.S. Navy, due to conservatism and Congressional stinginess, remained surprisingly backward until founding of Naval Observatory in 1844. After that navigation in navy was firmly founded on sciences that reduced its risk. Work of Bowditch, scientific studies of Maury gave it great reputation. (Moore's Solar System, left.)

452. NAVIGATION IN EARLY DAYS of navy was a difficult art. Since ancient times men had been able to find position north and south by height of sun or Pole Star. Compass gave direction of ship's heading. Approximate speed was obtained by chip log—a buoy tossed overboard

DEVELOPMENT OF
Navigation

452.1. MARINER'S COMPASS is key nautical instrument. Magnetic lines of force running between two poles near geographic poles of earth make needle fixed under compass card lie in rough north-south direction.

Difference between true and magnetic north, called *variation*, changes with different longitudes. Navigators of 17th century attempted to find longitude by comparing known variation with true north shown by Pole Star. Idea was impractical, but research enabled compass to be used more accurately on long voyages. Mariners used *parallel sailing* to run down destination east or west on known latitude; or used *middle latitude sailing*, a combination of observed latitude and "departure" (estimated course and distance made good east or west).

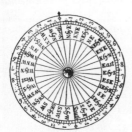

Late eighteenth century compass rose

1790 Danish hanging compass at left Above, Captain Cook's compass

Astrolabe, Nocturnal,
Cross-staff and Backstaff

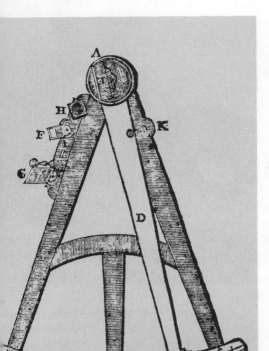

The principal Parts of this Inſtrument are,

The Index   D
The Index Glaſs   E
The Horizon Glaſſes   G and F
The dark Glaſſes or Screens   H
The Sight Vanes   K and G

452.2. QUADRANT, forerunner of modern sextant, was used for observation of height of sun or stars above horizon. By accurate observation of these "beacons in the sky" related geographical position could be determined. Instruments in use before this time were astrolabe, used by Columbus, and handier cross staff, invented in northern waters and customary instrument of navigators like Drake. Neither approached accuracy of quadrant, which used reflecting mirrors to get observation of heavenly body and horizon together. Quadrant was invented simultaneously in London and Philadelphia in 1734. Used primarily for traditional latitude sights—the height of sun at noon, height of Pole Star when horizon beneath it was visible just after sunset and just before dawn—it was also accurate enough for measure of distance between moon and nearby stars. Theoretically, after publication of British Astronomer Royal Makeleyne's lunar method in *Nautical Almanac* of 1767, this could determine sidereal time (time by the stars), independent of motion of earth, so get east-west position of ship by relating it to that of known meridian. Actually technique was impractical and beyond abilities of most navigators. Final method was checking time of known meridian (kept by chronometer) against time in degrees of arc, east or west of it.

Plane Sailing, above, right
and Traverse Sailing, below, at right.
from Moore's "Practical Navigator"

devoted his mature life to building reliable chronometer, died a few years after final recognition by George III ("By God, Harrison, I'll see you righted"), old, blind, unable to accompany own watch to sea on final tests. He was finally awarded the £20,000 prize by British Government Board of Longitude—38 years after he had won it. Chronometer apparently came into use in U.S. navy in 1820s. Before that time it was costly, difficult to adjust, and not considered completely reliable as mechanism. Bowditch worked out simplification of Maskeleyne's lunar method in 1802.

By PROJECTION

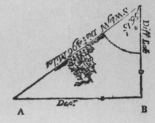

Draw the Meridian or Difference of Latitude, with the Chord of 60° in your Compaſſes, and one Foot in C, deſcribe an Arch, take 56° 15′ or 5 Points in your Compaſſes, and lay off that Diſtance upon the Arch from B C towards C A; through the Point where it cuts, draw the Diſtance C A; upon which ſet off 496: from A let fall the Perpendicular A B the Departure, and it is done; for A B being meaſured on the ſame Scale that A C was, will give the Departure 412.4, and B C 275.6 the Diff. of Lat.

The Calculation is the ſame as Problem 1. in TRIGONOMETRY.

I ſhall work this Caſe by making each Side Radius.

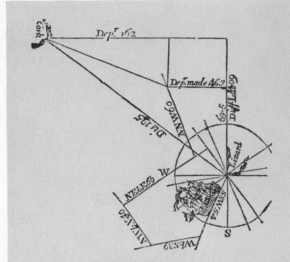

By the above Method any Traverse may be conſtructed, as alſo the Ship's Way pricked off on the Plane Chart.

452.3. HARRISON'S CHRONOMETER. Accurate timepiece of 1757, this mechanical wonder indicated way to solution of time problem at sea, led to modern solution of longitude. A navigator could get *local* time by celestial observation. To get his east-west position on spinning globe he needed to relate this apparent time to standard of some known meridian. Problem was to keep time, to within a few seconds, of known meridian in voyages lasting months out of sight of land and off known bearings. Later, less cumbersome model of Harrison's chronometer was used by Cook, effectively solved problem. Time solution to longitude by chronometer became standard as instrument was perfected for ordinary sea use in 19th century, is standard solution today. Harrison himself, son of Yorkshire carpenter,

Harrison's no. 3 timekeeper

Harrison's no. 1 timekeeper

Harrison's no. 4 Timekeeper, the prize-winner, and at right, Harrison

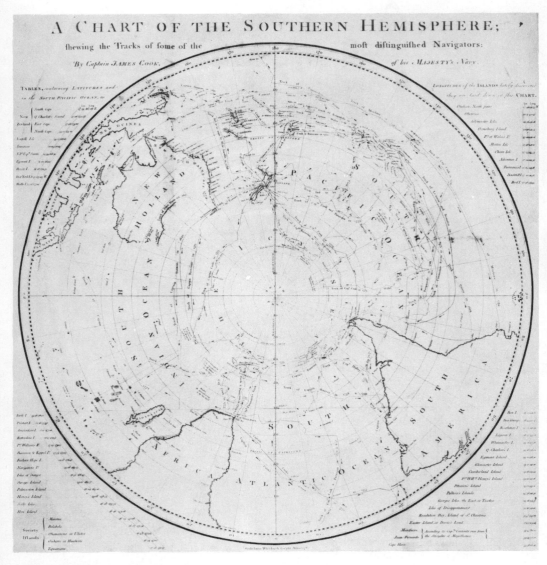

A CHART OF THE SOUTHERN HEMISPHERE;
shewing the Tracks of some of the most distinguished Navigators:
By Captain JAMES COOK, of his MAJESTY's Navy.

452.4. CAPTAIN JAMES COOK, R.N., last of great line of explorer-navigators. South Pacific explorations resulted in first charts of Australia, New Zealand. His Southern Ocean chart, same as that shown in portrait, gives track-lines of previous explorers, shows how his work completed the achievement of voyagers who went before him. Chart is an early example of polar projection (centered on pole), lately revived as "new" technique to meet needs of air age. Cook's first love was Royal Navy; early surveys helped in 1759 conquest of Canada. He died in its service, killed by Hawaiian natives who later worshipped him as a god, in 1779. (Above.)

452.5. FRENCH CHART SHOWING GRAND BANKS, 1632 (at right.) Best charts of this area were French, significant factor in early French mastery of these famous fishing grounds. Chart shown here is by the great explorer Champlain. In this period French *routiers*—chart collections—led the field, and known as "rutters," were highly prized and copied in England. Many names on this chart survive today. It was more than 200 years before Americans began officially charting their own waters!

452.6. BRITISH CHART OF BOSTON, 1781, shows workmanship of late 18th-century Admiralty surveys. Until long after the Revolution, best charts of American waters were British. This chart, from *Atlantic Neptune*—"For the Use of the Royal Navy of Great Britain"—shows waters in which Revolution actually started. Yankee mariners knew local waters, but British charts enabled their ships to use harbors as their own. (Left)

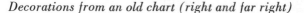

Decorations from an old chart (right and far right)

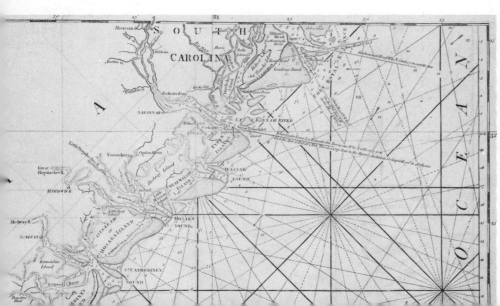

452.7. CHART OF SAVANNAH APPROACHES, 1794, is another example of British cartography in American waters. Range instructions on "Remarkable Tree" and notes on tide were printed on chart. Often skippers made their own drawings and notes on coast, corrections and additions from experience that made their sketch-books and chart collections valuable private possessions. Navy had no office for charts until 1830.

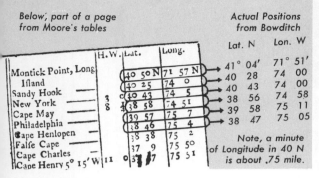

	H.W.	Lat.	Long.		Lat. N	Lon. W
Montick Point, Long Island		40 50 N	71 57 N	→	41° 04'	71° 51'
Sandy Hook		40 25	74 0	→	40 28	74 00
New York	3 8	40 43	74 5	→	40 43	74 00
Cape May		38 58	74 51	→	38 56	74 58
Philadelphia		39 57	75 7	→	39 58	75 11
Cape Henlopen		38 46	75 4	→	38 47	75 05
False Cape		38 38	75 2			
Cape Charles		37 9	75 50			
Cape Henry 5° 15' W	11 0	37 7	75 51			

Note, a minute
of Longitude in 40 N
is about .75 mile.

*Title page of J. H. Moore's
Practical Navigator, 8th Edition*

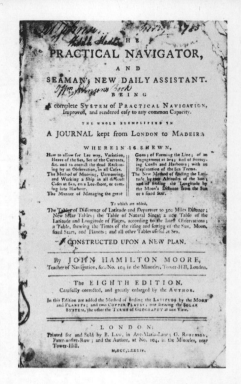

*Last portrait of
Mathew Fontaine Maury, aged 62*

THE NEW AMERICAN
PRACTICAL NAVIGATOR;
BEING AN
EPITOME OF NAVIGATION;
CONTAINING ALL THE TABLES NECESSARY TO BE USED WITH THE
NAUTICAL ALMANAC,
IN DETERMINING THE
LATITUDE;
AND THE
LONGITUDE BY LUNAR OBSERVATIONS;
AND
KEEPING A COMPLETE RECKONING AT SEA:
ILLUSTRATED BY
PROPER RULES AND EXAMPLES;
THE WHOLE EXEMPLIFIED IN A
JOURNAL,
KEPT FROM
BOSTON TO MADEIRA,
IN WHICH ALL THE RULES OF NAVIGATION ARE INTRODUCED:
ALSO
For the Demonstration of the most useful Rules of TRIGONOMETRY: With many useful Problems in NAVIGATION, SURVEYING, and GAUGING: And a Dictionary of Sea-TERMS; with the Manner of performing the most common EVOLUTIONS at Sea.
TO WHICH ARE ADDED,
(some GENERAL INSTRUCTIONS and INFORMATION to MERCHANTS, MASTERS of VESSELS, and others concerned in NAVIGATION, relative to MARITIME LAWS and MERCANTILE CUSTOMS.
FROM THE BEST AUTHORITIES.
ENRICHED WITH A NUMBER OF
NEW TABLES,
WITH ORIGINAL IMPROVEMENTS AND ADDITIONS, AND A LARGE
VARIETY OF NEW AND IMPORTANT MATTER:
ALSO
MANY THOUSAND ERRORS ARE CORRECTED,
WHICH HAVE APPEARED IN THE BEST SYSTEMS OF NAVIGATION YET PUBLISHED.
BY NATHANIEL BOWDITCH,
FELLOW OF THE AMERICAN ACADEMY OF ARTS AND SCIENCES.
ILLUSTRATED WITH COPPERPLATES.
First Edition.
PRINTED AT NEWBURYPORT, (MASS.) 1802,
BY
EDMUND M. BLUNT, (Proprietor)
FOR CALEB BINGHAM, BOSTON.
SOLD BY EVERY BOOK-SELLER, SHIP-CHANDLER, AND MATHEMATICAL-INSTRUMENT-MAKER,
IN THE UNITED STATES AND WEST-INDIES.

452.8. EARLY NAVIGATION BOOKS were dangerously inaccurate even for skipper who knew his position to a mile. Table (above at left) from John Hamilton Moore's *Practical Navigator* (published in London in 1784) shows accepted positions for vital coast features in approaches to New York. Montauk Point (east end of Long Island) is 14 miles south, 4 miles west of real position—hard luck to skipper groping way into Long Island Sound! Other errors show by comparison with actual positions. One error in this book actually caused loss of two ships. Yet this was standard, most reliable work available to shipmasters—until Bowditch revisions.

452.9. NAVIGATOR EXTRAORDINARY, young Nathaniel Bowditch started to revise Moore's work for second American edition on long sea voyage to East Indies, gave it up and wrote own book—*New American Practical Navigator*—which presented new, simple, accurate methods to seafaring world. Self-educated after age of 10, Bowditch came of poor Salem family ruined by wreck of father Habakkuk's sloop in 1775, later became wealthy as sea captain, shipowner, insurance executive. Like navy's M. F. Maury (*see later*) he was widely honored as one of world's outstanding men of science. (At right)

453. NEW AMERICAN PRACTICAL NAVIGATOR, 1802. Legend tells how every man down to the cook on Bowditch's ship learned "mystery" of navigation from this book and Bowditch's teaching. In 1866 U.S. Government bought rights to book, still issues revised versions known as plain "Bowditch" to all seamen—fitting monument to Salem lad who set out to overhaul system of navigation 150 years ago. Title page, right.

453.1. SIGNIFICANCE OF BOWDITCH'S WORK is indicated by recommendation by Salem merchants printed with early editions. To these wealthy men scientific achievement meant surer profits in lusty American sea economy. To seamen it meant something simpler—safety of their lives in a calling made less dangerous.

Report

Of the Committee, appointed by the East-India Marine Society of Salem, at their meeting on the 6th. of May, 1801, to examine a work called, "The New American Practical Navigator, by Nathaniel Bowditch, F.A.A."

AFTER a full examination of the system of Navigation presented to the society by one of its members, (Mr. Nathaniel Bowditch) they find, that he has corrected many thousand errors, existing in the best European works of the kind; especially those in the Tables for determining the latitude by two altitudes, in those of difference of latitude and departure, of the sun's right ascension, of amplitudes, and many others necessary to the Navigator. Mr. Bowditch has likewise, in many instances, greatly improved the old methods of calculation, and added new ones of his own. That of clearing the apparent distance of the moon, and sun or stars, from the effect of parallax and refraction, is peculiarly adapted to the use of seamen in general, and is much facilitated (as all other methods are) in the present work, by the introduction of a proportional table into that of the corrections of the moon's altitude. His table nineteenth, of corrections to be applied in the lunar calculations, has the merit of being the only accurate one the committee are acquainted with. He has much improved the table of latitudes and longitudes of places, and has added those of a number on the American coast hitherto very inaccurately ascertained.

This work, therefore, is, in the opinion of the committee, highly deserving of the approbation and encouragement of the society, not only as being the most correct and ample now extant, but as being a genuine American production; and as such they hesitate not to recommend it to the attention of Navigators, and of the public at large.

JONATHAN LAMBERT,
BENJAMIN CARPENTER,
JOHN OSGOOD,   Committee.
JOHN GIBAUT,
JACOB CROWNINSHIELD,
Approved.   BENJAMIN HODGES, President.

A true copy.   MOSES TOWNSEND, Sec'y.

Salem, May 13, 1801.

453.2. FERDINAND HASSLER,
brilliant author of first official survey
of U.S. coast, was colorful, tempes-
tuous character, devoted life in America to this work. His charm won
friendship of Jefferson and others, his
high-handed methods outraged Congress and old-line navy men who insisted they could handle job. (above)

**453.3. FIRST U.S. COAST SUR-
VEY CHART—1844!** In 1807 Jefferson invited Hassler, young Swiss political refugee, to begin scientific
survey of ill-charted U.S. coast. Congressional reluctance, navy jealousy
held up work until 1832, when survey
began on Long Island. First published
chart appeared after Hassler's death.
Importance of Gedney's channel, entrance to which is sketched on bottom
of chart, was recognized by New York
merchants, probably saved survey
from further delay. Coast Survey became U.S. Coast and Geodetic Survey
thirty four years later in 1878. (right)

**453.4. U.S. NAVAL OBSERVA-
TORY, FOUNDED 1844.** Central authority for navigation, founded belatedly to succeed Depot of Charts
and Instruments set up in 1830. Actual mission of Depot was to overhaul
charts and often worthless instruments, coordinate surveys, end chaos
in navigation in navy. Wilkes (*see
later*) was early superintendent.
Mathew F. Maury, first supervisor
of new Observatory, brought system
and eventual renown to navy navigation by wind charts and other work.
Founding of Naval Observatory,
which embodied functions of later
Hydrographic Office, marked establishment of scientific method, and the
coming-of-age of navigation in navy.

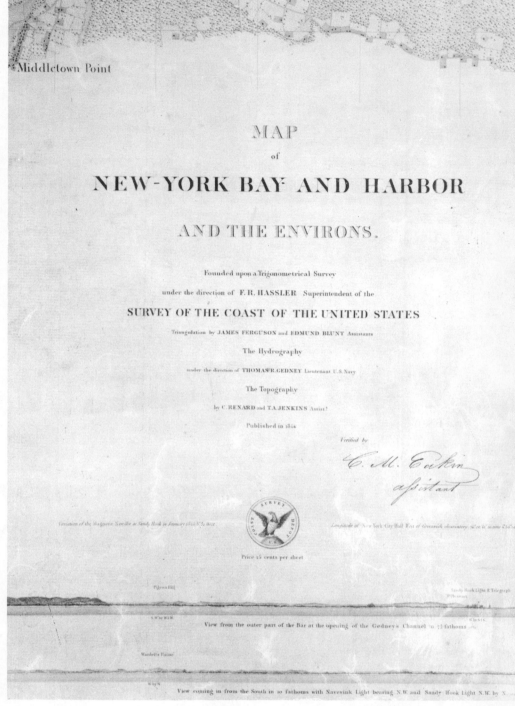

Middletown Point

MAP
of
NEW-YORK BAY AND HARBOR
AND THE ENVIRONS.

Founded upon a Trigonometrical Survey

under the direction of F. R. HASSLER Superintendent of the

SURVEY OF THE COAST OF THE UNITED STATES

Triangulation by JAMES FERGUSON and EDMUND BLUNT Assistants

The Hydrography

under the direction of THOMAS R. GEDNEY Lieutenant U.S. Navy

The Topography

by C. RENARD and T. A. JENKINS Assist.

Published in 1844

Verified by

Price 25 cents per sheet

View from the outer part of the Bar at the opening of the Gedneys Channel in 7½ fathoms

View coming in from the South in 10 fathoms with Navesink Light bearing N.W. and Sandy Hook Light N.W. by N.

Pigeon Hill

Sandy Hook Light & Telegraph

View from the outer part of the Bar at the opening of the Gedneys Channel in 7½ fathoms

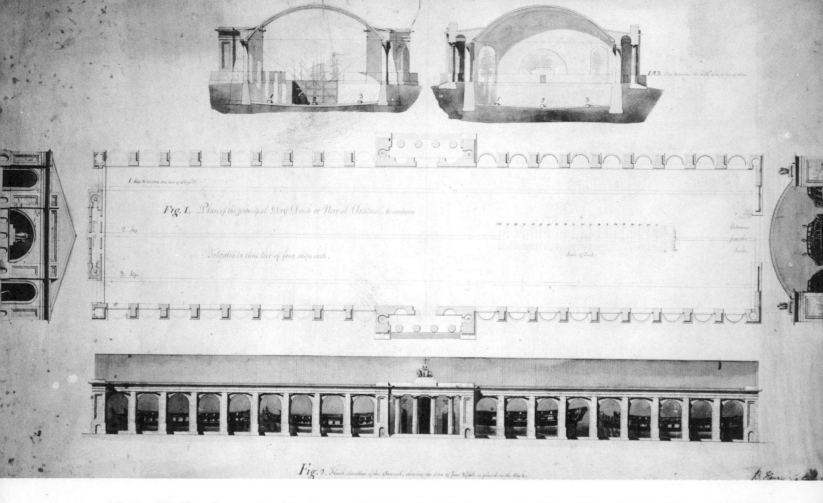

YARDS AND DOCKS OF THE SAILING NAVY

454. PRESIDENT JEFFERSON'S DRYDOCK. Political scientist, inventor, astronomer, educator, composer—Jefferson's genius was boundless. Called "the father of our national architecture," he is renowned as the designer of Monticello and the University of Virginia. Less well known is the fact that Jefferson also designed a Navy drydock (shown above) which was large enough to contain the entire American fleet of 1809.

Close-up, Washington Navy Yard.

455. WASHINGTON NAVY YARD (left above). Note shiphouse and sawmill on riverbank, old Capitol in background. Other Navy Yards of period: Portsmouth, Boston, New York, Philadelphia, Gosport, Charlestown, Pensacola. Enough to service the 37 ships of the United States Navy's 1837 fleet. At left, below, Mare Island Navy Yard, 1855. Selected for West Coast base after California was taken from Mexico (1847), Mare Island was last great yard opened by sailing Navy. Note big floating drydock. Pioneer yard commandant was David Glasgow Farragut, there 1854-1858.

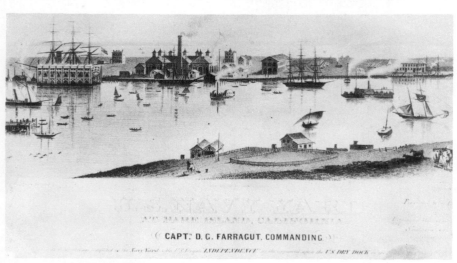

CAPT. D. G. FARRAGUT, COMMANDING

456. U. S. MEDITERRANEAN SQUADRON OF 1823. Assigned patrol duty between Gibraltar and Egypt, squadron employed Port Mahon, Minorca, as winter base. Old print "dedicated to Commodore John Rodgers" shows (left to right) line-of-battle ship *North Carolina* (flag), frigates *Constitution* and *Brandywine*, sloops *Erie* and *Ontario*. In 1825 Commodore Rodgers sailed flagship *North Carolina* to Constantinople to talk turkey with Sultan Mahmud II. Procuring favorable commercial treaties, Rodgers opened lively trade.

Foreign Station
STRONG ARM FOR U.S. COMMERCE

457. U. S. SHIP-OF-LINE *NORTH CAROLINA* bucking a blow in the Mediterranean. From painting in possession of Rodgers family at Sion Hill, Havre de Grace, Maryland. Original was inscribed "*North Carolina* weathering the Island of Zembla on 26 December, 1826. . . . Represented at the moment of splitting her jib in pieces, setting her foretopmast staysail, and brailing up her spanker." Canvasback U. S. Mediterranean Squadron was maintained until 1861.

458. CARIBBEAN PIRATES—JOB FOR NAVY. Masking skull-and-crossbones intentions with such phony colors as flag of "Richard Coeur de Lion," buccaneers made some 3,000 onslaughts on merchantmen in West Indies between 1815 and 1823. Murder, kidnap and rape were Jolly Roger pastimes. U. S. N. mustered strong force for extermination job.

459. U. S. WEST INDIA SQUAD-
RON, led by frigate *Macedonian*
(above), was organized in 1822 to
handle pirates raiding rich traffic
lanes off Florida, Hispaniola and
Puerto Rico. Under Commodore
James Biddle, squadron included
Macedonian, frigate *Congress*, four
sloops, two brigs, four schooners, two
gunboats. Mission: to sweep buccaneers from Spanish Main. For good.

460. WITH PORTER, FIGHTING
FOXES OF FOXARDO. Commanding West Indies Squadron in 1823,
David Porter pushed antipirate campaign at forced draught. Literally,
with 100-ton steam galiot *Sea Gull*
(above)—world's first steamer to go
on war duty. Purchased in New York
for $16,000, this dinky teakettle, a
converted ferry, served as Porter's
dispatch boat. Cracking down, Porter
waded into pirate haven at Foxardo,
Puerto Rico. When Spanish Governor
howled "neutrality violation," Navy
Department suspended Porter. Steam-
ing home in fury, he resigned from
U.S.N. and joined Mexican Navy.
Sea Gull went out of service in 1825.

462. YO-HO-HO, AND A YARD-
ARM'S END! Fitting end for such
cutthroats as Diabolito, Cofrecina
and ilk. Off Havana in 1825, Commo.
Warrington reported pirates no longer
extant around Cuba and Hispaniola.
By 1829 some 60 pirate craft had
been eradicated. Because Key West
was cesspool of yellow fever, antipirate station was moved north, Pensacola base was opened. West India
Squadron patrolled until 1861. By
that date, freebooting hadn't a leg to
stand on. Last pirate hanged by U. S.
was American Charles Gibbs who
went to gallows on Bedloe Island
(site of Statue of Liberty) in 1831.

461. PIRATE HUNTER IN STORM.
In 1825 *Constellation* (Commo. Lewis
Warrington) led West Indies patrol.
Area hurricanes proved worse than
pirates. Warrington lost no ships.
But World War II destroyer named
Warrington was sunk by Caribbean
hurricane—a peculiar turn of fate.

463. U. S. PACIFIC SQUADRON
was organized in 1821 to carry "Law
west of the Horn." U.S.S. *Constellation* was first frigate assigned to
station off Peru. Squadron expanded
to cover South Seas commerce and
California-Oregon-Alaska trade.
Maintained exactly 100 years. (left)

"Mad Jack" Percival

464. U. S. FRIGATE *CONGRESS*—China Opener. Crossing Pacific under Master Commandant J. D. Henley, *Congress* was first American warship to reach China via the East Indies. Prying open China's door with a show of cannon, Henley secured Cantonese port rights that paved way for China trade and many a Yankee fortune.

465. U. S. WAR-SCHOONER *DOLPHIN*—Hawaii Opener. Arriving at Honolulu in January 1826, *Dolphin* (Capt. Percival) procured concessions from King Kamehameha; gained foothold for American traders in Hawaii. Exploit was marred by conduct of "Mad Jack" Percival whose capers caused local missionaries to request his fast withdrawal.

466. BATTLE AT QUALLAH BATTOO. Dealing reprisal for murder of seamen from Salem pepper trader, frigate *Potomac* hit Sumatra port in February 1832. Combat sketch (below) was made on board ship. In battle Sultan Po Mahomet and 150 natives were killed; two American Navy men were killed, 11 wounded.

467. U.S.S. *VINCENNES* (above) —first American warship to cross Pacific and circumnavigate globe. Second-class ship-sloop; 18 guns; length 127; beam 34. Under Captain W. B. Finch, *Vincennes* reached New York in June 1830, heroine of three-year cruise. (Sketch by Lt. Charles Wilkes, soon to explore Antarctic.)

468. U. S. BRAZIL SQUADRON was established in 1820's to guard American commercial interests in South Atlantic at time Brazilians overthrew Portuguese rule. One of frigates attached to squadron was big 44-gunner *Hudson* (left). Ex-*Liberator*, she was built at Smith and Dimon's New York yard for Greek revolutionaries. As Greeks were unable to pay for frigate, builders sold vessel to U. S. Navy. (*Hudson* was last privately built frigate in U. S. service.) Brazil Squadron was maintained until Civil War. On typical mission in 1832 Commodore Melancthon Woolsey secured treaty with natives of the Falkland Islands.

469. U. S. AFRICA SQUADRON was organized in 1842 to reinforce the antislaver patrol established in 1819. Federal law of 1819 forbidding importation of slaves gave rise to odious game of "blackbirding." From West Africa kidnapped Negroes were smuggled to Cuba and other undercover stations, then into American South. Inhuman slave-runners were worst criminals on the sea. U. S. schooner *Shark* (above) conducted an early antislaver patrol under Captain Matthew Calbraith Perry.

471. "OLD IRONSIDES" ACTS FOR "OLD HICKORY." In 1832 South Carolina politicians threatened State secession if U. S. Government tried to enforce tax law. Medals appeared in Charleston with inscription, "John C. Calhoun, First President of the Southern Confederacy." President

470. PORT OF NEW ORLEANS IN HEYDAY OF SAIL. With Navy securing trade treaties and downing piracy, nation's foreign trade boomed. Between 1815 and 1860 imports rose from $113,000,000 to $362,000,000. Exports soared from $52,000,000 to $400,000,000. Keeping pace with commercial expansion, American merchant marine expanded. So did nation's great seaports. By 1828 "Queen City" on the Delta was America's second largest port (pop. 46,000). Small city, but doing big business.

Jackson acted swiftly. Under emergency orders *Constitution* sailed into Charleston Harbor with tompions out of guns. Carolina hotheads cooled off. Winner of first round of War Between the States, "Old Ironsides" is shown in painting (right) returning to "Constitution Wharf" at Boston.

472. "THE BLACKBIRDERS"—murder on the high seas. Pursued by naval patrols, slavers frequently pitched chained human cargo overside to lighten ship and rid vessel of

contraband. Navy showed such inhuman monsters short shrift; often wrecked captive slave ships on St. Helena. Royal Navy cooperated willingly. Antislaver drive ended in '61.

Slave Stowage

on a Guinea Man

473. MISSION TO NAPLES—BILL-ING KING BOMBA. When King of Two Sicilies welshed on debt to U. S., President Andrew Jackson called upon Navy to collect. U. S. frigate *Brandy-wine* (Captain M. C. Perry) put in at Naples. Then frigate *United States* arrived. Then U. S. sloop *Concord*. When it looked like bombardment for Bomba, the King paid up. Old print (above) shows *Concord* (left) and "Roaring Brandywine" off Malta.

SORROWS OF THE SEMINOLES—BANISHED FROM FLORIDA.

474. SEMINOLE WAR—NAVY OFF THE EVERGLADES. After Spanish Florida was ceded to U. S. in 1819, effort was made to transfer Florida Indians to western territory. Refusing to give up land, Seminoles finally rose under Chief Osceola, who killed General Wiley Thompson (when latter seized Osceola's wife as fugitive slave). Naval forces under Commo. Dallas were rushed to Tampa in 1835 to aid hard-pressed Army garrison. Osceola staged fierce resistance, but Indians were slowly driven deep into Everglades. Seized by Army at a truce conference, Osceola was imprisoned in Fort Moultrie where he died in chains. Lasting until 1842, Seminole War was most costly Indian conflict in which U. S. engaged. As expressed by caption to contemporary print, many Americans deplored treacherous treatment dealt Osceola.

Chief Osceola

475. "OLD HICKORY" DECAPITATED

—"murder" aboard "Old Ironsides." One of most controversial figures in American public life was Andrew Jackson, whose very figurehead became subject of raging controversy. When *Constitution* returned to Boston after South Carolina episode, Yard Commandant Jesse Elliott replaced ship's worn-out Hercules figurehead with figure of President Jackson. Campaigning against Jackson, anti-Democrats of Boston staged rally; demanded different figurehead for *Constitution*. And night of July 3, 1834, a marauder boarded "Old Ironsides" and beheaded "Old Hickory."

476. JACKSON'S HEAD REMOVED FROM *CONSTITUTION!*

Working with saw in dark and rain, headsman made clumsy decapitation. Offering $1,000 reward for discovery of perpetrator, Commandant Elliott described affair as "an insult to the United States Navy, if not to the entire United States." Losing own head, Elliott threatened to court-martial all hands in Boston Yard if vandal were not brought to book. But doer of deed escaped. (See his calling card—desperate rascal!—below.)

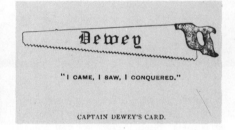

"I CAME, I SAW, I CONQUERED."

CAPTAIN DEWEY'S CARD.

COMMODORE J. D. ELLIOTT.

THE HEAD RESTORED.

477. MAHLON DICKERSON

—Naval Secretary who kept his head. One of Department's top leaders, Dickerson of New Jersey urged steam navigation, sponsored *Fulton II* and wasted no steam on teapot tempests, even when sailorman walked in and placed Jackson's head on his desk. Cool visitor stated there was nothing "unconstitutional" about beheading figurehead of warship *Constitution*. "Who are you?" Dickerson glared. Answer: "A Cape Cod skipper named Samuel Worthington Dewey." Dickerson scowled, then grinned. "Close the door, Cap'n Dewey, and tell me how you did it." When story was relayed to White House, "Old Hickory" roared. "I never did like that image! Give the man a postmaster's job!" Postmaster Dewey was collateral ancestor of George Dewey, hero of Manila, who also saw and conquered.

MAHLON DICKERSON.

THE UNITED STATES STEAM FRIGATE FULTON.

Enter the Engineers

478. *FULTON II*—Navy's second steam frigate. Built at New York Navy Yard under supervision of Commander Matthew Calbraith Perry. Propelled by 22-foot paddle wheels capable of 20 revolutions per minute for maximum speed of 11 knots. Engines on spar deck; copper boilers in reinforced hold. Cost of warship: $300,000. Although ineffi- ciently designed, *Fulton II* remained in service until 1859 when she was wrecked off Pensacola. Doughty Perry, her first skipper, became ardent advocate of steam frigates.

479. FIRST ENGINEER IN U.S.N. —Charles H. Haswell. Answering Perry's appeal for professionals, Mr. Haswell of New York became Chief Engineer of *Fulton II* on July 12, 1836. Over protests of Navy officers ("We will all be outranked!") he was appointed Engineer-in-Chief of Navy in 1840. As canvas-minded

480. SHOVEL COAL? NOT US! Called on to serve as firemen, Navy sailors staged "strike." As marlin-spike seamen proved inept as well as mutinous, Perry urged procurement of trained mechanics and engineers; sponsored creation of Engineer Corps which remained in Navy until 1899. Drive for engine-driven warships won him title "Father of Steam Navy."

captains thought steam-power exaggerated, Haswell had to combat mental inertia as well as that of machinery.

Commander Matthew Calbraith Perry, "Father of Steam Navy"

NAVY EXPANDS THE GLOBE

481. LEADER OF U. S. EXPLORING EXPEDITION—Commander Charles Wilkes. Launched by Congress in 1838, expedition pioneered Antarctic and Pacific frontiers. Elite naval crews and scientists manned U. S. squadron containing sloops *Vincennes* and *Peacock*, brig *Porpoise*, schooners *Flying Fish* and *Sea Gull*, storeship *Relief*. Explorers all.

482. PORTRAIT FROM WILKES' *NARRATIVE*—a Fiji princess. Laden with treasure trove of sketches, landscapes and charts, explorers reported to Congress. Wilkes recorded the expedition in a 19-volume opus rivaling Darwin's *Voyage of a Naturalist*. One of few masterworks authored by an American naval officer, its publication was marred by Wilkes' court-martial for cruelty to some of crew.

483. SOMEWHERE "OFF THE MAP." In storm off Antarctic Palmer Land, little *Sea Gull* was lost. She is shown (above) with *Porpoise* (from sketch by Commander Wilkes). After braving Antarctic limbo, squadron explored South Seas and North Pacific. Off Oregon, sloop *Peacock* was lost. Explorers charted American Northwest Coast, then crossed Oceania to Philippines. Then home in 1842.

PIONEERS ASHORE, 1840

484. LIEUTENANT MATTHEW FONTAINE MAURY—modernizer of navigation. While Calbraith Perry pushed steam engineering and Wilkes expanded world's horizon, Maury brought navigation up to date. Lame, he was given charge of Charts and Instruments Depot in Washington. Perhaps some hoped this a shelf for author of *Scraps from a Lucky Bag* —critiques on Navy life written by Maury. But Maury's nonconformist mind was not shelved. Assembling data on winds and currents, he produced scientific study of Gulf Stream; went on to found Naval Observatory and Hydrographic Office. By 1845 he had removed much "b'guess and b'god" from navigation. His North Atlantic Track Charts are standard today. Geographer, sponsor of Atlantic Cable, proponent of international amity, Maury was one of foremost thinkers of his time. But with tragic inconsistency his broad mind would contract under passionate pressures of 1861; his naval career would founder in effort to uphold Confederacy, aid Maximilian in Mexico.

485. ABEL UPSHUR—Secretary of Navy (1841-1843)—advocate of service reform. Virginia jurist in cabinet of President Tyler. Anticipated Mahan's global view of sea power. Sponsored naval expansion.

Dismayed idealists by describing war as struggle for commercial advantage. Urged revision of Navy Regs, abolition of flogging, academy for officer training—program stranded until Navy suffered series of grim disasters.

486. OFFICER OF 1840's—when time began to stale and custom wither. If this Lieutenant, U.S.N., has fixed stare, it could be because he has little to look forward to. Following Jackson's administration, caliber of Navy's officership showed marked shrinkage. Reason: stagnant promotion system that froze officers in grade and rank, killing incentive of those rooted at bottom and burdening service with antiques at top. By 1840, Navy was barnacled with mossbacks. Rugged individualists in youth who had aged into crusty know-it-alls resentful of any innovation that threatened their established authority. Sour characters of Elliott's jib. Martinets like Captain Thomas Wyman. Psychotic cranks like "Mad Jack" Percival. "We of the naval service are dead," wrote 40-year-old Lieutenant Raphael Semmes. "It is the cry of seniority which has killed us; that preposterous cry which insists a man's years and not his brains should be the test of promotion and employment. A more perfect system could not have been invented by our worst enemies to destroy us. It stifles talent, cripples energy, draws no distinction whatever between excellence and mediocrity." In day of steam such a system was bound to cause explosion.

The Somers Mutiny
PERSONNEL EXPLOSION

487. MIDSHIPMAN OF 1842—Youth bound to climb. Name: Stephen Bleecker Luce. With character clearly revealed in portrait (left)—one of oldest naval photographs in existence. "Who gave you a right to think on board my ship?" roared Captain Wyman of U.S.S. *Columbus* when Luce displayed initiative. So Luce began lifelong campaign for Navy brains. But similar repression wrecked more than one uniformed youngster of lesser caliber.

488. COURT-MARTIAL, 1840. Man who faced a deck court in Old Navy was lucky to be sentenced to the "brig." Punishment for average offense was flogging. Most officers insisted Draconian lash was necessary. "Our Navy crews," wrote Lt. L. C. Rowan, "are made up of thieves, gamblers, drunkards, play actors and circus riders. Many escaped jail by enlisting." But lash also fell on honest old salts and lads from good homes.

skinned boys who writhed in bunk for hours afterward. Although thoughtful officers deplored flogging, conservatives considered it necessary for discipline. But system gave cranky or sadistic captain chance for a Roman holiday. Such a captain was Alexander Slidell Mackenzie, commander of U.S.S. *Somers*. A "sun-downer."

490. SCENE TYPICAL ON BOARD U. S. WAR-BRIG *SOMERS*—cauldron that boiled over. New 10-gunner launched in 1841, this ship served as vessel for hell-broth that poisoned contemporary naval service with dose of appalling homicide. Ingredients: incompetent personnel performance spiced with "cat." Begin with martinet Captain A. S. Mackenzie, veteran of 1812 with trace of sadism in character. Add unhappy junior officers, plus 19-year-old Midshipman Philip Spencer, harum-scarum son of former Secretary of War. Instead of "gamblers, drunkards and circus riders," crew is largely made up of young apprentices on training cruise. But trouble formula is complete. As ship makes run to Africa, deck courts and floggings are daily affair. (below)

489. "ALL HANDS WITNESS PUNISHMENT, AHOY!" Bos'n advances with ominous green bag. From bag he produces nine-tailed scourge. "A fresh cat applied by a fresh hand" was privilege of every man-of-war culprit. (Used "cats" were blood-stained; liable to deal infection.) Following are typical sentences dealt on board one U. S. warship during cruise: "Pilfering rum from stores, 12 lashes; running in debt ashore, 12 lashes; spitting on man, 12 lashes; telling master-at-arms to 'go to hell,' 6 lashes; appearing naked on spar deck, 9 lashes. For drunkenness and mutinous conduct, 50 lashes; mutinous disrespect to officer, 40 lashes; slow to enter boat, 6 lashes; dropping bucket from aloft, 12 lashes; stealing officer's toupee, 12 lashes." As fourth lash usually drew blood, surgeon stood by to tend each victim. (Usual attention: bucket of salt water on slashed back.) Tough tars could take it standing up. However, multiple offenses were punished by series of flayings which might maim a man for life. And many of the "men" thus flogged were thin-

THE U. S. BRIG-OF-WAR SOMERS.

491. "A MUTINY WAS DISCOVERED on board this vessel Nov. 26th, 1842, on her homeward voyage from the coast of Africa. . . ." So reads the caption to foregoing contemporary print. But was it mutiny or prank on part of playboy Midshipman Spencer? A report from Purser's Mate Wales that Spencer was planning to seize ship and go on pirate cruise. A dime novel and a dirk found in Spencer's sea bag. A list of names (marked "Certain" and "Doubtful") ambiguously written in Greek. To Captain Mackenzie these were enough. When "mid" was seen whispering to Bos'n's Mate Sam Cromwell and Seaman Elisha Small, all three were put under arrest. Facing drumhead court, they swore innocence. They were ironed and bagged (canvas sack tied over the head) while Mackenzie and officers considered case. As crew seemed to "mutter mutinously" throughout day, four apprentices were put in irons. Mackenzie then recommended that "ringleaders" should be "put to death in manner best calculated to make a beneficial impression on the disaffected." Junior officers agreed. Following morning, crew was ordered to voice three cheers as Spencer, Small and Cromwell were swung aloft. After which, Mackenzie and officers coolly sat down at mess. Close-up of *Somers* picture (right)

shows hanging. Bodies were buried at sea. But when brig sailed grimly home to Brooklyn Yard, story leaked to press despite Mackenzie's efforts to suppress it. Hanging of young Spencer scandalized nation's capital. But execution of Small on scanty evidence, and Cromwell on none at all, outraged American public. Even case against Spencer seemed flimsy when Mackenzie stated verdict partly rested on fact that accused had "an odd glint in his eye" and "sometimes made music by squeezing his palms together." Critics noted that *Somers* was near St. Thomas on day of hangings; accused could have been tried in port. And could boys so easily disarmed have captured a ship? When Fenimore Cooper published booklet entitled *Cruise of the Somers, Illustrative of the Despotism of the Quarterdeck* the storm broke. Although Court of Inquiry upheld ship captain's action, Naval Secretary Upshur ordered Mackenzie charged with murder. He was acquitted by naval court-martial. But case remained subject of bitter controversy. For decades Navy officers were forbidden to mention it in public. As somber sequel, *Somers* capsized during Mexican War, drowning half her crew. In 1848 Mackenzie, aged 45, fell dead. One of *Somer's* officers committed suicide. One went insane. One drank himself to death.

492. MUTINY ON BARQUE *OSCAR* (below)—echo of *Somers* case. While Mackenzie trial made stormy headlines, episode at Ilha Grande was reported in the illustrated press. Composite picture shows shooting (on deck) and burial (coffin in smallboat) of mutineer on American naval vessel. Sensitive to public opinion, Navy leaders had made proud claim mutiny never occurred in U.S.N. Not on regular Navy list, *Oscar* could be ignored. But *Somers* case could not, especially with Mackenzie exonerated. For if men were not mutineers, Mackenzie was judicial murderer. So . . . no more death sentences executed in Navy without Presidential approval. Flogging abolished in 1850. Last hanging at yardarm in 1855. Last mutiny reported in Navy was in 1890. All told there were seven mutinies reported in Old U. S. N. Good record alongside other navies.

493. U.S.S. *MISSISSIPPI*—Navy's first steam-driven, ocean-going capital ship. Built at Philadelphia Navy Yard, and commissioned in 1841. A 1,732-tonner; length 225 feet; beam 40; depth of hold 23½. Carried two 10-inch and ten 8-inch shell guns. Despite Jonah engines she served valiantly, died in the War of '61.

Steam Up

HERE COME THE SIDEWHEELERS

494. TYPICAL SIDE-LEVER ENGINE used in steamers of 1840's. An unmitigated horror to Old Navy "stick and string" captains. But marvels of mechanical ingenuity. True, uneconomical. Using salt water, their boilers were limited to 15 pounds pressure. Machinery occupied much stowage space, and the furnaces were insatiable. As for repair bills—building cost of *Mississippi*, $567,000; cost of repairs first 12 yrs. service, $429,000. But engineer, fireman, coal-passer were in U.S.N. to stay.

495. U. S. PADDLE-SLOOP *MICHIGAN*—Navy's first iron-hull warship. Another Upshur-sponsored innovation, *Michigan* sailed in wake of English-invented iron barge (1787), French iron-hull *Aaron Manby* (1820), British iron ships *Phlegethon* and *Nemesis* (1839). Launched on Lake Erie in 1843, *Michigan* would establish record. Built at Erie, Pa., she was 582-tonner; length 165 feet, beam 27½, draft 9. Powered by two-cylinder, direct-acting condensing engine which developed 170 h.p., she could make 8 knots without using her barkentine rig. Cost: $165,000. Durable vessel. Name changed to *Wolverine*, she was still afloat in 1950.

496. SHIP'S ENGINEER OF 1840's. Regarded as unwelcome competitors, early engineering officers received chill wardroom reception from service traditionally resentful of "specialists." They shouldered monumental task of running as freakish an assortment of marine engines as ever escaped oblivion in the Patent Office.

497. NAVAL ENGINEER'S INSIGNIA—collar device (about 1850-1861). Like Chaplain's Corps or Medical Corps, Engineer's Corps was separate branch of service. Its members were called "engine-drivers." Most of them were technical geniuses. Could coax 5 knots from a teakettle.

Trial and Error

498. END OF U. S. PADDLE FRIGATE *MISSOURI*—at Gibraltar, August 26, 1843. Shock to nation was loss of *Mississippi's* sistership through fire which started when engineer's yeoman broke a demijohn of turpentine in vessel's storeroom. No help that Engineer Haswell had previously advised that inflammable liquids be stored in metal containers—a recommendation vetoed by higher naval authority. Although no lives were lost in disaster, opponents of steam made most of it. And pointed to operational failure of third paddle frigate, *Alleghany*—a monstrosity driven by water wheels which revolved merry-go-round fashion (invention of a naval officer with more political influence than talent). Undiscouraged, Secretary Upshur went full steam ahead; spurred construction of iron "Stevens Battery" and steam warship *Princeton*. Latter cost Mr. Upshur his life.

499. UNIQUE ENGINE IN U.S.S. *PRINCETON*. Modern engineers will see in this view (end elevation) a mechanical novelty. Unorthodox even for the unconventional, engine contained a steam box in which a plate was rocked back and forth by alternate spurts of pressure. Through system of arms and rods, rocking motion rotated the propeller shaft. Only engine of kind in history. (below)

500. JOHN ERICSSON, MASTER ENGINEER. Inventions of this Viking genius were talk of Victorian world. He was induced to work for U. S. Navy by Capt. Robert Stockton who met him in London. Ericsson set up shop in America in 1839. At Stockton's express urging, he designed power plant and propeller for *Princeton*—world's first screw-driven warship — launched Boston, 1851.

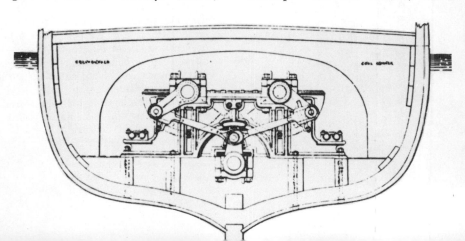

501. U. S. STEAM SLOOP *PRINCE-TON*—wonder cruiser of her day. Because huge paddle wheels were easily shattered by cannon fire, *Princeton's* underwater propeller was headline naval innovation. So were other Ericsson inventions for *Princeton*—furnaces for anthracite coal; steam-driven blowers; a telescopic smokestack to reduce silhouette. Ericsson also designed for *Princeton* a 12-inch gun (christened "Oregon") its barrel uniquely reinforced by metal hoops around the breech. Another 12-incher ("Peacemaker") was designed for *Princeton* by Captain Stockton. Ericsson warned Navy that Stockton's gun needed breech reinforcement. Navy ignored warning. Upshot: the 954-ton *Princeton* proved a lethal death-ship.

502. *PRINCETON* DISASTER! On trial run on Potomac, February 28, 1844, new warship treated President Tyler, cabinet members and guests to tragic excursion. On exhibition, Ericsson's "Oregon" boomed to loud applause. Stockton's "Peacemaker" then blew to pieces. Calamitous blast killed Abel Upshur (new Secretary of State), Naval Secretary Thomas Gilmer, two Congressmen, a deck officer. Wounded were Captain Stockton, 12 of ship's crew. Calling accident "Act of God," Navy Court of Inquiry exonerated Stockton. Buck was passed to civilian Ericsson. For refusal to whitewash Stockton's defective gun Ericsson was ostracized by Navy Dept., never paid for work on *Princeton*. (picture at right)

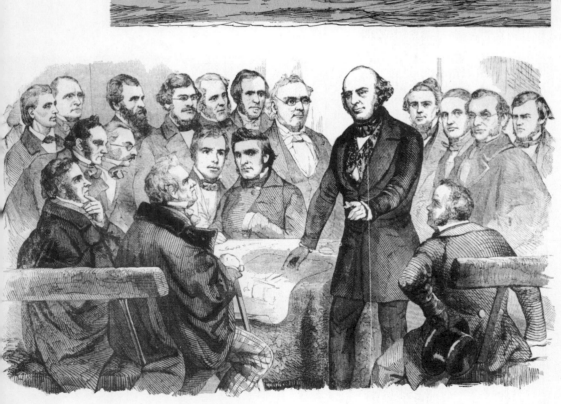

503. GENIUS SHELVED BY MEDIOCRITY. After *Princeton* blast Ericsson was denounced by Navy Captain Stockton as "presumptuous mechanic." Not the first scientist to suffer "brass poisoning," Ericsson was subjected to one of worst cases on record. Navy rebuilt damaged *Princeton* for $340,000, but lost million-dollar services of engineering genius. In New York workshop Ericsson pursued experiments. Caloric (hot air) engine. "Hydrostatic javelin" (torpedo fired from underwater gun). Late in 1850's he designed an ironclad turret vessel—offered to and rejected by France. Navy minds would not catch up with his creative intelligence until 1861. Then Ericsson's monitor, sponsored by Lincoln, would save nation's day.

Officer Education
ACADEMY AT ANNAPOLIS

Acting Midshipman circa 1850

504. CRADLE FOR FUTURE COMMANDERS—Old Fort Severn (from map of 1845). For 20 years Naval Secretaries had urged establishment of academy for officer training. *Somers* tragedy; *Missouri* conflagration; *Princeton* disaster—Congress learned the hard way. In 1845 appropriations were voted; Fort Severn, Annapolis, was procured as site of Naval Academy. Old Fort is shown at right.

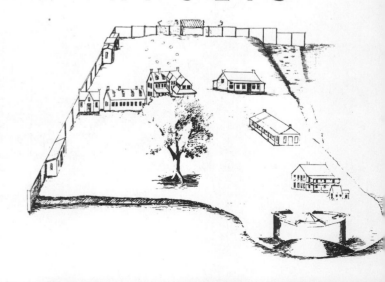

505. UNITED STATES NAVAL ACADEMY. Launched by Naval Secretary George Bancroft, school opened on October 10, 1845, under Captain Franklin Buchanan. First class, three midshipmen; first classroom, a shed. But Academy soon grew. Its success was manifest in character and skill of many Civil War line officers and mids.

506. FROM SAIL TO STEAM— "Old Ironsides" and U. S. paddle frigate in symbolic company at Newport, Rhode Island, on threshold of new era. By 1845 steam-power was recognized as naval imperative. Most important naval development since cannon, steam took the wind out of tactics; altered strategy by modifying

time-space (speed vs. distance) problem and by introducing factor of fueling stations; enhanced sea power of nations endowed with coal and iron and geared for mechanization. Henceforth the navies that ruled the wave would be built by industrial empires. And manned by skilled engineers as well as salty master mariners.

Chapter VI

THE MEXICAN WAR

INTRODUCTION

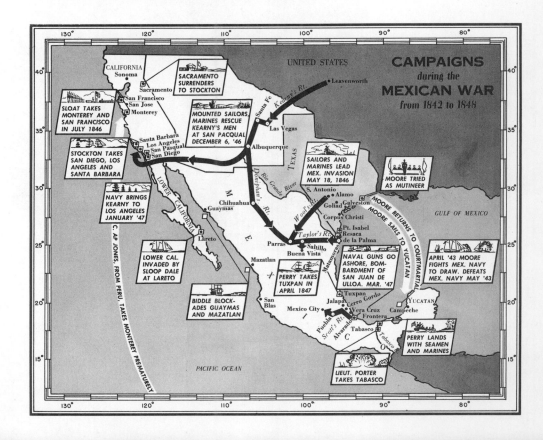

Naval Battery at Vera Cruz

American politicians called it "Manifest Destiny." The term is attributed to the editorial pen of one John L. O'Sullivan, whose journal approved the annexation of Texas on the theory that it was "our manifest destiny to overspread the continent." The term was popularized during the dispute with Britain over Oregon. It was used as an ideological excuse for the subsequent war with Mexico—the war by which the United States acquired California and the great Southwest. To such honest Americans as poet James Russell Lowell, Congressman Abraham Lincoln and soldier Ulysses S. Grant, "Manifest Destiny" was an empty phrase to cover a war of aggression. Certainly it was that to the Mexicans whose country was invaded and conquered.

The Mexican War has embarrassed American historians ever since. Modern grade-school histories play down the conflict. College texts treat it with relative indifference. One modern military historian commits the hypocrisy of calling the invasion campaign "defensive warfare." And a modern naval historian ties his text into semantic knots trying to justify the assault on Old Mexico on moral grounds. All such attempts to evade history or bring it morally into line with modern ethics amount to an erasure of the record. Cerro Gordo—Molino del Rey—Churubusco—Contreras—these names are virtually unknown to today's Americans. So are the details of the war effort that gained for the United States the nation's present Pacific Coast. That war effort was considerable. If it does not lend itself to modern moralizing (neither did slavery or the double standard), it remains a remarkable military and naval exploit. Mexico was the world's second largest republic, with a domain embracing vast expanses of mountain, desert and shore. Although disorganized and poorly equipped, the Mexican Army was much larger than the American, and had the advantage of fighting defensively on home soil. Given a navy, Mexico might easily have turned the war-tide. But the Mexican Navy was sunk before the war with the United States began—sunk by a vagabond American squadron in one of the most extraordinary naval engagements in history. That forgotten battle is only one of the incredible naval feats that led to the ultimate defeat of Mexico.

The Texas Navy
GUN SMOKE ON THE GULF

507. HEART OF TEXAS IN THE DEEP—war-schooner *Independence*, Texas Navy. Launched in 1836 under Provisional Gov't. of Lone Star Republic, behest of Sam Houston, original "Texian" flotilla contained war-schooners *Independence* (Commo. Wm. Brown), *Liberty* (Capt. Jeremiah Brown), *Invincible* (Capt. C. E. Hawkins), *Brutus* (Capt. Wm. Hard). Also armed raider *Flash* (Capt. Luke Falvel) and privateers *Thomas, Toby, Terrible*. Galloping down the Gulf these "Texians" rode herd on Mexican Navy at time of the Alamo. *Liberty* fought lively action. *Flash* rescued Provisional President David Burnet from coastal trap. But flagship *Independence* was captured by Mexicans. *Invincible* was seized by U. S. warship; charged with piracy for flying U. S. flag. When Texas Naval Secretary S. Rhoades Fisher was impeached for graft, pioneer Lone Star squadron was beached.

Sail plan of the revenue cutter "Jefferson," probably same as "Independence," built from same design, same yard in 1832. "Independence" was former revenue cutter, "Samuel D. Ingham."

508. WAR-BRIG *AUSTIN*—flagship of revived Texas Navy. Pioneer service was dissolved by President Houston. But in 1839, President Mirabeau B. Lamar revived T. N. for tidewater defense. New $800,000 fleet contained 20-gunner *Austin*, brigs *Wharton* and *Archer*, schooners *San Bernard*, *San Antonio*, *San Jacinto*, and 8-gun steamer *Zavala*. Crews imported from New Orleans; new commodore from Virginia. (Original *Austin* sketch by Midshipman Edward Johns, T.N., 1840.)

509. LONE STAR NAVAL LEADER —Commodore Edwin W. Moore, T.N. Former "mid" on sloops *Hornet* and *Boston*, this adventurous officer from Alexandria, Va., quit U. S. Navy to accept command ($200 a month) Texas Navy. Leading "Texians" on cruise from Galveston to Yucatan in 1843, he got into hot water. He liked hot water. To discomfiture of U. S., he reduced Mexican Navy to zero.

510. EARLY IRONCLADS—French iron fleet. First iron warships in American waters were frigates *Montezuma* and *Guadalupe* of Mexican Navy, 1842. Vessels were English-built, paddle-driven, smaller than French type shown. But extremely powerful for their day. *Montezuma* (1,164 tons) carried a 68-pound pivot gun, six 32's. *Guadalupe* (775 tons) carried two 68-pounders. Their sale

by British to Mexicans was obvious counter to Oregon dispute; encouraged Mexicans to hope Britain would intervene if U. S. invaded Mexico. Manned by English crews "on leave" from Royal Navy, Mexican ironclads worried Washington. But didn't faze Commodore Moore of Texas Navy.

511. WAR-SCHOONER *SAN ANTONIO*—"Texian" ghost. In autumn of 1842, revolution in Mexico dried up Mexican shipping. Prize-hungry "Texian" crews made trouble. T.N.S. *San Bernard*, mishandled, was wrecked off Galveston. Off Isle of Mugeres, Commo. Moore had to put down mutiny. *San Antonio* (Capt. Wm. Seeger) vanished in night; was later reported as "ghost ship" in Caribbean flying Jolly Roger. Early in 1843, Moore made port in New Orleans, two vessels missing, stores empty, crews penniless. Beginning of drama unmatched in naval annals!

Schooner "Rambler" (later "William Robbins"),
was the "Liberty" of the Texas Navy

512. SAM ("THE RAVEN") HOUSTON, again President, wanted no more of Texas Navy; ordered fleet home to Galveston for auction sale. Stranded in New Orleans, Moore rejected this directive. To pay sailors, finance provisions, he had rented Lone Star fleet to Yucatan agents for revolution against Santa Anna's Centralist Gov't. Ignoring President Houston's order, Moore sailed for Yucatan. Houston disavowed Texas fleet; denounced Moore and crews as mutineers, renegades, pirates. (left)

513. TEXAS LONE STAR FLAG—did it fly in first major sea battle involving ironclads? Or did "Texian" warships fly any national ensign? According to Houston they were pirates. According to Commo. Moore they were Texas Navy when (April 30, 1843) they attacked Mexican fleet of Don Tomas Marin off Campeche, Yucatan. Action featured *Austin, Wharton, Archer, San Jacinto* versus two brigs, two schooners, armed steamer *Regenerador*, and Mexican ironclads. Round one: a draw.

Texan Squadron

514. THUNDER ON THE GULF! Off Yucatan May 16, 1843, Moore's "Texians" lured iron warships into showdown. Or say Commo. E. W. Moore, ex-Texas Navy, lured Admiral Don Tomas, Mexican Navy, and Captains Cleaveland and Charlewood, on leave, British Navy. Whereby Moore's wooden brigs smashed Mexico's ironclads to junk. Score: *Austin*, 3 dead; *Wharton*, 2 dead; *Montezuma*, 40 dead; *Guadalupe*, 47. Thus fleet without country sank Mexico's Navy.

515. THE "TEXIAN" SQUADRON (left)—Moore's "Texians" at anchor. Hero to Yucatan rebels, Moore stepped from Gulf's hot waters into hotter diplomatic soup. Returning with victorious fleet to Texas, he was toasted by Galveston—and arrested as mutineer by President Houston. Moore was acquitted. But the orphan Lone Star fleet remained anchored until U. S. annexed Texas (1845) and vessels were adopted by U.S.N. Orphan Commo. Moore was not similarly adopted. Planning war on Mexico, U. S. leaders should have given him epaulets. Instead, fighting commodore, who defeated two ironclads 19 years before *Monitor* met *Merrimack*, got Navy brush-off. Although Raphael Semmes called him the star of Texas history, Moore died, forgotten, in New York. Few American histories mention fact that Moore's disowned "Texian" fleet sank Mexican sea power, thus clearing way for an invasion of Mexico.

516. EMBARRASSED BY "TEXIAN" NAVAL VICTORY? — John Slidell, U. S. envoy to Mexico. American President Polk wanted California. Dispatched to Mexico in spring of 1845, Slidell was instructed to offer Mexican Gov't. $25,000,000 for California and New Mexico—or else. When Mexicans refused to deal with Slidell, Polk planned war, confiding to his diary that if Mexicans didn't start it, he would. Since Mexico, minus a navy, could not offer serious challenge to U. S., Americans were compelled to invade Mexico, whitewashing war with term "Manifest Destiny." Term fooled nobody, least of all "Texians" who'd sunk Mexican Navy in honest combat. (Congress finally *did* vote Moore his back pay.)

UNITED STATES
Jumps the Gun

517. U.S.S. *UNITED STATES* featured in queer war preliminary in autumn of 1842. Under Commodore T. ap Catesby Jones, frigate was at Callao, Peru, when rumor came of break between U.S.A. and Mexico. Sudden departure of British squadron convinced Jones English intended to grab California. Jones raced north with *United States* and sloop *Cyane,* bent on seizing Monterey, California.

518. MONTEREY, CALIFORNIA— target of a "premature." Sailing with *United States* and *Cyane* into this harbor on October 19, 1842, Commodore Jones demanded its surrender to U.S.A. Mexican garrison offered no resistance as Americans seized Monterey Castle. Two days later Navy occupants were horrified to learn U. S. and Mexico were not at war. Although move by T. ap Catesby Jones evidently resulted from secret instructions, his act was disavowed by U. S. Government. Monterey was returned to Mexico with apologies. And Jones was detached from squadron command with official reprimand. The "ap," incidentally, is Welsh for "son of." Retiring from Monterey, Commodore Jones probably applied it to a good old American epithet.

519. AMERICAN ARMY AT CORPUS CHRISTI, TEXAS, October 1845. Just three years after ill-timed California attack, U. S. Army staged this scene on Gulf of Mexico. Force was under command of General Zachary (Old Rough and Ready) Taylor. When Texas was annexed by U.S.A. previous March, Mexico broke off diplomatic relations. Army's move to Texas-Mexican border was ordered by Naval Secretary George Bancroft, acting as Secretary of War *pro tem.* U. S. Gulf Squadron in scene was under Commodore David Conner.

Brevet Second Lieutenant U. S. Grant

520. BATTLE OF RESACA DE LA PALMA. Clash came on May 9, 1846, after Taylor pushed U. S. Army into disputed territory along Rio Grande and established sea base at Point Isabel. To Mexico this looked like first step of invasion. Someone opened fire when Mexican scouts encountered American. Defeated in fierce skirmish at Palo Alto, Mexicans were pursued, again beaten at Resaca de la Palma. On May 11, President Polk demanded war with Mexico, asserting: "After reiterated menaces, Mexico has invaded our territory and shed American blood on American soil. War exists, and notwithstanding all our efforts to avoid it, exists by the act of Mexico alone." Congress voted war.

521. MEXICAN WAR RECRUITING POSTER—an early broadside calling for volunteers. Despite such saber-rattling appeals, many Americans in North refused to respond. Outspoken objectors saw "Manifest Destiny" as mask for conquest and extension of slavery. In the *Biglow Papers*, James Russell Lowell wrote:

"They just want this Californy
So's to lug the slave states in."

But the war—perhaps the most unpopular in American history—had been declared. And the guns were already banging south of the border.

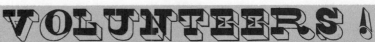

VOLUNTEERS !

Men of the Granite State!
Men of Old Rockingham !! the
strawberry-bed of patriotism, renowned for bravery and devotion to Country, rally at this call. Santa Anna, reeking with the generous confidence and magnanimity of your countrymen, is in arms, eager to plunge his traitor-dagger in their bosoms. To arms, then, and rush to the standard of the fearless and gallant CUSHING---put to the blush the dastardly meanness and rank toryism of Massachusetts. Let the half civilized Mexicans hear the crack of the unerring New Hampshire rifleman, and illustrate on the plains of San Luis Potosi, the fierce, determined, and undaunted bravery that has always characterized her sons. Col. THEODORE F. ROWE, at No. 31 Daniel-street, is authorized and will enlist men this week for the Massachusetts Regiment of Volunteers. The compensation is $10 per month---$30 in advance. Congress will grant a handsome bounty in money and ONE HUNDRED AND SIXTY ACRES OF LAND.
Portsmouth, Feb. 2. 1847.

522. COMMANDER-IN-CHIEF of the United States Army and Navy during the Mexican War—President James K. Polk. Southern Democrat. Lawyer. Former Congressman and Governor of Tennessee. First "dark horse" elected President. A shrewd politician, he had long advocated American expansion to West Coast; made California the principal objective of his war aims. Although an able executive and administrator, he mixed politics with war moves; antagonized State Department and U. S. Army chiefs. To his backers he was "empire builder." To opposing leaders of Whig (pre-Republican) Party, he was "Polk the Mendacious." Fortunately (from Navy's view) he meddled little with naval operations.

The

523. SECRETARY OF THE NAVY George Bancroft (1845-1846). Massachusetts-born writer, teacher, historian. Founder of U. S. Naval Academy at Annapolis. Frankly imperialistic, he favored war with Mexico to procure California; urged

Central Mexico invasion. He saw Navy was prepared; issued standing orders to Commodore Sloat to seize California ports as soon as war was declared. As Acting War Secretary he set military machinery in motion; sent Army across Tex border. (above)

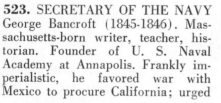

524. COMMODORE JOHN DRAKE SLOAT—"Conqueror of California." Veteran of 1812. Maneuvered frigate *United States* in famous battle with *Macedonian*. Captain of schooner *Grampus* during Caribbean antipirate campaign, he captured notorious picaroon Cofrecina, who was executed by firing squad in 1825. Replacing impetuous T. ap Catesby Jones, Sloat assumed command of U. S. Pacific Squadron in 1844. In July 1846 he took Monterey, California—repeat performance of drama previously staged by Catesby Jones.

By acting according to rulebook (i.e., after formal declaration of war on Mexico), Sloat made this conquest "official"—a legalistic farce which brought him promotion for doing what Jones had been demoted for in dress rehearsal. After Monterey capture, Sloat went on to seize San Francisco. But this winner of Pacific Coast empire for United States was soon to be forgotten by nation (and historians) eager to erase war with Mexico from public memory. Admiral Sloat died on Staten Island in 1867. Nation paid more homage to Farragut.

525. GENERAL ANTONIO LÓPEZ de SANTA ANNA—commander of Army of Mexico. Renowned as "Hero of Tampico" (for defeat of Spanish invaders in 1829) he led Mexicans at Alamo in attempt to quell Texas Revolution; was blamed for massacre of Texans at Goliad. Captured by troops of Sam Houston, he was released on promise to foster friendly Mexican Government. After battling French at Vera Cruz (1838) where he lost a leg, he became dictator, then President, of Mexico. Militaristic and harsh, he was ousted from office by Mexican liberals, then recalled from exile to lead army against American invasion forces. Recklessly he threw cavalry against artillery; failed to win a single battle. His wooden leg, captured at Cerro Gordo, made prize exhibit at Barnum's in New York.

Santa Anna in

full regalia

Leaders

Return of Santa Anna on Avon; Vera Cruz Harbor

with British Mail Steamer Avon saluting the forts, 1853

The Alamo March, 1836

527. COMMODORE DAVID CONNER—commander of Gulf Squadron at start of Mexican War. Veteran of 1812. Officer on board *Ontario* during Oregon exploit. Considered one of Navy's outstanding captains. He also enjoyed reputation of "best-dressed officer in the service." But lackluster tactics and his failure to storm and capture Vera Cruz fortress as French Admiral Baudin had done ten years before evoked a clamor from press and disappointed Congressmen. In March 1847 Conner was replaced by Commodore Matthew Calbraith Perry, steam sailor who pushed the Vera Cruz drive at forced draught.

528. COMMODORE ROBERT STOCKTON—credited by some naval historians as "Conqueror of California." Veteran of 1812 and Algerine War. Inventor of cannon which exploded on board *Princeton*. Arriving on West Coast in summer of 1846, he replaced Sloat (then ill) as commander of Pacific Squadron. Co-operating with "Bear Flag" revolutionists, his forces captured San Diego, Los Angeles, Santa Barbara and other California seaports; rescued an Army detachment in hot water at Agua Caliente. By arbitrarily installing Col. John C. Frémont, "Bear Flag" organizer, as governor of conquered territory, Stockton sparked explosive quarrel with U. S. Army General Kearny. After Frémont's court-martial (for defying Kearny), Stockton resigned from Navy to enter politics. Obituary in 1866 — then, like Sloat, forgotten.

529. GENERAL WINFIELD SCOTT —commanding general of U. S. Army. Nickname "Old Fuss and Feathers" nicely characterized this old-school soldier, who, in spite of vanity and temper, was highly capable leader. As he proved during War of 1812. Disliking Scott's politics, Polk called him "rather scientific and visionary." His "Martial Law Order" to govern conduct of troops (against looting, rape) was considered fussy. His plan to invade Mexico City through Vera Cruz was delayed when he injudiciously wrote, "I do not desire to place myself in that most perilous of all positions—a fire upon my rear from Washington, and the fire of the enemy in front." (left)

530. AT POINT ISABEL—Navy spearhead for Taylor. Rare woodcut shows invasion base at Rio Grande mouth near present site of Brownsville. Here Taylor's vanguard was menaced by Mexican force at Matamoros. Call for help brought squadron under Commo. Conner. First U.S. troops to invade Old Mexico, 500 seamen and Marines cleared road to Matamoros and Monterrey, boosting morale after some 200 U.S. soldiers deserted at Isabel. But Navy had own troubles. In area, young Lt. Grant saw a mutiny on Navy ship *Suviah*. Story came out years later, as did report of Commo. T. ap. C. Jones concerning mutiny on U.S. schooner *Ewing* and hanging of two seamen on West Coast.

American Dragoons before Fort Brown

Toops landing at Point Isabel.

531. GENERAL ZACHARY TAYLOR led U. S. Army invasion forces from Rio Grande into northern Mexico. Smashed army of General Pedro de Ampudia at Ciudad Monterrey. Drove on through wild Sierra Madre range to Buena Vista where he smashed Santa Anna's finest. He was stopped only when his victories threatened Polk's political machine by making popular general a possible rival candidate for President. Crude as tobacco juice, cactus-tough, an experienced Indian-fighter, "Old Rough and Ready" had little use for politics, less for rulebook warfare. When offered a copy of Scott's *Martial Law Order*, he threw it aside with comment, "Another of Scott's novels!" (Entirely possible Taylor thought Winfield Scott the author of *Ivanhoe*.) But Old Zach fully appreciated logistics problems; welcomed naval assistance at Point Isabel. First Americans to invade Mexican territory below Rio Grande were 200 sailors and Marines who crossed river on May 18, 1846, to clear enemy from village in path of Taylor's army. (Taylor's portrait at right.)

General Taylor at Buena Vista

532. "SAILOR'S FAREWELL"—popular lithograph of period—contributes one of few pictures of American blue-jacket at time of Mexican War. Accompanying poem "Black Eyed Susan" was much sighed over by belles of that day.

> "Oh Susan! Susan! lovely dear,
> My vows shall ever true remain,
> Let me kiss off that falling tear,
> We only part to meet again,
> Change as ye list ye winds! my heart shall be
> The faithful compass that still points to thee.
>
> "The Boatswain gave the dreadful word,
> The sails their swelling bosom spread,
> No longer must she stay aboard:
> They kiss'd, she sigh'd, he hung his head:
> Her less'ning boat unwilling rows to land,
> Adieu, she cries, and wav'd her lily hand."

533. HE WENT AWAY A BOY, came back a man. Lithographs (above and left) by N. Currier of New York authentically record uniform, ship, and sentimentality of 1846. Note the chin whiskers—new item for American Jack Tar.

534. WAR-GOING AMERICANS had lively sense of humor, as displayed by cartoon with caption "As You Were!" published in New York in 1846. Enlistments were brisk after "Rough and Ready" won victory at Monterrey, capital of Nuevo Leon. Exact figures on armed forces during Mexican War went unrecorded. But Army mustered largest force in nation's history to that date. Navy probably totaled less than 5,000. Armed forces total: 104,000.

Brevet Lt. U. S. Grant goes

for ammunition, Monterrey

VOLUNTEERS FOR TEXAS

535. FORTRESS AT VERA CRUZ—Mexico's major defense bastion. Considered strongest *castillo* in America, and impregnable barrier to invasion by sea, ancient stronghold of San Juan de Ulloa guarded Vera Cruz harbor; blocked the mountain road inland to Mexico City. Fort's capture by French in 1838 suggested that battlements (partly built in 16th century) had softened. Parapet guns were mostly antiques, but fortress remained formidable barrier for U. S. naval batteries to crack. And Mexicans on Gulf had powerful ally in yellow fever; counted on delay and Yellow Jack to save Vera Cruz. *Vomito* was dreaded by Americans.

Vomito!

536. MEXICAN LANCER. Army of Mexico contained motley infantry, but Mexican cavalry was excellent. Typical Mexican lancer was sketched in California by Gunner Wm. H. Meyers of U. S. sloop-of-war *Dale*—a sailor artist whose sketch-pad recorded for history some of best contemporary pictures of Pacific Squadron invading California. Naval brigades ashore were assailed by Mexican lancers. But horsemen frequently made fatal mistake of charging headlong into American artillery. Mexican Army lacked trained artillerymen, possessed few good field guns.

M e n

Charge of the Mexican Lancers at Buena Vista

U.S.S. Mississippi

537. U. S. PADDLE FRIGATE *MIS-SISSIPPI*. Bulwark in blockade which closed Mexico's Gulf ports. Led U. S. fleet at Vera Cruz. Largest of eight steam vessels Navy possessed at start.

538. U. S. FRIGATE *SAVANNAH* —flagship of Pacific Squadron. One of 14 American sailing frigates, she led U. S. invasion forces which seized California. With Sloat at Monterey.

WARSHIPS AND WEAPONS

539. U. S. WAR-SLOOP *SARA-TOGA*—one of nine new heavy sloops in American fleet. Built at Kittery, Maine. Largest of class in service—an 882-tonner; length 150 feet; beam 36¾; depth of hold 16½. Carried seven 8-inch guns and eighteen 32-pounders. Cost: $160,000. In Gulf Squadron she was captained by Commander Farragut. Navy possessed 23 sloops, eight brigs for war.

540. U. S. STEAM GUNBOAT *SPITFIRE*. With sister *Vixen*, she was originally built for Mexican Government by Brown and Bell of New York; commandeered into U. S. service. Both were 241-tonners, 118 feet long, with 22½ beam, 9¼ depth. Their 18½-foot paddles could wheel them at 7 knots. Each carried an 8-inch Paixhan shell gun (68-pounder) on bow; two 32-pounder

carronades in broadside aft. Navy also acquired Gulf side-wheelers *Scorpion* and *Polk* for war duty. Navy's nine big "liners" and super-battleship *Pennsylvania* were superfluous for war against dusty Mexico.

541. NAVAL GUN OF MEXICAN WAR PERIOD. Although rifling had been invented and Paixhan shell gun widely adopted by French and British, the U. S. N. of 1846 favored solid shot and old trusty (if musty) smoothbores. A few shell guns went to war. But fleet cannon at Vera Cruz were mostly the type used in 1812. Sufficient against Mexican antiques.

California
CAMPAIGN

542. COLONEL JOHN C. FRÉMONT—leader of "Bear Flag" revolt. Explorer. Secret agent extraordinary. One-time teacher of mathematics in U. S. Navy. Won fame as "Path-finder" in Oregon and California. With scout Kit Carson, he was at Yerba Buena (San Francisco) in spring of 1846. Urging American settlers to rise against Mexican authorities, he seized Sonoma; proclaimed a Republic of California. Arriving on scene in July, frigate *Congress* (Commo. Stockton) found Frémont in control. Navy and "Bear Flaggers" joined forces to conquer northern California. An exploit shared by U. S. Army under Kearny.

543. U. S. WAR-SLOOP *CYANE* participated in capture of Monterey on July 7, 1846. In early water color she is shown at Santa Barbara with frigate *United States*. When war news came, *Savannah* (Commo. Sloat) *Cyane* and *Levant* took possession of sleepy California capital. No contest.

544. BATTLE OF SAN PASQUAL (December 6, 1846). Setting out from Kansas with army 1,700 strong (including 500 Mormons) General Stephen Kearny headed for California *via* Santa Fe trail. Only a tattered remnant reached Los Angeles area. At Agua Caliente, U. S. regulars and Latter Day Saints were surrounded. Forty mounted sailors and Marines arrived just in time to rescue survivors at San Pasqual. Sketch is by Gunner Wm. Meyer of U.S.S. *Dale*, whose sloop was at nearby port.

Naval Sketches of the War in California — Meyers   No — 5

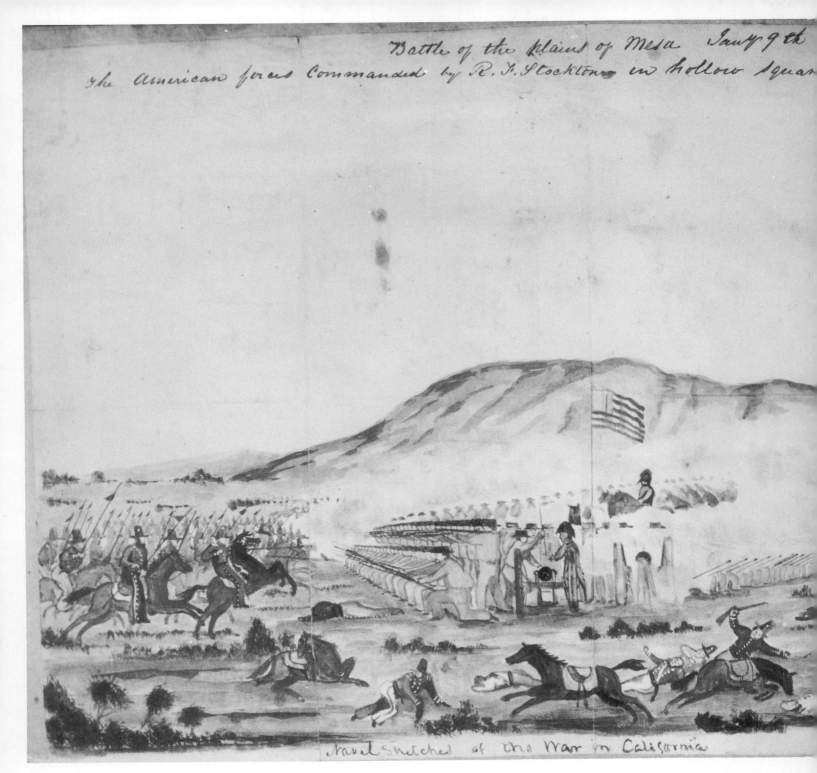

Battle of the Plains of Mesa Jan'y 9th. The American forces Commanded by R. F. Stockton in hollow Square

Naval Sketches of the War in California

BATTLE OF SACRAMENTO, FEB. 28TH 1847,
TERRIFIC CHARGE OF THE MEXICAN LANCERS.
Drawn from a sketch taken on the battle ground by E. B. Thomas, U. S. N.

545. BATTLE FOR LOS ANGELES. Summoned by Ensign E. F. Beale and Kit Carson, who stole through enemy line at San Pasqual, Navy reinforcements brought Kearny to San Diego. On Jan. 9, 1847, sailors, dragoons and settlers defeated forces of General Flores near Los Angeles. Sketch by Meyer.

546. BATTLE OF SACRAMENTO ended Upper California campaign. (Early lithograph by N. Currier, from on-the-spot sketch by "E. B. Thomas, U.S.N.") By Treaty of Cahuenga, defeated Mexicans surrendered all Upper California to Commodore Stockton. Victorious Americans had won huge jackpot.

charged by Gen'l Floras on to side

CENTRAL MEXICO
Invasion

547. BATTLE OF BUENA VISTA (February 22, 1847). After Taylor took Ciudad Monterrey, Polk shifted half his army to Vera Cruz expedition. Left in hole, "Rough and Ready" stubbornly drove to Buena Vista where his abbreviated force crushed the army of Santa Anna. Defeat left Mexico helpless.

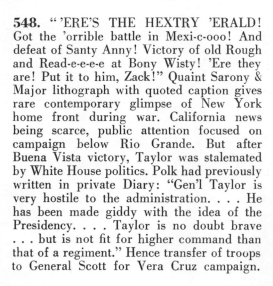

548. "'ERE'S THE HEXTRY 'ERALD! Got the 'orrible battle in Mexi-c-ooo! And defeat of Santy Anny! Victory of old Rough and Read-e-e-e-e at Bony Wisty! 'Ere they are! Put it to him, Zack!" Quaint Sarony & Major lithograph with quoted caption gives rare contemporary glimpse of New York home front during war. California news being scarce, public attention focused on campaign below Rio Grande. But after Buena Vista victory, Taylor was stalemated by White House politics. Polk had previously written in private Diary: "Gen'l Taylor is very hostile to the administration. . . . He has been made giddy with the idea of the Presidency. . . . Taylor is no doubt brave . . . but is not fit for higher command than that of a regiment." Hence transfer of troops to General Scott for Vera Cruz campaign.

THE ISLAND   OF LOBOS.

Rendezvous of the U.S. Army under General Scott, previous   to the Attack on Vera Cruz, February 9th 1847.

Drawn on the spot by   Lieut. C C Barton U.S Navy.

Published by P.S.Duval. N°7   Reade Alley, Philadelphia

550. FIRST LARGE-SCALE AMPHIBIOUS OPERATION IN U.S.N. history—and first major American landings on foreign soil—the Vera Cruz invasion! After conference between Commodore Conner and General Scott at Anton Lizardo fleet anchorage, Navy assumed charge of landings. Covered by gunboats, troops were placed on beach three miles from Vera Cruz. Begun morning of March 9, 1847, landings were concluded evening of 10th; 12,000 men safely ashore to tune of "Alice Gray," "Some Love to Roam" and "Hail Columbia!" Drawing by Lt. C. C. Barton, U.S.N. Rare print. (right)

549. ISLE OF THE WOLVES (LOBOS)—a rendezvous point for U. S. convoys off Vera Cruz. Above scene, dated February 9, 1847, was "Drawn on the spot by Lieut. C. C. Barton, U.S.N." and published by P. S. Duval, Philadelphia. Shown are four transports and (right) U. S. sloop *St. Mary's*. Part of Scott's invasion force. Ships under Com. Conner.

Vera Cruz
CAMPAIGN

551. GUNS GO ASHORE. Unopposed at beachhead, Scott's army went in with bands playing, colors flying under eye of Fortress San Juan de Ulloa (Contemporary litho.)

552. PADDLE FRIGATE *MISSISSIPPI* RIDES STORM. Down from Norfolk with Commodore M. C. Perry (replacement for Conner), Navy's No. 1 steam warship encountered a "norther." Frequent in area, storms had already downed brigs *Somers* and *Truxtun*. In tempest soon after one pictured, 23 transports were wrecked. *Mississippi* is shown going to relief of steamer *Hunter*, French blockade-runner (prize), off Vera Cruz. Contemporary Sarony & Major print is from drawing by Lt. Henry Walke, U.S.N., Navy's finest artist. (right)

March 24th	Potomac Gun 32 lb	St Mary's Gun 68 lb	Albany Gun 68 lb	Mississippi Gun 68 lb	Potomac Gun 32 lb	Barrican Gun
Capt J. H. Aulick	Comr A. S. Mackenzie	L C. H. A. H. Kennedy	L O. H. Perry	L S. S. Lee	L A. S. Baldwin	L H. Ingersoll
March 25th	ordinance officer					
Capt J Mayo	L J. S. Biddle	L C. Steedman	L S. B. Bissell	L Jr De Camp	L J. M. Frailey	L R. Semmes
			Mast Jn. Crossan			

553. ASSAULT ON VERA CRUZ—naval batteries. Six heavy naval guns were landed to support Army artillery under Captain Robert E. Lee. Navy's guns, commanded by Captain J. H. Aulick, included 8-inchers.

554. VERA CRUZ BOMBARDED—a contemporary view. City's defenses were feeble. During lulls in firing attackers could hear church bells ringing. In Mexico City, Santa Anna was vainly trying to raise relief army. "The enemy is but a handful; we are millions!" But neither church bells nor appeals could save Vera Cruz.

555. GUNBOATS OFF VERA CRUZ. Flotilla under Josiah Tattnall included (l. to r.) schooners *Falcon* and *Reefer*, steam gunboat *Vixen*, schooners *Petrel* and *Bonita*, steam gunboat *Spitfire* (flagship) and schooner *Tampico*. Close inshore they loaned fire support to Army. (From sketch by "J. M. Ladd, U.S.N.")

556. BLASTING OF SAN JUAN DE ULLOA. Sarony & Major lithograph picturing height of bombardment (morning of March 25th) inaccurately shows heavy ships close in.

Actually steam frigates (with vulnerable paddle wheels) and sloops kept distance. Close-range fire was delivered by Tattnall's gunboats. Disregarding Perry's retirement signal, Tattnall with little gunboat *Spitfire* hammered fort for half hour at 800 yards. Defenders surrendered Vera Cruz on afternoon of March 29th. Road to Mexico City lay wide open.

VERA CRUZ SEQUEL

557. INVOLVED IN RODEO AT ALVARADO—no horses, but a Navy goat. After fall of Vera Cruz, the road to Mexico City lay open, but American army lacked horses. Some 3,000 wagons coming ashore, and less than 1,000 draft animals available! Serious transport problem was accentuated by onset of yellow-fever season; to escape dreaded *vomito* on Tierra Caliente coast, Scott's army must hit highroad for mountainous interior as soon as possible. To overcome horse shortage, General Scott and Commodore Perry launched joint operation to capture port of Alvarado, 30 miles to south of Vera Cruz, where large horse herds had been reported. Overland marched General Quitman, his troops well supplied with halters and lassos. Down from Vera Cruz sailed Perry, flags flying, bands playing, guns loaded for heavy bombardment. As two previous attempts to seize Alvarado by sea had failed, Perry led a full-dress naval expedition. It was strategy dear to the Commodore's heart—Army to outflank the town while Navy's fleet blocked the harbor and sailors stormed in to the beach.

Then, surprise! On reaching objective, Perry found port in hands of little blockade gunboat *Scourge*, whose captain, a young Lieutenant Hunter, had on own initiative accepted town's surrender the day before. Above scene (excellent display of period uniforms) suggests meeting between Commodore and eager lieutenant. Perry's common sense deserted him; he had youthful officer court-martialed for acting without orders, also on claim that gunboat's intrusion had scared horses from Alvarado vicinity. Reviewing case, President Polk disapproved Lieutenant Hunter's dismissal from Navy, doubtless perceiving that if single gunboat could scare horses, Perry's fleet would have caused a stampede. Alvarado episode evoked wry verse from New York *Sun:*

> *"But not a soul was there to whip,*
> *Unless they fought a shadow,*
> *And so was spoiled the pretty sport,*
> *Of taking Alvarado."*

Sick Bay, Naval Vessel, 1845

558. NAVY VERSUS YELLOW JACK. Two sinister diseases plagued Navy in tropics. One, fought largely with futile method of censorship, would not be beaten until advent of penicillin in 1940's. Murderous Yellow Jack was conquered in Cuba 50 years after Mexican War. In both cases, Navy medicine contributed to ultimate victory. Bureau of Medicine and Surgery, founded in 1842, sent to Vera Cruz front such valiant men as Navy surgeon John Wright of brig *Somers* and Dr. Elisha Kane. Yellow Jack grinned at these doctors with their "loblolly boys" (pioneer Corps Men) fighting blindly against the Unknown. In Perry's fleet, losses mounted at alarming rate. Ship's doctors themselves were ready victims— at one time a single surgeon remained to serve seven warships. Blockading Tuxpan, Farragut reported ghastly struggle with Yellow Jack. Attacked by forces of "His Saffron Majesty," Navy fought the most heroic battles of the Mexican War. A costly effort.

U. S. Brig "Somers", of mutiny fame, goes down in "Norther" while blockading Vera Cruz; Raphael Semmes in command

Tabasco
CAMPAIGN

559. NAVAL ATTACK ON TUXPAN, MEXICO. While Scott's army drove for Mexico City, Navy tightened grip on Mexican coast. In April 1847 Perry led gunboats up Tuxpan River (left) to assail town. Flagship *Spitfire* is shown in lead of column below fort. As General Cos fled, sailors captured Tuxpan. (This and following Sarony & Major lithographs of Tabasco campaign record art work of Lt. Henry Walke, U.S.N. Art critics might agree naval line officer, talented, missed his calling.)

560. U. S. GUNBOATS ENTERING TABASCO RIVER (June 14, 1847). Navy had previously captured port of Frontera at river mouth. But guerilla activities brought Perry to this backwater in southern Mexico with expedition to seize Tabasco, 70 miles up river. Tabasco proved peppery. And Commo. Perry could now use some of power displayed to no purpose at Alvarado. But—gunboats forward! Those towing barges are *Spitfire* (flagship), *Vixen*, *Scorpion* and *Scourge*. ("Designed and drawn on stone by H. Walke, Lt., U.S.N.") (below)

561. UPSTREAM PUFFED THE STEAMERS towing small craft and boats laden with men from frigates *Mississippi, Raritan,* sloops *John Adams, Albany, Germantown,* brig *Decatur.* Note Mexican guerillas watching from concealment. (above)

562. U. S. GUNBOAT *SCORPION* UNDER FIRE. About 16 miles below Tabasco, Mexicans in jungle opened fire on lead steamer and bomb-brigs *Vesuvius* and *Washington. Scorpion's* heavy bow and pivot gun soon eradicated ambush. (picture, upper right)

563. JUNGLE BATTLE developed at point 9 miles below Tabasco where Mexicans had blocked river with obstructions. Perry promptly landed with 1,064 seamen and Marines, determined to fight way through chaparral to town. (picture in center)

564. *SCORPION* AND *SPITFIRE* TAKE TABASCO. While Perry's force slogged through jungle, Lt. David Dixon Porter of *Spitfire* blew barrier out of channel. Gunboats then raced to Tabasco. When Perry arrived town was under Porter. (far right)

565. U. S. ARMY ENTERING MEXICO CITY (Sept. 14, 1847). Cerro Gordo—Contreras—Churubusco—Molino del Rey—Scott's forces won battle after battle. After fall of Chapultepec, Santa Anna fled; Mexicans sued for peace. (below)

Sketches of the War in California Meyer

Lower California
C A M P A I G N

566. *DALE* FITTING OUT TENDER *LIBERTAD*. Vessel was chartered by *Dale's* skipper, Commander T. O. Selfridge; placed under Lieutenant T. A. M. Craven to operate as raider. Note scuttled Mexican vessel *Madelena* in background. (Sketch by Gunner Wm. Meyer of the *Dale*.)

567. U. S. WAR-SLOOP *DALE* at Lareto. Waging one of least-known campaigns in American history, Navy's Pacific Squadron invaded Lower California in autumn of 1847. Sketches of this campaign, perhaps only ones in existence, are by Gunner Wm. Meyer of *Dale* on locale.

568. U. S. SHIP-OF-LINE *COLUMBUS* (Commodore Biddle), returning from Japan, reinforced Pacific Squadron. Ship-of-line *Independence* also joined squadron; blockaded Guaymas and Mazatlan in autumn, 1847.

569. BATTLE IN GUAYMAS was fought by *Dale* men; sketched by Gunner Meyer. Mazatlan fell next. San Blas was captured in January 1848. War with Mexico ended where it began—California. Golden prize.

Ship of the line "Columbus"

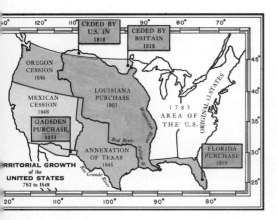

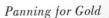

570. CALIFORNIA, HERE WE COME! Covered wagons rolled westward even as ink dried on Treaty of Guadalupe Hidalgo. Formally ending Mexican War, treaty was diplomatic freak. Nation's only major treaty which bears but one American signature, it was negotiated unofficially by private citizen. (American envoy to Mexico, Nicholas Trist had been re-called by President Polk at Scott's request. However, Trist mended quarrel with General by gift of jar of jelly, whereupon Scott regretted envoy's dismissal; urged him to deal with Mexicans *ex officio*.) When Senate voted to accept Trist's terms, U. S. gained title to vast western domain— millions of acres at less than three cents an acre! Entire Southwest!

571. AMERICA COAST TO COAST. Gaining vast area shown, United States spanned the continent. With refreshing candor War Secretary W. L. Marcy coined maxim, "to the victor belong the spoils," proposing that U. S. take all of Mexico and seize Cuba in bargain. Public reaction was adverse. Mexico was paid $15,000,000 for lost territory; additional sum was paid for strip of southern New Mexico (Gadsden Purchase). But a cloud hung over new territory—would it be slave or free? Question led up to the greatest conflict in nation's history.

572. AMERICAN CONSCIENCE WAS TROUBLED by Mexican War. No argument or military excuse could alter fact U. S. invaded Mexico. Honest Americans deplored conquest

MEXICAN WAR
Aftermath

as one aimed to expand South's slave empire. Congressman Abe Lincoln called it "a war unnecessarily and unconstitutionally begun by the President." Years later Grant wrote: "I do not think there was ever a more wicked war than that waged by the U. S. on Mexico." And John C. Calhoun (no pacifist) observed he could "plunge a dagger into his heart" before he blamed Mexico as aggressor. Hence grim cartoon of General Scott when he entered presidential race.

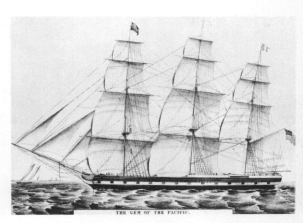

THE GEM OF THE PACIFIC.

573. EXPRESSING APPROVAL OF NAVAL EFFORT, ship lithographs by N. Currier were popular in 1849. Navy's Mexican War record was not marred (as was Army's) by vandalism of troops or by political finagling of top leaders. Blockade operations— logistics effort which maintained 900-mile Pensacola-to-Vera Cruz supply line—amphibious work at Vera Cruz —California invasion operations— Navy's endeavors were up to mark. By opening West Coast ports to lively foreign and domestic trade, Navy pushed great shipping boom. (above)

Panning for Gold

574. "THERE'S GOLD IN THEM THERE HILLS!" Nuggets as big as bullets! Dust for everybody! On January 24, 1848 (just nine days before peace treaty with Mexico was signed) a settler at Sutter's Mill hit jackpot. Scouts had previously reported gold in California. Franciscan monks had espied it. But nothing like this bonanza! For six weeks the strike at Sutter's was guarded secret. Then news exploded as billion-dollar bombshell. It was El Dorado—Treasure Land—Rainbow's End! To Californy raced the "Forty-Niners." And 'Frisco Harbor became a Sargasso of abandoned vessels as shown in this 1852 daguerreotype view—ships rotting at anchor, crews over the hill from cabin boy to skipper. Sail the sea with all that pay dirt inland? All hands ashore to pry open Golden Gate!

575. 'FRISCO HARBOR DURING GOLD RUSH. In July 1848 Lieutenant E. F. Beale, U.S.N., raced overland from West Coast to Washington to confirm news nation had struck it rich. Greatest gold rush since days of Coronado turned sleepy California into bedlam. Rioting gold hunters slew Sutter family in battle to stake out claims. Miners, tinhorns, outlaws, prospectors swarmed into territory. Some speculators (like Frémont) made fortunes out of land. Others profited on lumber and supplies. Within five years of Mexican surrender, San Francisco was boom city complete with harbor ferries, hotels, Barbary Coast. While merchant crews deserted on waterfront, Navy continued to sail. (In 1850, Government procured Mare Island in San Pablo Bay 35 miles NE of 'Frisco for base.)

MEXICAN WAR AFTERMATH. California gold mines were worth $166,000,000—total cost of war to United States. Cost to Mexico, including territories, left vanquished country bankrupt. About 10,000 Mexicans died in battle defending their homeland. According to modern Defense Department, U. S. Army losses were about 2,000, plus 11,000 dead of disease; U. S. Navy lost only one man killed in action, three sailors wounded. (Commodore Knox and other naval historians suggest Navy's battle deaths numbered 15 or 20.) Authorities agree Yellow Jack took surprisingly light toll in U. S. fleet. As for territory gained, never had American armed forces won so much at cost of so little. But slavery issue remained— a deadly due bill awaiting final settlement—an economic drag on nation.

The Fabulous '50's

NAVY IN MID-NINETEENTH CENTURY

The U.S.A. was going places in 1850. From Maine to everywhere. The West teemed with covered wagon's (California's population grew from 82,000 in 1850 to 207,000 in 1852.) Southern rivers came alive with cotton-hauling steamboats. Fast becoming industrialized, the free-state North also boomed. The American was Aladdin, and an inquiring mind was his wonderful lamp. Vulcanized rubber, the sewing machine, gaslights, the telegraph, the rotary press— Washington's Patent Office was swamped with mechanical marvels, amazing gadgets, miraculous inventions. To Europe went Mr. Goodyear with rubber boots; to England went Mr. McCormick with his reaper. Manufacturing, importing, exporting, Americans of the 1850's garnered the largest foreign trade in the nation's history. And U. S. Navy took the stage in a new, dramatic role. Sea warrior and home defender, commerce protector, diplomat, explorer, policeman, the Navy man now assumed still another character. In 1850 the sailor became a salesman.

Naval Salesmanship

PERRY OPENS JAPAN

576. WHALING OVERTURE. For 200 years the Japanese had remained world's champion isolationists. When Yankee whalers in hot pursuit of Moby Dicks were wrecked on Japan's shores, they were jailed. In 1846 Commo. Biddle was ordered to Nippon to investigate affairs. (above)

577. PIONEER VISITOR TO NIPPON—Commodore James Biddle, U.S.N. Skipper of *Hornet* in War of 1812, captain of sloop *Ontario* dispatched to claim Oregon territory in 1817, Biddle led Navy's East India Squadron to Japan. As a forceful "salesman," he almost opened door.

578. *COLUMBUS* AND *VINCENNES* AT YEDO. As shown in old print, Japanese warcraft surrounded Biddle's boats and politely asked American visitors to depart. (right)

579. COMMODORE MATTHEW CALBRAITH PERRY—"Opener of Japan." President Millard Fillmore selected sagely when he chose Perry for leader of full-dress expedition to Nippon. At stake: lucrative foreign trade—American pots and pans in exchange for Japanese trinkets and silks. Study of Nipponese customs convinced Fillmore's advisers theatricals were in demand. American lead must be played by someone capable of pomp and circumstance—a mastodon of dignity. Only such an envoy could out-face the inaccessible Mikado. As photograph suggests, in "Father of Steam Navy" the U. S. Government had its man. Made from an early Brady daguerreotype, this 1848 portrait is fine character study of officer known as "Old Bruin."

580. U.S.S. *MISSISSIPPI* off the Bonin Islands (June 1853). Carrying on where Biddle and Captain James Glynn, U.S.N., left off, Perry was instructed to "explore coasts of Japan" as a possible "means of extending our commercial relations." And to "use force only as last resort." As Japs received but one ship (Dutch) per year, Perry had a "selling" problem.

581. PERRY'S SQUADRON IN YEDO (TOKYO) BAY—July 8, 1853. Colors flying, Perry sailed boldly in with frigates *Susquehanna* (flagship) and *Mississippi*, war-sloops *Saratoga* and *Plymouth*. Accompanying views are by expedition artists.

582. OUTDOING GILBERT AND SULLIVAN THEATRICALS, American naval officers and Japanese Pooh-Bahs staged fantastic meeting at Gora-Hama. Calling himself "Lord of the Forbidden Interior," Perry played high "face cards," demanded prompt reception by top princes of the realm.

583. PERRY MEETS THE PRINCES
—July 14, 1853. Condescending to
deliver letter from U. S. President to
Japanese Mikado, Commodore Perry
landed at Gora-Hama to meet the
Princes Idzu and Iwami. Displaying
stupendous pomp and devastating
dignity, "Old Bruin" out-princed
both princes. Next year he returned.

584. PERRY LANDS AT YOKU-
HAMA—March 8, 1854. Squadron
now contains *Susquehanna, Mississippi*, new steam frigate *Powhatan*,
and sail warships *Macedonian, Vandalia, Southampton* and *Lexington*.
Perry is tipping hat to Imperial party.

585. PARADES AND FOLDEROL
climaxed signing of first Japanese-
American treaty on March 31, 1854.
Scene shows Perry marching back to
ship after visit to Prince Regent.
Treaty contained trade agreements,
opened Jap ports to U. S. vessels.

586. EXERCISING U. S. TROOPS
IN SIMODA TEMPLE GROUNDS.
Perry purposely flaunted military display; ordered numerous broadside
salutes. Rightly he suspected Sho-
guns would be impressed by gunnery.

587. U. S. PADDLE SLOOP *POW-HATAN*—"show ship" of Perry's squadron. Commissioned in 1851, she was Navy's finest. Visiting Japs went bug-eyed at splendid vessel; then (in sailor lingo) pie-eyed after banquet.

As Japanese Saw It

588. A M E R I C A N S THROUGH JAPANESE EYES. Exhibiting fine artistry, a "Son of Heaven" produced this lively picture of visiting "barbarians" on parade. Although highly stylized, Japanese art compared favorably with European and American. But culture, based on Emperor-worship, was ultra - nationalistic, warlike.

589. JAPANESE POR-TRAIT OF PERRY. Artist flattered great "Western Lord" by endowing him with Japanese features. Japan flattered him by signing valuable commercial treaty.

590. SAMPLING WEST-ERN CIVILIZATION. "Tom Thumb" railroad charmed Japanese. So did pistols, telegraph, farm tools, whiskey. After bibulous *Powhatan* banquet, one Nip assured Perry, "Japanese and Americans all one same heart!"

Barge of the

Commissioners

591. FIRST JAPANESE EMBASSY TO UNITED STATES—Washington Navy Yard, May 1860. Ambassador Shinni (third from right) and entourage were brought from Japan by U.S.S. *Powhatan* and *Roanoke*. Arrival of Japs in Washington occasioned more Gilbert and Sullivan ceremony. No one guessed at time Nippon would soon rule Far East; that U. S. Navy had opened a "Pandora's Box." Notable Navy figures in picture: Lt. D. D. Porter (at left in civvies, full beard, straw hat); C. H. McBlair (two-striper beside Porter); Captain S. F. Du Pont (center in civvies, stovepipe hat); Captain Franklin Buchanan, Commandant Navy Yard (behind Ambassador). Shinni seems intelligently interested, but other Japs eye camera as though expecting sinister explosion. Or were they staring with clairvoyance into 20th century? (Assumed Brady photo.)

China Conflict

592. IN BATTLE AT CANTON IN 1856—U. S. war-sloop *Portsmouth*. Opposed to despotic Manchu regime, Chinese peasant leader Hung Hsiu-chüan, proclaiming himself "Younger Brother of Jesus Christ," roused insurrection. U. S. supported British policy favoring Manchu rule. When Chinese forts below Canton fired on British warships, U.S.S. *Portsmouth* and *Levant* were ordered into action. Americans stormed the forts; captured 176 cannon. Chinese lost 250 men in hot bottle; U. S. Navy, 29.

593. BOMBARDING CANTONESE FORTS—U.S.S. *Portsmouth* and *Levant* in action. Note steam tug in foreground towing landing barges in to beach. Assault was led by Commander Andrew H. Foote. (below)

Chinese war junks

594. U. S. STEAM SLOOP *SAN JACINTO* (Commo. James Armstrong) led squadron in China waters. Late in 1856, she hovered near Tientsin while American envoy, Dr. Peter Parker, dickered with Manchu rulers. (Parker wanted U. S. to seize Formosa at this time, but Government under President Pierce said no. Japs took island in 1895.)

595. U. S. STEAM FRIGATE *MINNESOTA* joined U. S. squadron off China coast in 1858. New screw-driven 40-gunner, she served under

Commo. Josiah Tattnall, who aided British naval forces attacking Tientsin. After Chinese resistance collapsed, Americans came in on favorable port rights, commercial treaty.

Special Missions

STEAM-CANVAS NAVY TROTS GLOBE

596. TO PRUSSIA AS NAVAL ADVISOR went U. S. frigate *St. Lawrence* in 1849. Mission: to help found German Navy. As in Japan's case, U. S. unwittingly fostered a Frankenstein which would one day have to be drowned. The invisible future!

597. TO NICARAGUA in 1854 went U. S. war-sloop *Cyane* (Commander G. N. Hollins) to settle affair in which American Minister Solon E. Borland had been hit over head with a bottle. Hollins avenged this insult by blowing British Greytown off the map. A bombardment rather rough on natives who were innocent bystanders to British-American struggle to control Nicaragua, Mosquito Coast and possible Trans-Isthmian canal.

598. TO ARCTIC WENT NAVY-LED GRINNELL EXPEDITION in search of English explorer. American Henry Grinnell eased Nicaragua tension by offering vessels *Advance* and *Rescue* for expedition to find Sir John Franklin, lost in polar Canada. Neither first expedition, led by Lt. E. J. de Haven, nor second, led by Dr. Elisha Kane, could find Franklin. Kane group (in photo) set "farthest north" record. (Kane with telescope.)

599. TO EGYPT FOR CAMELS went Navy storeship *Supply* in 1856. Resembling Noah's Ark, vessel returned to Indianola, Texas; unloaded 35 camels. Animals were sent to Fort Defiance, N. M., for experimental transport work in Army. As top sergeants and camels did not get along, herd was eventually sold. Startled Americans later saw camels in remote corners of Southwest—probably descendants of "desert ships" brought in by Lt. D. D. Porter (picture above).

600. TO PARAGUAY ON POLICE MISSION went U. S. squadron in 1859, demanding redress for shots fired at U. S. gunboat *Water Witch* (below). Assailed while surveying Paraná River (after Paraguayans had given permission) *Water Witch* was hulled ten times, her helmsman killed. Supported by seven warships, and 12 gunboats, *Water Witch* and *Fulton II* steamed to Asunción. Dictator Lopez promptly paid indemnities; hastily signed new U. S. trade agreement.

601. TO NICARAGUA FOR WILLIAM WALKER went U. S. war-sloop *St. Mary's* (at left). With "unofficial" U. S. support, soldier-of-fortune Walker launched revolution in Nicaragua, then went too far by seizing transit line controlled by Cornelius Vanderbilt. He was deported by Commodore Hiram Paulding, who was punished for action by President James Buchanan. Paulding was returned to command by Lincoln.

602. TO DAVY JONES' LOCKER in 1854 went U. S. war-sloop *Albany* —one of 14 Navy vessels lost through disaster in decade and half preceding Civil War. Losses included paddle frigates *Missouri* and *Fulton II*, steam cruiser *Princeton*, sloops *Concord*, *Peacock*, *Boston*, *Yorktown*, *Levant*, *Albany*, brigs *Porpoise*, *Truxtun*, *Somers*, schooners *Shark* and *Grampus*. Fire and explosion finished two largest of these men-o'-war; rest were lost through storm or navigational error—reminder that "Old Devil Sea" was and ever shall be Navy's first enemy. In gale like that pictured in N. Currier lithograph (below right), *Albany* foundered with all hands. Another battle lost in interminable war against forces of wind and wave.

603. TO AFRICA VERSUS SLAVERS went U. S. steam sloop *Mohican* in 1860 (right) one of new screw-driven 10-gunners of type corresponding to today's light cruiser. Armed with 11-inch smoothbores, she made powerful reinforcement for antislave patrol squadron which at time included heavy sloop, *San Jacinto*, sail sloops *Constellation*, *Portsmouth* and *Saratoga*, steam gunboats *Sumter* and *Mystic*. Big boom in Southern cotton spurred slave-running. But capture of 12 slave-runners in 1860 put decided crimp in odious "blackbirding" game.

604. TO SEATTLE TO FIGHT INDIANS went U. S. war-sloop *Decatur* in 1856 (below) when Nez Percé, enraged by treaty, attacked Puget Sound settlement. After shore bombardment, Jack Tars landed to drive Red Men from coastal area. Cutlass against tomahawk—one of Navy's last Indian fights. *Decatur* vs. Old Joseph.

605. BATTLEWAGON OF LATE 1850's—U.S.S. *Wabash*. Commissioned at decade's end, this screw-driven, auxiliary-sail, 3,274-ton steam frigate was finest of class which included new *Minnesota, Merrimack,* *Roanoke* and *Colorado*. Back-acting tandem engines and Martin boilers of water-tube "superheater" type comprised power plant which could drive her at 9 knots. She mounted 44 guns. "Palace ship" of fleet. (left)

IMPROVED
Weapons

606. BIGGER BANG FOR A BUCK —in late 1850's. Scene: Washington Navy Yard, Experimental Ordnance Test Battery. Basically primitive until mid 19th Century, naval ordnance was given sudden boost by Army Captain T. J. Rodman, who devised gauge to measure explosive forces of cannon powder; designed a tapering barrel to conform with "pressure curve." He also devised foundry method of cooling gun's bore so that exterior metal, hardening slowly, would shrink to reinforce the interior. Soon adopted by Navy, the Rodman 15-incher was largest gun afloat. Simultaneously the rifled gun appeared. An ancient device, rifling was reintroduced by ex-artillery officer R. J. Parrott. Parrott also exploited the hooped or "built-up" gun breech patented by Harvard

Professor Daniel Treadwell in 1842. Meantime, best of new naval guns was designed by Navy's own ordnance expert, Comdr. John A. Dahlgren, who had reported to Washington Navy Yard in 1847. In charge of department manufacturing Hale's rockets, Dahlgren discovered "curve of pressure" through independent experiments; in 1850 designed a bottle-shaped smoothbore which combined best features of Rodman metallurgy and reinforced breech. As shown in old print (below) new guns were tested by practice battery in Washington Yard. Note experimental breech-loader (at left) which set design for future. Like Rodman and Parrott guns, the Dahlgren was a muzzle-loader with fire-control operation of Paul Jones vintage. But the 11-inch Dahlgren "soda bottle" (big gun in picture), firing solid shot with 30-pound charge, made Navy's 1860 batteries most authoritative on sea.

607. NEW YORK NAVY YARD— masthead from *Gleason's Weekly*. Popular in Navy of late 1850's, *Gleason's* was largely devoted to nautical subjects. However, in hot-tempered era, *Gleason's* maintained a highly nationalistic tone, beating drum for American imperialism. At this stage of American history, Britain was held to be U. S. Enemy No. 1. Propaganda—newly used as a "cold war" weapon—aimed many a broadside at England. Example: accompanying article from *Gleason's* of November 1858, recalling horrors of Red Coat prisons, Revolutionary War.

13, 1858.

NAVY YARD AT BROOKLYN, N. Y.

Our spirited picture of the Brooklyn Navy Yard conveys a correct idea of that greatest of American Naval depots—or rather we should say of a portion of it, for the entire yard covers an area of forty-five acres, and it would require a whole series of illustrations to do justice to the numerous objects of interest which are to be seen there. The location is on the south side of Wallabout Bay, the original Dutch name of which was *Waalbogt*. By the way—the first settlement of Brooklyn was made in 1625, near this spot, by the Dutch West India Company, who called the town *Breukelin*, and established there a colony of Walloons, to cultivate the soil. And we may as well mention now that from 1776 to 1782, the British kept in Wallabout Bay the pestilential prison hulks in which during that time, more than eleven thousand five hundred American sailors and citizens miserably perished of disease and starvation.

The bodies of that immense multitude of victims were flung promiscuously into holes made upon the sandy beach, or, with even greater indecency, thrown overboard. Washed by the tide, the sand soon gave up the putrifying remains, and many of the corpses which had been consigned to the sea, were cast upon the shore— a disgusting reproach to the inhumanity of the British officials. The most earnest representations and remonstrances were made by the American Commander-in-Chief, Gen. Washington, to the British General in regard to the prison hulks; and the dirt and filth and bad ventilation of those vile dens, and the treatment of the Americans confined there, were contrasted with the comfortable quarters and good treatment of his British prisoners, but in vain.

The quantities of cannon, cannon-balls, and other munitions of naval warfare, in the Brooklyn Navy Yard are immense. More than enough men are kept daily at work, there, than would be necessary to populate a good-sized town. The two buildings on the extreme left of the picture are ship-houses. Each of these is 250 feet long, 125 feet wide and 120 feet high, and is sufficient to admit of the largest size man-of-war's being built within it. But the grandest feature is the Naval Dry Dock. The construction of it occupied a large number of workmen sixteen years. Its foundation is 406 feet long by 120 feet wide. The bottom of its basin is 286 feet long and 30 feet wide; and the top 307 feet long by 98 feet wide. An admirable Naval Lyceum and a Marine Hospital are connected with the Yard.

PAGING
Jules Verne

608. ROCKET TO THE MOON? SUBMARINE? Rivaling Jules Verne fantasy is vessel shown above in one of rarest marine photographs in existence. This is Winan's Iron Steamer or "Cigar Ship," launched in Baltimore in 1858. Displacing 350 tons, vessel was 180 feet long, 16 wide in midsection. Steered by rudders at either end, she was powered by four engines; driven by flanged "ring" which circled her amidships. Note topside observation deck; vents for exhaust. Designed to operate semi-submerged, "Cigar Ship" carried 20 passengers on fast run to England in 1859. Pre-Civil War marvel, craft has the earmarks of a 20th-century sub.

Dark Horizon, 1860

609. TRANSATLANTIC TELEGRAPH. In 1854 American engineer Cyrus Field conceived idea; won assistance of Navy Department and Commander Maury. With services of U. S. steam sloop *Niagara*, hydrographic information from Maury and aid from Royal Navy, cable was laid by 1858. In mutual effort, U.S.S. *Niagara* and H.M.S. *Agamemnon* are shown completing job on cross-ocean telegraph line. (Picture from cover of "Atlantic Telegraph Polka" which set event to music.) British cooperation might have healed old wounds left by Revolution, inaugurated era of good feeling, but for sour notes of Oregon squabble and Tory diplomacy during Civil War. Even so, cable proved tie to England. Field said Maury "furnished brains" for job.

610. ARGUMENT OVER A PIG almost exploded war between U. S. and England in 1859. Property of Hudson Bay Co., pig was shot by American settler on tiny island near Vancouver. Resulting row raised echoes of old Oregon-border dispute; American troops were rushed to island; Britain sent five warships to scene. Perhaps presence in Pacific of new U. S. steam cruiser *Lancaster* (right) calmed Vancouver waters and invited peaceful arbitration. Pig incident, reflecting hair-trigger tempers of period, was soon forgotten by nation in throes of dire upheaval.

Ship-types in Boston Harbor, circa 1855

611. STORMCLOUDS OVER AMERICA. While frontiersmen settled West, baleful dissension steadily undermined the Republic. Was Federal Government to be more powerful than State Government? Could a Democracy tolerate Negro slavery? With industrial North outstripping South's backward social system, nation was developing "split personality." Most Navy men were remote from situation. But in 1850's Navy wardrooms were worried by rumors of the widening North-South rift.

612. BROADSIDES ON HOME FRONT, posters (above) stirred New England in early 1850's. In Missouri guns flamed as Abolitionist fought slaveowner. John Brown stalked in Kansas. While fugitive slaves were sheltered in Washington, D. C., across the Potomac in Alexandria, Virginia, Negro girls were sold like horses at auction. Navy men, uneasy, read *Uncle Tom's Cabin,* or discussed *The Impending Crisis*—book published in 1857 by North Carolinian who noted that South was going bankrupt through plantation-slave economy. Everyone quoted Abe Lincoln of Illinois. Campaigning for President in 1860, Lincoln observed: "This government divided into free and slave states cannot long endure."

614. NAVY ON THE EVE. As nation broke asunder and Confederacy formed, storm rocked the U. S. Navy. After Confederates opened fire on Fort Sumter in Charleston harbor, war was inevitable. Thanks to sub-

VOTERS, Read This!

EXTRACT FROM A
SPEECH
DELIVERED BY THE
Hon. Daniel Webster,
IN THE SENATE OF THE UNITED STATES,
ON THE 7th OF MARCH, 1850.

"If the infernal Fanatics and Abolitionists ever get the power in their hands, they will override the Constitution, set the Supreme Court at defiance, change and make Laws to suit themselves. They will lay violent hands on those who differ with them politically in opinion, or dare question their infallibility; bankrupt the country and finally deluge it with blood."

versive work by Secretary Toucey, few U. S. naval vessels were in American waters in fatal April of '61. Of Navy's 90 ships, 48 were not in commission. Only 12 were at home. Picture by "Jas. La Jones" of *Dale*

RALLY SPIRITS OF '76!

ALL CITIZENS OF
LEOMINSTER,
without distinction of party, who disapprove of the
"Nebraska Iniquity,"
are requested to meet at the
TOWN HALL,
Monday Evening, July 10th,
AT 7 O'CLOCK,
to choose delegates to meet in a
Mass Convention,
at Worcester, the 20th inst., to teach the "South" we have a "North," and will maintain our CONSTITUTIONAL RIGHTS.
CALEB C. FIELD, LEONARD BURRAGE, MERRITT WOOD.
Leominster, July 6, 1854.

613. COMMANDER HENRY WALKE struck one of first naval blows against disunion. When South Carolina leaders, outraged at Lincoln's election to Presidency, announced State's secession in December 1860, Florida politicians directly followed suit. On January 12, 1861 (three months before Sumter) a small rebel force seized Pensacola Navy Yard from doddering Commodore James Armstrong. Commanding U. S. storeship *Supply* at Pensacola, Walke resisted seizure; rushed ammunition to nearby Fort Pickens. He was immediately court-martialed by Naval Secretary Isaac Toucey, a secret secession sympathizer. But artist who created finest pictures of Mexican War soon won renown in Civil War

portrays warship types in Navy at nation's zero hour—screw-driven steam sloop, paddle gunboat, paddle frigate, sail sloop. Wooden vessels on eve of Iron Age, these were ships that sailed for the Union into Civil War.

Chapter VII

THE CIVIL WAR

Was it the duty of a Navy man to go with his state or stay with the nation? With this enormous question the Civil War split the Navy. A number of officers formally resigned. A number of captains relinquished their warships to Federal authorities. But some merely quit the national service and headed South. Enlisted men were induced to desert. From Carolina to Texas, naval stations were freely delivered to "Secesh" militia. Pensacola was handed over by Commodore James Armstrong. When U.S.S. *Brooklyn* arrived to support Fort Pickens, Captain H. A. Adams signed a meek truce with Confederate General Bragg. A Mobile mob hanged a man sent there to purchase supplies for *Brooklyn*. Adams sat inert. So did Commodore C. S. McCauley when Marines and seamen at Norfolk staged open mutiny. In Washington the Navy Department was riddled with subversion. Directives smothered—bases sabotaged—vessels abandoned—arsenals looted! All this before the shooting at Fort Sumter sparked the Secession effort to overthrow the U.S. Government by force of arms.

Sixteen captains, 39 commanders, 76 lieutenants, 111 midshipmen —one-sixth of the Navy's officer corps went over to the Confederacy. Departees included Commander Matthew Maury of the Naval Observatory; Captain George A. Magruder, Chief of the Ordnance Bureau; Captain Josiah Tattnall of Mexican War fame; Captain Franklin Buchanan, Commandant, Washington Navy Yard. But there were Southerners who stood by the "old flag." Among them: Captain David G. Farragut, Tennesseean, and Captain Percival Drayton of South Carolina. Also Captain John A. Winslow, Carolinian, and Captain S. P. Lee (General Lee's cousin) of Virginia.

The U.S. Navy, hard hit, was far from scuttled. For the fleet remained. And behind it, Northern industry. The Confederacy's leaders monstrously miscalculated the sea-power factor. It was as simple as the inventory of a country store. To stay in business the South had to import manufactured goods and export cotton. This meant shipping. With only a sketchy merchant service, and no means to defend it, the Confederates blindly opened fire. They meant to create a navy? Build warships? In all the South there wasn't a single plant which could manufacture a marine engine!

Overlooking evidence that harbor forts were sitting ducks for fleet bombardment, Southern leaders believed the Southern seaports could withstand naval invasion. But how was the Confederacy's ocean-going foreign trade to be maintained? No one in Richmond had adequate answer, for blockade runners were not enough. Ultimately Confederate commerce was ruined and the South was sunk—at sea and in the waterways—by Mr. Lincoln's blockade and by the jugular thrust through the Mississippi . . . The Civil War story in a gun-shell.

615. MATHEW B. BRADY, GREATEST CIVIL WAR PHOTOGRAPHER, produced first photographs of Navy in action. Without Army-Navy aid, Brady financed and conducted a camera campaign which left him bankrupt. But his efforts gave the world a new art. His war photos (and those taken by Alexander Gardner, G. N. Barnard, Timothy O'Sullivan and other Brady assistants) remain classics. And his documentary coverage of the War of '61 stands as a work without parallel.

616. PROBLEM FACING U.S. NAVY is shown by chart. From Chesapeake to Brownsville, Texas, extends 3,549 miles of sea frontier, containing the great Southern seaports—Norfolk, Wilmington, Charleston, Port Royal, Savannah, Fernandina, Pensacola, Mobile, New Orleans, Galveston. Plus vast problem of the Mississippi. Blockade and river campaigns demanded major naval operation— launched with 8 available warships!

For four years, the armies of the Potomac and Northern Virginia fought a futile war of maneuver, first one and then the other threatening each other's capital. (Both Lincoln and Davis were hyper-sensitive about Washington City and Richmond). Thus a bloody stalemate. The effective strategic strangleholds were applied on the waterways—the Gulf-Atlantic Blockade, the Mississippi amputation and the thrusts through gulf ports.

So many millions of words have been written about the battles of Virginia that to most people this spells out the Civil War. Actually there were two wars as shown by the mini-charts (right and below). One was the BATTLES FOR THE CAPITALS, the other, the less-publicized but far more important war of attrition.

As to the effectiveness of the Blockade itself, a theory (more sensational than factual) has been recently advanced re, the Blockade "that failed." Mahan gave the best answer to this in 1889. Said he, (1.) ". . . extent of a sea-coast is a source of strength or weakness . . . Had the South had a people as numerous as it was warlike, and a navy commensurate to its other resources as a sea-power the great extent of its sea coast and its numerous inlets would have been elements of great strength." (2.), "The . . . United States . . . justly prided themselves on the effectiveness of the block-ade of the whole Southern seacoast. It was a great feat, a very great feat; but it would have been impossible had the Southerners been more numerous, and a nation of seamen." (3.), "Scattered unsupported along the coast, the U. S. ships kept their places singly or in small detachments . . . Had there been a Southern navy to profit by such advantages . . . the latter could not have been distributed as they were . . . But as the Southern coast, from its extent and many inlets, might have been a source of strength so from those very characteristics, it became a fruitful source of injury." And finally Mahan said, (4.), "Never did sea power play a greater or more decisive part than in the contest which determined . . . the existence of one great nation, instead of several rival States, in the North American continent."

MAP SHOWING SOUTHERN STATES IN ORDER OF SECESSION. BLACK LINE SHOWS NORTHERN BOUNDARY OF CONFEDERACY. TONE SHOWS TERRITORY CONTROLLED BY U.S. FORCES IN JULY 1861. PERTINENT ACTIONS SHOWN ARE FOR PERIOD TO END OF 1861. ANCHOR INDICATES NAVAL ACTIONS.

BULL RUN — RICH MOUNTAIN — BATTLES FOR THE CAPITALS — HATTERAS INLET — PORT ROYAL — TYBEE ISLAND — BLOCKADE

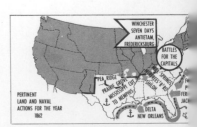

WINCHESTER — SEVEN DAYS — ANTIETAM, FREDERICKSBURG — BATTLES FOR THE CAPITALS — PEA RIDGE — PRAIRIE GROVE — MISSISSIPPI CITY — MEMPHIS — SHILOH — DELTA — NEW ORLEANS — PERTINENT LAND AND NAVAL ACTIONS FOR THE YEAR 1862

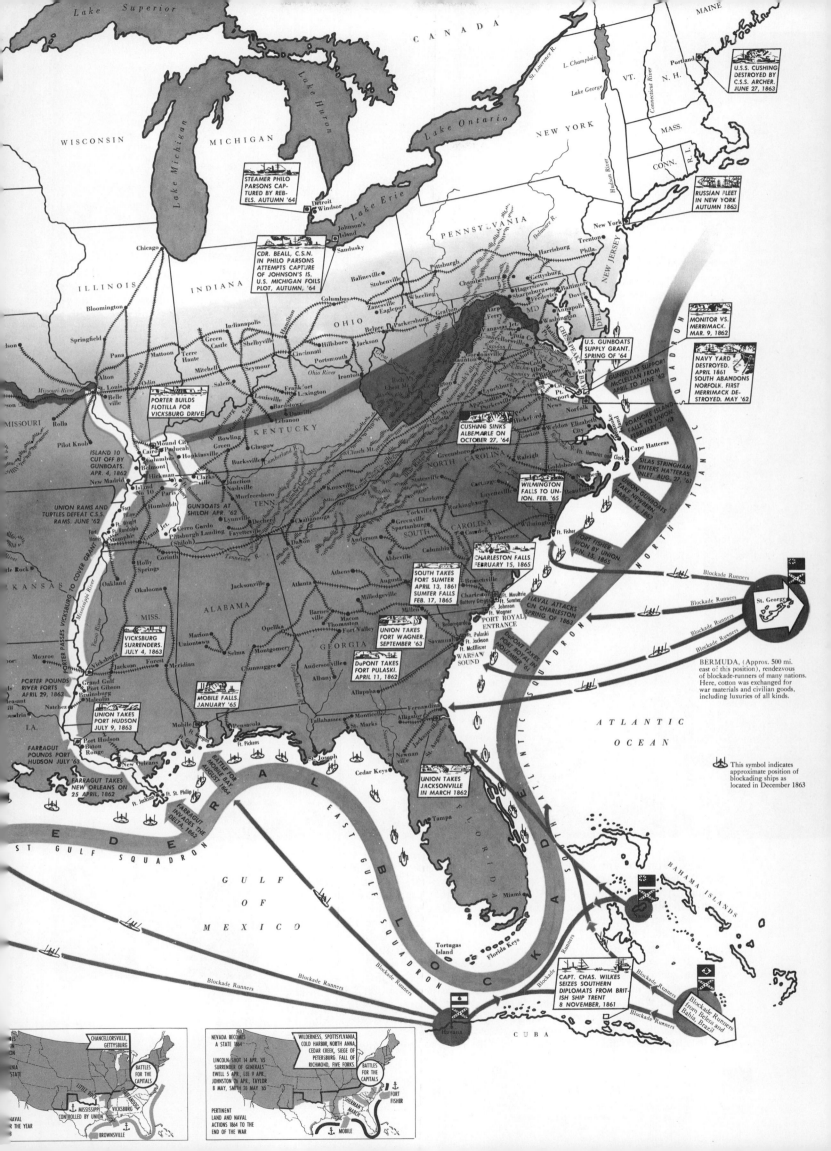

U.S.S. CUSHING DESTROYED BY C.S.S. ARCHER. JUNE 27, 1863

RUSSIAN FLEET IN NEW YORK AUTUMN 1863

STEAMER PHILO PARSONS CAPTURED BY REBELS. AUTUMN '64

CDR. BEALL, C.S.N. IN PHILO PARSONS ATTEMPTS CAPTURE OF JOHNSON'S IS. U.S. MICHIGAN FOILS PLOT, AUTUMN, '64

MONITOR VS. MERRIMACK. MAR. 9, 1862

U.S. GUNBOATS SUPPLY GRANT. SPRING OF '64

NAVY YARD DESTROYED. APRIL 1861 SOUTH ABANDONS NORFOLK. FIRST MERRIMACK DESTROYED. MAY '62

PORTER BUILDS FLOTILLA FOR VICKSBURG DRIVE

CUSHING SINKS ALBEMARLE ON OCTOBER 27, '64

ROANOKE ISLAND FALLS TO UNION. FEBRUARY 7, '62

SILAS STRINGHAM ENTERS HATTERAS INLET. AUG. 27, '61

ISLAND 10 CUT OFF BY GUNBOATS. APR. 4, 1862

UNION GUNBOATS TAKE NEWBERN MARCH 14, 1862

UNION RAMS AND TURTLES DEFEAT C.S.S. RAMS. JUNE '62

GUNBOATS AT SHILOH APR. '62

WILMINGTON FALLS TO UNION. FEB. '65

FORT FISHER WON BY UNION. JAN. 15, 1865

Blockade Runners

St. George

CHARLESTON FALLS FEBRUARY 15, 1865

SOUTH TAKES FORT SUMTER APRIL 13, 1861 SUMTER FALLS FEB. 17, 1865

NAVAL ATTACKS ON CHARLESTON SPRING OF 1863

Blockade Runners

Blockade Runners

PORTER POUNDS RIVER FORTS APRIL 29, 1863

VICKSBURG SURRENDERS. JULY 4, 1863

UNION TAKES FORT WAGNER. SEPTEMBER '63

PORT ROYAL ENTRANCE

DuPONT TAKES PORT ROYAL IN NOVEMBER '61

Blockade Runners

BERMUDA, (Approx. 500 mi. east of this position), rendezvous of blockade-runners of many nations. Here, cotton was exchanged for war materials and civilian goods, including luxuries of all kinds.

UNION TAKES PORT HUDSON JULY 9, 1863

DuPONT TAKES FORT PULASKI. APRIL 11, 1862

MOBILE FALLS. JANUARY '65

WARSAW SOUND

ATLANTIC OCEAN

FARRAGUT POUNDS PORT HUDSON JULY '63

FARRAGUT TAKES NEW ORLEANS ON 25 APRIL, 1862

BATTLE FOR MOBILE BAY AUGUST 1864

This symbol indicates approximate position of blockading ships as located in December 1863

FARRAGUT INVADES THE DELTA 1862

UNION TAKES JACKSONVILLE IN MARCH 1862

GULF OF MEXICO

EAST GULF SQUADRON

WEST GULF SQUADRON

B L O C K A D E

BAHAMA ISLANDS

Blockade Runners

CAPT. CHAS. WILKES SEIZES SOUTHERN DIPLOMATS FROM BRITISH SHIP TRENT 8 NOVEMBER, 1861

Blockade Runners from Belize and Bahia, Brazil

Tortugas Island

Florida Keys

Havana

CUBA

CHANCELLORSVILLE, GETTYSBURG

BATTLES FOR THE CAPITALS

MISSISSIPPI CONTROLLED BY UNION

BROWNSVILLE

NEVADA BECOMES A STATE 1864

LINCOLN SHOT 14 APR. '65 SURRENDER OF GENERALS: EWELL 5 APR, LEE 9 APR, JOHNSTON 26 APR, TAYLOR 8 MAY, SMITH 26 MAY '65

PERTINENT LAND AND NAVAL ACTIONS 1864 TO THE END OF THE WAR

WILDERNESS, SPOTTSYLVANIA, COLD HARBOR, NORTH ANNA, CEDAR CREEK, SIEGE OF PETERSBURG; FALL OF RICHMOND, FIVE FORKS.

BATTLES FOR THE CAPITALS

FORT FISHER

SHERMAN'S MARCH

MOBILE

617. COMMANDER-IN-CHIEF of the United States Army and Navy during Civil War—President Abraham Lincoln. Stanton, his devious War Secretary, snubbed him to his face and called him "ape" behind his back. His Secretary of State had temerity to suggest that he, Seward, run the government. Chase, Treasury Chief, quit on him. But Naval Secretary Gideon Welles, staunch friend in Cabinet of intriguers, stood by him from the outset. Lincoln responded by trusting Welles and the U.S. Navy.

For a former backwoodsman and prairie lawyer, Lincoln displayed a remarkable grasp of sea power and naval strategy. Two weeks after Sumter, he proclaimed formal blockade of the entire Confederate coast. He observed that this decree "would be like the Pope's bull to the comet; trade would go on in spite of . . . the executive proclamation." But he saw that the blockade would eventually bottle up Confederate shipping, crush Southern commerce and leave Old King Cotton dying on the vine.

The

 T H E   N O R T H

618. JEFFERSON DAVIS, President of the Confederacy. Former West Pointer (veteran of Monterrey and Buena Vista), Mississippi planter and Senator, War Secretary in Pierce's Cabinet, Davis was "old school," a conventional thinker, inclined to be autocratic. Experienced artillerist, he backed Lee to the limit, but it could be said his horizon was bounded by the Confederacy's coastline. He chose astute Naval Secretary in Stephen Mallory. But naval strategy seemed to baffle Davis. He took relatively little interest in the C.S.N. Fatally shortsighted, he assumed harbor forts could stop invasion by sea. His dictatorial methods hampered Mallory's expansion program. Compared with Lincoln, a mediocre Commander-in-Chief.

Leaders

Major General R. E. Lee, Commander of the Military and Naval Forces of Virginia, April to June, 1861 With Capt. Mathew F. Maury he planned naval defenses of State of Virginia (before she joined Confederacy), at Aquia, Yorktown, James River, etc. Later Lee defended Port Royal Sd. against Federal Fleet. (He grew beard Sept.-Oct., 1861, at Valley River.)

619. GIDEON WELLES—Secretary of the U.S. Navy during Civil War. Entering office in March '61, he found Department inefficient, collapsing, undermined by subversion. Energetic, splenetic, honest, "Uncle Gideon" (former Hartford newspaper editor) had what it took under his henna wig to bring order out of chaos. Land-side "Old Man of the Sea"—perhaps the nation's greatest Naval Secretary —he guided the U.S.N. through worst storm in its entire history. (right)

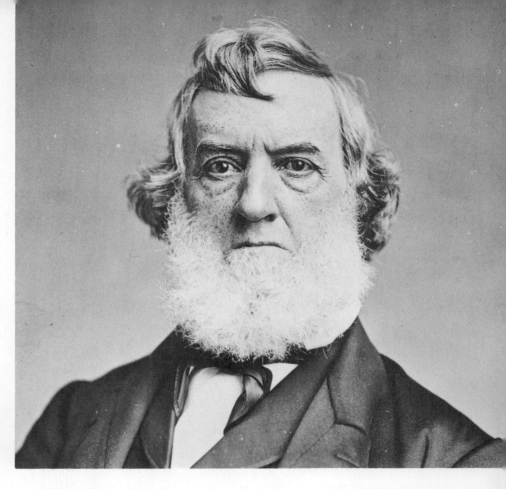

620. GUSTAVUS V. FOX—Welles' right hand. Ex-naval officer who had entered Massachusetts textile indus-try, Captain Fox rushed to Washing-ton at war's onset, volunteered to lead relief expedition to Sumter. Thanks to State Department meddling and other interference, Fox's expedi-tion was stymied. But Welles made him Assistant Naval Secretary. Loyal, aggressive, imaginative, Fox assisted by procuring merchant steamers for blockade duty, urging ironclad con-struction, obtaining stores, pushing campaigns. Welles devised U.S. Navy's moves. Fox energized them.

621. FLAG OFFICER SAMUEL F. DU PONT, U.S.N. (lower right)— in charge of blockade operations. Jersey born. Navy bred. Veteran of California. On Welles' Strategy Board. Then (autumn of '61) given command of fleet blockading South's Atlantic Coast. Port Royal (Beau-fort), Fort Pulaski (Savannah) soon fell to his guns. But Charleston!

622. CAPTAIN JOHN A. DAHL-GREN, U.S.N.—Navy's ordnance ex-pert. Made commandant of Washing-ton Navy Yard shortly after war's outbreak, then Chief of Ordnance Bureau, Dahlgren labored tirelessly to arm Union vessels with best in weapons. Some authorities credit his "soda bottle" gun with winning war.

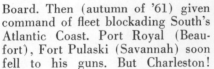

623. CONFEDERATE NAVAL SECRETARY Stephen R. Mallory—perhaps best mind in Richmond Cabinet. Former Florida Senator, Chairman of Naval Affairs Committee, Trinidad-born Mallory thought in terms of machinery and metal. Pushing construction of ironclad warships, he strove to build a modern, mechanized navy—impossible endeavor. Starting from scratch, Confederacy lacked credit, material, technicians. To most Southerners, "horsepower" meant cavalry. (left)

624. CAPTAIN JAMES D. BULLOCH of Georgia (above)—Mallory's right hand. Steamship expert, ex-Navy officer, he was secretly dispatched to England in May '61 with $2,000,000 to purchase warships, preferably ironclads. Ace diplomatic intriguer, he procured such vessels for Confederacy as cruiser *Florida* and famous *Alabama*—raiders which played hob with Northern shipping. Bulloch's acumen was family trait. He had 3-year-old nephew named Teddy Roosevelt. Future Bull Moose.

625. COMMODORE GEORGE N. HOLLINS, C.S.N. (below). Veteran of 1812 and Mexican War, skipper of *Cyane* when she bombarded Greytown, Nicaragua, Hollins was personification of fiery Southern officer. With squadron containing ironclad *Manassas*, he scored Confederate Navy's first victory over Federal. Facing irate Confederate Congressional Committee which investigated ultimate fall of New Orleans, he inadvertently spoke the Confederate Navy's obituary. Question: "Was your machinery in good condition?" Answer: "Yes, sir, but of course not equal to theirs." Situation, C.S.N.

626. CAPTAIN JOHN N. MAFFITT, C.S.N. (below right), skipper of raiding cruiser *Florida*. As set of his cap suggests, this "Rebel" breezed into action with superb elan. Before her capture in 1863 *Florida* bagged some forty Northern merchantmen.

627. CAPTAIN RAPHAEL SEMMES, C.S.N. (below)—star under Stars and Bars. Vera Cruz veteran who had quit Navy to practice law. Virtual "period piece" imbued with provincialism of Southern aristocrat. But sea warrior unexcelled. Courteous. Cool. Deadly. "Old Beeswax" to his crew, he proved hornet on ocean; with raiders *Sumter* and *Alabama* paced an anti-shipping campaign which all but wrecked the North's salt-water commerce. Confederacy's last admiral at war's end, he fought to hold the last ditch at Richmond.

628. FLAG OFFICER FRANKLIN BUCHANAN, C.S.N. (left)—of *Merrimack* and Mobile. Former Naval Academy head, in charge Washington Navy Yard at war's outbreak, this Marylander dealt North sharp blow by "going South." In his wake, Potomac yard was found sabotaged. Man of confused principles, he endeavored to rejoin U.S.N. when Maryland remained in Union. Rejected, he dodged to Richmond to accept command of ironclad *Merrimack-Virginia*. Destined to meet Farragut.

629. FLAG OFFICER DAVID GLASGOW FARRAGUT, U.S.N.—battle leader at New Orleans and Mobile Bay. Born in Tennessee, married to a Virginian, this veteran was living quietly in Norfolk when Sumter was fired upon. Secession? Not for man who had served as "mid" in 1812 under legendary "Logan" Porter. Within two hours of news that Virginia had seceded, Farragut packed wife and family in carriage, thrust loaded pistols into coat and raced to waterfront to board

a North-bound steamer. Of unassailable integrity, iron courage, granite convictions, he came as crucial reinforcement to Navy Headquarters. Given command of Western Gulf Blockading Squadron in December '61, he led power drive on Confederacy's southern seaboard. Delta forts would not stop Farragut, nor mines (and Buchanan) at Mobile. Perhaps first American naval officer to comprehend modern fleet tactics, he became U.S. Navy's first admiral. An all-time inspiration to the service.

Buchanan meets Farragut at Mobile

630. COMMODORE BENJAMIN F. ISHERWOOD—Engineer-in-Chief of U.S. Navy. Big, gruff, outspoken, Isherwood (seated second from left) was as hard-driving and sometimes as cantankerous as a monitor's engine. Unexcelled at his profession, he knew marine machinery as did few other technicians of his time; literally put the steam in Union Navy's punch. In July '62 Lincoln placed him in charge of new Bureau of Steam Engineering. There, with rank of Commodore (base pay $3,500 a year) Isherwood engineered a program that drove the Federal warships to victory over the limping, mechanically inferior naval vessels of the stranded Confederacy.

631. LIEUTENANT DAVID DIXON PORTER, U.S.N.—ace in Navy's shuffled deck. Although son of old Commodore Davy, he was at first mistrusted by Welles, who heard he had been a house guest of Senator and Mrs. Jefferson Davis. But Porter had gone ardent Unionist after Mrs. Davis confided at a tea party, "We shall now have a monarchy in the South." Following brief duty on a Gulf blockader, he rushed to Washington to propose drive on New Orleans with Farragut as its leader. Applauding Porter's "dash, energy and audacity," Welles agreed—one of war's major strategic decisions.

 T H E   N O R T H

632. MIDSHIPMEN AT U.S. NAVAL ACADEMY, NEWPORT. Because of subversive Maryland atmosphere, Navy Department in 1861 transferred the Academy from Annapolis to Newport, R.I. Many Newport lads graduated to officer U.S. steam cruisers, monitors and ironclads in Civil War. (picture, left)

633. UNION BLUEJACKETS (at left) Backbone of U.S.N. in Civil War—enlisted men. It was a day of transition—a cox'n might be called upon to man a shovel, a coal passer ordered to lend a hand with sail. When duty was tough and shipboard luxuries nonexistent (Jack Tar of '61 munched his hardtack and salt horse, sitting tailor-fashion on deck, oil-cloth apron in lap). There was chance for prize money. But many of lads who "rallied 'round the Flag," were impelled to fight for Freedom. One wrote, "After seeing a group of slaves led in chains through Alexandria, I was ready to volunteer." Of such stuff, the Boys in Blue who manned wooden ships and ironclads.

Call for Naval Volunteers (at right,
One of War's earliest recruiting poster

634. COMMANDERS AND LIEU-TENANTS, CONFEDERATE NAVY. Photographed as war prisoners confined in Fort Warren near Boston, Confederate naval officers in picture are not so smartly uniformed as some who sat for cameras at home. Dress is typical working costume, however. And this group is perhaps more exemplary than the Daguerreotype and other specimens rigidly posed for parlor photography. Picture, too, contains rare portraits of some of Confederate Navy's outstanding line officers. Following served on Confederate ironclad ram *Atlanta*: (17) Master-mate N. McBlair, (19) Lieutenant A. Bobot, (20) Pilot Austin, (23) Midshipman Williamson, (24) Lieutenant Joseph W. Alexander (who had just escaped, been recaptured after long chase), (25) Commander William A. Webb, *Atlanta's* captain. Central figure (21) is Lieutenant C. W. Read, captain of C.S.S. *Tacony*—daring raider who sailed from Hatteras to Maine in spring of '63; captured 22 Northern merchantmen en route; then boldly breezed into Portland Harbor and seized, blew up, U.S. Revenue Cutter *Caleb Cushing*. (Others are army Rebs.)

The Men

635. CONFEDERATE SAILORS (below). Confederate raiding cruisers were manned largely by foreigners. But hundreds of Southern lads volunteered for C.S.N. While shortage of skilled mechanics hampered service, there was no lack of able seamen for deck and gun crews. Rallying to Stars and Bars, they sang "Bonny Blue Flag." Poorly equipped, underpaid, they hung on long after hopes for victory and bounty were sunk. When many Southerners were calling it "rich man's war and poor man's fight," the sailors of the Confederate Navy, impoverished in everything but spirit, went on fighting. (Pictures of Confederate naval enlisted men are very rare. Published 40 years after war, this photograph was captioned as picturing Union seamen. However, original plate recently found in Richmond bears notation identifying sailors as Confederate. Regulation enlisted uniform, C.S.N., was gray with black pie hat, or summer white with white hat. But men wore anything available. Group in photograph may be captives on Union ship.)

636. U.S.S. *WABASH* — "palace ship" of the U.S.N. One of five steam frigates available at war's outbreak, she was out of commission, minus crew, in April '61. Similarly unready were *Roanoke, Colorado, Minnesota, Merrimack.* Before Welles could get them to sea, *Merrimack* was lost. *Wabash* became Du Pont's flagship.

637. U.S.S. *PENSACOLA.* Carrying twenty-eight 9-inch smoothbores, this handsome 3,000-ton steam sloop, commissioned in December 1859, was prototype for U.S. cruisers. Built at Warrington Navy Yard, Fla., she was about 230½ feet long, with 44½-foot beam, 15-foot depth. Speed: about 9½ knots. She was one of seven heavy screw sloops which, with eight light, formed nucleus of Federal fleet. Readied for action in April '61, *Pensacola* is seen off Alexandria, Va., all polished up to the nines, awaiting inspection by the President. (below)

Warships

638. TYPICAL CONFEDERATE RAIDER — C.S.S. *GEORGIA.* Of same breed as *Alabama* and *Florida,* she was British-built iron screw cruiser of 600 tons. Sailing from Scotland in April 1863, she ran up Stars and Bars, ran out her guns, and captured nine prizes before faulty engines sent her back to shipyard. Other British-built Confederate raiders of note were *Georgiana* (whose career was nipped in bud off Charleston) and *Shenandoah* (nemesis of Yankee whaling fleet). American vessels also served as Confederate raiders. Notably the *Nashville,* the converted blockade-runner *Archer* (vessel that invaded Portland), and *Tallahassee* (killer of 26 vessels).

and Weapons

639. CONFEDERATE ARMORED RAM *MANASSAS*—first American ironclad. Incredible overconfidence which led Confederate leaders to start war without a single warship in South's possession seemed almost justified by creation and early triumph of this odd little vessel. Ex-steam tug *Enoch Train,* she was procured by private subscription in New Orleans; rebuilt into a sort of aquatic armadillo, boiler-plated, her bow carrying a ploughlike underwater ram. Her one hatch served also as port for her only gun (an ancient 32-pounder) which was shielded by an iron eyelid. Completed five months before famous *Merrimack,* this pugnacious pigmy (387 tons) steamed into action under Capt. John Stevenson, C.S.N., night of Oct. 12, 1861. The armadillo was looking for bear. Leading squadron of Commo. Hollins, she charged down the Delta and panicked a Federal blockade force by ramming and disabling U.S.S. *Richmond* and driving U.S. sloop *Vincennes* hard aground. Living up to her name, little *Manassas* contrived a fast naval "Bull Run."

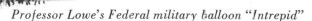

Professor Lowe's Federal military balloon "Intrepid"

640. *PENSACOLA* "MANNING THE YARDS" FOR LINCOLN. Brady was on hand with his little black wagon to get this camera-shot.

641. U.S.S. *BROOKLYN*—screw sloop (right)—one of few ships on duty in home waters at start of war. Stationed with sail frigate *Sabine* at Pensacola, Fla., she flunked at outset when her commander, Captain H. A. Adams, stood supinely by while Confederate General Braxton Bragg seized Pensacola base. Under new captain *Brooklyn* redeemed herself.

642. U.S. GUNBOAT *SENECA*— one of 23 gunboats built on rush order for blockade duty. Called "ninety-day wonders," these 691-ton vessels pitched into the war like so many bantams. Mounting one 11-inch Dahlgren gun, one 20-pound rifle, and two 24-pound howitzers, *Seneca* type was the destroyer of its day.

643. A CONVERTED NEW YORK FERRYBOAT. Craft shown (right and below) served with makeshift flotilla mustered during early days of the blockade. Many an unlikely boat was purchased for Navy by George D. Morgan, dynamic New York business man commissioned by Welles to buy any vessel available. Scraping barrel (or harbor) bottom, Morgan acquired 79 craft in record time. Specimens like this ferry waddled to sea to join a fleet which Confederates contemptuously dubbed "Abe Lincoln's Soapbox Navy." But "Soapbox Navy" stubbornly held the blockade, giving North time to assemble heavy sea forces and produce such powerful warships as U.S.S. *New Ironsides*.

 T H E N O R T H

644. C.S. IRONCLAD RAM *AR-KANSAS* (above). While U.S. Navy's Ironclad Board was still debating, Richmond leaders ordered two iron-clads for defense of upper Missis-sippi. In August 1861 the contracts went to J. T. Shirley of Memphis. Begun at Memphis and completed in Yazoo, *Arkansas* was formidable vessel; length 165, beam 33, draft 11½. Twin-screw-driven, good for 10 knots, she was coated with railroad iron; carried eight heavy guns and underwater ram. Cost: $76,000. Federals didn't give Shirley time to build sister ironclad ram *Tennessee*.

646. C.S. GUNBOAT *PATRICK HENRY*. Originally steamer *York-town*, this 1,300-ton sidewheeler was seized by Virginia Secessionists in March 1861; later taken into C.S.N.

645. C.S. IRONCLAD RAM *PAL-METTO STATE* (at left). Built with companion ram *Chicora* at Charles-ton from fund raised by local sub-scription. Both vessels were armored with 4-inch plating and powerfully armed (*Palmetto* with ten 7-inch rifles); cost about $250,000 each. Confederates built ten of this "ram" type for coastal and harbor defense. Floating iron barns, they were slug-gish, hard to maneuver, tough on sweltering crews. Under Flag Officer Duncan N. Ingraham, *Palmetto* struck one solid blow for Charleston. Then (chronic with type) she conked.

In company with gunboat *Jamestown* and tug *Teaser*, she served as escort for ironclad *Merrimack*. Then to Richmond for duration as training ship of Confederate Naval School.

647. CONFEDERATE BLOCKADE RUNNER (left) — mainstay of South's war effort. Absolutely de-pendent on imports (iron, chemicals, machinery, guns) and on exports (cotton, turpentine, hides, tobacco), to pay for the imports, the Con-federacy's life depended on shipping, which perforce meant blockade-run-ning. Out of South's 189 Atlantic and Gulf harbors and estuaries raced speedy "runners" of type shown. Carrying vital exports to return with lifeblood imports—ships with fate of the Confederacy in their holds.

648. C.S. RAM *GENERAL STER-LING PRICE*. Numerous river steamers were taken into Confederate Navy for duty on inland waters. Fitted with iron rams and patchwork

armor, they galloped into battle to butt the enemy under. Charge was usually ended by point-blank fire.

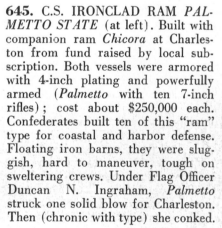

649. CONFEDERATE COAST ARTILLERY—defending Southern seaboard against Federal invasion. Rare photograph shows Confederate "water battery" at Pensacola, Fla. (note Pensacola Lighthouse in distance), cannoneers loading, while drummer boy with bass drum stands by to beat rataplan. Vintage of 1812, these old Columbiad guns on Gribeauval carriages should have been easy marks for U.S. naval forces in area at war's outbreak. Muddled orders and treason cost Navy Pensacola Base which Confederates held until spring of 1862. (Taken by N. O. or J. D. Edwards of New Orleans, photograph was probably captured by Farragut at Mobile. Southern camera experts took numerous photos of Farragut's ships in Gulf and Union vessels elsewhere. Early example of camera espionage.)

650. GUARDING VITAL HARBORS which Confederacy could not afford to lose, batteries similar to these at Yorktown defended Charleston, Wilmington, Savannah, Mobile and other Southern ports. Guns shown are Dahlgren 11-inchers of "soda-bottle" type seized at Norfolk arsenal. Their iron muzzles argued to support opinion of Mallory and R. E. Lee that Confederate naval inferiority might be "compensated by invulnerability." U.S.N. argued no.

651. GUNS AT FORT JOHNSON, S.C., guarding Charleston. Unlike most in Confederacy's coast-defense system, these proved very tough.

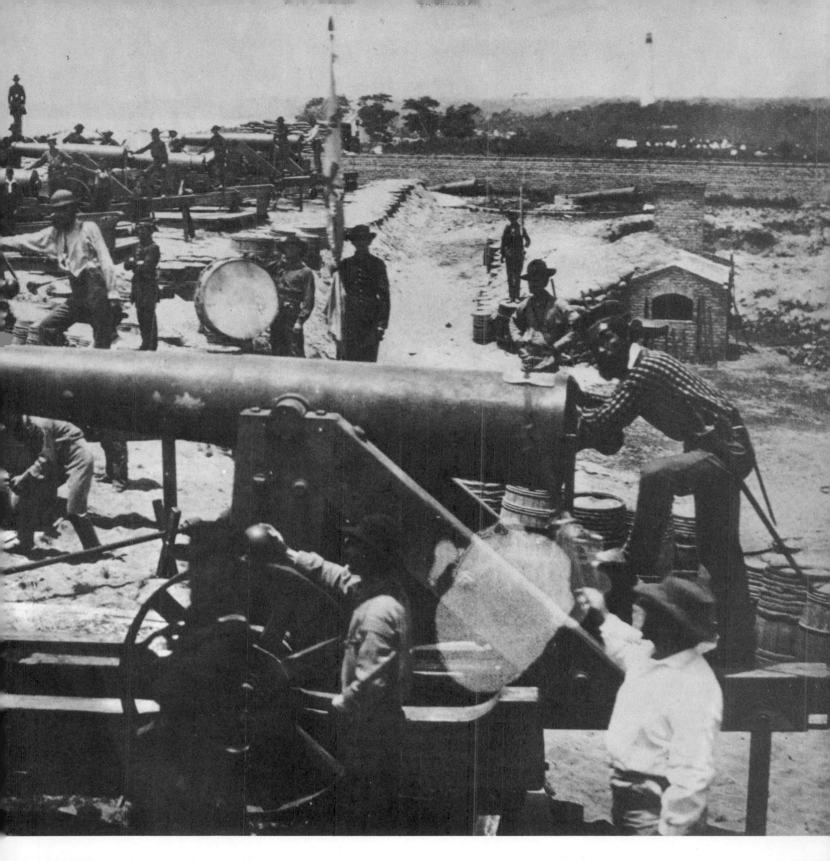

At left: Confederate Mortar Battery on Morris Is. (after a photo)

652. PARROTT GUNS were among lighter artillery pieces employed in Confederate sea and river inner-defense fortifications. Not as dependable as "pressure-curved" Dahlgren gun, the Parrott was a nasty weapon to operate, but one of earliest to throw an explosive shell. The 30-pounder Parrott rifle packed a punch particularly devastating to wooden ships and those targets euphemistically labeled "personnel." Union landing forces faced such batteries.

653. U.S.S. *NEW IRONSIDES* (bow and full-length view)—Navy's first armored capital ship. Ordered by Welles' Ironclad Board in September '61, and completed in August '62, she was frigate similar to England's *Warrior*—wooden hull shielded by armor plate, guns enclosed in an iron "battery box." Built by Merrick & Sons of Philadelphia for $865,000, *New Ironsides* displaced 3,486 tons; was 230 feet long, with 15¾ draft;

8-knot speed. She mounted fourteen 11-inch Dahlgrens, four heavy rifles and a 12-pound howitzer. Veritable floating fort, she proved strong link in the blockade's chain in Civil War.

654. TYPICAL UNION MONITOR —U.S.S. *MAHOPAC.* North's answer to Southern ironclads. Thanks to genius of inventor John Ericsson. "When the first monitor was built, many naval men sneered 'humbug,'"

Welles wrote. "Afterwards I was abused for not preparing to build more." By late '63, Navy owned squadrons of these unique turret vessels. Built of wood plated with iron, average was 1,500-tonner; double-turret specimens were bigger. Their construction boomed such plants as Novelty Iron Works of New York, Globe Works of Boston, Vulcan of Baltimore, Secor & Co. of Jersey. They were spearheads of U.S. Fleet.

655. U.S. IRONCLAD GUNBOAT *CINCINNATI.* On "Western Waters" of upper Mississippi seven river gunboats of this type were spawned. North's first ironclads, they were designed by Naval Constructor S. M. Pook; rush-jobbed by J. B. Eads of St. Louis. Stern-wheelers, 175 feet long with 50-foot beam, they were plated with 2½-inch iron; carried 13 guns. "Pook Turtles," led Union drive on "Old Man River" that eventually split the South in twain.

656. BEHIND UNION FIRE-POWER—Northern industry. South could not compete with industrialized North geared to produce big guns, machinery, engines, munitions. Backing Civil War offensives waged by U.S. Army and Navy were scores of factories, foundries and mills—literally the forges of victory. Shown: Du Pont Powder Plant on the Brandywine, where much of Navy's firepower was manufactured. (Note powder mills on riverbank, their wooden roofs facing stream to direct force of accidental explosion toward water.) In South few manufacturing plants existed. In some circles, labor was thought "ungentlemanly" and machines were held a menace to society. (As late as 1840, citizens of Charleston, S.C., voted to outlaw steam engines in city.) Only Tredegar and Anderson-Delaney of Richmond, Leeds & Co. of New Orleans, and a few others could handle heavy metals work. War-going Confederates, short of tools for job, strove to make up for South's industrial lack with desperate valiance, ingenuity and bluff —as witness "dummy guns" below.

658. CONFEDERATE MINE-TORPEDO — surprise naval defense weapon. Mines ("torpedoes" in Civil War vernacular) were planted in Southern harbor entrances and rivers. In charge of Confederate harbor defenses, Captain Matthew Maury, famous naval scientist, invented an electric mine in summer of '61, but could not obtain insulated wire for its production. First encountered in July '61 at Aquia Creek (Potomac tributary 35 miles below Washington), Confederate contact mines (mechanical type) were an ugly menace to Federal warships. Mine shown is of electrical type devised by G. J. Rains, Hunter Davidson and Lieutenant Beverly Kennon, C.S.N., late in '63. Mine warfare took heavy toll of Union fleet. But material shortages badly hampered Confederate torpedo manufacture.

657. BEHIND THE DIXIE DEFENSE—Confederate dummy guns. Short of foundries and forges for cannon manufacture, and facing iron famine, "Johnny Reb" resorted to desperate bluff. These wooden jokers at Centreville, Va., not far from Wash., fooled McClellan for weeks.

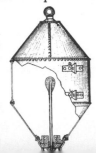

T H E   S O U T H

Tug Yankee.   Cumberland.   Merrimac.

659. WASHINGTON NAVY YARD (below) at hour of crisis. All seemed quiet on the Potomac after Sumter. Too quiet. Visiting capital yard, Lincoln found gates unguarded. Commandant Buchanan gone—guns dismantled—what did it mean? Lull before storm. It broke at Norfolk.

Norfolk

FLASH

660. HOLOCAUST AT NORFOLK (April 20, 1861). In charge at Norfolk Navy Yard was Commodore C. S. McCauley, senescent leftover of 1812, who thought best answer to Confederate challenge was another quart of rum. Rushed to Norfolk to get up steam in immobilized fleet, Engineer Isherwood found McCauley hiccuping in his cups, everything at sixes and sevens. Marines abandoned post; Southern crews mutinied; before ships could be readied to sail, Virginia was out of Union. When Isherwood reported McCauley "under the influence of liquor and bad men," Welles promptly dispatched sloop *Pawnee* (Captain Hiram Paulding) to trouble scene. Finding Rebel militia closing in, situation hopeless, Paulding ordered yard blown up, fleet scuttled. Thus America's largest naval base and ten valuable warships were lost to Union. Confederates saved drydock (one of nation's two best), salvaged frigate *Merrimack*, and gained hundreds of cannon, including some 300 Dahlgren guns. "Great as was the loss of our ships," wrote Porter, "it was much less than the loss of our guns!" For Dahlgren cannon went into Southern fortifications that would take months and years to crush. And capture of base gave Confederacy a naval powerhouse. Norfolk was Civil War "Pearl Harbor"—a demonstration which conclusively proved to Navy that "soda bottles" were more to be prized than rum bottles. (picture at left)

Pawnee.   Pennsylvania.

D e b a c l e

B A C K !

661. U.S.S. *PENNSYLVANIA*, Navy's largest sailing warship, was cremated at Norfolk. A sorry loss.

662. U.S.S. *DELAWARE*, 74-gunner burnt in the Norfolk debacle, She is pictured (right) in a better day, in peaceful regalia. Her burning left a charred hole in the U.S. fleet.

663. RUINS OF NORFOLK NAVY YARD (lower right)—a gratuitous victory for the Confederacy. Lost to U.S. Navy in this rummage of devastation were line-of-battle ships *Pennsylvania, Delaware, Columbus, New York*; frigates *Columbia, Raritan, United States*; steam frigate *Merrimack*; sloops *Germantown* and *Plymouth*. Also lost was brig *Dolphin*.

664. BURNING OF U.S.S. *MERRIMACK* (directly below). Best of ten warships lost to Navy at Norfolk, brand-new steam frigate, a 50-gunner, was caught in yard, her guns ashore, boilers opened for repairs. After Isherwood managed to start her engines and assemble emergency crew, crapulous McCauley ordered the ship's fires drawn. Confederates were able to salvage *Merrimack* hulk.

665. U.S. GUNBOAT *THOMAS FREEBORN*—first to open fire for Navy in Civil War. Early in May '61 Confederate batteries emplaced at Aquia Creek, Va., began shelling Potomac River traffic below Washington. At insistence of Commo. Paulding a "soapbox" squadron was dispatched down-river to abolish this Rebel strongpoint. Under Commander James H. Ward, U.S.N., little squadron included 250-ton paddle boat *Thomas Freeborn* and two smaller steamers. On May 29, 1861, the *Freeborn* opened on enemy's works; was credited with firing Navy's first offensive shots in War of Rebellion. Supported by sloop *Pawnee*, she chugged down-river again to attack the enemy at Mathias Point. Hot action developed on June 26 when a *Pawnee* landing party was repulsed. While in act of sighting *Freeborn's* bow gun (as demonstrated for camera by officer wearing straw hat) Commander Ward was killed in action.

Opening
FIRST SHOTS

666. COMMANDER JAMES HARMON WARD—first U.S. naval officer slain in Civil War. "Wounded in the abdomen, he soon expired," reads the terse account. Aquia Creek assaults failed to dislodge the Confederate guns. They continued to badger Potomac River shipping until General "Joe" Johnston, C.S.A., voluntarily abandoned the area. But Ward would be remembered by U.S. Navy men for resolution with which he led jerry-built squadron against formidable shore batteries. Action at Mathias Point was also memorable for episode in which enlisted man won Navy's first Medal of Honor.

THE BLOCKADE ON THE "CONNECTICUT PLAN".

667. SOAPBOX BLOCKADE—a Currier & Ives View. *Nashville* was one of Confederate blockade-runners that easily eluded Navy patrols in first months of war. Frustration of blockaders is suggested in dialogue of above lampoon, while jubilance of runners is expressed in manner not usually associated with Southern gentlemen. Unable to tag such vessels as *Nashville*, Navy needed more cruisers for game of catch-as-catch-can. And as blockade operations are strategically static, demanding many vessels to snare few, U.S. leaders determined to stop Confederate shipping at source; launched campaign to seize the South's major seaports.

Operations
FIRST BLOOD

668. CIVIL WAR MEDAL OF HONOR. Navy's highest award, Medal of Honor was approved and authorized by Congress on December 21, 1861. As originally created, it was special award for enlisted men ("petty officers, seamen, landsmen and Marines") cited for service "above and beyond the call of duty." On April 3, 1863, Naval Secretary Gideon Welles awarded the medal to some 30 Union sailors. Among the first citations approved was that of John Williams, captain of the maintop, U.S.S. *Pawnee*, "for conspicuous gallantry in action during the attack on Mathias Point." It was noted that Williams had gone in with the landing party. His commanding officer had reported, "I must call attention of the Department to the bravery of John Williams . . . who told his men while lying off in the boat that every man must die on his thwart sooner than leave a man behind, and when the flagstaff of his boat was shot away and the ensign fell, he, although suffering a gunshot wound in the thigh, seized it in his hand and bravely waved it over his head." Dated June 26, 1861, this was earliest action to win famed Congressional Medal. (Medal of Honor awards for officers were granted in 1915.)

THE

EAGLE

STRIKES

669. TO GET AT THE KERNEL one must first crack the shell. But where? Question of target for immediate strike on Confederate seaboard proved knotty for Union naval leaders. Lincoln urged swift attack. The U.S. Army's July defeat at Bull Run demanded a counteracting victory. Navy's Strategy Board finally decided Hatteras Inlet on North Carolina coast the likeliest initial target. On August 26, 1861, Flag Officer Silas Stringham sailed from Fortress Monroe with steam frigates *Wabash* and *Minnesota*, two sloops, a gunboat and two transports. Objective was reached on 27th. As illustrated (left) Forts Hatteras and Clark were pounded into submission by naval bombardment. Forts were then occupied by landing forces under General Ben Butler. Navy thus scored the North's first major victory.

670. PORT ROYAL (above)—a setback to Robert E. Lee. Midway between Charleston and Savannah, Port Royal was ideally located for blockader base. So Flag Officer Du Pont was dispatched with invasion expedition. With frigate *Wabash,* two big sloops, six armed steamers, four old and four new gunboats of *Seneca* type, Du Pont struck on November 7, 1861. By circling his warships in harbor entrance, he succeeded in hammering Port Royal forts into surrender. A shock to General R. E. Lee who had devised the fortifications.

671. CONFEDERATE BATTERIES at Port Royal. Du Pont's bombardment tactics wrecked these imposing coast-artillery cannon. Stunned by Royal's collapse, Lee recommended that such coastal batteries be shifted out of naval-fire range. Port Royal advised Confederacy that "invulnerability" was easier to say than realize.

672. FIRST NAVAL AIRCRAFT CARRIER. In November 1861 this scene was staged in lower reaches of Potomac River. Behold world's first "flattop" — U.S. steamer *George Washington Parke Custis* raising observation balloon *Washington* near Budd's Ferry below Mount Vernon. Mission: aerial search for blockade-runners. Army first employed balloons in summer of '61. Balloonists' failure to identify Confederate dummy guns subsequently led to discontinuance of Army Aeronautics Corps in 1863. Navy's pioneer aeronautics effort was similarly "written off." Fledgling born before its time.

NAVY in the UPPER MISSISSIPPI

CMDR. RODGERS IN ST. LOUIS TO MUSTER NAVAL FORCES. AUG. '61

PORTER BUILDS FLOTILLA FOR VICKSBURG DRIVE

GRANT'S RETREAT COVERED BY CONESTOGA AND LEXINGTON. SEPT. '61

UNION TAKES NEW MADRID, MARCH 1862

"TURTLES" SPEARHEAD ASSAULTS ON FORTS HENRY AND DONELSON. FEB. '62

SHOT BURSTS BOILER ON ESSEX. FEB. 1862

ST. LOUIS TAKES 59 HITS. FEB. '62

UNION TAKES RIVER FORTS IN JUNE 1862

TYLER, CONESTOGA, LEXINGTON, CAPTURE REBEL RAM EASTPORT. FEB. '62

673. THE MISSISSIPPI—artery or jugular vein. While Potomac front made headlines, strategists saw the Mississippi as war's biggest problem. To the South the vast river was a vital transport system for Confederate commerce. To the North it could prove a highway for a drive to the Confederacy's heart. With Federal troops mobilizing in "Western Area" under General John C. Frémont, Welles rushed Commander John Rodgers II to St. Louis to muster naval forces for amphibious campaign. All hands realized rough fighting was in prospect. And "Old Man River" himself — muddy, floody, meandersome and malarial—was no mean opponent. A giant on any map.

674. COMMANDER JOHN RODGERS II, U.S.N. Son of 1812 Commodore, he proved as flinty. Clashing with pompous Frémont whose H.Q. was mare's-nest of graft, Rodgers blew up. Recalled, he was given command of new ironclad *Galena*. West went Flag Officer Foote Frémont's match. And Mississippi's.

"Catfish" Front

Commodore Foote's Gunboat Flotilla on the Mississippi

Water Battery at Fort Donelson

675. U.S. "TIMBERCLAD" *CONESTOGA*—one of three river boats procured by Rodgers in June '61. Served in September with Union forces under unknown general named Grant, attacking Rebel base at Belmont, Missouri. When Grant was driven back, *Conestoga* and sister *Lexington* covered the retreat. But iron was needed on "Catfish" front.

676. U.S. GUNBOAT *ST. LOUIS*—first of Foote's river ironclads. Prototype for "Pook Turtles" built by Eads of St. Louis, she was launched 45 days from contract date. Iron plate from Pittsburgh; timber from Minnesota forest; cannon from Youngstown. She carried three 8-inch Dahlgrens forward, four 42- and six 32-pounders in broadside, plus small howitzer. "Turtles" were slow going upstream. But South was down.

677. U.S. GUNBOAT *LOUISVILLE*. Like sisters, she was heavily armored on bow to meet Dahlgren's axiom: "A warship's business is to enter action, not retire from it." Attacking Confederate forts guarding rivers into Kentucky, "Turtles" entered action.

679. U.S. GUNBOAT *PITTSBURG*—another "Turtle" on "catfish" front. Others were *Cincinnati, Mound City, Carondelet, Cairo, Louisville*. By February '62 Foote's flotilla was ready for drive with Grant into Tennessee. "Turtles" spearheaded assault on flinty Forts Henry and Donelson.

678. COMMODORE ANDREW H. FOOTE, U.S.N.—veteran of antislave patrol and China campaign—supplied driving leadership for Union flotilla on upper Mississippi. Rigid teetotaler and sermonizer (officer who put end to Navy's grog ration), the Yankee counterpart of Stonewall Jackson, this old sailor was not one to tolerate graft or incompetence. Shortly after Foote's arrival at St. Louis base, Frémont was dismissed by Lincoln; Grant came to fore. Foote wanted ironclad gunboats; got them. "Let not your heart be troubled," he is said to have preached one Sunday. "Ye believe in God; believe also in gunboats."

Mississippi Amphib

680. U.S. "TIMBERCLAD" *TYLER* (below)—a tinderbox, but iron-hearted. Scouting in van of amphibious drive on Forts Henry and Donelson, she made diversionary run down the Tennessee with wooden *Conestoga* and *Lexington*. At Cerro Gordo, Tenn., they captured Rebel ram *Eastport*. First prize in West.

681. U.S. RIVER IRONCLAD *ESSEX* (right). A "center-wheeler" procured from Wiggins Ferry Co.; rebuilt into ironclad by Eads. Fort Henry's last shot smashed into *Essex*, burst her boiler, scalding 28 of crew.

At Donelson "Turtle" *St. Louis* took 59 hits. Foote was seriously injured, but lived to see Kentucky and northern Tennessee fall to Union forces.

682. CANNON WHEELS made hash of Dixie's red clay roads. Rain turned hash into tapioca. Great ally of Confederacy was General Mud, everywhere complicating U.S. Army's logistics problem. Nowhere more so than in domain of Mississippi mud.

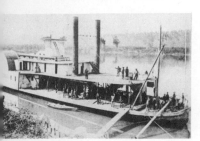

683. TRANSPORT DUTY—Navy legs for Army. Term "logistics" was unknown in Civil War. But problem was familiar. Since battles are won by "getting there fustest with the mostest," logistics could be defined as "delivery of the necessary sufficiency." Navy on "catfish" front helped to solve the delivery stickler.

684. MULES, MIRE, IMMOBILITY —common Civil War fix. Stuck supply cart. The sergeant threatening to shoot if driver doesn't "git that team a-goin'!" Tableau of frustration in which even Sarge's trigger finger can't move. But Navy could. And did.

685. SUPPLY BOAT (below left) —answer to General Mud. Sailors on inland waters carried U.S. Army forces and supplies past miles of canebrake, roadless forest, bottomless swamp. Navy's gunboats escorted.

686. CREW OF GUNBOAT *CARONDELET* (right). Under fighting artist-skipper, Captain Henry Walke, these men reduced Confederate stronghold Island No. 10 to zero.

Civil War

687. GENERAL FLOOD—another Confederate ally. After fall of Forts Henry and Donelson, Confederates retreated to southern Tennessee defense line anchored at Island No. 10 in the Mississippi. Driving down through Tennessee, Grant left Island No. 10 to Foote's flotilla and forces under General Pope. As shown (above) floods slowed Army's advance. But water was Navy's element.

688. SAWING A CHANNEL—one way to go through swamp. It was tried as means of bypassing Island No. 10, Confederate stronghold blocking the Mississippi near New Madrid, Missouri. Island (no longer in existence) was located at bend of oxbow "U" which was lined with Rebel guns and flanked by dense swampland. Defenses included huge floating battery *New Orleans* armed with 8-inch Columbiads. So bypass seemed discreet. At Foote's suggestion, Pope's troopers tried to cut a detour canal across top of "U." Meantime, Navy mortar boats bombarded the "Johnny Reb" batteries.

Navy Mortar Boats

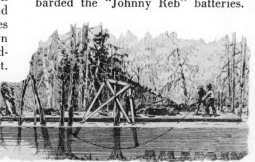

Sawing a channel

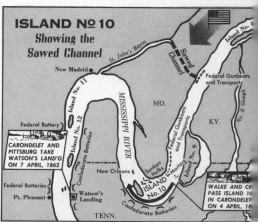

ISLAND No 10
Showing the Sawed Channel

CARONDELET AND PITTSBURG TAKE WATSON'S LAND'G ON 7 APRIL, 1862

Federal Battery

New Madrid

Island No. 11

Island No. 12

New Orleans

Federal Batteries

Pt. Pleasant

Watson's Landing

Sunken Hulks

ISLAND No. 10

MISSISSIPPI RIVER

MO.

KY.

Island No. 9

No. 8 Slough

Island No. 8

WALKE AND PASS ISLAND IN CARONDELET ON 4 APRIL, 18

St. John's Bayou

Sawed Channel

Federal Gunboats and Transports

Confederate Batteries

TENN.

Logistics

690. "TURTLES" bombarding Island 10. Which finally succumbed after Walke and crew volunteered to run "U" gantlet with gunboat *Carondelet*. She made it around the loop on night of April 4th. Cut off by naval guns at both ends of "U," island garrison was trapped. Confederacy lost its Mississippi anchor.

691. U.S.S. *RED ROVER*—Navy's first hospital ship. Fitted in St. Louis, summer of '62, she had operating rooms, bathtubs, water closets, elevators, ice vault. Even "volunteer female nurses." She would have been blessing at Shiloh. And might have saved Flag Officer Foote who died in '63 of wounds dealt by Donelson.

689. CONFEDERATE SHARP-SHOOTERS banging at Union mortar boats. Nonstop sniper fire stung Foote's sailors. But Navy finally got "10's" number. A hard one to solve.

Walke's sketch of "Carondelet" at Is. #10.

Commissary depot on the Tennessee,

692. PITTSBURG LANDING—Grant's anchorage for Shiloh. Peaceful scene does not reflect earthquake battle which exploded at nearby Shiloh Church when combined U.S. armies of Grant and Buell advanced to this point far down the Tennessee River. Surprised by Confederate forces under Generals A. S. Johnston and P. G. T. Beauregard, Union troops were threatened with annihilation. Battle raged for two days (April 6-7, 1862). Only desperate fighting saved the day for Union. And two little gunboats (see below) helped to turn the tide for Grant's army.

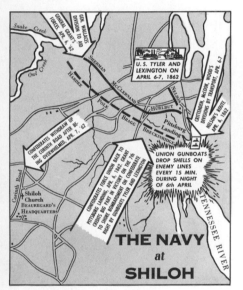

THE NAVY
at
SHILOH

Grant at Shiloh, death of Carson, Grant's scout

Shiloh!

693. SHILOH! Recalled with horror by every Blue and Gray trooper who lived to remember it. To that date greatest battle ever fought on American continent, costing some 20,000 dead and wounded. At crucial climax Confederates almost seized Pittsburg Landing (above), Grant's transport base. Whereupon gunboats *Tyler* and *Lexington*, serving under Grant, waded in to blast Rebels on riverbank (as shown in Navy artist's sketch below). Grant credited old "timberclads" with big part in Shiloh victory. Their fire support saved day.

694. BATTLE FOR ROANOKE ISLAND (February 7, 1862) opened Union campaign to gain control of South's ocean seaboard. In first large-scale amphibious effort on Atlantic coast, U.S. naval forces under Flag Officer L. M. Goldsborough placed army of General Burnside on this Carolina beachhead. Although Goldsborough's fleet was of much-despised "soapbox" variety, it easily squelched the sketchy Confederate defenses. In rapid sequel, Union forces took Elizabeth City (seaport just below Norfolk); went on to seize Beaufort and New Berne, N.C. Before end of March, Jacksonville, Fla., meekly surrendered to U.S.S. *Wabash*. In April, Du Pont's squadron crushed and captured Fort Pulaski, sea-guardian of Savannah. The Confederates determined to hold Wilmington, N. C., Charleston, Norfolk. Navy was fencing South in.

Atlantic Amphib
CLOSING SOUTH'S SEABOARD

695. CAPTURE OF NEW BERNE, N.C. (March 14, 1862)—sequel to Roanoke Island. Rare Major & Knapp lithograph shows New Berne waterfront and Fort Totten (background) in grip of Union flotilla. Miscellany of "soapboxes" contains wonderfully-named gunboats *Jeremy Blue, Dudley Buck, Shawsheen* and *John Faron* (little paddle-boats at left) and U.S.S. *Hetzel* (big paddle-boat at right). Tiny tug in right foreground is U.S. "Lilliputian Steamship" *Slaght*. Big showboat-type vessel in center is U.S.S. *Hunchback*. Union forces might have converged at this time to take Wilmington, N.C. But on Virginia coast to north a thunderhead had exploded. Leaving "soapboxes" to hold New Berne, Goldsborough rushed to Hampton Roads to blockade deadly *Merrimack*. His failure to check the behemoth's sortie incensed Gideon Welles.

Goldsborough's expedition crossing Hatteras Bar.

"Merrimack" before conversion   *"Merrimack" after conversion to the "Virginia"*

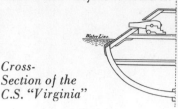

Cross-Section of the C.S. "Virginia"

696. THE *MERRIMACK* (C.S.S. *VIRGINIA*). While gray and blue forces battled on the Dixie line, South's commerce felt pinch of blockade. To break the "Anaconda," Confederates rebuilt *Merrimack*, salvaged at Gosport Yard in Norfolk. Cruiser's superstructure was replaced by barn-like casemate armored with 2-inch layer of iron. A 1500-pound iron ram was bolted to her bow. New length, 263 feet; draft 23; mounting six 9-inch Dahlgrens, two 6.4 rifles and a 7-incher fore and aft. First ocean-going ironclad made in U.S.A.

697. PLANS FOR *MONITOR* (*below*). When Union spies and Richmond newspapers reported the *Merrimack*, Gideon Welles called for armored warship capable of meeting the ironclad menace. Prevailed upon to forget previous abuse by Navy, inventor John Ericsson submitted unique *Monitor* design. A turret on a raft! Only two guns! Welles and canny Hiram Paulding approved, but orthodox heads on the Navy's Ironclad Board were horrified. Commodore Joseph Smith thought Ericsson's vessel "quixotic." Commander C. H. Davis thought it "like nothing on earth or in the waters under the earth." Lincoln settled it. Shown design, he chuckled, "There must be something in this as the girl said when she put her leg in a stocking."

Monitor and

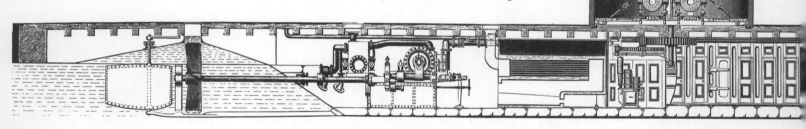

698. INSIDE *MONITOR*. Hull was built in 100 days by Continental Iron Works at Greenpoint, L. I. Aptly named Novelty Iron Works of New York built turret. Engine (Delameter & Co. of N.Y.) was two-cylinder, double-trunk type with rocking arms. She was 776-tonner, 172 feet long, beam 41½, draft 7½. Made 7 knots. Commissioned February 25, 1862. Doubters jeered: "Ericsson's Folly."

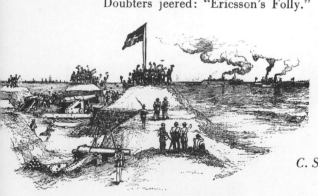

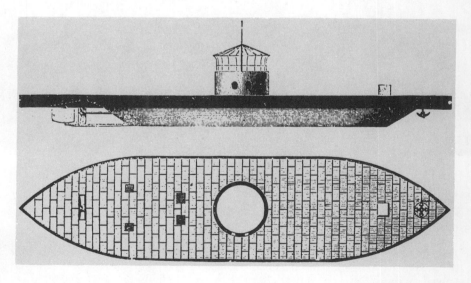

C. S. "Virginia" passing C.S.A. works on Craney Is. en route to attack Federal fleet.

Inside "Monitor" Turret

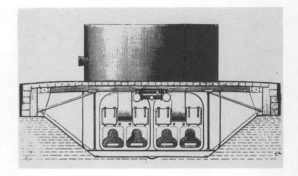

699. CROSS-SECTION *MONITOR*. Two-gun turret was 9 feet high, 20 in diameter, armored with 8 inches of laminated wrought-iron plate. Like *Merrimack's* casemate, it had an overhead grating of iron rails. Mounted on a brass ring inlaid in the middle of the deck, the turret could move in slow merry-go-round, machinery driven. When the twin guns (11-inch Dahlgrens) were withdrawn for loading, the gunports were closed by iron lids that swung automatically into place. Other Ericsson innovations: blowers for the ventilators, an ammunition hoist, and a small pilothouse with shuttered peephole (forerunner of the modern conning tower) about 40 feet forward of the turret. Navy specified mast and sails. Ericsson ignored specification.

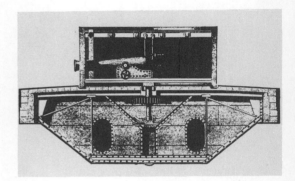

Turret Machinery

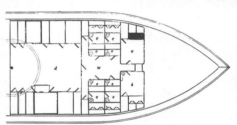

Captain's Cabin on the "Monitor"

Merrimack

Plan of the "Monitor" berth Deck

Launching the "Monitor"

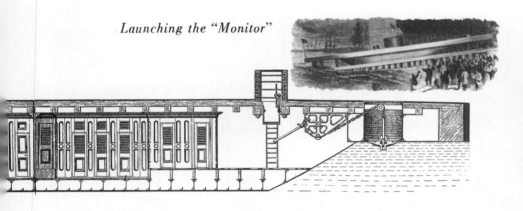

"Monitor" in storm en route

Berth deck on the "Monitor"

Engine Room of the "Monitor"

Pumping and bailing en route to battle

700. *MONITOR'S* CREW—iron men of an iron vessel. She was captained by Lt. John L. Worden, U.S.N.—returnee from a Confederate prison and an ardent Union officer. On March 6th she was ordered top speed to Hampton Roads. Storm off Delaware—waves flooding blowers and turret—engine crew stifled—voyage a nightmare. But ship and crew managed to survive; leaking, clanging, banging, *Monitor* got there in time.

701. *MONITOR* MEN AT MESS. Most of her 10 officers and 46 men were volunteers from old frigate *Sabine*. A gritty lot. Maiden voyage was comparable to present-day trial of atomic sub. But in combat.

Lt. G. U. Morris,
acting commander
of the "Cumberland"

702. *MERRIMACK (VIRGINIA)* RAMMING U.S.S. *CUMBERLAND.* Captained by Flag Officer Franklin Buchanan, the Confederate ironclad made her blockade-busting sortie on March 8, 1862. Midday. Escorted by bevy of small craft, the behemoth steamed out of Elizabeth River and headed for Union squadron across Hampton Roads. Mission: to smash blockaders at mouth of James and release Confederate James River Squadron. Immediate target: old warships *Cumberland* and *Congress* anchored off Newport News Point. Federal commander, Flag Officer Goldsborough, was not on scene. Caught with sails down, the Union ships maneuvered desperately to evade while small craft fired furiously at oncoming Rebel ironclad. Cannonballs caromming from her casemate, *Merrimack* rammed sloop *Cumberland.*

703. *CUMBERLAND* GOES DOWN (right). *Cumberland* was 1,700-ton wooden sloop, armed with twenty-two 9-inch smoothbores. Her speed without sails up was zero. *Merrimack* (*Virginia*) was 3,800-ton ironclad carrying 9-inch Dahlgrens, modern Brooke rifles and cast-iron ram. Her speed, about 6 knots. When they saw her coming, *Cumberland*'s crew raced to battle stations, cheering. *Merrimack* got a full broadside. But the shots bounced. And the ironclad's ram smashed home, exploding *Cumberland*'s bow gun, "killing ten men including the Quarter Gunner who had his arms and legs blown off." As *Cumberland* sank, Lt. T. O. Selfridge, U.S.N., shouted final order. "Give her a broadside boys, as she goes!" Down she went with guns firing.

704. MASSACRE OF U.S.S. *CONGRESS* (right). On Union side everything went askew. Running to *Cumberland*'s rescue, steam frigate *Minnesota* slammed hard aground off Fortress Monroe. Lamed by engine trouble, steam frigate *Roanoke* couldn't get across the Roads. Ironclad *Merrimack* enjoyed Roman holiday. Having sunk *Cumberland*, she

Lt. J. B. Smith,
acting commander
of the "Congress"

blasted an Army transport, then headed for *Congress* which had run aground nearby off Newport News. Buchanan's younger brother was an officer in this helpless frigate, which surrendered after two murderous broadsides. When Federal troops ashore then fired at *Merrimack*, elder Buchanan, enraged, ordered *Congress* shot to pieces. He himself was shot in thigh while directing the firing.

Explosion of the "Congress"

The New-York Times.

VOL. XI—NO. 3264.　　　　NEW-YORK, MONDAY, MARCH 10, 1862.

HIGHLY IMPORTANT NEWS.

Desperate Naval Engagements in Hampton Roads.

Attack Upon our Blockading Vessels by the Rebel Steamers Merrimac, Jamestown and Yorktown.

The Frigate Cumberland Run Into by the Merrimac and Sunk.

Part of Her Crew Reported to be Drowned.

SURRENDER OF THE FRIGATE CONGRESS.

Engagement of the Rebel Steamers with the Newport's News Batteries.

The Minnesota and Other Vessels Aground.

CESSATION OF FIRING AT NIGHT.

Opportune Arrival of the Iron-Clad Ericsson Battery Monitor.

A Five Hours' Engagement Between Her and the Merrimac.

The Rebel Vessel Forced to Haul Off.

THE MONITOR UNINJURED.

FORTRESS MONROE, Saturday, March 8.

The dullness of O'd Point was startled to-day by the announcement that a suspicious looking vessel, supposed to be the *Merrimac*, looking like a submerged house, with the roof only above water, was moving down from Norfolk by the channel in front of the Sewell's Point batteries. Signal guns were also fired by the *Cumberland* and *Congress*, to notify the *Minnesota*, *St. Lawrence* and *Roanoke* of the approaching danger, and all was excitement in and about Fortress Monroe.

There was nothing protruding above the water but a flagstaff flying the rebel flag, and a short smokestack. She moved along slowly, and turned into the channel leading to Newport's News, and steamed direct for the frigates *Cumberland* and *Congress* which were lying at the mouth of James River.

As soon as she came within range of the *Cumberland*, the latter opened on her with her heavy guns, but the balls struck and glanced off, having no more effect than peas from a pop-gun. Her ports were all closed, and she moved on in silence, but with a full head of steam.

In the meantime, as the *Merrimac* was approaching the two frigates on one side, the rebel iron-clad steamers *Yorktown* and *Jamestown* came down James River, and engaged our frigates on the other side. The batteries at Newport's News also opened on the *Yorktown* and *Jamestown*, and did all in their power to assist the *Cumberland* and *Congress*, which, being sailing vessels, were at the mercy of the approaching steamers.

The *Merrimac*, in the meantime, kept steadily on her course, and slowly approached the *Cumberland*, when she and the *Congress*, at a distance of one hundred yards, raised full broadsides on the iron-clad monster, that took no effect, the balls glancing upwards, and flying off, having only the effect of checking her progress for a moment.

After receiving the first broadside of the two frigates, she ran on to the *Cumberland*, striking her about midships, and literally laying open her sides. She then drew off, and fired a broadside into the disabled ship, and again dashed against her with her iron-clad prow, and, knocking in her side, left her to sink, while she engaged the *Congress*, which laid about a [...] of a mile distant.

[...] officers on the point that both had been considerably damaged. These statements, if meant to borne in mind, are all based on what could be seen by a glass at a distance of nearly eight miles, and from a few panic-stricken non-combatants, who fired at almost the first gun from Newport's News.

In the meantime darkness approached, though the moon shone out brightly, and nothing but the occasional flashing of guns could be seen. The *Merrimac* was also believed to be aground, as she remained stationary, at a distance of a mile from the *Minnesota*, making no attempt to attack or molest her.

Previous to the departure of the steamer for Balti [...]

LATER AND BETTER NEWS.

A Five Hours' Engagement Between the Ericsson Battery and the three Rebel Steamers.

The Rebel Vessels Driven Off—The Merrimac in a Sinking Condition.

705. NORTHERN HEADLINES—reflecting alarm in Washington after *Merrimack* rampage. At emergency cabinet meeting War Secretary Stanton wailed in panic. "The *Merrimack* will come up the Potomac! . . .We (may) have from one of her guns a cannonball in this very room!" Lincoln and Welles remained calm.

706. *MONITOR* ARRIVES! She reached scene in time to see *Congress* blow up, midnight of March 8th. With iron beak broken off (in *Cumberland*), captain wounded, *Merrimack* had retired to safe anchorage near Norfolk. Lying low, little *Monitor* waited. When *Merrimack* came out next dawn, *Monitor* intercepted.

TERRIFIC ENGAGEMENT BETWEEN THE "MONITOR" AND "MERRIMAC."

707. *MONITOR* VS. *MERRIMACK.* Rushing in where wooden ships feared to tread, little *Monitor* maneuvered to protect stranded *Minnesota*, the *Merrimack's* next target. Confederates thought *Monitor* a "floating water tank." Surprise! As big ironclad closed in, the "water tank" spat flame. A stunning salvo struck *Merrimack's* casemate, hurling her gunners across interior deck like bloodstained tenpins.

CONFEDERATE BATTERY, SEWELL'S POINT.　　CONFEDERATE BATTERY, CRANEY ISLAND.
CONFEDERATE STEAMERS "YORKTOWN" AND "JAMESTOWN."　　CONFEDERATE BATTERIES AT PIG POINT AND BARREL POINT.　　JAMES RIVER.

GOSPORT.　　UNION BATTERY RIP-RAPS.　　FRENCH MAN-OF-WAR.　　"MONITOR" AND "MERRIMAC."　　"MINNESOTA."　　WRECKS OF "CONGRESS" AND "CUMBERLAND"
PORTSMOUTH.　　U. S. FRIGATE "ROANOKE" AND TRANSPORTS AND STORE-SHIPS.　　UNION BATTERIES AND CAMP AT NEWPORT
NORFOLK.　　　　FORT MONROE.　　HAMPT[...]

GRAND MARCH,
COMPOSED BY
E. MACK.

708. *MONITOR* AND *MERRIMACK* —sheet music title page. Battles were popular theme for Civil War composers. This tune should have been Anvil Chorus as ironclad and turret vessel went at it, hammer and tongs. "I laid the *Monitor* alongside the *Merrimack,* and gave her a shot," Captain Worden subsequently reported. "She returned our compliment by a shell weighing 150 pounds . . . which struck the turret squarely. (But) it did not start a rivet or a nut." *Monitor* veered off; her turret revolved; she dealt *Merrimack* another two-gun salvo. For next hour the two antagonists jockeyed, firing almost muzzle to muzzle. Attack bewildered Lieutenant Catesby ap. R. Jones, who was now commanding *Merrimack* as Buchanan's successor.

709. TURRET VS. CASEMATE: Big ironclad found little turret vessel an elusive target. "Aim for her ports," shouted Catesby Jones. "Sir," reported Gunnery Officer J. R. Eggle-ston, "I can do as much damage by snapping my fingers." Shells from the big Brooke rifles merely burst like giant eggs on *Monitor's* armor. But *Monitor's* solid shot cracked *Merrimack's* iron, drove great splinters from the 22-inch planking of the casemate wall, jarred the ironclad's engines. Beam to beam, the big and little titan slugged it out furiously.

710. BATTLE OF IRONCLADS. *Monitor's* gun crew (16 men under Lt. S. Dana Greene) worked like sons of Vulcan. On board *Merrimack* "all was bustle, smoke, grimy figures and stern commands, while down in the engine and boiler rooms the 16 furnaces belched fire and smoke." Battle lasted over two hours. *Monitor* men fired 41 shots for 20 hits. *Merrimackers* hit *Monitor* with 22. After futile attempt to ram *Monitor* under, the Confederate ironclad, damaged, leaking badly, veered off and headed for home. Norfolk newspapers called *Monitor* "cheesebox on a raft." But *Merrimack* had met her match.

711. POINTBLANK HIT! During
battle, a *Merrimack* shell struck *Monitor's* pilot house, blinding Captain
Worden. Fainting, he gasped, "Have
I saved the *Minnesota?*" Told *Merrimack* was licked, he replied, "Then
I don't care what becomes of me."
Monitor's pilot house, contrary to spaciousness shown in contemporary
prints, was only 2 ft. 8 in. wide by 3
ft. 6 in. long internally. Side walls
above deck plate were 9 in. thick by
12 in. deep—wrought-iron blocks
held at corners by 3 in. bolts. Original design called for 5/8 in. viewing
slit all around pilot house by placement of packing between top and
second iron bar (would give 360 degree view up to 80 ft. in height).
Despite proximity of enemy guns,
chances are Worden would not have
been hurt had not some Naval arm
chair expert (over designer and ship's
company objection) increased the
viewing slit so that shell's concussion
bent the bars. Top of the pilot house
had 2 in. thick plate made removable
from within to act as escape hatch.

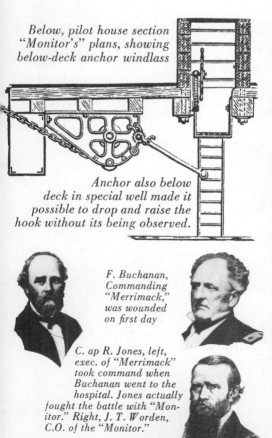

*Below, pilot house section
"Monitor's" plans, showing
below-deck anchor windlass*

*Anchor also below
deck in special well made it
possible to drop and raise the
hook without its being observed.*

*F. Buchanan,
Commanding
"Merrimack,"
was wounded
on first day*

*C. ap R. Jones, left,
exec. of "Merrimack"
took command when
Buchanan went to the
hospital. Jones actually
fought the battle with "Monitor." Right, J. T. Worden,
C.O. of the "Monitor."*

© Fred Freeman, 1956

712. OFFICERS OF *MONITOR*— after battle. Captain Worden (center) wears glasses to shield eyes temporarily blinded by powder burns. Hero of North, he was visited by Lincoln, who took his hand, told him he had saved the nation. Also honored was Ericsson, *Monitor* designer. Both sides proclaimed victory in world's first engagement between armored ships. But battle, a tactical draw, was strategic defeat for South. *Merrimack* failed to break blockade. And, sorely hurt in action, she would never fight again. Retiring to Norfolk, she left James River open to Union invasion.

713. INSPECTING *MONITOR*'S TURRET. Captain Worden (wearing straw hat) examines dent in turret's armor. With her smokestack riddled, bow bashed, casemate cracked and

engines crippled, *Merrimack (Virginia)* had been harder hit. Noting that *Monitor* was *Merrimack's* "equal," Buchanan reported to Naval Secretary Mallory that the Confederate ironclad was unseaworthy. "Should she encounter a gale or a very heavy swell, I think it probable she would founder." While *Monitor* waited in Hampton Roads, *Merrimack* remained in Norfolk. There she posed as bugaboo, but *Monitor* had her number.

714. FIRST FIGHTERS OF THE TURRET — gunners who stopped *Merrimack*. Conqueror of U.S.S. *Cumberland* and *Congress*, the Confederacy's great ironclad spelled ultimate death of wooden warships. But these Union turret-fighters spelled death of Confederacy's ironclad casemate rams. Holding *Merrimack* at

bay, *Monitor* gunners cleared way for McClellan's army to enter area. They cheered *Merrimack's* finale when she was finally blown up at Norfolk to prevent capture. In *Monitor*, they fought again at Drury's Bluff, spearheading McClellan's drive up the James, and again at Malvern Hill. Then many of these iron men in picture went down with *Monitor* in December '62 when, en route to Charleston, she foundered in gale.

S. D. Greene, 22 years old, exec. on the "Monitor"

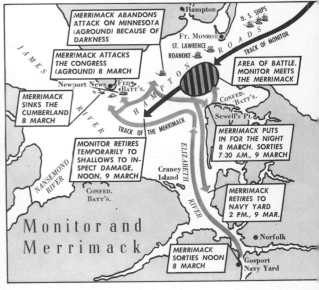

Monitor and Merrimack

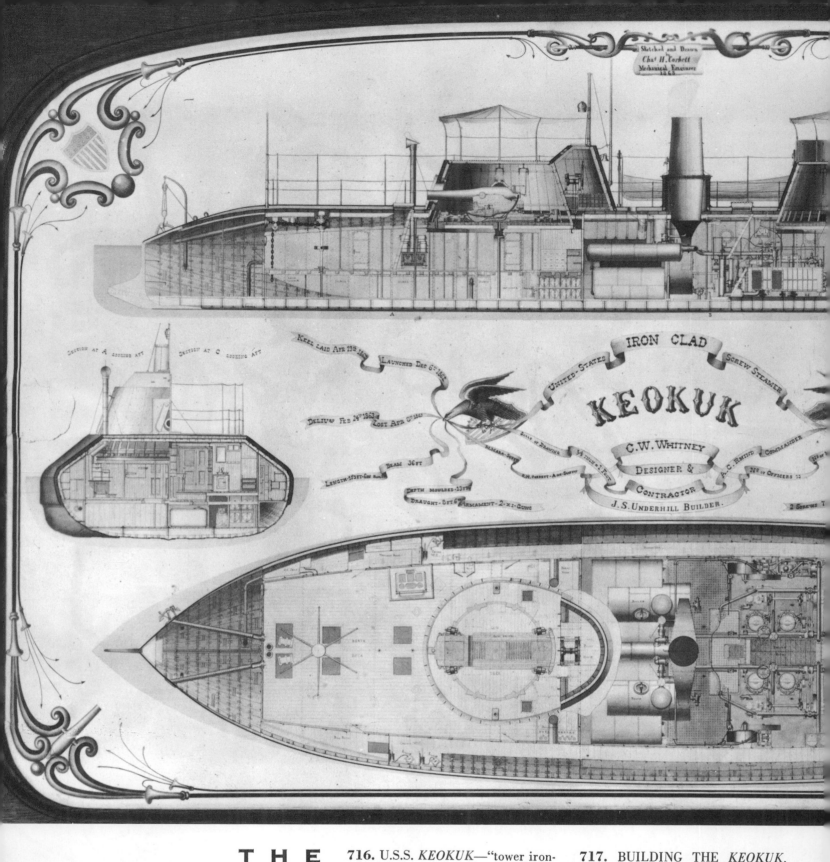

Sketched and Drawn
Chas H. Corbett
Mechanical Engineer
1863

UNITED STATES   IRON CLAD   SCREW STEAMER

KEOKUK

C. W. WHITNEY
DESIGNER &
CONTRACTOR
J. S. UNDERHILL BUILDER.

A. C. RHIND COMMANDER

KEEL LAID APR 13th 1862
LAUNCHED DEC 6th 1862
DELIV'D FEB 24th 1863
LOST APR 9th 1863

SECTION AT A LOOKING AFT
SECTION AT C LOOKING AFT

BEAM 36 FT
LENGTH 172 FT 6 IN
DEPTH MOULDED 13 FT
DRAUGHT 8 FT 6
ARMAMENT 2 × 11 GUNS

2 SCREWS

THE
MONITOR
NAVY

**715. TURRET PLAN OF LATER
MONITOR.** Overnight "Ericsson's
Folly" became naval wonder—prototype for turret vessels which took
original's name as generic. Some 35
monitors were ordered by Navy in
1862 and 25 were ordered in '63.

716. U.S.S. *KEOKUK*—"tower ironclad." Navy rush-ordered a fleet of
turret vessels after *Monitor's* success.
Odd number in novel fleet was 677-
tonner built on above plan. Mounting
two 11-inch guns in igloo-shaped
nonrevolving turrets, she could not
match "rafts" of Ericsson design.

717. BUILDING THE *KEOKUK*.
Designed by C. W. Whitney and constructed by Dry Dock Iron Works of
New York at cost of $228,000, vessel
was launched in December 1862. A
clumsy performer, her shortcomings
added up to her obituary in spring
when she went down off Charleston.

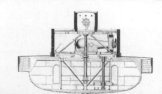

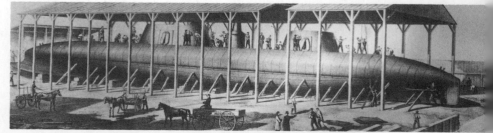

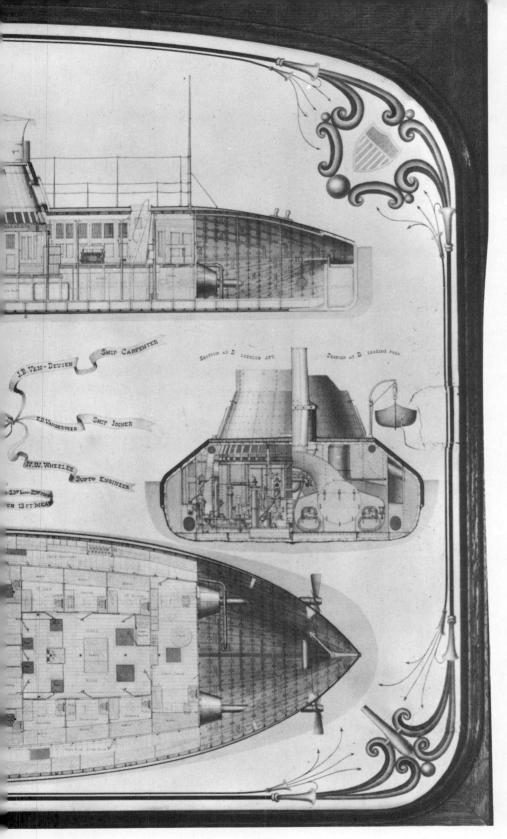

719. U.S.S. *WEEHAWKEN*—typical coastal monitor. Built by Zeno Secor & Co. of Jersey City, at cost of $465,-000. Launched November 5, 1862. An 844-ton vessel, she carried one 15-inch and one 11-inch Dahlgren gun. In addition, Navy soon acquired oceangoers of *Catskill* class—single-turret, 1,875-tonners armed with one 11-inch Dahlgren and one 15-inch Rodman gun. In 1863 came the larger *Canonicus* class—single-turret, 2,100-tonners carrying two 15-inch Rodmans. For "catfish" front Navy acquired river monitors of 614-ton *Klamath* and 970-ton *Kickapoo* class. Firing wrought-iron shot instead of cast iron used at Hampton Roads, any of these monitors could have massacred the ironclad *Merrimack.*

720. U.S.S. *ROANOKE*—first turret battleship. While Confederacy favored ironclad rams of *Merrimack* design, Union concentrated on monitors. Neither of famous prototypes survived Civil War. Original *Merrimack-Virginia* was burned by her crew at Norfolk in May '62 when McClellan's forces closed in. Following December, original *Monitor* foundered in gale off Hatteras. Noting that both types were plagued by poor sea-keeping qualities, Northern naval designers attempted to combine good features of each in converting steam frigate *Roanoke* (onlooker at *Monitor-Merrimack* fight) into an armored, turret-gunned capital ship. With her three turrets carrying 15-inch guns, this vessel, direct descendant of Ericsson's *Monitor*, was forerunner of the modern battlewagon.

718. DOUBLE-TURRET MONITOR *ONONDAGA* (bottom right). Built by G. W. Quintard, this $760,-000 oceangoer (1,250 tons) carried two 15-inch Dahlgrens and two 150-pounder Parrott rifles. Navy ordered five of these double-turret specimens; only *Onondaga*, *Monadnock* and *Tonawanda* were completed during war. Largest monitors acquired during war were million-dollar "sea elephants" *Dictator* and *Puritan*, 3,000-tonners completed in 1864. Five other big monitors, including 6,000-ton giants *Kalamazoo* and *Shakamaxon* were nearing completion in 1865.

721. FARRAGUT ON BOARD HARTFORD. Scheduled for April 1862 was invasion of South's largest seaport by Farragut's forces. To pit against Delta forts and harbor defenses which included an ironclad and a flock of small rams, he had four wooden steam sloops, an old steam frigate, three corvettes, 15 small gunboats. "Success," he wrote his wife, "is the only thing listened to in this war. I must sink or swim by that rule." Farragut planned to stay afloat. He sent Porter in with mortar fleet to annoy enemy forts.

New Orleans

722. U.S. STEAM SLOOP HARTFORD—Farragut's flagship during Delta invasion when "Queen City" was kingpin for a Union naval strike.

723. DEFENDING NEW ORLEANS, Forts Jackson and St. Philip (below) guarded the Delta. Jackson boasted bombproof vaults, big guns.

724. PARROTT RIFLES at Mississippi's mouth. Forts dominating channel below New Orleans made iron fists in the gantlet to be run.

725. ROUND SHOT AND GRAPE (cannonball cluster) were fired by smoothbores. Parrott rifles fired shells. New Orleans wasn't gun-shy.

727. C.S.S. *STONEWALL JACKSON*—a "cotton clad." One of 12 Orleanean gunboats. A seedy improvisation. But Confederates believed the Delta forts would stop Farragut before he reached harbor.

728. UNION MORTAR SCHOONER in flotilla employed to soften Delta forts. David Dixon Porter's idea. An 11-inch mortar could lob 200-pound shell 4,000 yards. Porter used 13-inchers. Navy supplied 28 schooners; "iron pots" came from Pittsburgh.

726. TYPICAL HOT-SHOT FURNACE used to heat cannonballs. Red-hot reception was prepared for Farragut and his wooden warships.

Federal mortar Schooners in action

Campaign

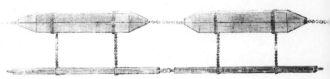

732. CHANNEL BOOMS (above) and nets (below) used to block Mississippi approaches to New Orleans. Defenders believed harbor secure.

729. GABIONS (above)—Civil War barricades. Wicker cylinders were filled with sand and employed to form beach traps or make a wall (gabionade). Landed on Delta, army of Ben Butler encountered such barriers. Of French origin, gabions and abatis were common at New Orleans.

730. ABATIS (right)—the Civil War equivalent of barbed wire. Guarded land approaches to the forts.

731. CHAIN ARMOR (below) was used by Farragut to protect the sides of his ships from cannon shot.

Confederate Iron-clad "Louisiana"

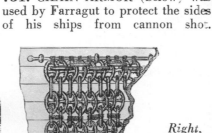

Right, plan of the "Louisiana"

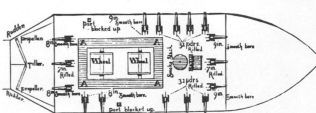

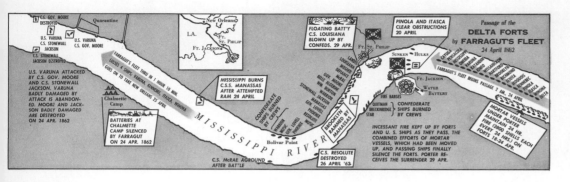

733. PASSING THE DELTA FORTS (left)—before dawn, April 24, 1862. Although Porter's mortars had battered them for six days, St. Philip and Jackson thundered a wicked crossfire as Farragut's ships started upriver. Lead gunboat *Cayuga* took 42 hits. But Union fleet got in.

734. FIRING THROUGH THEIR OWN BOW, desperate sailors of C.S.S. *Governor Moore* slammed a disabling shot into U.S. gunboat *Varuna* of Farragut's van. A "cotton clad" of New Orleans squadron, the *Moore* (Capt. Beverley Kennon, C.S.N.) was soon demolished in furious melee in the harbor entry.

736. MIDGET RAM *MANASSAS* (above). Leading defense force of 12 vessels under Commo. J. K. Mitchell, C.S.N., she charged into thick of fray, attacked big cruisers.

735. SHELL-HIT on U.S. gunboat *Iroquois.* Someone muddled an order and sent her veering alongside the *Louisiana* — unfinished ironclad moored as a floating battery near Fort St. Philip. Both *Iroquois* and Union gunboat *Pinola* were blasted.

737. *MANASSAS* MAULS U.S.S. *MISSISSIPPI.* Ramming, the "pigmy monster" gashed the old sidewheeler's hull; dealt her a carronade shot. As ram veered, Union ship's exec—Lt. George Dewey—was peering overside, as shown at right. *Manassas* next sideswiped *Brooklyn.* Then, hard hit, she ran aground, blew up.

738. GENERAL "BEN" BUTLER, U.S.A. As civilians stoned retreating Confederate troops, Butler marched in (May 1st) to rule city. He soon offended Orleaneans by posing as conqueror. Also U.S. Navy. Someone's verse reminded him Farragut and Porter defeated enemy General Lovell before Butler entered city.

"Oh, tarry, Lord Lovell!" Sir Farragut cried.
"Oh, tarry, Lord Lovell!" said he.
"I rather think not," Lord Lovell replied.
"For I'm in a great hur-ree.
"I like the drinks at St. Charles Hotel,
"But I never could stand strong Porter.
"Especially when it's served on the shell,
"Or mixed in an iron mortar."

739. BATTLE OF NEW ORLEANS (left)—carnage in inner harbor. "The river and shore were one blaze, and the sounds and explosions were terrific," wrote a Union officer. But by noon of April 25th the Stars and Stripes flagged over great seaport. Dazzling victory won by U.S. Navy.

740. FEDERAL HEADQUARTERS, New Orleans—symbol of Farragut's victory. Won at cost of 37 Union sailors, it deprived South of great seaport, vital cotton center, strategic naval base, two big ironclads (one burned to prevent capture) and whole Mississippi Delta. A mortal blow.

741. STRIPPED FOR ACTION— *Hartford* and *Brooklyn.* While Butler struck attitudes in New Orleans, Farragut prepared to strike Vicksburg. Both he and Porter urged immediate drive on Mobile, but Washington ordered them up Mississippi to Vicksburg where Farragut was to meet Union gunboats coming down from north. With "Old Man River" and "Rebs" in ugly mood, it was rough assignment for weary fleet.

FIRST STRIKE AT
Vicksburg

BRILLIANT NAVAL VICTORY ON THE MISSISSIPPI RIVER, NEAR FORT WRIGHT, MAY 10TH 1862.
By the Union Flotilla of 6 Gunboats, commanded by Com. C. H. Davis, and the Rebel fleet of 8 Iron clads, under Hollins. The action lasted one hour. Two of the Rebel gunboats were blown up, and are sunk, when the remainder retired precipitately under the guns of the fort.

742. RAMS VS. TURTLES. On May 10, 1862, Captain J. E. Montgomery, C.S.N., led Vicksburg squadron north to waylay Union gunboats approaching Memphis. Under Commo. C. H. Davis (Foote's replacement) "Turtles" were ambushed near Fort Wright. Rams disabled *Cincinnati* and *Mound City*, slowed Union drive.

743. BATTLE FOR MEMPHIS (lower left). After emergency repairs, Davis' squadron resumed down-river push. Reinforced by Army rams under Col. Charles Ellet, "Turtles" were off Memphis on June 6th. Rebel rams intercepted. In wild melee U.S. rams and "Turtles" demolished Reb rams. But missed big ironclad.

744. FARRAGUT'S GUNNERS off Vicksburg. Arriving below the city late in May, Farragut found it a Mississippi Gibraltar. On June 28th *Hartford* and seven other warships succeeded in passing the forts. Awaiting Davis' squadron upstream, Farragut reported the mission "purposeless." His position was risky.

LCDR. Cummings, exec. of the "Richmond," "I would willingly give my other leg, if we could but pass those batteries!"

745. MEMPHIS CAPTURED. As last of Montgomery's eight rams went down, Stars and Stripes rose over Memphis. South lost a vital river port and industrial center. But Rebel rams slowed Union gunboats; gave incompleted ironclad *Arkansas* chance to reach Yazoo haven near Vicksburg.

746. MEN WHO RAN VICKSBURG GANTLET—sailors of U.S. gunboat *Wissahickon*. According to picture's original caption, they were "always ready for a fight or a frolic." However, as photograph suggests, Farragut's men did little frolicking in Vicksburg's vicinity. Then or later.

747. *ARKANSAS* ESCAPES (below). Bursting out of her Yazoo lair, the Rebel ironclad charged through Farragut's fleet and dodged into Vicksburg sanctuary. Disgusted, Farragut led his ships downriver that same night (July 15th); returned to Delta. Vicksburg was to be had.

THE PIVOT-GUN OF THE "WISSAHICKON" AND ITS CREW

Confederate commerce-destroyers. She was in the fleet of Admiral Farragut at New Orleans and ran the batteries at Vicksbur Late in 1862 she was in Carolina waters and in January, 1863, participated in the first attacks on Fort McAllister. She was Admiral Dahlgren's fleet during the stirring operations in Charleston harbor and returned to South Carolina waters toward the clo of 1864, where she captured numerous prizes, enriching her officers and crew. The sailors on few of the Federal vessels had a mo varied and adventurous experience of the war than did those of the "Wissahickon," and the faces in the picture, both old and youn are those of men ready at any and all times for a fight or a frolic on their beloved ship.

748. FEDERAL SHIPS IN HAMPTON ROADS (above). With *Merrimack* checkmated, Union invasion forces were rushed to Hampton area for drive up James Peninsula. Objective: Richmond. Shipped to Fort Monroe, army of General G. B. McClellan began drive in April '62.

Action on
PENINSULAR

749. PEACEFUL JAMES RIVER— a deceptive scene. Water highway from Hampton Roads to Richmond, placid stream, in spring of '62, became road to Avernus. Union squadron entered river to cover McClellan's flank on Richmond drive.

750. THROUGH DISMAL SWAMP (below) Union naval forces jabbed at Norfolk from Elizabeth City while McClellan assembled army for siege of Yorktown at eastern end of James Peninsula. Abandoning Norfolk as untenable, Virginians blew up *Merrimack*; retreated toward Richmond. Confederate capital lay only 75 miles up the James. Not far on a small map. But a long way in Rebel country.

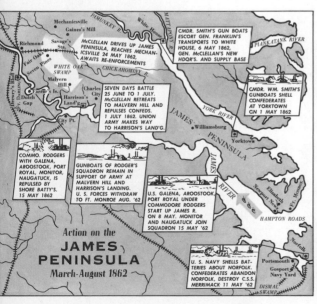

McCLELLAN DRIVES UP JAMES PENINSULA, REACHES MECHANICSVILLE 24 MAY 1862, AWAITS RE-ENFORCEMENTS.

CMDR. SMITH'S GUN BOATS ESCORT GEN. FRANKLIN'S TRANSPORTS TO WHITE HOUSE, 6 MAY 1862, GEN. McCLELLAN'S NEW HDQR'S. AND SUPPLY BASE

SEVEN DAYS BATTLE 25 JUNE TO 1 JULY. McCLELLAN RETREATS TO MALVERN HILL AND REPULSES CONFEDS. 1 JULY 1862. UNION ARMY MAKES WAY TO HARRISON'S LAND'G.

CMDR. WM. SMITH'S GUNBOATS SHELL CONFEDERATES AT YORKTOWN CN 1 MAY 1862

COMMO. RODGERS WITH GALENA, AROOSTOOK, PORT ROYAL, MONITOR, NAUGATUCK, IS REPULSED BY SHORE BATT'S. 15 MAY 1862

GUNBOATS OF RODGER'S SQUADRON REMAIN IN SUPPORT OF ARMY AT MALVERN HILL AND HARRISON'S LANDING. U. S. FORCES WITHDRAW TO FT. MONROE AUG. '62

U.S. GALENA, AROOSTOOK, PORT ROYAL UNDER COMMODORE RODGERS START UP JAMES R. ON 8 MAY. MONITOR AND NAUGATUCK JOIN SQUADRON 15 MAY '62

Action on the
JAMES
PENINSULA
March-August 1862

U. S. NAVY SHELLS BATTERIES ABOUT NORFOLK. CONFEDERATES ABANDON NORFOLK, DESTROY C.S.S. MERRIMACK 11 MAY '62

the James
CAMPAIGN ★★

751. BLUEJACKETS ON JAMES. Gunboat sailors engaged in drill on board U.S.S. *Philadelphia,* serving with squadron which covered McClellan's flank. Note neat little "powder monkey" soberly holding cartridge bucket. Boy fighting a man's war.

752. UNION MORTARS AT YORKTOWN—pots with nothing to cook. Not to be caught like Cornwallis, Confederates abandoned Yorktown. McClellan laid siege to a "ghost town." First blunder in campaign of errors. Pulled punch of Union drive.

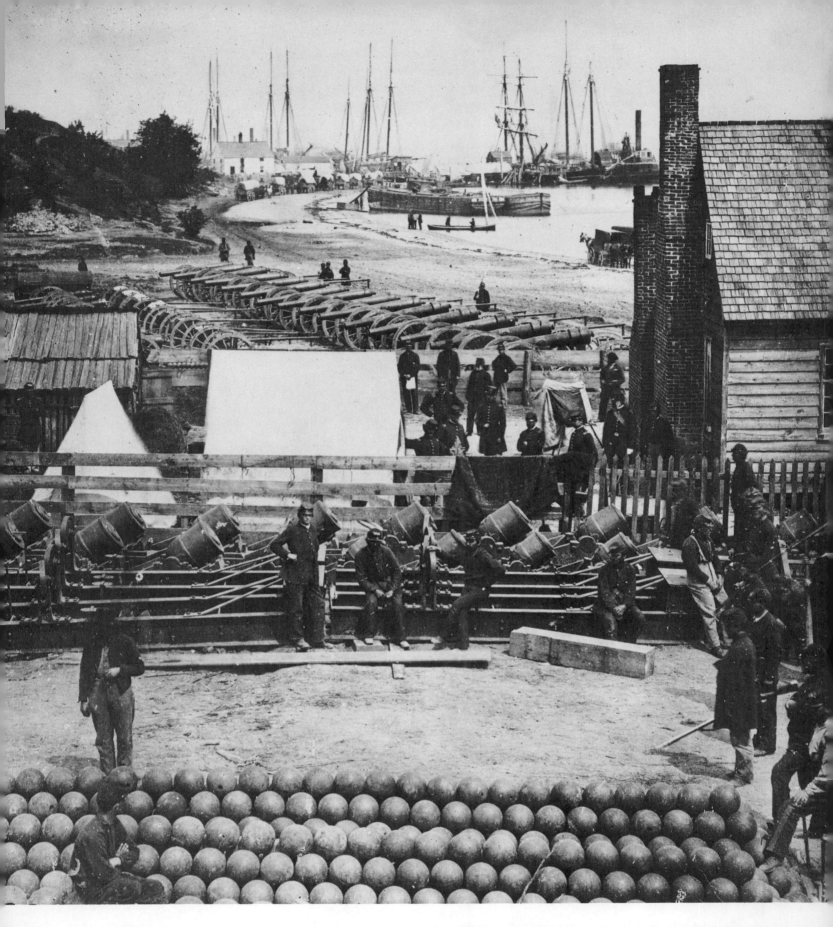

753. BOUND FOR RICHMOND— McClellan on Peninsula. Scene is study in Civil War logistics—Coehorn mortars, cannonballs, Parrott guns and caissons on beachhead. Army wagons ready for overland haul. Naval transports in the background.

754. WAITING UP THE JAMES— big guns at Fort Darling on Drewry's Bluff. While McClellan laid futile siege to Yorktown, Confederates worked to strengthen river defenses near Richmond. To no oncoming Yankee would Darling endear herself.

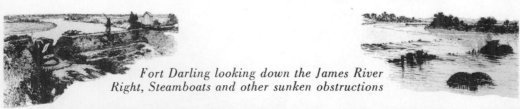

*Fort Darling looking down the James River
Right, Steamboats and other sunken obstructions*

755. McCLELLAN COMING UP. As sketched by witness, "Little Mac's" forces landing near Hampton were beautifully drilled, splendidly equipped. Best dressed troops in U.S.

756. U.S.S. *GALENA*—experimental armored sloop—led Rodgers' squadron in drive up James. Built by C. S. and H. L. Bushnell at Mystic, Conn., vessel was considered invincible ironclad. Underestimating river defenses and overestimating *Galena*, Flag Officer Goldsborough ordered Rodgers to push upstream to Richmond and if possible "shell the place into surrender." On May 15th flagship *Galena*, famous *Monitor*, Stevens battery *Naugatuck* and escorting gunboats reached Drewry's Bluff, eight miles below Richmond. In duel with Darling, *Naugatuck's* rifle burst, *Galena's* 3⅛-inch armor was punctured by 13 hits. *Monitor*, struck three times, couldn't elevate her guns to fire back at Darling's (cannon from *Merrimack*). Retreating, Rodgers dryly noted that *Galena* "was not shot-proof." Wanted: more Navy!

757. CONFEDERATE GUNBOAT *TEAZER*. Ordered to advance upstream, Federal squadron under Commo. John Rodgers II encountered mine-torpedoes, sniper fire and this one-gun tug which rushed at Yankee column like a bulldog barking at a parade. Disabled by an answering shot, *Teazer* was captured and posed for this Brady. Skipper looks as taciturn as gun. Portrait of a Reb.

758. HARVEST OF DEFEAT—McClellan beaten. Within sight of Richmond in June, he got there "lastest with mostest"—115,000 men, miles of wagon trains and siege guns. On hand "firstest with least," Generals J. E. Johnston and R. E. Lee flung 90,000 men in counteroffensive. In series of murderous battles, Union army was hurled to Malvern Hill.

Retreat from Malvern Hill

759. NAVY AT MALVERN HILL —Union gunboats and *Monitor* covering McClellan's retreat. Exerting usual military influence, Chance and Blunder were the Generals in top command on James Peninsula. Victory went to side which committed fewest errors. Despite overwhelming superiority at start, McClellan waited for reinforcements. War Secretary Stanton withheld them. Then (Chance!) General Johnston was severely wounded before Richmond; Confederate command fell to Robert E. Lee—a fatal upshot for McClellan. Opposing South's greatest soldier, "Little Mac" found war too big to handle. Mechanicsville—Gaines' Mill —White Oaks Swamp—Savages' Station—Union army reeled back. Then Lee's staff work tangled; Stonewall Jackson pulled inexplicable fluke, giving McClellan chance to reach Malvern Hill on James River. As Death rampaged at Malvern, McClellan held frantic conference with Commo. Rodgers on *Galena*; decided to retreat to Harrison's Landing. "The Army is in a bad way," Rodgers reported to headquarters. He concluded, "the gunboats may save them." But the situation "demands immediately all our disposable forces."

760. McCLELLAN COMING DOWN. Covered by Navy, Union Army made stand at Harrison's Landing. Then exhausted troops were shipped off in remarkable Civil War Dunkirk. Retreating masterfully, McClellan had cost Confederates some 19,000 dead and wounded; Federals lost about 10,000. But Peninsular defeat was expensive for Union. War Office replaced McClellan with Pope (bad). Union Army launched an inland drive for Richmond (worse). Had North's leaders spent equivalent on naval effort at this time, Mobile, Wilmington and Charleston might have fallen like New Orleans at minimum cost. Then the South's commerce would soon have expired which would have meant end of the Confederacy. But the Navy voices went unheard.

GUERRE DE CHASE

761. U.S.S. *WYOMING* (above) pursued *Alabama* to East Indies. At Singapore raider eluded pursuer, dodged to Indochina, then backtracked to Europe. *Wyoming* went on to Far East to investigate trouble with war-like Samurai in Japan.

762. FEDERAL BLOCKADER. While Confederates cheered spectacular exploits of *Alabama, Florida, Tacony* and other sea raiders, U.S.N. tightened the blockade. Southern commerce felt chill of creeping paralysis as cotton rotted ashore.

763. C.S. RAIDER *ALABAMA* (left)—Raphael Semmes in action. Mysterious "290" built by Laird's, she sailed as British cargoman to Azores for delivery to Captain Semmes, who provided her with guns and English-Irish crew described as "most reckless sailors from groggeries and brothels of Liverpool." Soon she was bagging rich prizes. To North, a pirate. To South, valiant raider—the "Scourge of the Seas."

764. SOUTHERN BLOCKADE-RUNNER under British flag (right). Accusing raiders of "piracy," U.S. Government also declared flag deceptions "illegal." But warfare, always antithesis of law, bows to expediency.

765. THE *R. E. LEE* (right)—blockade-runner with telescopic stacks. This British-built ship could shorten funnels to reduce silhouette. Slim, gray, fast, such vessels would point stern toward enemy, pull down stacks, go haring off in surface haze.

766. BLOCKADE-RUNNER *VANCE* (right). Like others, she raced between Southern ports and Bahamas. She was caught carrying a million-dollar cargo. (Runners also carried agents. Famous spy Rose Greenhow perished on runner *Condor*.)

767. *ALABAMA* SINKING U.S.S. *HATTERAS* (above). During last half of '62, Semmes' raider snared 28 Union merchantmen. Then (January 11, 1863) her Blakely pivot guns and 32-pounder broadsiders massacred Union blockader *Hatteras*, lured into fatal chase off Galveston.

Federal Blockader

768. U.S.S. *SANTIAGO DE CUBA* (above)—Union's champion ship-catcher. Converted merchantman, she proved expert blockader, bagged nine runners including *Vance* and *Lee*. In day of prize money she hit jackpot, with crew sharing over $1,500,000.

769. RACING YACHT *AMERICA* —aristocrat of fleet. Winner of "America's" cup in 1851, she skimmed into Jacksonville early in war; was sold by Lord Decie to Confederacy for $60,000. Groomed to carry agents Slidell and Mason to England (a mission canceled), she was eventually scuttled by Rebels when Federals invaded Florida. Later raised, repaired, she served as U.S. blockader. No "Reb" yacht could outspeed *America*. Thoroughbred racer.

THE CONSCRIPT BILL!
HOW TO AVOID IT!!
U. S. NAVY.
1,000 MEN WANTED, FOR 12 MONTHS!

Seamen's Pay,	- - - - - - -	$18.00 per month.
Ordinary Seamen's Pay,	. . . . .	14.00 " "
Landsmen's Pay,	. . . . .	12.00 " "

$1.50 extra per month to all, Grog Money.

$50,000,000 PRIZES!

Already captured, a large share of which is awarded to Ships Crews. The laws for the distributing of Prize money carefully protects the rights of all the captors.

PETTY OFFICERS,—PROMOTION.—Seamen have a chance for promotion to the offices of Master at Arms, Boatswain's Mates, Quarter Gunners, Captain of Tops, Forecastle, Holds, After-Guard, &c.
Landsmen may be advanced to Armorers, Armorers' Mates, Carpenter's Mates, Sailmakers' Mates, Painters, Coopers, &c.
PAY OF PETTY OFFICERS,—From $20.00 to $45.00 per month.
CHANCES FOR WARRANTS, BOUNTIES AND MEDALS OF HONOR.—All those who distinguish themselves in battle or by extraordinary heroism, may be promoted to forward Warrant Officers or Acting Masters' Mates,—and upon their promotion receive a guaranty of $100, with a medal of honor from their country.
All who wish may leave HALF PAY with their families, to commence from date of enlistment.
Minors must have a written consent, sworn to before a Justice of the Peace.

For further information apply to U. S. NAVAL RENDEZVOUS,

E. Y. BUTLER, U. S. N. Recruiting Officer,
No. 14 FRONT STREET, SALEM, MASS.

770. JOIN NAVY, AVOID DRAFT —more manpower for Northern sea power. In South volunteering broke down in 1862, compelling Richmond to order first draft in American history. North began draft in 1863. In South and North alike, army draft proved unpopular. Hence appeal of above Navy recruiting poster—much resented by heads of U.S. Army. (In 1952, Pentagon official ordered prints of this poster destroyed. A little late in day to censor Civil War history.)

771. "KING COTTON"—a falling monarch. Bales futilely waiting on wharf for shipment tell story of Confederacy's downfall. In 1860 some 6,000 ships entered and cleared from Southern ports. First year of wartime blockade reduced number to about 800. By 1862 cotton exports, financial blood of the Confederacy, dropped from $200,000,000 to under $4,000,000. South was dying on the vine.

(William Growman, drafted in Michigan, escaped the provost-marshal by hiding under the crinoline of his intended. When he emerged he wanted—out of gratitude probably—to marry the girl on the spot, and did so.)

Growman

772. "OLD MAN RIVER"—road to Deep South. As of autumn 1862 this Dixie highway—plugged by Union forces at New Orleans and Memphis, and blocked midway by Confederate Vicksburg—remained closed to both Rebel and Yankee traffic. Union strategy called for clearance of Vicksburg block. Dynamite was ordered.

Ripping The

773. DAVID DIXON PORTER—Navy's "second admiral"—gained gold stars in October 1862 when Welles dispatched him to Cairo, Ill., to rejuvenate the Western Flotilla for amphibious drive on Vicksburg. Porter wrote that he "enjoyed the promotion immensely." He would.

774. CARTOON BY ADMIRAL PORTER reveals impatience with "high brass." Caption reads: "Engineer-in-Chief Foxy explaining to the Hon. Sec'y and Board of Admirals the merits of Watt's steam engine." Quacking geese remain unidentified.

775. MOUND CITY—Porter's naval base near Cairo. Here he found slovenly vessels, sick sailors, rusty equipment. At once he installed a rigid clean-up, repair and inspection program. "The comfort and health of the men must be the first thing looked after." While old cannon were replaced and tired engines tuned up, new crews were recruited and trained. Smart uniforms were ordered. Porter himself "liked to dress up like a flaming drum major." But he could puncture pomp with a chuckle. "Fresh-water Navy" became salty under dynamic, unconventional Admiral. And prepared to go.

Cotton Curtain

777. MISSISSIPPI FLOTILLA at anchor off Mound City (above). "Tinclads," "Pook Turtles" and river ironclads of new design. Buying vessels right and left, Porter built up old Foote-Davis squadron into minor armada. Vicksburg would need it. Confederate ironclad *Arkansas* had been sunk during summer by gunboat *Essex*. But forts won't sink.

776. U.S.S. *BLACK HAWK*—Porter's flag-vessel. Gaudily painted, she bore more resemblance to showboat than gunboat. Typical Porter. First boat to carry repeating guns.

778. MAN-O'-WAR'S MEN. Type with Farragut below Vicksburg. (Banjo: favorite instrument on Mississippi River. In forage caps: U.S. Marines.) Salts on muddy water.

779. U.S.S. *CAIRO*, veteran "Turtle," was lost in reconnaissance up Yazoo River before Vicksburg drive began. Victim of electric mine-torpedo. Sunk December 12, 1862.

780. GENERAL ULYSSES S. GRANT, U.S.A. — commanding Union Army in amphibious Vicksburg drive. Wearing grubby "civvies," he met Porter at Cairo in December '62 to plot campaign. Porter wrote: "While I looked earnestly at Grant, trying to make out how much . . . there was under the plain exterior, he regarded me to see what amount of work lay under the gilt buttons and gold lace." Each saw in other a hard-hitter with no illusions about rule-book warfare.

781. VICKSBURG DEFENDER (left)—"Whistling Dick." Thickets of Rebel guns lined river bluffs where Vicksburg lay at base of a horseshoe bend. General J. C. Pemberton, C.S.A., thought city's defenses impregnable. Thinking otherwise, Grant launched stubborn effort to outflank river forts; began canal across open end of horseshoe for a wide bypass.

782. "MONSTER IRONCLAD" *CHOCTAW* (above)— one of new gunboats in Porter's flotilla. Designed by Admiral's brother, Lt. W. D. Porter, U.S.N., this 1,000-tonner was built at St. Louis in '62. Carried three 11-inch guns; two 30-pound rifles; two howitzers. Her side-wheels worked independently; could turn her on dime. Not up to Eads boats.

Original caption to spot (right), "Bress de Lord!"

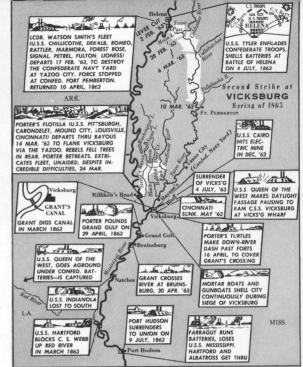

783. JUBILO!—come the gunboats! At Memphis and other river towns, Yankees were greeted by throngs of liberated colored people. Banjos thrummed song of the day.

Say, darkies, have you seen de massa,
Wid de muffstash on his face,
Go long de road some time dis mornin',
Like he gwine to leave de place?
He see de smoke way up de ribber,
Where de Linkum gunboats lay,
He tuk his hat an' he left very sudden,
And I 'spec he's runned away. . . .
De massa run, ha ha!
De darkey stay, ho ho!
It mus' be now de Kingdom comin'
In de year of Jubilo.

784. YAZOO MORASS (left) ensnared Yankee forces trying to penetrate swamps north of Vicksburg to strike city's eastern flank. Convoying army transports, Porter's gunboats were clawed by forest and foe at every turn. "Turtles" finally managed to extricate army from Yazoo trap.

785. AMPHIBIOUS TRESTLE (below)—one way to cross flooded wilderness. From January to March 1863, Grant, Porter and W. T. Sherman sought a path through Yazoo swamps to Vicksburg's "back door." Sherman waded in to save Union gunboats ambushed in one bayou.

786. FAKE IRONCLAD (right)—Vicksburg joker. While Grant's army worked on bypass, new ironclad *Indianola* dodged past Vicksburg to cut supply line below forts. Haplessly she was captured by C.S. ram *Webb* and consorts near Natchez. Meanwhile, Porter built bogus warship of logs and barrels; sent her downstream, carrying skull-crossbones flag and large sign: "Deluded People, Cave In!" Surprisingly delusive, fake ironclad drew heavy Vicksburg fire; caused panicky Confederates to blow up captive *Indianola*. A Richmond newspaper raged: "Laugh, O Yankeedom—!" And Admiral Porter roared.

787. POUNDING PORT HUDSON
—Farragut coming up. Unaware of her demise, Farragut headed north from New Orleans to rescue *Indianola*. At Port Hudson, 300 miles below Vicksburg, his ships were savagely flogged by shore guns. Old side-wheeler *Mississippi* was shot to ruin; only *Hartford* and one gunboat got through. Farragut went on with two lonely vessels to blockade the *Webb* in Red River. Ram *Webb* discreetly took cover and lay low.

788. "TURTLES" VS. VICKSBURG
(center)—night, April 16, 1863. Frustrated in canal attempt, Grant, at Porter's suggestion, decided to march army down west side of river, cross below Vicksburg, and attack from south. Porter's ironclads were to cover the lower crossing—hence this run down-river past Vicksburg's palisades. Shielded by coal barges, seven ironclads, a small ram and three transports made fiery dash. One transport was lost, but not a sailor was killed. Jubilantly Porter wrote, "It was really a jolly scene. Vicksburg never got a better pounding."

789. BOMBARDING GRAND GULF.
Forty miles below Vicksburg, Porter's ironclads slugged at Confederate river forts which blocked Grant's crossing at this point. During daylight action of April 29th, "Turtles" received severe punishment— 24 sailors killed, 56 wounded. Struck by a shell fragment, Porter himself was slightly injured. Deciding to avoid Grand Gulf, Grant moved further downriver to cross at Bruinsburg. Confederates evacuated Grand Gulf. Caught between Grant and Sherman, Vicksburg was in a vice.

790. TRUCE TO BURY DEAD—
common scene on Vicksburg front where stench of corpses became unendurable. Meeting in strange fellowship, gravediggers who had only yesterday snarled atrocity stories (of Yankee plunder, or of captive Union officers crucified for leading Negro troops) now consorted as friends. In exchange for tobacco and food, "Reb" soldiers confided inside information. Advised city was starving, Porter ordered propaganda leaflets dropped by kites flown from the *Price*. "Think of one small biscuit . . . !"

791. TRENCHES BEFORE VICKSBURG. Familiar to many of Porter's sailors and Marines who joined soldiers besieging city's outskirts. Fearing arrival of relief forces under "Joe" Johnston, Grant welcomed bluejacket help. From river, ironclads hurled shells at Vicksburg bluffs. Late in May, gunboat *Cincinnati* was sunk by shots from "Whistling Dick." But city slowly crumbled while desperate populace rioted for bread. Starving citizens lived in cellars, tended wounded.

792. VICKSBURG LEVEE—Union steamboats at landing. Gripped by forces of Grant and Sherman, bombarded from river, Vicksburg was doomed. To end useless slaughter, General Pemberton surrendered 31,000 troops on July 4, 1863. Emerging from ruins, starved populace welcomed relief from worst siege ever endured by American city. Coincident with Lee's defeat at Gettysburg, Vicksburg decisively spelled finis for the Southern Confederacy.

793. "UNVEXED TO THE SEA" flows Father of Waters. So Lincoln phrased it after Vicksburg's fall and the consequent seizure of Port Hudson (July 9, 1863), by Farragut's ships and army forces from New Orleans. Capture of entire Mississippi opened vast waterway to Union traffic (below); cut off Arkansas and Texas from Confederacy; cleared way for Sherman's march into Georgia. With the Cotton Curtain irreparably torn, the Deep South was wide open to Federal forces.

795. RUSSIAN ADMIRAL LESSOVSKY—good-will visitor to Washington and New York during Civil War. Russia was sole European power openly favoring the U.S.A. Angered by "*Trent*" Affair" (seizure of two Confederate diplomats from British steamer *Trent* in Bahama waters by U.S.S. *San Jacinto*) British massed troops in Halifax in spring of 1862. Simultaneously French Army entered Mexico. Whereupon Tsar Alexander sent friendly Russian fleet to United States on diplomatic visit.

794. NAPOLEON III—opportunist. While Union and Confederacy were at death grips, French Emperor sent army to Mexico to plant Austrian Archduke Maximilian on puppet throne. New try at old "Holy Alliance" game. Tragic for Maximilian.

796. RUSSIAN FLEET IN NEW YORK HARBOR (below)—sensation in autumn of 1863. Russian warships also visited Golden Gate, Admiral Popov reaching San Francisco just as city was threatened by a Confederate raider. Lavishly entertained there, Russian sailors won immense popularity by manning bucket brigades when the city was ravaged by conflagration. Modern historians point out that Russian motives were not purely altruistic; fleet's visit was a counter to British imperialism. But it served as tremendous morale-boost to war-weary North at time Britain was aiding Confederacy and French were breaching Monroe Doctrine. Gideon Welles' contemporary sentiments: "Thank God for the Russians."

INTERNATIONAL
SITUATION

Charleston
NUT THE NAVY

797. HOLDING U.S.N. AT BAY at Charleston, S.C. Defending South's largest Atlantic port were such guns as this 220-pounder Parrott in Fort Gregg on Morris Island. Similar heavies in Forts Moultrie, Sumter, Wagner, Beauregard, Marion, Bee, Johnson and Glover roared defiance at Union from "Cradle of Secession." (Note gunners at poker game.)

798. GUN DECK OF U.S.S. *PAW-NEE*—with Du Pont's squadron laying off (and for) Charleston. Naval attack was scheduled for spring of 1863. Du Pont called for ironclads to hammer at harbor's maze of forts.

799. POWDER MONKEY ON U.S.S. *New Hampshire*. Union Navy contained dozens of iron youngsters.

800. "PET PARROTT ESCAPES on U.S. vessel." Episode could have occurred off Charleston where Du Pont's "soapboxers" fought many a winter gale. Also fought enemy rams.

801. CHARLESTON RAMS VS. BLOCKADER. Action exploded on January 31, 1863, when ironclad rams *Palmetto State* and *Chicora* steamed out of Charleston to attack Union blockade line. After bashing and capturing U.S. armed steamer *Mercedita*, rambunctious rams assaulted blockader *Keystone State*. As illustrated, they caught tiger by tail. Wooden "soapboxer" turned tables by ramming *Palmetto State* twice and again. Union vessel took ferocious scorching—one shot beheaded three Marines; another burst her steam chest, scalding the engine crew. Then U.S.S. *Housatonic* came up; Confederate rams fled back to base. Bombastic General Beauregard issued manifesto declaring the blockade broken. British Prime Minister Gladstone stated Confederacy was now "a nation." And North rushed ironclads to Charleston front for naval smash.

Campaign
COULDN'T CRACK

802. MONITOR *MONTAUK* DESTROYS *NASHVILLE*. Old Rebel met sorry end when new monitor reached Carolina front. Du Pont sent her to Warsaw Sound to shell Ft. McAllister. There she waylaid and blasted famous raider, night of February 25th. Captained by John L. Worden, No. 1 *Monitor* skipper, *Montauk* blew hole in Reb bombast.

803. U.S. IRON FLEET OFF CHARLESTON—*New Ironsides* and consorts in action. Ordering capture of defiant stronghold, Secretary Welles rushed new monitors *Montauk, Weehawken, Patapsco, Catskill, Nantucket, Nahant, Passaic,* and turret vessel *Keokuk* to Charleston front. With flagship *New Ironsides,* Du Pont now commanded Navy's entire ocean-going iron fleet. Picture in *Illustrated London News* may have impressed Gladstone. But Du Pont hesitated before iron-jawed harbor.

804. DIVINE SERVICE on board U.S. monitor *Passaic.* On evening of April 6, 1863, Du Pont's men-o'-war girded for battle. All-out assault on Charleston was slated for next day.

805. ASSAULT ON CHARLESTON FORTS—score: nothing for Navy. Prodded by Welles, Du Pont attacked on April 7th. Monitors were ordered to bombard Sumter "beyond precedent." But everything went wrong. Able to fire only 139 shots in all, "fighting rafts" were lambasted by some 2,200 shots from Sumter and Moultrie. On sidelines big *New Ironsides* fired just one salvo. In confusion Du Pont retired with only one sailor killed but every monitor damaged or disabled. Weird *Keokuk,* riddled, rolled over and sank next morning. Du Pont reported failure.

806. DAHLGREN WITH STAFF off Charleston. "Du Pont," wrote Welles, "seems determined Charleston shall not be captured by the Navy." Determined to the contrary, "Uncle Gideon" replaced Du Pont with Dahlgren. Time and again Dahlgren pushed the attack (he was wounded on monitor *Passaic*). But Navy's famed gun-inventor could do little against forts bristling with his own big-calibered "soda bottles."

807. MONITOR *WEEHAWKEN* VS. RAM *ATLANTA*. In this action (June 17, 1863) prestige was regained for blockade fleet and for Ericsson-type monitor. Patrolling with sister *Nahant* off Warsaw Sound, *Weehawken* caught Georgia ram in sortie. Expertly handled by Capt. John Rodgers, monitor scored four smashing hits. Holed, the brand new Confederate ironclad surrendered after 15 minutes. A valuable prize

808. CAPTURED RAM *ATLANTA*. She is shown in Union possession, working as minesweeper (note fender on bow) with James River Flotilla. Her cumbersome casemate displays basic weakness of Confederacy's *Merrimack*-type ironclads — bulk which made slow vessel an easy target. Agile monitors of *Weehawken* class (armed with one 11-inch rifle, one 15-inch smoothbore) couldn't miss. Casemate in point: *Atlanta*'s.

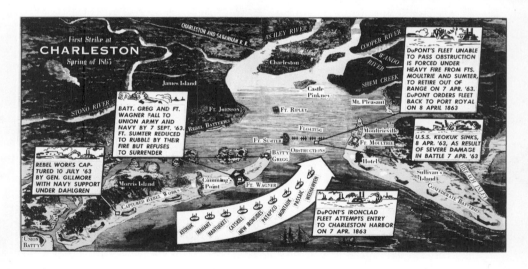

809. MONITOR *CATSKILL* off Charleston. Time out for camera pose was rare for monitors on Charleston front. During July-August '63 *Catskill* alone fired 559 shots at enemy forts; was struck by 86 projectiles. Bombarding Fort Wagner, shortly after this photo, Capt. G. W. Rodgers (shown seated on turret) was killed.

810. UNION SAILORS IN FORT WAGNER. "Rebs" abandoned outermost fort in September after assault by monitors and landing forces of General Gillmore. This was nearest Navy came to entering Charleston. But if Navy could not break in, defenders could not break blockade, even by desperate submarine effort.

CIVIL WAR
Submarines

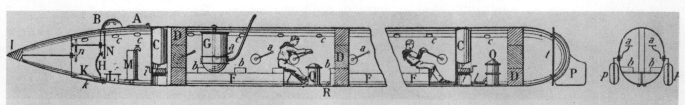

811. FEDERAL SUBMARINE ALLIGATOR

811. FEDERAL SUBMARINE ALLIGATOR—U.S. Navy's first. By 1861 both Germany and Russia possessed submarines; French inventors were building a third. Suddenly remembering Bushnell and Fulton, U.S. Government hired French engineer De Villeroi to design and build sub for Navy at Philadelphia—one that could blow up ironclad *Merrimack* then at Norfolk. Born was *Alligator*, 47 feet long, 6 in diameter, "built of steel plates." Critics described her motive power as "absurd arrangement 'of hand-worked, duckfoot paddles in age of screw propeller." The paddles which "opened and shut like the leaves of a book" were worked by 16 men sitting two by two. Air was produced by "two machines—a bellows passing over a chamber of lime, the other producing oxygen." She was armed with a "spar torpedo." But she never made an attack. Failing construction deadline, De Villeroi absconded. Government seized vessel for completion. Under a Mr. Eakins, "Gator" left Philadelphia in June '62, during storm, she was abandoned off Virginia Capes. (Diagram below)

Diagram from "La Navigation Sous-Marine," By Maurice Delpeuch, Felix Juven, Paris

DIAGRAM OF VILLEROI'S SUBMARINE, 1863

The labels are as follows: A, hatch; B, conning tower; C, buoys; D and F, solid and liquid ballast; G, air purification apparatus; K, watertight compartment, from which diver exits under water by port k; a, levers to operate oars or paddles. (See page 845.)

C. S. N. SUBMARINE FORCE

812. RAM AND SPAR TORPEDO (below)—Confederate design. Weapon carried by submarine *Alligator* indicates Union ordnance men experimented with similar torpedoes. But Confederates contrived first successful devices for torpedo warfare. Barrel-shaped "ram torpedo" was merely contact bomb affixed to underwater ram. "Spar" or "outrigger torpedo" (at right) was simple contact bomb fastened to end of long pole or spar which was thrust at target. Chief draw-back: torpedo-blast which sank victim was liable to sink user as well. Case of being hoist on own petard.

813. DESIGN FOR CONFEDERATE SUBMERSIBLE (below). Early in war Confederate Sec'y of State Benjamin received letter from a Mr. J. K. Scott requesting naval commission for "submarine boat called the *Pioneer*." Scott wrote: "Said vessel, built at New Orleans in March 1862, is 34 feet in length, 4 in breadth, 4 feet deep. She measures about 4 tons, has round conical ends and is painted black. She will carry explosive matter, and will be manned by two or more men." *Pioneer* was first of a number of remarkable Rebel subs. Below is plan of an undersea boat that was designed and built at Charleston in 1863 by St. Julien Ravenel, M.D.

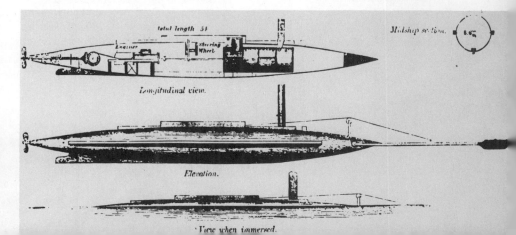

814. AMAZING CONFEDERATE SUBMERSIBLE (above)—a coal-burning "David." South's subs were named for Biblical giant-killer. This privately built specimen was donated to C.S.N. by Mr. Theodore Stoney of Charleston. Manned by four volunteers, she sortied on night of October 5, 1863; in surprise attack jabbed 65-pound torpedo into U.S.S. *New Ironsides*. Blast disabled big warship, and swamped little sub. Stunned Union sailors captured *David's* captain, Lt. W. T. Glassell, C.S.N., and Fireman Sullivan. But her engineer and pilot (aptly named Tomb and Cannon) bailed her out, started engine, steamed her home to Charleston—first sub in history to torpedo an enemy warship. Camera found her on beach after war.

815. C.S.S. *HUNLEY*—first submarine to sink an enemy ship. Nicknamed "David," "fish torpedo-boat" and "floating coffin," *Hunley* was first sub constructed for deep submergence. Designed by H. L. Hunley with aid of Baxter Watson and J. R. McClintock (inventors of *Pioneer*), she was built in shops of Park & Lyons at Mobile. Her hull an old boiler, she had diving fins, ballast tanks for submersion. Was powered by elbow grease, eight men working hand-cranked propellor. During Mobile trials, volunteer crew and designer drowned in *Hunley*. Expressed to Charleston, she made four more fatal trials. However, Lt. G. E. Dixon of 21st Alabama Infantry volunteered to serve as sub's captain. On night of February 16, 1864, "floating coffin" tried daring surface raid; succeeded in ramming spar torpedo into U.S. steam sloop *Housatonic*. Blast which sank surprised warship also downed little sub and crew of nine—sixth crew to perish in *Hunley*. (at left)

816. "DAVID" SUB IN CHARLESTON HARBOR. As Confederate sub operations were highly secret and records were burned to prevent exposure at war's end, no one knows exact number of submarines built by South. Impavid little "Davids." They failed to break blockade, but their challenge worried North's naval "Goliaths" no end. And 35 years would pass before the U.S. Navy acquired a comparably successful submarine. (at left)

"River Devils" for carrying on the war.

CHARLESTON POSTSCRIPT

817. RECRUITING CONFEDER-ATE LADIES for "Seaboard Service." According to some historians, poster which appeared in Southern cities during Civil War indicated shortage of manpower for coast de-defense. Others say poster was only hoax. But authorities on social customs of day point to evidence indicating that ladies wanted may have been those usually associated with the adjective "evening." (right)

A valiant warrior you are
You talked exceeding fine.
But shirked when bullets flew about
You're not my Valentine.

818. CIVIL WAR COMIC VALENTINE (above). Published in 1863 and doubtless popular on February 14, 1864. Navy's failure at Charleston made this jape a probable favorite in the Captain's mail. Also for Sailor Boy who had talked a big fight.

YOUNG LADIES WANTED
IN THE
ENGINEER CORPS

A Few Places Yet Left!

GREAT INDUCEMENTS!
Are offered YOUNG LADIES in the Engineers.

TRY IT!

COME INTO THE ENGINEERS & BE HAPPY!

NO HUMBUG!

The ENGINEER CORPS are stationed exclusively on the SEABOARD! Young ladies fond of *Oysters! Crabs! Eels! Turtles! Catfish!* or *Clam Soup!* may enjoy this diet all the year round by securing a husband in the ENGINEERS!! LARGE FORTUNES considered *no objection* in the Engineer Corps! Consumptive and delicate YOUNG LADIES of large means, *try the Engineer Corps and the Sea Air!* YOUNG LADIES mourning the loss of wealthy and indulgent parents, and with no sympathising brothers and sisters, *seek consolation in the Engineer Corps.* A hearty welcome is offered; the pleasures of a home by the sounding sea are secured; sympathising hearts are found, and true happiness is warranted only in the ENGINEER CORPS! TRY IT! TRY IT!

APPLY EARLY. Offers received for a few days only.

N. B.—Grass and California Widows need not apply.

819. UNION ADMIRAL'S HAT—uneasy lies the head. Valentine lampoon was mild compared to jabs given top-rank Navy officers by acidulous Secretary Welles. No respecter of braid, "Uncle Gideon" had scolded Farragut for *Arkansas'* escape from Yazoo. After *Merrimack's* first sortie he scathed Goldsborough for "wordy pretensions, but no courage." Du Pont got it for Charleston. "He prefers living in his palatial flagship." Navy's Civil War admirals (first in U.S. service) found jobs no sinecure. (at left)

820. C. S. RAIDER *CHICAMAUGA.* Unable to break Union lock on Charleston, Confederates labored to build new ironclads. A big one at Charleston—two at Wilmington— *Albemarle* up Roanoke River—another at Savannah—three at Richmond—two giants at Mobile. Meantime, such merchantmen as *Chicamauga* went out as ocean raiders. All proved forlorn hopes. (at left)

*Commodore Duncan Ingraham, C.S.N.
Commander of Confederate Naval Forces
defending Charleston*

MISSISSIPPI MOP UP

821. U.S. TURRET STEAMER OUACHITA. Soon after fall of Port Hudson, Farragut was awarded rest leave; Porter was placed in command of Mississippi from Cairo to New Orleans. "Old Man River" was in Union to stay. But her lower tributaries and deep bayous made haven for remnant Confederate squadrons. In concealed backwater lurked C.S. ram *Webb*. Deep South, Confederacy was dying hard. Porter worked overtime to build up flotilla depleted by Vicksburg campaign ("Turtles" *Cairo* and *Baron de Kalb* torpedoed in Yazoo; *Cincinnati* and *Indianola* sunk in battle). Purchased in Cairo in September '63, big sidewheeler *Ouachita*, armed with 39 cannon, was largest Civil War gunboat on Mississippi. She was needed on dangerous occupation front. (left)

822. U.S. RIVER RAM *VINDICATOR*—more reinforcement for Porter's flotilla. Built with sister ram *Avenger* at New Albany, Ind., she was 750-tonner carrying 13 guns. But rams were obsolescent by autumn of 1863. At Cincinnati, St. Louis, Pittsburgh, great iron works were hammering out river monitors. Navy would need them. Below Vicksburg thousands of tons of cotton awaited salvage. Snipers and raiders plagued the valley. Example: at Rodney, Miss., guerillas captured captain and crew of gunboat *Rattler*, surprising them in church. Porter planned mop-up. (below, right)

823. U.S. DOUBLE-TURRET RIVER MONITOR *KICKAPOO*. By fall of '63, Mississippi Flotilla contained three small monitors—*Neosho, Ozark, Osage.* Coming were heavies: *Kickapoo, Milwaukee, Manayunk, Winnebago, Shiloh, Chickasaw, Catawba, Klamath, Umpqua, Yuma, Tippecanoe.* By autumn of '64, flotilla would boast 107 vessels. But Western Confederates jumped the gun on these heavy reinforcements. In spring of '64 Louisiana was menaced. Storming out of Texas came Rebel army under savage General Bedford Forrest. Porter prepared to meet foe half way. (below)

824. PORTER'S SQUADRON UP RED RIVER

824. PORTER'S SQUADRON UP RED RIVER—precarious position. In March 1864, Union forces launched amphibious drive for Shreveport, La. Purpose was three-fold: to pin down a Rebel army, isolate Texas, and counter French threat below the Rio Grande. Porter led Navy squadron, pacing Union army under General N. P. Banks. Bungling at outset, Banks failed to make rendezvous on schedule. While Rebel scouts on Red reported, "The Yankee gunboats are thicker than fiddlers in hell," General Banks (political appointee known as the "Dancing Master") fiddled in New Orleans, attending banquet. Delay gave enemy time to stiffen defenses. Also gave Red River time to go low.

Red River
N A V Y   U P   A

825. U.S. "TIMBERCLAD" LEX-INGTON (left). One of 12 vessels in Red River drive, old "Lex" showed guts behind her timber. Because start was delayed until April 3rd, spring floodwater ebbed, threatening to strand squadron in shallow river. Then Banks, ambushed at Pleasant Hill, retreated pellmell, leaving Porter up the creek. During crisis, monitor *Osage* ran aground. In gun battle with "Rebs," *Lexington* rescued her.

826. U.S. RIVER MONITOR *OSAGE* (above). One of three Eads-type "rafts" in Red River campaign, this odd little 500-tonner met Porter's appeal for vessel which could float "wherever there is enough dew." But up the Red there wasn't enough dew. Grounding in midstream (April 12th), *Osage* was attacked by 5,000 Rebels. Just in nick, *Lexington* arrived. Wild battle cost "Rebs" 700 dead. *Osage* won and hauled clear.

Porter's Expedition starting from Vicksburg for the Red River

U.S.S. OSAGE GOES AGROUND DURING SIEGE AT PLEASANT HILL, SAVED BY LEXINGTON 12 APRIL, 1864

PORTER LOSES U.S.S. CRICKET AND EASTPORT IN RUNNING BATTLE DOWN RED RIVER WITH CONFED. LAND FORCES

RIVER TOO LOW FOR PORTER'S FLEET TO PASS. DAM BUILT, BOATS FLOATED THRU TO SAFETY, MAY '64

RED RIVER

Shreveport
Sabine Cross Roads
Pleasant Hill
Alexandria
Ft. DeRussy

Expedition on the RED RIVER
Spring of 1864

GEN. BANKS' ARMY WITH ADM. PORTER'S FLEET OF 19 VESSELS LEAVES ALEXANDRIA FOR SHREVEPORT 3 APR. '64. AMBUSHED AT SABINE CROSS ROADS, BANKS RETIRES TO PLEASANT HILL, FIGHTS OFF CONFEDS. 12 APRIL, DECIDES TO RETURN TO NEW ORLEANS, LEAVES PORTER IN RED RIVER

NORTH

LA.

827. U.S. "TINCLAD" *CRICKET* (right)—Porter's flagship in Red. Shown at Alexandria, La., she was blistered in hot fighting as squadron retreated downstream toward that base. Porter himself took helm when she ran into river ambush. With bullets literally combing his beard, Admiral steered down tricky channel swept by shore guns and sharpshooters. *Cricket*, riddled, was finally abandoned. So was gunboat *Eastport*, after striking mine. Rest of squadron reached Alexandria to find local rapids too shallow for navigation. When General Banks suggested abandoning all vessels, Porter went apoplectic. The answer was "Dam!"

Fiasco
CREEK

828. DAM TO THE RESCUE! Suggestion from Col. Joseph Bailey, a former lumberman. Block the river! When water rose, gunboats could go through! So! While *Osage* and other vessels fought off attacks, Union troops and bluejackets desperately played beaver. Dam-job went forward, as shown in rare photograph.

829. DOWNSTREAM SWIM THE "TURTLES" (below). At crucial climax dam was blown. "Jumping over sand bars and logs," gunboats got through. Porter punned bitterly, "If damning helped, I'd have been afloat long ago." Behind remained two crippled "tinclads." Also crowds of helpless Negroes who were rounded up and butchered by vengeful Confederate militia. With squadron safe on Mississippi, Porter blamed Banks for costly fiasco. He never forgave Banks for leaving him in the Red.

830. HUNTERS OF THE RAIDER. Officers of U.S.S. *Kearsarge*, ship that caught up with the *Alabama*. Catch was at Cherbourg, France, where Rebel cruiser put in for repairs in June 1864. Spy reports brought Yankee *Kearsarge* down from Holland, bone in teeth. Former shipmate of Raphael Semmes, Capt. John A. Winslow, U.S.N. (third from left), was determined to trap famous raider. *Kearsarge* was there in time. Happy schoolchildren would soon recite: "In Cherbourg Roads the pirate lay, On the morn of June, like a beast at bay. . . ." Yankee accent.

831. ACE CAPTAIN OF CONFEDERATE NAVY — Semmes on board the *Alabama*. Rare photograph (below) was taken in Jamaica, West Indies, before raider's run to Orient. By time she reached Cherbourg, *Alabama* had sunk one U.S. warship, bagged immense haul of 63 Northern merchantmen. Ordered by French to quit neutral port, Semmes sent message out to Winslow, proposing old-fashioned ship duel. "My intention is to fight the *Kearsarge*. . . . I beg she will not depart before I am ready." Winslow grimly cleared decks, prepared for showdown with "Falcon of the Seas." Semmes told raider crew, "Defeat is impossible!"

Kearsarge

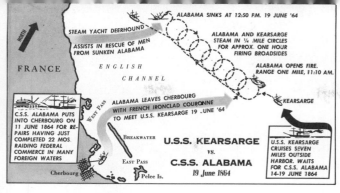

U.S.S. KEARSARGE
vs.
C.S.S. ALABAMA
19 June 1864

ALABAMA SINKS AT 12:50 P.M. 19 JUNE '64

ALABAMA AND KEARSARGE STEAM IN ¼ MILE CIRCLES FOR APPROX. ONE HOUR FIRING BROADSIDES

ALABAMA OPENS FIRE. RANGE ONE MILE, 11:10 AM.

STEAM YACHT DEERHOUND ASSISTS IN RESCUE OF MEN FROM SUNKEN ALABAMA

C.S.S. ALABAMA PUTS INTO CHERBOURG ON 11 JUNE 1864 FOR REPAIRS HAVING JUST COMPLETED 22 MOS. RAIDING FEDERAL COMMERCE IN MANY FOREIGN WATERS

ALABAMA LEAVES CHERBOURG WITH FRENCH IRONCLAD COURONNE TO MEET U.S.S. KEARSARGE 19 JUNE '64

U.S.S. KEARSARGE CRUISES SEVEN MILES OUTSIDE HARBOR. WAITS FOR C.S.S. ALABAMA 14-19 JUNE 1864

832. *ALABAMA-KEARSARGE* MEETING (top left)—Sunday, June 19, 1864. Flags flying, officers in full dress, raider steamed out of harbor escorted by French ironclad *Couronne* and English pleasure yacht *Deerhound*. Crowds lined Cherbourg cliffs, cheering. Winslow, no romanticist, cleared *Kearsarge* for show-down. Semmes opened fire at mile range. *Alabama's* tough Limey tars may have chanted foc's'le song below.

We're homeward bound; we're homeward bound,
And soon we'll stand on English ground,
But ere our native home we see,
We first must fight the Kearsargee!

vs. Alabama

833. BLASTING *ALABAMA* (top right). Winslow opened fire at close range. Two wooden sloops were fairly matched: *Alabama*, 8 guns; *Kearsarge*, 7. But *Kearsarge* had heavier guns (two 11-inchers), better gunnery. Firing methodically, Union sailors hit hard while enemy shots missed.

834. *ALABAMA* HARD HIT. As ships reeled along French coast, *Kearsarge* shots riddled raider's hull, ripped her decks, uprooted her guns. When 11-inch shell exploded in *Alabama's* engine-room, Semmes, in despair, turned crippled vessel toward shore. *Kearsarge* closed in.

835. DEATH OF THE *ALABAMA* —drama of a dying era. Of wooden warships (*Kearsarge* was chain-armored). Of outmoded formalities (the challenge to duel). Of bravura theatricals (Captain Semmes hurling his sword into the sea). Twenty-one of crew died with *Alabama*. As raider sank Semmes escaped on yacht *Deerhound*. Sea victory braced North, just shaken by shock of Cold Harbor.

836. 100-POUNDER IN *KEARSARGE* STERNPOST — *Alabama's* story in a dud shell. Deadhead came from raider's Blakely rifle. Duds explain *Kearsarge* loss of only one man.

NAVY
SUPPORTS
Grant

837. PETTY OFFICERS OF U.S.S. *HUNCHBACK*—sharp as you please. Civil War Navy chiefs holding that pose for Brady are typical gunboaters of James River Flotilla which supported Grant's drive on Richmond.

838. UNION GUNBOAT VETERANS—type who held the lower James open for Grant. Hardy specimens, they show the wear and tear of arduous duty on river road to Richmond. Hazards beset every bend—Confederate snipers, shore batteries, channel traps, torpedoes. They got old gunboat *Shawsheen* (artillery fire) and old gunboat *Commodore Jones* (a mine). But this old gunboat (probably U.S.S. *Hunchback*) seems to have been immune to everything but contemporary camera shots.

839. LIEUTENANT AND ENSIGN OF *HUNCHBACK*. All rigged for shore leave. The ladies won't mind those costumes—*nobody's* trousers are pressed in 1864. But pipe classy headgear! Bring on the hoopskirts!

JAMES RIVER

OPERATIONS, 1864

B-5226

840. CITY POINT ON JAMES RIVER—where Grant moved U.S. troops after Cold Harbor disaster. Brought east by Lincoln to command Potomac Army in spring of '64, Grant promptly launched massive drive on Richmond. Although heavily outnumbered, Lee struck crushing blow at Cold Harbor, ten miles from Confederate capital. (In one-hour battle Federals lost 7,000 killed; Confederates about 600.) Instead of retreating, Grant swung southeast to cross James and establish City Point base. Navy's James River Flotilla covered move to outflank Richmond.

841. MINE STRIKE!—Confederate torpedo in James River blasts U.S. gunboat *Commodore Barney*. Episode of August '63 warned Rear Admiral S. P. Lee, U.S.N., that Rebel mine experts were on the scene. An old "soapboxer," *Barney* barely managed to survive. After elderly *Commodore Jones* was blasted (May 1864) Welles reinforced James Flotilla supporting Grant with new gunboats and monitors. Navy rigged mine sweeps.

842. U.S. "DOUBLE-ENDER" *MENDOTA*—new-type gunboat on James. One of 25 built for Navy in 1863, she could operate like two-way ferryboat—a facility which eliminated turn-around maneuver in narrow river channels. These agile 10-gun vessels were welcomed in James Flotilla. Some had iron hulls.

845. GUNBOAT *AGAWAM* AND MONITOR *SAUGUS*. Picketing James River, U.S. vessels guarded against counterattack by Richmond ironclads under Commo. J. K. Mitchell, C.S.N. — an ugly threat.

846. DRIFTING MINES (Confederate model). Type shown below swam downstream with little head poked above surface, harder to spot than a blacksnake. Specimen at right has propeller device ingeniously geared with mechanism to explode powder demijohn after timed run in swift current. Mines were sown in James by Hunter Davidson, captain of C.S.S. *Torpedo*. Converted tug, she was one of most intrepid minelayers in American naval history.

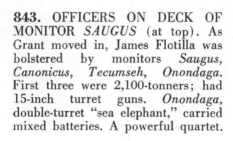

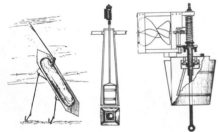

843. OFFICERS ON DECK OF MONITOR *SAUGUS* (at top). As Grant moved in, James Flotilla was bolstered by monitors *Saugus*, *Canonicus*, *Tecumseh*, *Onondaga*. First three were 2,100-tonners; had 15-inch turret guns. *Onondaga*, double-turret "sea elephant," carried mixed batteries. A powerful quartet.

844. MONITOR *CANONICUS* ON JAMES (above). Photographed on duty below Drewry's Bluff, she may have been taking on supplies, or examining suspicious vessel. While Grant's transports unloaded at City Point, monitors upstream stood guard against disguised minelayers and spy boats sent down from Richmond.

847. *SAUGUS* ON MINE-SWEEPING DETAIL (below). Note "torpedo fender" on her bow. Up James she picketed Richmond ironclads *Virginia II*, *Richmond* and *Fredericksburg* hemmed upriver. Ironclads hurled long-range fire at monitors in summer and fall of 1864. But kept their distance. Big rams at bay.

EAGLES THEY FLY HIGH AT

Mobile!

boats, ocean-going monitor *Manhattan,* and twin-turret river monitors *Chickasaw* and *Winnebago.* But barging into Mobile won't be easy.

848. FARRAGUT OFF MOBILE. With Captain Percival Drayton on board *Hartford.* Date: July 1864. Mission: to capture South's last major Gulf port. Farragut's squadron contains flagship *Hartford,* seven other steam sloops, three double-ender gunboats, three light gun-

849. *HARTFORD'S* GUN DECK— 11-inchers aiming for Mobile. Three years a-building, Mobile defenses were ready. Forts Morgan, Gaines and Powell guarded the bay. In harbor was defense squadron led by new ironclad ram *Tennessee* under Admiral Buchanan, former captain of *Merrimack-Virginia.* And channel chock-a-block with mines. Farragut was grim, but resolute. He wrote his wife, "Any man who is prepared for defeat would be half defeated before he commenced." Defeatist? Farragut?

Federal Fleet in Mobile Bay

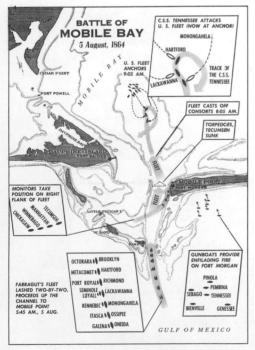

BATTLE OF
MOBILE BAY
5 August, 1864

MOBILE BAY

C.S.S. TENNESSEE ATTACKS
U. S. FLEET (NOW AT ANCHOR)
MONONGAHELA
HARTFORD
LACKAWANNA
U. S. FLEET
ANCHORS
9:05 AM.
TRACK OF
THE C.S.S.
TENNESSEE

CEDAR POINT
FORT POWELL

FLEET CASTS OFF
CONSORTS 8:05 AM.

TORPEDOES,
TECUMSEH
SUNK

DAUPHINE ISLAND
FORT GAINES

MONITORS TAKE
POSITION ON RIGHT
FLANK OF FLEET
MANHATTAN
TECUMSEH
WINNEBAGO
CHICKASAW

MOBILE POINT
FORT MORGAN

LITTLE PELICAN I.

W. BAND

BAND

FARRAGUT'S FLEET
LASHED TWO-BY-TWO,
PROCEEDS UP THE
CHANNEL TO
MOBILE POINT
5:45 AM, 5 AUG.

OCTORARA ● BROOKLYN
METACOMET ● HARTFORD
PORT ROYAL ● RICHMOND
SEMINOLE ● LACKAWANNA
LOYALL
KENNEBEC ● MONONGAHELA
ITASCA ● OSSIPEE
GALENA ● ONEIDA

GUNBOATS PROVIDE
ENFILADING FIRE
ON FORT MORGAN

PINOLA
● PEMBINA
SEBAGO ● TENNESSEE
BIENVILLE ● GENESEE

GULF OF MEXICO

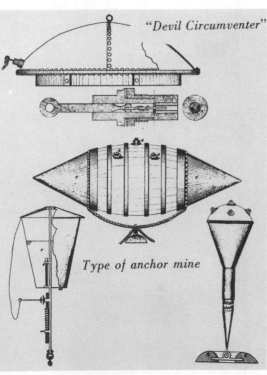

"Devil Circumventer"

Type of anchor mine

850. "DEVIL CIRCUMVENTER"
AND ANCHOR MINES—types used
at Mobile. Priming rods (tubes of
sulphuric acid) exploded the powder
demijohns when jostled. Some models
trailed long tentacles to foul ship's
propellers. Mobile minefields (over
200 mines) were planted in pattern
which forced ships to enter bay
through narrow channel directly
under heavy guns of Fort Morgan on
Mobile Point. Scouting in for telescope view of bay, Farragut sighted
the buoys which marked lethal fields.
But risk had to be run. Mobile blow
was timed to coincide with Sherman's
drive through Georgia. Troops of
General E. R. S. Canby were on hand
to seize beachheads. Farragut landed
them on schedule. Monitor *Tecumseh*
arrived as late reinforcement. He
started in. Confident of victory.

*Other types of anchor mines used at M
Bay, showing priming rods and contact*

851. "DAMN THE TORPEDOES, FULL SPEED AHEAD!"—Farragut going in. Wooden ships are hung with chain armor as at New Orleans; lashed two-by-two as at Port Hudson (if one engine is smashed, other can keep going). Fleet in double column; monitors on the inside (nearest fort), wooden vessels keeping pace outside. Date: August 5, 1864. Time: 7:00 A.M. Fort Morgan opens volcano fire; Union warships roar answer. Then, leading the monitor column, the *Tecumseh*—newcomer from James Flotilla—veers out of line (against orders) and strikes mine. Tragic blunder! Down goes monitor, drowning captain and 112 of crew. Union vessels hesitate, *Brooklyn* swerves, fleet stalls in confusion. "Captain Drayton, go ahead!" shouts Farragut. "Damn the torpedoes! Go on!"

852. QUARTERMASTER RICHARD KNOWLES, U.S.N. Fierce old fellow when photographed in 1870, he was one of iron men on wooden ship *Hartford* at Mobile. During crisis in torpedo-blocked channel, Farragut climbed to masthead for a better view. Knowles scrambled aloft to tie Admiral to rigging lest he be wounded and lose hold. Farragut did not fall. Battering its way past Fort Morgan, his fleet went on. Luck escorted him. Mines bobbed up around the Union ships, scraped their keels. But faulty triggers jammed; defective powder squibbed. Advancing from under cover of Fort Morgan, Admiral Buchanan with ironclad *Tennessee* (at left above) hoped to see Farragut's fleet pile up in disaster. Instead, he saw Farragut pass the fort and enter Mobile Bay.

853. *TENNESSEE* COMES OUT TO FIGHT (right). Pride of Mobile, casemated ironclad was 1,273-tonner, 209 feet long with 38 beam, 14 draft. Vaunted as "most powerful vessel of Confederacy," she was slabbed with 6-inch iron, armed with six Brooke rifles. As Farragut's van brushed aside the mines, Buchanan drove *Tennessee* to intercept. "We met the leading Union vessels and fought them face to face," recalled Dr. D. B. Conrad, *Tennessee* surgeon. "But their fire was so severe, our top deck was swept absolutely clean." Unable to ram speedy U.S. ships, the 3-knot ironclad withdrew to shelter of Fort Morgan. Crew glumly munched breakfast as "Buchanan, grim and silent, stumped up and down the deck." Then abruptly he ordered *Tennessee* up the bay to attack the invaders. One ironclad against three monitors, 14 ships. When Farragut saw *Tennessee* coming, he growled, "I didn't think old Buchanan was such a fool." Attack was suicidal.

854. "AN AUGUST MORNING WITH FARRAGUT"—*Hartford* vs. *Tennessee*. As *Tennessee* came up, Farragut ordered his steam sloops to ram her. In turn she was struck by *Monongahela*, *Lackawanna*, *Hartford*. Famous painting (center) shows wooden flagship and ironclad firing beam to beam. As vessels staggered apart, monitors moved in to hammer ironclad. Blacksmiths around anvil.

855. INSIDE IRONCLAD *TENNESSEE* (below). One of few pictures of Confederate sailors in battle, drawing shows *Tennessee* blasted by 15-inch shot from monitor *Manhattan*. As described by Lt. A. D. Wharton, C.S.N., "A thunderous report shook us all while . . . 440 pounds of iron impelled by 60 pounds of powder shattered our side. . . . Inside netting caught the splinters; there were no casualties." But carnage ensued as other monitors blasted *Tennessee*. Wrote Surgeon Conrad: "Suddenly there was a dull sounding impact. Men whose backs were against the casemate shield were riven to pieces. All of the gun's crew and the Admiral [Buchanan] were covered with blood, flesh and viscera. Fragments of the dead were shoveled into buckets and stuck below." Buchanan lay writhing. Bitter luck! Right thigh drilled on *Merrimack*; now left leg broken by 11-inch monitor shot.

856. CAPTURE OF *TENNESSEE.* Pounded by ships and monitors, ironclad was hammered to junk. Hugging enemy's stern, monitor *Chickasaw* slammed finishing shots. *Tennessee's* funnel toppled, her steering chains went, her plates caved. Up went white flag. "We'd have beaten you," Buchanan rasped, "if it hadn't been for that damned black hulk astern." He meant the *Chickasaw.* But ironclad's 7-inch guns and wooden-gear engines were no match for U.S. products. Nor was Buchanan match for Farragut. So Mobile was lost.

857. *BROOKLYN* AFTER BATTLE. Lead ship of Farragut's wooden column, she was clawed by Fort Morgan batteries when she balked at sight of *Tecumseh* sinking. Navy suffered heavy casualties at Mobile: 335 dead and wounded compared to Confederate loss of 30. But poor defensive strategy and Buchanan's reckless tactics cost Confederacy Mobile.

858. END OF FORT MORGAN—finale by Farragut's forces. Smaller Forts Powell and Gaines fell to hard-hitting monitor *Chickasaw* and army troops day after naval battle. With 69 guns Fort Morgan held out until August 23rd, then collapsed under fire of Union monitors and army artillery. City of Mobile resisted siege until January 1865. Mines in area sank six more U.S. vessels, including monitors *Osage* and *Milwaukee.* But Mobile Bay was in Farragut's hands day he entered. Mission accomplished. Alabama sealed by blockade.

Buchanan, severely wounded in the leg, gives up his sword in surrender to a staff officer sent by Farragut; it was reported Buchanan "yielded with bad grace."

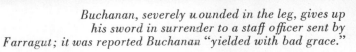

859. IRONCLAD GROWING IN CORNFIELD—the C.S.S. *Albemarle*. Far up Roanoke River she was built in winter of 1863-64. A *Merrimack*-type ram designed to smash Federal blockade clamped on North Carolina seaboard. Union spies and Richmond newspapers promptly reported the project. Gideon Welles took note.

860. RIPPING UP RAILROAD TRACKS — iron for *Albemarle's* casemate. Scavenging Carolina for metal, ram's builder, Commander

J. W. Cooke, C.S.N., won nickname of "Iron-Monger Captain." State was already stripped of everything down to iron deer. So railroad had to go.

861. C.S. IRONCLAD RAM *ALBE-MARLE* (top right). Completed in April 1864, she snorted down the Roanoke looking for battle. Casemate of iron rails. Cast-iron ram on bow. Two 100-pounder rifles (only guns available). But bellicose as a rhino.

862. GUN CREW OF U.S.S. *MIAMI* (below) — "double-ender" gunboat blockading Roanoke estuary. With "soapboxer" *Southfield* she stood guard against sortie by *Albemarle*. In charge of the wooden vessels, Commander C. W. Flusser hitched them together with length of chain; planned to catch ironclad in between, then board, fling powder down Rebel's funnel. Meantime, gunners held frequent drill. Note sailor with sponger, men at elevating gear, Marine at breech, gunner holding lanyard, netting to prevent boarders.

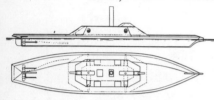

Bagging the

ot. J. W. Cooke C.S.N.
of the "Albemarle"

Gun has compression friction recoil system; fires spherical shell and solid shot. All set to meet "cornfield ram."

863. *ALBEMARLE* VS. *MIAMI AND SOUTHFIELD* (April 19, 1864). As ironclad charged out of river, Union gunboats tried to snare her as planned. But ram's beak cut the chain. Captain Cooke swerved her smash into *Southfield*. Down went *Southfield* as pictured, while *Miami* fired point-blank at the foe. *Miami's* shots bounced. Commander Flusser

Albemarle

was killed, Marines died in boarding attempt, riddled gunboat retreated. *Albemarle* rampage ended when engine trouble forced her to retire upriver. After repairs, another try.

864. U.S.S. *SASSACUS* RAMS *ALBEMARLE* (May 5, 1864). Returning down-river, ironclad was promptly attacked by *Miami* and by three "double-enders" which had been rushed to Roanoke estuary. Charging to trample the wooden quartet, ironclad herself was rammed by *Sassacus*. Collision smashed the "double-ender's" prow; a shot burst her boiler; she staggered off, wrecked But *Albemarle*, hurt, again retired.

865. SPAR GEAR FOR TORPEDO BOAT (below)—antidote for *Albemarle*. Needed at Mobile and Charleston, Navy's heavy ships could not be spared for Roanoke menace. How to squelch the ironclad? Messrs. Wood and Lay, engineers at New York Navy Yard, proposed fast steam launch with spar torpedo that could be manipulated for undersea thrust.

866. WOOD-LAY TORPEDO BOAT (right). Launch was 30-footer carrying 29-foot spar. Midget to pit against a ram. But big enough for Lt. W. B. Cushing, U.S.N., dispatched to Hampton Roads with group of three. One foundered at sea. One ran ashore, was captured. Low man in his class, but tallest daredevil in Navy, Cushing scored with No. 3.

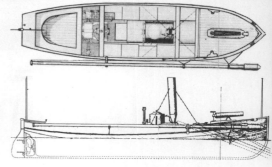

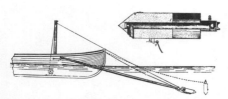

Below, Cushing torpedoes the "Albemarle"

867. *ALBEMARLE* IN HER LAIR. Replacing S. P. Lee as head of North Atlantic fleet, Admiral Porter wanted Roanoke ironclad eliminated. Cushing volunteered for job. In black drizzle, night of October 27, 1864, Lieutenant and party prowled up Roanoke in launch; surprised *Albemarle* at her berth. Double explosion roared as launch drove spar-torpedo into ironclad and *Albemarle*'s guns blasted launch. Only Cushing and one man escaped. *Albemarle* didn't.

868. DAREDEVIL WHO DOWNED *ALBEMARLE*—Commander William B. Cushing, U.S.N. For valiant exploit, he was commended by Welles and Lincoln, given command of Porter's flagship. After daring feat at Wilmington, where he piloted dummy monitor to draw enemy fire, he was lauded as are few national heroes. At crest of fame Cushing's wave of fortune would collapse. Awarded $56,000 for *Albemarle* sinking, he was to be dragged into grubby postwar row over prize money. In 1874 he went insane. But he would be recalled as man who sank ironclad.

869. *ALBEMARLE* DOWN (below) —a dead leviathan. The second Civil War vessel killed by torpedo driven at target—naval weapon of future.

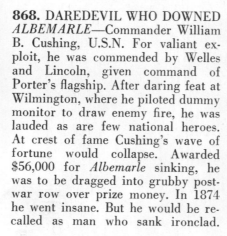

Fort Fisher
EXPEDITION

870. PORTER AND STAFF—on flagship *Malvern*, eve of Fort Fisher expedition, December 1864. Admiral poses in center. Cushing holds coat at left. Captain K. R. Breese, ärms folded, faces Porter. Comdr. T. O. Selfridge (*Osage* veteran) stands hand in bosom ahead of Marine.

871. ARMSTRONG GUN IN FORT FISHER—sample of late-war ordnance. Presented to Jefferson Davis by inventor, this British 150-pounder, shows new "hooped barrel" design. A formidable weapon in fort guarding Cape Fear River, door to Wilmington, N.C.—Lee's supply port.

872. OFFICERS OF MONITOR *MAHOPAC.* For Fisher campaign Welles gave Porter largest U.S. fleet thus far assembled. It included monitors *Mahopac, Saugus, Canonicus* and twin-turret *Monadnock*, armored *New Ironsides*, 26 wooden warships, and squadron of armed steamers. Fly in ointment: expeditionary army was under General Ben Butler who wanted "powder ship" to blow up Fisher. Porter fumed. More politics!

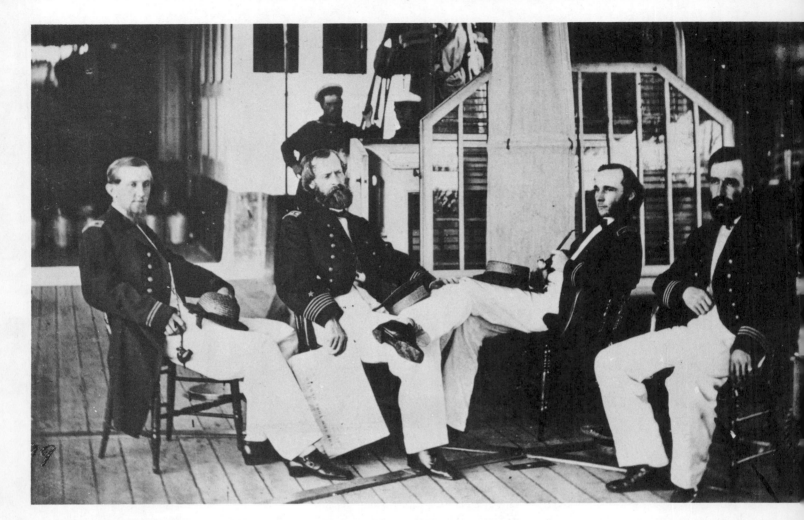

873. EMBARKING FOR FORT FISHER (above)—Union fleet at Hampton Roads. Bad weather and Butler delayed expedition while Porter raged. "Political generals!"

874. OFFICERS OF GUNBOAT *AGAWAM*. Holding newspaper is Captain A. C. Rhind, former skipper of *Keokuk*. At right, Lt. George Dewey, future admiral. Rhind was in charge of Butler's "powder ship," an old vessel loaded with 300 tons of explosive. As fleet approached Fisher (night of December 23rd) Rhind towed "powder ship" close in to fort. Set off by clockwork, huge blast killed fish; failed to hurt Fisher.

875. BOMBARDMENT OF FORT FISHER (below). Massing over 600 naval guns, Porter opened fire on target midday December 24th. Monitors moved in close to blaze point-blank at Fisher batteries. On arc of outer circle, rest of fleet hurled long-range bombardment. At peak Union armada was delivering 115 shots per minute. But Fisher, under command of Col. William Lamb, C.S.A., was steeled for last-ditch stand. Alerted by blast of futile "powder ship," defenders were ready. Confederacy's last Atlantic outlet would die hard.

876. FISHER FIGHTING BACK—Mound Battery in action. From this bastion, nicknamed "The Pulpit," Confederate big guns roared at Union armada. Fleet was harder hit by bursting of own Parrott guns and "bust" caused by General Butler. Landing on Christmas morning, Butler's troops could have easily flanked beach batteries (shown in background of picture). But Butler suddenly lost heart, quit battle, sailed away, leaving Porter to hold bag. Porter blew up like "powder ship."

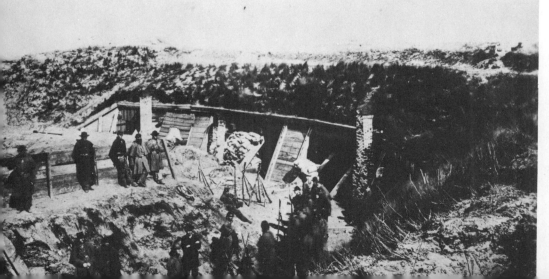

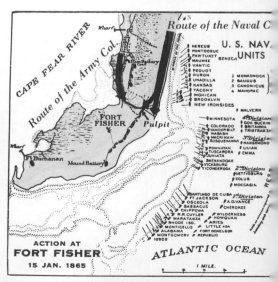

ACTION AT
FORT FISHER
15 JAN. 1865

877. NAVY STORMS FORT FISHER (above and left). On January 15, 1865, naval brigade of 1,600 bluejackets and 400 Marines were landed for frontal assault on fort's main bastion. Sailors were ordered to scale terraces and take Mound Battery. By someone's stupid order bluejackets were armed only with revolvers and cutlasses. On beach they were massacred wholesale by light artillery, riflemen and Armstrong gun. Attack ended in bloody welter.

878. ARMY TAKES FORT FISHER. Aided by covering fire from fleet, troops of General A. H. Terry (Butler's successor) stormed into fort. Murderous battle ensued.

879. ARMSTRONG GUN AND CAPTURED CONFEDERATES. Fort fell on evening of January 15th. Survivors were lucky. Fisher was a charnel house. A war correspondent wrote of "breakfasting on horrors ... Rebel dead in almost every shape and position, some standing on their feet and others on their heads, all glaring and grinning ghastly alike." Naval barrage had exacted heavy toll.

880. CAPTURED CONFEDERATES IN "THE PULPIT" (facing page). Fisher cost Union needlessly heavy casualties. But fort's fall killed the South. Entering Cape Fear River, Porter sealed off Wilmington—Confederacy's last port supplying Lee.

881. CAPTURE OF WILMINGTON (bottom right)—Union advance up Cape Fear River. Through Wilmington in autumn of '64 Confederates

had imported 69,000 rifles, tons of meat, lead, chemicals, clothing and coffee. Stoppage of this vital supply line doomed Lee's army to eventual starvation. Desperate Confederate leaders refused to confess defeat, even planned to free all slaves and conscript them for army service. Southern people were kept in dark concerning dire situation. At Richmond, Lee fought on as Grant closed in and Sherman came up from Georgia.

*"Cap'n, this is my first command
and I'll ride upon the quarter-deck."*

MELODRAMA ON LAKE ERIE

882. TARGET OF WEIRD PLOT —U.S. paddle sloop *Michigan* guarding Johnson's Island, Sandusky. In late autumn of '64, vessel and fort (sketched by soldier on locale) featured in one of war's strangest dramas—eleventh-hour attempt by Confederates to gain control of Lake Erie. Plan called for raid on Johnson's Island by Confederates from Canada. Object: to release some 4,000 war prisoners from this Erie "Alcatraz." Escapees were to capture warship *Michigan*, then bombard Buffalo, Cleveland and Detroit. Leader of "Erie Expedition," Commander John Y. Beall, C.S.N., mustered 18 volunteers at Windsor, Ontario. Meantime secret agent Charles Cole, aided by spy known as "Irish Lize," tried to bribe *Michigan* officers at Sandusky. Plot was foiled by counter-intelligence of J. W. Murray, *Michigan* petty officer ordered to shadow mysterious Cole. When Beall's raiders seized steamer *Philo Parsons* off Detroit, and crossed lake to strike at Johnson's, defenses were ready. Raiders fled back to Canada. Stars and Bars were gone with the wind on blue Lake Erie.

883. HANGING OF COMDR. J. Y. BEALL, C.S.N.—last act of Erie melodrama. In wake of Sandusky fiasco, Beall was caught at Niagara while attempting to derail a prisoner train. Hustled to Fort Lafayette at New York, he was condemned to die for "piracy and sabotage." Numerous Northern officials interceded in young officer's behalf. But attempt by Confederate saboteurs to burn New York City militated against reprieve. On Feb. 24, 1865, he was hanged on Governor's Island in manner illustrated. Subsequent rumor said Booth shot Lincoln to avenge friend Beall.

Power Drive on

884. DEFENDING RICHMOND— heavy Confederate gun overlooking Dutch Gap on James River. During war's final winter, cannon of this caliber denied Union forces the last few miles of river below the Confederate capital. Grant simply avoided these fortifications by pushing westward from City Point to Petersburg to outflank Richmond's southern defenses. Move caught Lee off guard.

Signaling the Ships

885. ANOTHER RIVER GUN. This 10-inch Columbiad in "Battery Semmes" had range of 2½ miles. Battery was named for captain of *Alabama*, who now commanded ironclads penned up at Richmond base.

888. FREAK VESSEL ON RICHMOND FRONT (below)—U.S. semi-submersible *Spuyten Duyvil.* Built by Wm. Wood and John Lay (designers of Cushing's launch), strange craft and sister *Stromboli* made debut on James early in '65. Vessels were designed to wade into action with deck awash—half steamboat, half submarine. Unique feature was bow tube through which mechanical spar torpedo was thrust like underwater javelin. New type of torpedo-boat.

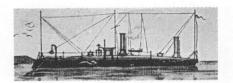

886. CITY POINT SENTINELS. U.S. gunboat and double-turret monitor *Onondaga* were two of depleted James Flotilla which guarded Grant's river base while Union fleet was at Wilmington. On January 24, 1865, Flag Officer J. K. Mitchell brought

Richmond ironclads down-river to menace City Point. As usual, balky engines plagued the Confederates. Gear jammed and steam leaked. The sluggish ironclads grounded on river obstacles, fired a few random shots and retired. Swan song of C. S. N.

887. C.S. IRONCLAD *RICHMOND* —watchdog of doomed city. In company with new ironclads *Virginia II* and *Fredericksburg* she was both guard and prisoner at gates of besieged capital. Taking command of squadron in February '65, Admiral Semmes found engines rusting, crews deserting, new ram *Texas* incompleted.

889. RAILROAD YARD AND DOCKS AT CITY POINT—power house for Grant. Had Richmond ironclads come within gun-range of this terminal they might have wiped out Grant's supply system, lifted Petersburg siege. Too late work was spurred on new ram *Texas*—behemoth in a bottle. City Point was safe.

Richmond

890. LANDING A LOCOMOTIVE (below). Heavy U.S. goods for U. S. Grant. Even railroads were convoyed up the James by U.S. Navy. Inland drive for Richmond went forward on iron wheels. Which arrived by water.

891. MORE GOODS FOR GRANT — monster 17,000-pound seacoast mortar bound for Petersburg front. Special delivery by river transport and salt-water haul from North. Belatedly Confederate leaders realized importance of naval transport in relation to logistics. Had they assessed importance of Navy to begin with, they might not have opened fire in '61 when cotton empire lacked ships.

Inflating the pontoons

892. U.S. RAILROAD MORTAR "DICTATOR" at Petersburg front. Via spur from City Point. Via water transport up James River from points north. Brady photograph nicely summarizes the logistics picture before Richmond. This is the end of the line. It might have been reached sooner had Northern leaders spent less on cavalry boots, more on boats. In 1862, for instance, when little James Squadron wasn't big enough for Fort Darling and Drewry's Bluff.

893. CHARLESTON EVACUATED —Confederacy collapsing. With Wilmington gone and Sherman charring Georgia's seaboard, South's case was hopeless. But Quixotic leader of the Confederacy urged a fight to the last man. So boys in gray died in useless stand at Charleston. And boys in blue died in Union monitor *Patapsco*, lost with all hands to mine off Sumter in mid-January '65. Then Sherman's vanguard cut city's rail communications, and Charleston resistance died overnight. On February 15, 1865, Sherman's veterans met Dahlgren's sailors in battered city.

894. RUINS OF FORT SUMTER (below left)—incorrigible in "Cradle of Secession." Although South Carolina was now moving to secede from Confederacy itself, Sumter held out until Charleston fell. Union effort to crack city by naval siege was costly mistake. Early in '63 spies had reported that all her defenses faced ocean. But she was setup for flank assault by land. As Sherman proved.

895. "SEA ELEPHANT" BELOW RICHMOND—double-turreted monitor *Onondaga*. Built by G. W. Quintard at Greenpoint, N.Y., she was 1,250-tonner packing two 150-pounder Parrotts and two 15-inch Dahlgrens. Bigger sisters *Tonawanda* and *Monadnock* were needed elsewhere. But this "elephant" and companion "fighting raft" *Lehigh* were big enough to stymie Semmes' ironclads while Grant's forces crashed Petersburg. When Petersburg front collapsed in March, Lee fell back on Richmond. James Flotilla pushed closer to wharves of beleagured city.

*Embalming Establishment
before Richmond*

896. HAMMERING OUT UNION VICTORY—monitor men at work. Photograph of dungaree navy in action symbolizes naval technology which forged victory for North. No "marlinspike" seamanship on deck of monitor *Lehigh* facing Richmond up the James. Facing monitors down the James, Richmond ironclads were weakened by mechanical defects which had plagued C.S.N. from start. On land, South had balanced military disparity with brilliant generalship. At sea, South was beaten from outset in warfare demanding engineering and technical know-how. The defeat was inevitable. Slavery and American technology didn't mix.

897. ABE LINCOLN SLEPT HERE (right)—Porter's flagship *Malvern*. With Wilmington secured, Porter returned to City Point. There he met top-flag visitors—President and Mrs. Lincoln. Porter to Gustavus Fox (March 29th): "Mrs. Lincoln got jealous of a lady down here, and rather pulled his wig. We put him through the Navy to make him forget [his] cares." When wife huffily returned to Washington, Lincoln was quartered on the *Malvern*. As guest's bunk proved uncomfortably short, Porter had it rebuilt next day while Lincoln was ashore. Following morning Lincoln observed, "I must have shrunk in length and sideways!"

898. RICHMOND, APRIL 1865—King Cotton down in ruins. Lee retreated to Appomattox on the 3rd. On same day Admiral Semmes blew up his ironclads. He was last top-rank Confederate to quit South's capital. Porter escorted Lincoln into city on 4th. They landed on wharf near Libby Prison not far from this gray scene.

Affecting appeal to the Union Commissary

War's End

899. THE MIGHTY *STONEWALL* ship that never came in. Displaying dreadnaught silhouette of the future, this formidable ironclad cruiser was built in France for the C.S.N. Sold as diplomatic "blind" to Denmark, she was transferred to Confederate agents in Copenhagen. Flying Stars and Bars in January 1865, she took on stores at El Ferrol, Spain (where photo was made). Watching her, U.S.S. *Niagara* and *Sacramento* (Flag Captain Henry Walke) wisely let her go undisturbed. Four engines—13-knot speed—Armstrong guns—she was probably superior to any Union ship afloat. So she reached Cuba in April, only to find war over. Interned, she was later handed over to U.S. Ultimate fate: sold to Japan.

900. GHOST RAIDER *SHENAN-DOAH*—ship that never came home. One of the Confederacy's 12 commerce raiders, this British-built cruiser left England in October 1864 on mission to destroy Yankee-whaling fleet operating in the North Pacific. Entering Bering Sea in March '65, she downed 29 vessels. She had inflicted $6,000,000 damage before July, when she heard that the war was three months over. Disguised as a cargoman, *Shenandoah* returned to Europe by way of the Antipodes. Now become a ship without a country, she reached England in November '65. The "ghost raider" was destined to cause an uproar (see text #901.)

901. "OLD RIP OF THE *SHENAN-DOAH*"—Yankee jibe at Captain J. I. Waddell, C.S.N., "ghost raider's" skipper. When ship reached Liverpool she was handed over to U.S. by embarrassed British. Her post-war rampage contributed much to anti-English sentiment which resulted in "Alabama Claims"—U.S. demand that British pay for damages wrought by British-built raiders. Last warship to fly Stars and Stripes, *Shenandoah* was sold by U.S. Government to Sultan of Zanzibar.

902. VICTORY PARADE—Farragut's squadron at New York. Guns muzzled, cutlasses stowed, *Hartford* led victorious Mobile squadron on parade in nation's biggest harbor. Farragut awarded promotion to vice admiral. But the celebration was tempered by remembrance of combat loss. Of the 380 men who sailed in *Hartford* from Philadelphia in 1861, only 40 remained. Total U.S. Navy losses in Civil War eventually numbered 95 vessels, over 2,100 sailors. (below)

THE OLD *RIP* OF THE "SHENANDOAH."

CAPTAIN WADDELL (AS RIP VAN WINKLE). "Law! Mr. Pilot, you don't say so! The war in America over these Eight Months? Dear! dear! who'd ever a' thought it!"

Name	Tonnage	Builder	Approx. Cost		Disposition
Monitor *Catawba*	1,034	Niles Works, Cincinnati, '65	$ 625,000		Eventually sold out
Monitor *Catskill*	1,875	Ericsson, New York, '63	$ 427,700		Eventually sold out
Iron Steamer *Cherokee*	600	Purchased, Boston, '64 (as prize)	$ 75,000		Sold at war's end
Double-Turret *Chickasaw*	1,000	T. G. Gaylord, St. Louis, '64	$ 390,000		Sold at war's end
Ironclad Gunboat *Chillicothe*	400	J. Brown, Cincinnati, '62	$ 92,000		Sold at war's end
Monitor *Chimo*	600	Aquila Adams, South Boston, '64	$ 630,000		Scrapped, '74
Ironclad Gunboat *Choctaw*	1,000	Built St. Louis Yd., '62	$ 100,000	Designed by Lt. W. D. Porter	Laid up at war's end
Ironclad Gunboat *Cincinnati*	600	J. B. Eads, St. Louis, '62	$ 50,000		Sunk, Vicksburg, '63
Iron Steamer *Circassian*	1,750	Purchased, Key West, '62 (as prize)	$ 107,000		Sold at war's end
Iron Steamer *Clyde*	300	Purchased, New York, '63 (as prize)	$ 40,000		Sold at war's end
Monitor *Cohoes*	600	M. F. Merritt, Phila., '64	$ 600,000		Scrapped, '75
Iron Steamer *Columbia*	500	Purchased, Key West, '62 (as prize)	$ 66,000		Wrecked, Masonboro Inlet, N. C., '63
Iron Steamer *Cornubia*	600	Purchased, Boston, '63 (as prize)	$ 99,000		Sold at war's end
"Galvanized" Iron Tug *Dandelion*	100	Purchased, New York, private owner	$ 18,000		Sold at war's end
Iron Steamer *Delaware*	350	Purchased, Wilmington, Del., '61	$ 45,000		Sold at war's end
Monitor *Dictator*	3,000	Ericsson, New York, '64	$1,400,000		Eventually sold out
Iron Steamer *Don*	400	Purchased, Boston, '63 (as prize)	$ 66,000		Sold at war's end
Iron Steamer *Donegal*	1,000	Purchased, Phila., '64 (as prize)	$ 140,000		Sold at war's end
Iron Steamer *Dumbarton*	700	Purchased, Boston, '64 (as prize)	$ 145,000		Sold at war's end
Ironclad Ram *Dunderberg*	5,000	Aetna Iron Works, New York, '65	$1,250,000		Sold to France, '70
Ironclad Gunboat *Eastport*	700	Purchased, War Dept., '63 (as prize)	$ 9,000		Sunk, mine-torpedo, Red River, '64
Iron Steamer *Emma*	350	Purchased, New York, '63 (as prize)	$ 50,000		Sold at war's end
Ironclad Gunboat *Essex*	614	Wiggins Ferry Co., St. Louis	$ 20,000	Converted by U.S.N., '61	Sold at war's end
Monitor *Etlah*	600	C. W. McCord, St. Louis, '64	$ 581,000		Eventually sold out
Iron Tug *Fortune*	400	James Tetlow, Boston, '65	$ 128,000		Commissioned after war
Iron Steamer *Frolic*	900	Purchased, New York, '64 (as prize)	$ 120,000		Sold at war's end
Ironclad Sloop *Galena*	750	Bushnell, Mystic, Conn., '62	$ 250,000		Wrecked off Martha's Vineyard, '90
Iron Steamer *Gertrude*	350	Purchased, New York, '63 (as prize)	$ 45,000		Sold at war's end
Iron Steamer *Gettysburg*	950	Purchased, New York, '63 (as prize)	$ 90,000		Sold to Italy after war
	450	Purchased, New York, '64 (as prize)	$ 55,000		Sold at war's end

906. *Navy graves at Port Hudson. (above)*

907. *Lincoln's body lying in state; commander-in-chief of U. S. Army and Navy, killed April 14, 1865 (below)*

Name	Tonnage	Builder	Approx. Cost	Disposition
Monitor *Monitor*	987	Ericsson, Green Point, N. Y., '62	$ 280,000	Foundered en route Charleston, '63
Iron Double-Ender *Monocacy*	1,370	Denmead & Son, Baltimore, '64	$ 275,000	Sold to Japanese, '03
Monitor *Montauk*	750	Ericsson, Green Point, N. Y., '62	$ 400,000	Damaged, Charleston, mine-torpedo, Feb., '63 Repaired, in service until '04
Iron Double-Ender *Muscoota*	1,000	Continental Iron Wks., N. Y., '64	$ 275,000	Eventually sold out
Monitor *Nahant*	1,875	H. Loring, South Boston, '62	$ 400,000	Eventually sold out
Monitor *Nantucket*	844	Atlantic Works, Boston, '63	$ 400,000	Eventually sold out
Monitor *Napa*	614	Harlan, Hollingsworth & Co., Del., '64	$ 500,000	Eventually sold out
Monitor *Naubuc*	614	Wm. Perine, Williamsburg, N. Y., '64	$ 500,000	Eventually sold out
Monitor *Nausett*	614	Donald McKay, Boston, '64	$ 560,000	Eventually sold out
Floating Battery *Naugatuck*	200	E. A. Stevens, Princeton, N. Y., '61	donated	Eventually decommissioned
Monitor *Neosho*	523	J. B. Eads, St. Louis, '63	$ 195,000	Sold at war's end
Ironclad *New Ironsides*	3,500	Merrick & Sons, Phila., '62	$ 865,000	Destroyed, accidental fire, Phila., '66
Iron Tug *Nina*	350	Reaney & Archbold, Chester, Pa., '65	$ 128,000	In service many years
Steamer *Niphon* (wood & iron)	475	Purchased, private owner, Boston, '63	$ 75,000	Sold at war's end
Monitor *Oneota*	1,034	Swift Co. and Niles Wks., Cin., '64	$ 620,000	Sold at war's end
Double-Turret Monitor *Onondaga*	1,250	G. W. Quintard, New York, '64	$ 760,000	Returned to builder at war's end
Monitor *Osage*	623	J. B. Eads, St. Louis, '63	$ 119,700	Sunk, mine-torpedo, Blakely River, Ala., Mar., '65
Monitor *Ozark*	578	Geo. Bestor, Mound City, Ill., '63	$ 225,000	Sold at war's end
Iron Steamer *Palos*	350	Jas. Tetlow, Chelsea, Mass., '65	$ 128,000	Launched after war
Double-Tur. Monitor *Passaconaway*	2,300	U.S.N. and C. H. Delameter, N. Y., '65	$1,062,000	Incompleted at war's end
Monitor *Passaic*	1,875	J. Ericsson, Green Point, N. Y., '62	$ 400,000	In service until '00
Monitor *Patapsco*	1,875	J. Ericsson, Wilmington, Del., '62	$ 400,000	Sunk, mine-torpedo, Charleston, Jan., '65
Iron Steamer *Philadelphia*	500	Commandeered, War Dept., April, '61	None	Sold at war's end
Iron Tug *Pilgrim*	170	Pusey, Jones Co., Wilmington, '64	$ 100,000	In service until '89
Iron Tug *Pinta*	350	Reaney & Archbold, Chester, Pa., '64	$ 128,000	In service, '89
Ironclad Gunboat *Pittsburgh*	512	J. B. Eads, St. Louis, '62	$ 50,000	Sold at war's end
Semi-Ironclad *Poppy*	100	Purchased, Phila., private owner, '63	$ 20,000	Sold at war's end
Iron Steamer *Preston*	430	Purchased, New York, '64 (as prize)	$ 65,000	Sold at war's end
Monitor *Puritan*	3,265	J. Ericsson, Green Point, N. Y., '64	$1,486,000	In service until about '00
Iron Steamer *Queen*	630	Purchased, Boston, '63 (as prize)	$ 65,000	Sold at war's end
Double-Tur. Monitor *Quinsigamond*	3,000	Atlantic Works, Boston	$ 425,000	Incompleted at war's end
Triple-Turret Ironclad *Roanoke*	3,435	Novelty Iron Wks., New York, '63	$ 820,000	Converted from frigate Sold in '83
Ironclad Gunboat *St. Louis*	512	J. B. Eads, St. Louis, '62	$ 50,000	Changed, *Baron de Kalb.* Sunk, mine-tp., Yazoo, '63
Ironclad Gunboat *Sandusky*	480	Tomlinson, Hartupee Co., St. Louis, '65	$ 235,000	Sold in '73
Monitor *Sangamon*	1,875	J. Ericsson, Chester, Pa., '62	$ 107,000	In service until '00
Monitor *Saugus*	1,034	Harlan, Hollingsworth Co., Del., '63	$ 525,000	In service until '89
Double-Turret Monitor *Shakamaxon*	3,000	Pusey, Jones & Co., Wilmington, '65	$1,300,000	Scrapped, '74
Iron Double-Ender *Shamokin*	1,030	Reaney & Archbold, Chester, Pa., '65	$ 275,000	Sold at war's end
Monitor *Shawnee*	614	Curtis & Tilden, Boston, '65	$ 582,000	Scrapped, '75
Monitor *Shiloh*	614	Geo. Bestor, St. Louis, '65	$ 589,000	Decommissioned, '74
Semi-Ironclad *Shokokon*	710	Purchased, private owner, Phila., '63	$ 100,000	Sold at war's end
Iron Steamer *South Carolina*	1,165	Purchased, Boston, '63, private owner	$ 172,500	Sold at war's end
Iron Tug *Speedwell*	350	J. Tetlow, Boston, '65	$ 127,000	Incompleted at war's end
Monitor *Squando*	614	McKay & Aldus, Boston, '65	$ 574,000	Scrapped, '74
Monitor *Suncook*	614	Globe Works, South Boston, '65	$ 593,500	Scrapped, '74
Iron Double-Ender *Suwanee*	1,030	Reaney & Archbold, Chester, Pa., '64	$ 171,000	Wrecked, '68
Monitor *Tecumseh*	1,034	Secor & Co., New York, '63	$ 640,000	Sunk, mine-torpedo, Mobile Bay, '64
Monitor *Tippecanoe*	1,034	Miles Greenwood, Cincinnati, '64	$ 635,000	Eventually sold out
Double-Turret Monitor *Tonawanda*	1,536	Merrick & Sons, Phila., '64	$ 806,000	Changed, *Amphitrite.* In service, WWI period
Iron Tug *Triana*	350	Wm. Perine, New York, '65	$ 129,000	Eventually sold out
Iron Steamer *Tristram Shandy*	444	Purchased, Boston, '64 (as prize)	$ 58,000	Sold at war's end
Monitor *Tunxis*	614	Reaney, Son & Archbold, Chester, '64	$ 632,000	Eventually sold out
Ironclad Gunboat *Tuscumbia*	915	Joseph Brown, Cincinnati, '63	$ 227,000	Sold at war's end
Monitor *Umpqua*	614	Snowden & Mason, Pittsburgh, '65	$ 595,000	Sold for $9,000, '74
Iron Steamer *Virginia*	581	Purchased, New York, '63 (as prize)	$ 47,000	Sold at war's end
Iron Steamer *Wando*	645	Purchased, Boston, '64 (as prize)	$ 121,000	Sold at war's end
Iron Steamer *Wasp*	521	Purchased, New York, '65 (as prize)	$ 83,360	Sold, '76, Uruguayan firm
Monitor *Waussuc*	614	G. W. Lawrence, Portland, Me., '65	$ 547,000	Eventually scrapped
Iron Gunboat *Wateree*	974	Reaney & Archbold, Chester, Pa., '63	$ 130,000	Wrecked, tidal wave, '68
Ironclad *Waxsaw*	1,000	A. & W. Denmead, Baltimore, '65	$ 592,000	Eventually scrapped
Monitor *Weehawken*	844	Zeno, Secor & Co., Jersey City, '63	$ 400,000	Sunk, leakage, off Charleston, Dec., '63
Double-Turret Monitor *Winnebago*	970	J. B. Eads, St. Louis, '63	$ 381,000	Sold out, '74
Iron Double-Ender *Winnipec*	1,030	H. Loring, Boston, '64	$ 275,000	Sold at war's end
Monitor *Yazoo*	614	Merritt & Sons, Phila., '65	$ 556,000	Sold out, '74
Monitor *Yuma*	614	A. Swift & Co., Cincinnati, '65	$ 602,000	Sold out, '74

Chapter VIII

FROM IRON TO STEEL

909. NAVY ON THE SHELF. These monitors in "mothballs" (term in those days was "in ordinary") graphically represent general condition of U.S.N. in post-Civil-War decade. Within the year following Appomattox, the U.S. Fleet was whittled from 626 vessels to 30. Most of Navy's 65 ironclads were scrapped or sold out. A few monitors were retained for coast defense. Those in photograph are moored at League Island Yard, Philadelphia. First in line is U.S.S. *Nahant*, famous veteran of Charleston blockade. Line probably includes the *Montauk*—vessel which featured in dark drama of war's aftermath.

Civil War Aftermath

910. MONITOR *MONTAUK* — GUARDIAN OF BOOTH'S BODY. On night he killed Lincoln, Booth escaped across Potomac over Navy Yard Bridge. After assassin was trapped and slain near Bowling Green, Va., body was carted to Washington Navy Yard (April 27, 1865); placed on U.S.S. *Montauk*. Following autopsy on board monitor, remains were secretly buried in Penitentiary grounds. Other assassination conspirators, captured by Secret Service, were held prisoner on Navy gunboats.

911. RETURN OF CONSPIRATOR JOHN SURRATT — Washington Navy Yard, 1867. Booth's friend and accomplice, John Surratt escaped to Europe after Lincoln murder, joined the Papal army, then fled to Egypt where he was captured. Returned to States on board U.S.S. *Swatara*, he faced trial by Army court which had hanged four other conspirators including Mrs. Mary Surratt. Because military court proved unreliable, young Surratt (shown in costume of Papal Zouave) was later released.

INTERNATIONAL
Influence U.S.N.

912. U.S. MONITOR *MIANTONO-MOH*—"Missioner to Moscow." In 1866 *Miantonomoh* made good-will voyage to Russia, bearing Assistant Naval Secretary Fox to St. Petersburg with greetings to country which had aided United States at critical hour of Civil War. The same year monitor *Monadnock* steamed around Horn to Pacific. Surprise to European experts, ocean voyages of two monitors went far to convince French Emperor Napoleon III he could not maintain imperial foothold in Mexico.

One of "Miantonomah's" breech-loading rifles

913. U.S.S. *FRANKLIN* "SHOWED FLAG" to Europe (right). Symbolizing a reunited America, she made European cruise in 1867-68 as flagship of Admiral Farragut. Old 1815 ship-of-line, converted to steam in 1864, also symbolized naval service devoted to protection of American commerce. Ambassador of good will, Farragut was everywhere acclaimed.

914. U.S.S. *WAMPANOAG*. Driven by Isherwood-designed power plant (first to use superheated steam) this 4,215-ton cruiser set speed record of 23 knots in 1869. So Britain decided to pay *Alabama* Claims—big sum to U.S. for damage wrought by English-built Confederate commerce-raiders.

915. "SEWARD'S ICE BOX"— Navy's nethermost frontier. The williwaws almost blew through President Andrew Johnson's cabinet when Secretary of State Seward negotiated purchase of Alaska from Russia in 1867. For years Russian Government had been angling to sell Alaskan Territory to U.S.A. Deal was considered by many Americans as utter folly. But Alaska and Aleutians (territory twice the size of Texas) went to United States for bargain at $7,200,000. This was last big real-estate deal on American continent.

916. STEAM-FRIGATE *COLORADO*—flagship of U.S. Asiatic Squadron in 1870's. Squadron included screw-cruiser *Benicia* and steam gunboats *Alaska*, *Monocacy* and *Palos*. Commanded by Rear Admiral John Rodgers of Civil War fame, squadron was ordered with American diplomats to Korea in 1871 to negotiate commercial treaty and investigate hostile attitude of natives of "Hermit Kingdom" who had declared their coastal waters closed to foreign shipping and had fired on American trading vessel.

First Korean War

917. U.S. NAVY AT KOREA, 1871. On board gunboat *Benicia*, fatherly Admiral Rodgers (leaning over table) plans assault on native fort which had fired on U.S. expedition.

918. U.S. MARINES ATTACKING FORT CH'OJIJIN, KOREA (June 10, 1871). Demanding apology for wounding of two men, Rodgers waited ten days, then launched an assault.

919. NAVAL LANDING PARTY. Sailors in redoubt (left) are holding mud flats shown on chart (facing page). Some 650 seamen and Marines were put ashore "to chastise hostile Koreans" in the fortified Seoul area.

930. U.S. TORPEDO-RAM *ALARM* —"dream boat" of David Dixon Porter. Success of Cushing's ironclad-killing launch inspired invention by Admiral Porter. Upshot: strange vessel equipped with three spar-torpedoes. An 800-tonner, *Alarm* was 172 feet long (including 32-foot ram), with 27½ beam, 11-foot depth. Novel side-spars for sideswiping enemy were 18 feet long. As indicated in plan drawing, the bow torpedo was controlled by tackles and winch. Vessel contained other Porter novelties. She was built of iron on bracket-plate system (double hull) with compartmented bottom. Carried electric light, rapid-fire guns. Weak features were plough-shaped ram (hard to steer) and Fowler Wheel ("feathering paddle wheel" that turned horizontally). *Alarm* sired larger torpedo-ram *Intrepid*. Self-guiding steam torpedo soon made Porter's rams obsolete. But bells, gadgets and gizmos on *Alarm* and *Intrepid* kept Navy officers alert to scientific invention in day when Department was run by backward anti-intellectuals.

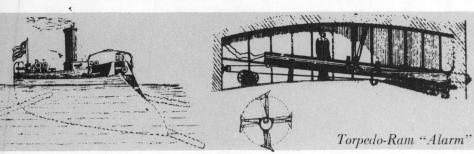

Torpedo-Ram "Alarm"

Navy in Decline

931. DOLDRUMS AT PENSACOLA —picturing naval decline of 70's. Grant's Administration. Heyday of

marrow by political hacks. At time of international tension with England, France and Spain, the Navy was

Cock-pit, yacht "America"

As Secretary I made such a name,
That a millionaire I soon became.
I sold new ships for the price of junk,
And those I repaired invariably sunk,
Or went out of sight so effectualee
That soon I demolished the whole navee.

935. SECRETARY OF NAVY GEORGE M. ROBESON—grafter on duty. Elected President in 1868, General Grant proved one of poorest judges of human nature ever to sit in White House. When mythologist Mr. Borie resigned in huff at realistic Admiral Porter, Grant replaced him with Mr. Robeson. Described as "first-rate judge of wines, second-rate trout fisherman, and third-rate New Jersey lawyer," Robeson soon reduced U.S.N. from first-rate navy to twelfth-rate. Typical graft during Robeson regime: new U.S. super monitor *Shackamaxon* (cost $1,300,-000) sold as junk for $18,500; new U.S. ironclad *Waxsaw* (cost $600,-000) sold as scrap for $3,000; new U.S. steam sloop *Piscataqua* (cost $1,000,000) sold for $5,000; prize racing yacht *America* sold to Ben Butler for $5,000. Robeson also dealt extravagant repair jobs to friend John Roach who all but bankrupt the service. By decade's end Congressional investigators were asking how, during eight years as Naval Secretary, he had boosted private bank account from $20,000 to $325,000. Answers were never vouchsafed. But American comic weekly *Puck* stated case in verse (accompanying portrait).

936. NAVAL EXTRAVAGANCE—U.S. steam frigate *Tennessee*. Beautiful two-stacker, built by Government at New York Navy Yard, engines by Allaire Works, was launched July 8, 1865. Originally christened *Madawaska*, she was 3,281-tonner, 355 feet long with 23-foot depth of hold. Power plant featured two vibrating-lever surface-condenser engines, eight Martin boilers and four boilers of tubular superheating type. Vessel cost $1,673,000. But first cost was not last. During Robeson regime she cost Navy (meaning American taxpayers) over $865,000 in ship repair bills.

FLAG
Alaska and
he resistance of
Navy's admiration.

U.S. DIPLOMATS at Korea.
Envoys Drew (seated) and Low with
Chinese interpreters on *Colorado* at
Seoul. Koreans refused to sign treaty
at gun point. In 1882 velvet glove
succeeded where iron fist had failed.

all but beached. Blow to service was

U.S.S. Colorado underway

NESS...
mid-Victo...
magnificent...
son's jobbery, wa...
private firm for...
Robeson deals: new tur...
Chickasaw (cost $390,000) s...
$8,000; new $1,000,000 steam si...
Chattanooga sold for $18,600; new
$600,000 monitor *Klamath* sold for
$7,400; new $700,000 steam frigate
Nevada given to John Roach as "part
payment" for repairs on monitor
Puritan — a $475,000 repair job.

938. U.S. STEAM SLOOP *CON-GRESS*—another throw-away. Built
by Government in 1865 for $1,000,-
000, this 3,000-ton cruiser, originally
named *Pushmataha*, served in U.S.
Med Squadron during 1870's. Fine
ship, she could ride out a tempest in
Naples harbor as shown below. But
could not survive Robeson regime.
Decommissioned in 1876, she was
sold out in 1883 for mere $26,000.

939. U.S.S. *QUINNEBAUG*—one of six 1,900-ton wood-hull steam gunboats remodeled after Civil War. Photographed while on mission to Venice (above), she was pretty as a yacht, and as unsubstantial. She was sold at junk prices before decade's end with sisters *Resaca, Albany*.

940. U.S.S. *MONONGAHELA*—retrogressively tying on the knots. Commissioned as steam sloop in 1863, she survived freak tidal wave which carried her over housetops, beached her at St. Croix, West Indies, in 1867. Fate even more bizarre overtook her in 1884 when Government converted her into sail ship.

941. VICE ADMIRAL DAVID DIXON PORTER—aging, but no mossback. Head of Naval Academy during postwar decade, he restored school at Annapolis, abolished classroom spying for honor system, ousted such empty subjects as "moral philosophy," installed classes in engineering, planned the future Naval Institute. In 1869 he was made assistant to Naval Secretary Borie, who soon resigned declaring, "The Department is managed by Porter." Eased out by slippery Mr. Robeson, Porter was retired with rank of Admiral of the Navy. In retirement he wrote amusing but candid war history that enraged General Ben Butler, who stupidly accused him of cowardice at New Orleans. But nation justly honored Porter as valiant naval leader when he died in 1891.

Engineering department at Annapolis

The Courant.

COLVOCORESSES.

MURDER OR SUICIDE?

The Bridgeport Tragedy Reviewed.

New and Important Facts and Circumstances Presented.

A STRONG SUPPORT OF THE SUICIDAL THEORY.

The whole story of the Colvocoresses tragedy, together with the chief points of interest preceding it, has never been told. At the outset THE COURANT, representing itself and

942. NAVY'S STRANGEST MURDER MYSTERY—the Colvocoresses sensation. While service disintegrated under Robeson, Navy wardrooms were shocked by baffler involving distinguished officer. Author of bestseller *Four Years in Exploring Expedition*, exec on *Levant* in Far East; commander of *Saratoga* on Civil War blockade duty, Greek-born George M. Colvocoresses made notable record in U.S.N. Sponsorship by Partridge family of New England, marriage to an Eliza Halsey, then (widower) to Adeline Swasey, took him to top of social as well as service ladder. Trouble began in 1867 when retired Captain threatened to sue Gov't. for extra prize money. Farragut had received $56,000 for capturing Mobile; Admiral S. P. Lee $109,000 in blockade awards; Lt. Cushing $53,-000 for sinking *Albemarle*. Protesting award of $17,000, Colvocoresses demanded bonus. Facing bankruptcy after stock market gamble in autumn of 1871, he acquired numerous life policies in New York, insuring himself for $185,000. Following spring, he made mysterious trips to Bridgeport, Conn. On night of June 4, 1872, he was found shot dead on back street of Bridgeport, an ancient horse pistol lying nearby. It looked like a holdup murder. But victim had not been robbed, nor could police find trace of assailant. As reported by Hartford *Courant*, dubious evidence pointed to flimflam—fake murder to gain insurance money. Life agents charged suicide fraud. When rumor suggested stooge was shot in Captain's stead and Colvocoresses was hiding in exile, affair was hushed, insurance settled "out of court." Murder? Suicide? Or vanishing act? Unsolved case remained enigma in Navy's Family Album. Page Sherlock Holmes!

943. CAPTAIN GEORGE DEWEY on bridge of U.S.S. *Pensacola*—two Navy stalwarts. In 1880's when this photograph was taken, Dewey was well up promotion ladder. Veteran of Gulf and Vicksburg campaigns, teacher at Academy under Porter, he forged ahead in naval career at time when service morale was low ebb and Navy's progress was largely backward. Backward headquarters leadership can mean poor pay, discontented crews. As told in Dibble's book, *Strenuous Americans*, Dewey had to put down mutiny on board *Pensacola*. A mutinous gang refusing to answer roll call. Dewey facing them, pistol in hand. "I see you, Seaman Johnson. Answer or you'll be a dead man!" No answer, so Dewey shot. End of Johnson. End of mutiny. Navy denied episode. But censorship tells no tales, and incident fits character of times—and of George Dewey.

944. JUNIOR OFFICERS OF *PENSACOLA*. Like Dewey, they found themselves at sea in difficult transition period of a navy half sail, half steam. To old-timers pictured on following page, they were merely youngsters still wet behind the ears.

945. RHYME OF AN ANCIENT MARINER—old salts of the 80's (plus Marine Corps skeptic) on board U.S. screw-sloop *Richmond*.

*He took the anchor on his back
And leaped into the main;
Through foam and spray he clove his way
And sank and rose again.*

*Through foam and spray a league away
The anchor stout he bore,
Till safe at last he made it fast
And warped the ship ashore.*

*Such was the tale that was told to me
By that modest and truthful son of the sea,
For he ain't like some of the swabs I've seen
As would go and lie to a poor Marine.*

                              Anonymous

946. TIME DID NOT STALE NOR CUSTOM WITHER these grand old sea vets serving on board U.S.S.

Mohican in the Pacific Squadron of 1888. Standing in center is Seaman Gilbert Purdy (age 60 plus). At left, arms folded, Seaman David Ireland (age 55). Seated on ditty box, smoking pipe, Chief Gunner's Mate John King, mere lad of 54. Reclining on tub, hands behind head, Chief Carpenter's Mate John T. Griffith, 64. Ready to retire? Not these sailor boys! Purdy eventually served under Dewey in the Spanish-American War —a bluejacket 71 years young. Or maybe 81. (No one in service knew Purdy's actual age or christened name, which wasn't Gilbert Purdy. Like many contemporaries, after numerous re-enlistments old sea dog employed an assumed name, a *nom de guerre*, to conceal age or previous record. Legendary figure in service, Purdy contributed to Navy lingo the term "Gilbert hitch," applied to third, fourth or ad infinitum re-enlistment.)

Naval Explorers
OF THE EIGHTIES

947. ON ARCTIC RELIEF EXPEDITION—U.S.S. *Alliance* (left) sought steamer *Jeannette*. Presented to Government by newspaper tycoon James Gordon Bennett, *Jeannette* with Navy crew had failed to return from Arctic exploration voyage. Hunting lost ship in winter of '81, the *Alliance* found only polar ice.

948. TRAIL'S END—Siberia (below). While *Alliance* turned back from Spitzbergen, U.S.S. *Rodgers* trailed *Jeannette* across Bering Sea. *Rodgers* met disaster by ice and fire. But members of her crew, exploring Siberian coast, found camp of *Jeannette* party—Commander G. W. LeLong and ten men frozen to death. A few *Jeannette* men survived; with rescuers made Homeric journey home via Northern Siberia and Moscow.

949. U.S.R.C. *BEAR* IN ROADSTEAD AT NOME. Veteran polar explorer, *Bear* served in Greenland Relief Expedition dispatched in 1884 to search for Lieutenant A. W. Greely and Army explorers lost in icy limbo of Grinnell Land. Navy rescue squadron under Commander W. S. Schley included vessels *Thetis*, *Bear*, *Alert*. Greely's party was found at Cape Sabine. Navy sailors blazed a trail that opened way to the Pole.

U.S.S. Thetis

950. NAVY ON PACIFIC STATION IN 80's—old stick-and-stringer, youngster and obsolescent gun on board U.S.S. *Mohican*. Sharing letter from home, sailors may be reading that Cleveland has been elected President, that New York City has elevated railway, or that a Mr. Holland is inventing a new-type submarine. The late 80's are full of inventions. Why, it's been ten years since Professor Ritchie flew over Hartford, Conn., in a flyin' machine. But out here in the Pacific it's kind of slow. Old *Mohican* still carries cannon like this big rope-hauled, muzzle-loaded smoothbore Civil War "soda bottle."

Pacific Showdown

951. EXPONENT OF BLOOD AND IRON, and ready to back his program with steel—Prince Otto von Bismarck, Chancellor of Germany. Creator of German Empire, this Prussian Junker is a militarist who demands that when he dies he be buried with a pistol in his coffin. For Germany he demands living-space— "a place in the sun." His Prussian armies take what they want by force —Alsace-Lorraine, a piece of Denmark, a slice of Austria-Hungary. By 1885 Bismarck's shadow stretches from Berlin across the Pacific.

952. HARBOR OF PAGO PAGO, Tutuila Island, Samoa—way stop on ocean road to Australia. Coveted for a coaling station, Samoa was target for competing world powers in the 80's. In 1878 Samoan chiefs signed treaty granting U.S.A. the right to use Pago Pago as a naval station. At same time British were granted similar rights, and Germans acquired a concession in Samoan Group. Samoa then became jackpot in underhanded international Pacific poker game.

953. GERMAN BATTLESHIP *DEUTSCHLAND*—one of big guns in Bismarck's holster. In 1889 Bismarck called the deal on Samoa. An "incident" was manufactured; a native chieftain deposed for "insulting the Kaiser." When islanders rose against German puppet chief, warships *Olga, Adler* and *Eber* arrived to quell "rebellion." Backing them up were such German Fleet heavyweights as formidable *Deutschland*.

An ill wind that blew fair for the Navy of the United States

954. U.S.S. *VANDALIA*—one of American squadron rushed to Samoa at time of German-made crisis. Wooden hybrid (half steam, half sail) she was 1,900-ton sloop rebuilt as gunboat. Carrying guns similar to *Mohican's*, she entered Apia Bay in March 1889, accompanied by U.S.S. *Trenton* and *Nipsic*. Samoa had been guaranteed independence by Western Powers. But on that point the *Berliner Tageblatt* (Bismarck's mouthpiece) stated: "These little islands cannot remain independent forever, and it is therefore urgently wished that Germany should . . . take Samoa while it is to be had."

955. PREPARED TO ARGUE— U.S.S. *Trenton* (below). Flagship of Rear Admiral L. A. Kimberly leading Pacific squadron at Samoa, wooden frigate *Trenton* unlimbered for possible showdown. Pivot gun was new model for U.S.N.—a breech-loader elevated by hand wheels. But (as shown) it was trained by old block-and-tackle system involving 19-man crew. No match for German naval guns of '89. And war was close with Germans glaring at Americans at Apia. Very atmosphere was hair-trigger—glass was falling— when—! The storm! Wild hurricane!

U.S.S. Nipsic, another hand-me-down gunboat at Samoa.

Vandalia

*End of U.S.S. Vandalia
(U.S.S. Trenton alongside)*

Samoans of the nineties

956. AFTER SAMOA HURRICANE
—U.S.S. *Trenton, Vandalia* and
Nipsic on the rocks. Witness to blow
which struck Apia in March 1889,
Robert Louis Stevenson noted that
warships were thrown on beach "as
schoolboys' caps tossed on a shelf."
With sails shredded and engines
swamped, the old American vessels
were wrecked with loss of 50 lives.
Wrecked too were German *Olga,
Adler* and *Eber*—plus Bismarck's
plot to grab Samoa. Storm also
wiped out last of Robeson influence
in Washington as scared Congress
voted to modernize obsolescent Navy.

*End of Bismarck's Pacific am-
bitions. (S.M.S. Adler on beach.)*

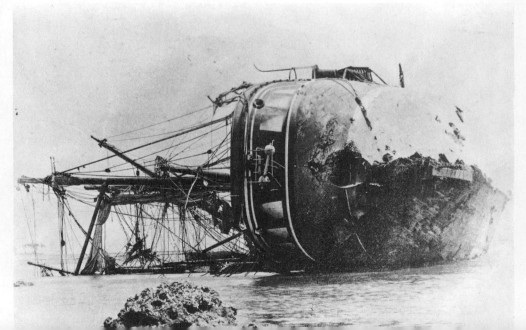

Old Order Passeth

957. "MUTINY" ON U.S.S. *ENTERPRISE.* Known during 80's as "Old Blood Tub," gunboat *Enterprise* (above) was unhappy ship under captaincy of Bowman McCalla. Expert at seamanship, McCalla fouled out on leadership, inept at human relations. Unmitigated martinet, he was detested from bridge to engine room. Men put in strait jackets, gagged with chunks of wood, triced up by their thumbs, chained in coal bunkers. When he sword-whipped a handcuffed fireman and third of *Enterprise* crew deserted during Baltic cruise in '89, Court of Inquiry sat on McCalla. Service storm ensued.

958. "OLD BLOOD TUB" COURT-MARTIAL—Bowman McCalla (three-striper front and center) and officers at time of *Enterprise* trial. When ensigns, Chief Engineer and seamen testified that vessel was hell-ship, McCalla countered with mutiny charges. Defended by celebrated lawyer Joseph Choate, he later changed story, claiming he was victim of grudge plot rigged by Lt. T. B. M. Mason, aide to Naval Secretary Tracy. But Court suspended McCalla for three years, advising Service sundowners would not be tolerated.

Sailors and Marines sound "Tattoo," circa 1890

959. LAST OF AN OLD GUARD —*Kearsarge* wrecked on Roncador Reef. She was on her way from Port au Prince, Haiti, to Bluefields, Nicaragua, on mission to protect American interests threatened by local "mosquito coast" war. Night of February 3, 1894. White combers suddenly foaming dead ahead. Cry from startled lookout. Too late the helm was thrown hard over. With jarring crash the cruiser steamed full tilt on shark-toothed Caribbean snag. Victim of navigational error, famed conqueror of *Alabama* was finished. Her loss culminated a series of marine disasters which had gradually abolished veteran ships of the "Old Navy" and cost lives of several hundred American officers and bluejackets. Disaster toll included:

Sacramento lost Godavery River, India, '67.
Monongahela tidal-waved, St. Croix, '67.
Fredonia by tidal wave, Arica, Peru, '68.
Wateree by tidal wave at Arica, Peru, '68.
Oneida by fatal collision off Japan '70.
Saginaw wrecked on Ocean Island—1871.
Idaho wrecked on coast of Japan—1874.
Huron lost on North Carolina coast, '77.
Trenton by hurricane at Samoa—1889.
Vandalia by hurricane at Samoa—1889.
Nipsic by hurricane at Samoa—1889.

Time and tide were taking care of the antiques which had been scorned by Robeson's auctioneers and rejected by junkman Roach. The "Old Navy," half wood, half iron, was going out. Day of "New" steel Navy was in.

INTELLECTUAL RENAISSANCE
Emphasis on Brains

960. "POOR LITTLE HOUSE, I christen thee United States Naval War College." So spoke founder Luce, at opening of this old mansion at Coaster's Harbor, Newport, R.I. For many years and while Commandant at Annapolis, Luce had advocated a War College where officers might exchange ideas and pursue advanced naval studies. In 1885 this institution—first of its kind—was opened. Launched on a starvation budget, it would live to become indispensable to modern Navy. Pioneer superintendent was Commander Alfred T. Mahan, naval scholar.

961. COMMODORE STEPHEN B. LUCE, U.S.N. — Navy educator, this far-seeing leader inaugurated program to lift Navy's intellectual level. To change his-not-to-reason-why sailor into a think-for-yourself Jack able to master complex guns and gear on modern warships. To change rulebook officer into one capable of solving complicated tactical and strategic problems of modern naval warfare. Such was the mission (largely self-appointed) of Captain Luce, who, more than anyone, brought Navy into step with march of science in modern Age of Steel.

962. COMMANDER ALFRED THAYER MAHAN, U.S.N.—first head of Naval War College, genius of Navy's intellectual renaissance. Lecturer on naval history and strategy, Mahan won fame in 1890 by epochal work, *The Influence of Sea Power Upon History*—a recognized classic. Unique in service which had been conspicuously short of writing talent, Mahan's literary ability made him Navy's No. 1 spokesman.

Naval War College, circa 1900

963. NAVAL ACADEMY IN THE 90's. Under David Dixon Porter, Annapolis made transition from "marlinspike" to steam navigation school. Under Luce, Academy assumed status of good university, its graduates qualified to sail (or fight) steel ships and lead the skilled technicians who would man "New Navy." Cadets of the 90's were drilled as usual in marksmanship and seamanship. But brains were the underlined requisite in formula which had previously emphasized discipline and target practice, "yours not to reason."

INTRODUCING
Naval Intelligence
ENTER THE O.N.I.

964. WAS ABOVE THE WORK OF A SPY? Since forewarned is forearmed, gathering of information concerning actual or potential enemy is as old as warfare. Early naval intelligence consisted largely of coastwatching, reporting movements of enemy ships. Although American secret agents competed with British during Revolution, U.S. naval intelligence remained haphazard until "New Navy" era. During Civil War, however, Confederate espionage service was well organized and extensive. In North, where security was slovenly, enemy secret agents had field day. In South, Confederate spies photographed U.S. ships at New Orleans, Pensacola and elsewhere. Obviously drawn by skilled artist, above sketches by unidentified hand may have been work of Confederate spy at Hampton Roads. Drawings are of U.S.S. *St. Lawrence, Colorado* and *Minnesota*. Bottom line reads: "I send these various ships to —. They may all be of value sooner or later—"

Two views of "Maj. E. J. Allen" (Allan Pinkerton) right, at Secret Service Headquarters. Pinkerton, North's Chief of S.S. misinformed McClellan as to Lee's strength on the Peninsular by 50,000 men, was cause of many of North's faulty assumptions.

965. LIEUTENANT THEODORUS B. M. MASON, founder of Office of Naval Intelligence. Through his urging, U.S. Navy in 1882 established an agency to study and assess data on foreign navies reported by observers. Soon O.N.I. was training agents for secret missions overseas.

966. OFFICE OF NAVAL INTELLIGENCE, 1890. At desk is Commander C. H. Davis, early O.N.I. Chief. National aversion for "spy warfare" tended to inhibit project at that time. But American espionage in Madrid was to pave way for victory in war with Spain. And exploits of secret agent Victor Blue would prove O.N.I. an indispensable naval arm.

 # "New Navy" Men

967. TRAINING, TRAINING, AND MORE TRAINING. John Paul Jones said it. Farragut said it. Future naval commanders would continue to say it. But like all aphorisms, it was senseless unless properly applied. "Old Navy" thought of training as drill—to develop mechanical obedience and manual reflexes. "New

Navy" added mental reflexes to training objective. Campaigning for sailors who could use their heads, Commodore Luce established Naval Apprentice Training System to train seamen for both Navy and Merchant Marine. Apprentices in photo (left) are learning ropes—and being told "whys" as well as "what and how."

968. SMALL ARMS DRILL on deck of U.S.S. *Constellation*. Anchored at Portsmouth, century-old frigate serves as training ship in the new Luce program (below left). Not that the drills were new. Luce's originality lay in idea that men in "New Navy" should be led rather than driven.

969. DECK TRAINING—how to handle gear. Luce advocated schools for enlisted men as well as officers. Tough, tarry and tattooed, Marlinspike Jack had learned by monkey-see-monkey-do. Modern warships, weapons and engines required bluejackets with brains under pie hats.

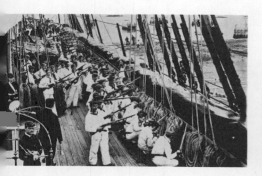

970. BOAT DRILL—an old exercise under eye of new warship. Vessel is one of "ABCD" group completed during energetic regime of Naval Secretary Whitney. May be U.S.S. *Boston* — new "protected cruiser."

971. "ON GUARD!" — seagoing swordsmen. Physical culture for the men was another Luce innovation. Pain in neck as calisthenics drill; fun as competitive sport, the Luce way.

972. NAVAL RESERVES—more innovation. Reinforcing State Naval Militia, Reserves organized in the 90's were a new muscular arm for the U.S.N. Ship is old *Vermont*.

973. ROUND ONE! Popular feature of Luce sports program. Also good means of settling fo'c'sle disputes.

974. CHIEF PETTY OFFICERS of the 90's—off duty. Dice in 1776. Keno in 1861. Now it's cribbage. "New Navy" Chiefs up to old tricks. And Marine sarge at head of the table is getting the usual treatment.

975. BANDSMEN AND BARBER SHOP BALLADES! What's Navy coming to? Well—shaves and haircuts. And popular music. By 1890's whiskers of Civil War genre were obsolescent as tarred queues. So were hornpipes. Sailors of 90's liked Sousa marches and such tunes as "Daisy."

Visitors' Day

976. BEER CALL—favorite of all "New Navy's" shipboard musters. Old grog ration is taboo, but a Gay 90's crew can have a holiday to wet its whistle. Line up, boys! Lager or ale?

977. SHIP'S STORE, 1890. Postcards? Cigars? Emy's Fine Chocolates? Old Navy Tars were eternally "working off dead horse" to pay bills owed the ship's "slop chest." New Navy "geedunk" was boon to bluejackets. In picture: Apprentices.

978. "SWEETHEARTS AND WIVES!" Favorite toast of junior officers in "New Navy." And it was champagne at such collations as this one on board U.S.S. *Newark*—1892 cruiser. Gentlemen, down the hatch!

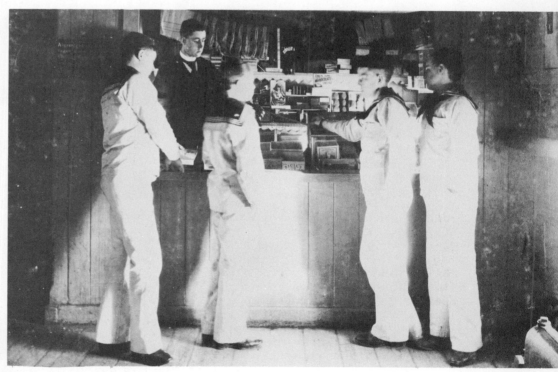

Take her away, cox'n!

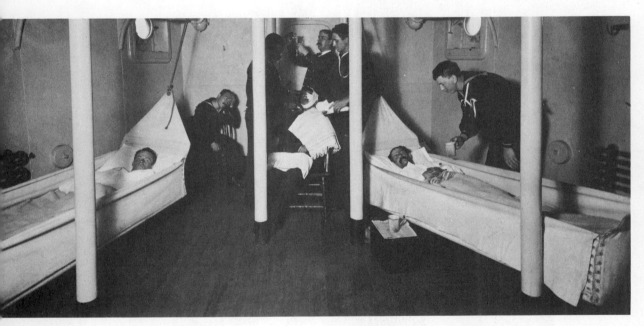

"Columbia" in dry-dock showing her 3 props.

979. JOIN NAVY, SEE WORLD! Well-run liberty party was another innovation of 90's. Sphinx stares at men from U.S.S. *Raleigh*, a protected cruiser of 1890's.

980. SICK BAY on "New Navy" cruiser suggests some shore leaves could be rugged. But men on "binnacle list" never had it better. Far cry from frigate's gory cockpit.

981. LADY WITH LAMP—a new favorite with Navy men. She arrived in U.S.A. in 1876, an immigrant like all the founding mothers of America. Born in Paris studio of French sculptor Bartholdi, she was originally christened "Progress," designed to stand at entrance of Suez Canal. Rejected by Suez officials, she was given by France to America. World's largest bronze statue (225-ton figure 150 feet tall), she created problem for U.S. authorities—where to place her? Bedloe's Island in New York Harbor, once site of a gallows, proved available. Unveiled in October 1886, Goddess stands there today on star-based pedestal, beloved by every sailor who sees her. Her official American name: "Liberty Enlightening the World."

En route to the unveiling

"NEW NAVY" Ships

982. U.S.S. *ATLANTA*—first of the ABCD warships in "New Navy's" steel fleet. Authorized 1883, *Atlanta, Boston, Chicago, Dolphin* marked end of iron hulls. Built by John Roach Shipyards, 3,000-ton *Atlanta* and sister *Boston* were planned as iron-hullers. But Lt. Robley Evans, Navy metallurgist, inserted steel specifications. Roach protested; Navy Department transferred Evans, but kept steel. Classified "protected cruisers," ABCD ships were badly jobbed, too slow, too expensive. Reason: Roach. Abecedarian.

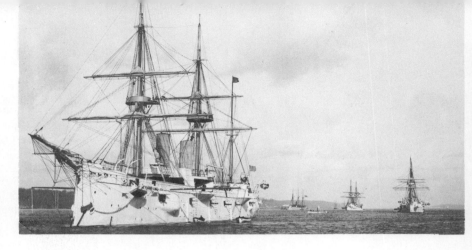

983. PROTECTED CRUISER *CHICAGO* — largest of ABCD's — shown in "Squadron of Evolution" with contemporaries. A 4,500-ton hybrid steam sailer, *Chicago* sacrificed speed (she made 14 knots) for firepower; carried four 8-inch; eight 6-inch guns. So-called Squadron of Evolution was tactical innovation. Whereas Old Navy squadrons often tackled enemy on a free-for-all, devil-take-hindermost basis, New Navy ships trained for group teamwork.

984. U.S. DISPATCH BOAT *DOLPHIN* — "D" of ABCD group. A 1,485-ton steam hybrid with schooner rig. Could do 13 knots; carried one 6-inch gun. Vessel's poor construction incurred wrath of honest Secretary Wm. C. Whitney who ended all dealing with avaricious John Roach.

985. PROTECTED CRUISER *NEWARK* — last U.S. warship fitted with sail. A 4,098-tonner, with 3-inch deck and 2-inch turret armor. Twelve 6-inch guns. Speed: about 19 knots.

986. ADMIRAL FIFE BOARDS new protected cruiser *San Francisco*.

987. OFFICERS' PANTRY, U.S.S. *Newark*. No hardtack-and-bully-beef menus in Navy of the 90's. With tablecloths for the men and napery to go with wine for officers' mess, life on the rolling main could be fancy. Especially when (note pantry decorations) Christmas was in air.

988. COLUMBIAN NAVAL REVIEW (April 1893). By this date U.S. Fleet boasted 15 light steel cruisers including new *Baltimore, Charleston, Philadelphia, Columbia, Olympia*. Also heavy armored cruiser *New York;* small battleships *Maine* and *Texas* built on English design.

Watching the great "Review"

989. COALING SHIP—the dungaree Navy. To veterans of sailing days the smokes which soiled a hybrid's canvas were clouds without silver lining. Onerous, too, was task of storing fodder for gluttonous engines.

990. CREW AFTER COALING. Tired, but fairly cheerful. Blackface minstrels were popular in the 90's.

991. COAL GANG OUT OF COSTUME. Does that feel good! And by noon entire ship will have had a bath.

992. SAILORS, MAN YOUR MOPS! On armored cruiser *New York:* cleanliness next to godliness.

993. SUNDAY SERVICE on *Texas* —new 1890 battleship. Visiting ladies are Methodist "King's Daughters."

994. U.S. ARMORED RAM *KATAHDIN*—a throwback. Built in the 90's for coastal defense, this vessel was a turtle-like freak with 6-inch side and deck armor, workhorse engines, no guns. Armed only with ram, she was supposed to drive her steel beak into enemy warship as rhino would gore elephant. But it would have to be a sitting elephant. Sluggish *Katahdin* could hardly catch a buoy. Ram was outmoded weapon.

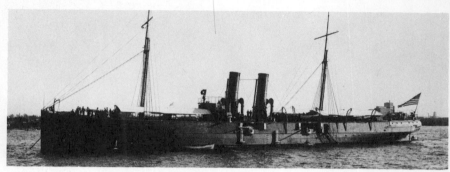

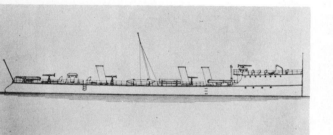

995. U.S. TORPEDO BOAT *DUPONT*. When long-range torpedo made debut in 1890's, Navy acquired 16 fast T-B's. Largest: *Porter*, *Rowan* and *DuPont*, 185-tonners capable of 27 knots. Smallest: *Stiletto*; 31-tonner; 18 knots. Designed for high-speed attacks with mobile "fish," bantam T-B's proved too thin-skinned for job. But torpedo was feared.

996. U.S. GUNBOAT *TOPEKA*—(above). A new 1,180-tonner. Six 4-inch guns. Speed 14 knots. No great warship. Distinction lay in her purchase from Brazil, along with cruisers *New Orleans* and *Albany*. New weapon in Navy arsenal—strategic dollars. A potential enemy, Spain wanted the Brazilian warships. U.S. "captured them" with a higher bid.

"New Navy" Weapons

997. 6-INCH NAVAL GUN OF THE 80's. Weapon is breech-loader rifle; trains and elevates by wheel and gear; has simple recoil system. Gun was called "quick-firer" because projectile and powder charge were encased in single cartridge; breech-lock worked rapidly; recoil mechanism returned gun to firing position.

998. 6-INCH NAVAL GUN OF THE 90's. Strengthening Navy's ordnance arm, inventors in 90's made rapid progress. Gun in picture (left) has new "interrupted screw" breech-plug—faster and safer than earlier type. Splinter shield, gun carriage and recoil gear are ultramodern for Victorian Era. Given sights and range-finder, gun would look 1941.

999. GUNNERY PRACTICE OF THE 90's. On board protected cruiser *Newark*, gun crew operates 6-incher. Note unique training and elevating gear, loaders standing by, gun captain ready to jerk lanyard. Gun is still aimed by primitive method of sighting along barrel by eye. Gunnery Officer's sword (theatrical and expensive) and fire-hazard wood lockers were anachronisms soon to go. (Swords were reintroduced, 1954.)

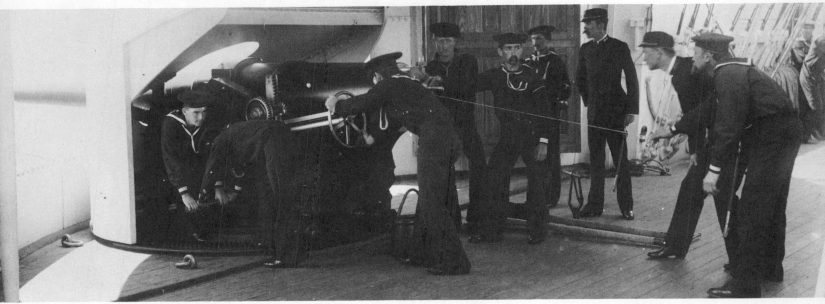

1000. GUN DECK OF U.S.S. *BROOKLYN*—new armored cruiser of mid 90's. Nothing antiquated about these trim batteries. Latest in the day of Harvey-processed steel.

1001. 8-INCH NAVAL GUN OF THE 90's. Cruisers *New York* and *Brooklyn* mounted these big ones.

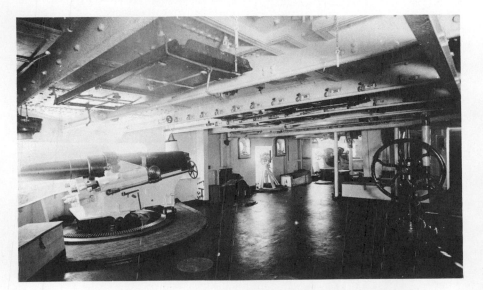

8-in. gun of the "Baltimore"

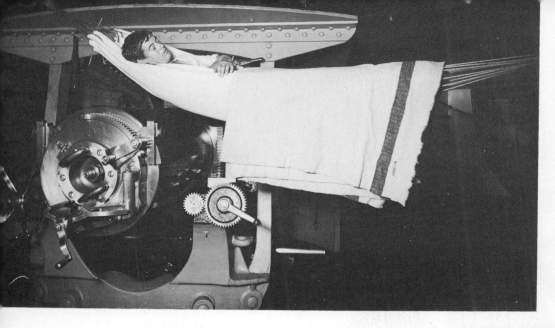

1002. 10-INCHER IN BATTLE-SHIP TURRET. Breech mechanism exhibits fine mechanical tooling of mid 90's as gun captain exhibits *élan*. The *Maine* carried four 10-inchers. *Texas* toted two 12-inch guns. "New Navy's" 12-incher (heavyweight of 45 tons) could puncture at 1,000 yards some 26.7 inches of iron.

1003. MACHINE GUN OF 1890's. "New Navy" featured Gatling and Maxim guns. Overgrown derringer with revolving barrels, the Gatling (below) could fire 1200 shots p.m.

1004. MAXIM MACHINE GUN had automatic cartridge-feed. Maxim crew on gunboat (below) aims blanks at *Brooklyn*. Fast gun for close work.

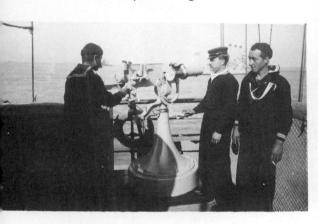

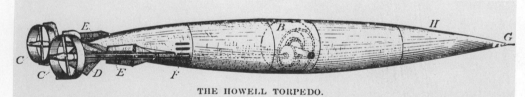

THE HOWELL TORPEDO.

B, fly-wheel. *C, C*, screw propellers. *D*, diving rudder. *E, E*, steering rudders. *F*, water-chamber containing automatic apparatus. *G*, firing pin. *H*, position of gun-cotton magazine.

1005. THE HOWELL TORPEDO. Mystery weapon of the 70's was the self-propelled torpedo which expanded torpedo warfare from sparring bout to long-range combat. Invented by Austrian naval officer and British engineer Whitehead, this torpedo remained hit-or-miss until 1885 when Lieutenant J. A. Howell, U.S.N., invented gyroscopic rudder device for steering control. By 1890 Howell torpedo was standard weapon in U.S.N. Early model was manufactured by Hotchkiss Ordnance Co.; cost $1,835. It was 11¼ feet long; 14 inches in diameter; contained explosive charge of 81 lbs. of guncotton. Steam driven at 25 m.p.h.; range of 400 yards.

1006. ARSENAL OF "NEW NAVY" —Gun Factory, Washington Navy Yard. New guns of the steel fleet were built by technicians at Naval Gun Factory. Coming off the line, this big-caliber weapon was one of most formidable of its day. Navy's late-90's battleships would carry 13-inchers. Highest fire-power afloat.

1007. WHARVES OF BROOKLYN NAVY YARD—in mid 90's. Originally called New York Naval Shipyard, Brooklyn Navy Yard was no longer forest of masts supporting nests of canvas. Gunboats at wharf contribute to yard's "New Navy" silhouette, as styled in day of soup-strainers and leg-o'-mutton sleeves.

"New Navy" Navy Yard

1008. LAWN AND OFFICES, BROOKLYN NAVY YARD—new armored cruiser *Brooklyn* in background. Note sailors at ferry slip, perhaps bound for Manhattan weekend—the Bowery, China Town, a trip down Bay to see Miss Liberty, or up Broadway to see Louise Heppener —"The Flatbush Brunehilde."

1009. U.S. FLEET OF 1890's at Hampton Roads—introducing the modern Navy. Highspeed warships, long-range guns, squadron battle-tactics, Mahan strategy—U.S.N. has shed canvas swaddling clothes for-ever. Forged of nickel-steel "face-hardened" armor, Fleet is stout weapon of nation approaching the mechanized Twentieth Century.

1010. NEW ENGINE FOR "NEW NAVY" BATTLESHIP. One of "vertical triple-expansion" engines which drove late-90's battlewagon. Unlike "White Fleet" hybrids, new battleships *Indiana*, *Massachusetts*, *Iowa*, *Oregon* were engine-power moderns averaging 16 or 17 knots.

New Navy Officer:
Ensign on board U.S.S. Texas

1011. "NEW NAVY" LEADER—Captain Robley D. (Fighting Bob) Evans. Product of Naval Academy. Wounded at Fort Fisher (scars he bore through life). Skilled navigator. Expert skipper. Construction specialist. Metallurgist. Schooled in tactics and strategy. Student of history and foreign affairs. Scientific sailor, engineer, executive—Evans exemplified the versatile officer professionally qualified for modern naval leadership. In 1891 a liberty party from new cruiser *Baltimore* went ashore at Valparaiso, Chile. A brawl in the True Blue Saloon. Then riot, two U.S. seamen killed, 18 wounded. With hotheads of both nations demanding war, Navy dispatched new gunboat *Yorktown* (Captain Evans) to scene. An old-time Barron, Hollins or Percival, full of chauvanistic fervor, might have opened fire. So might a fiery young D. D. Porter. But this was eve of a new, more adult century. In '87 Capt. T. O. Selfridge had faced court-martial for endangering Japanese lives by careless battery practice near Ike-Shima beach. In Chile incident, Evans lived up to adult responsibilities. Recognizing two sides to controversy, he salved anger with tact, prevented costly U.S.-Chilean War with diplomacy. In 1898 he was (as shown) far up ladder; captain of new battleship *Iowa*. Commanding by virtue of competence. And by meeting those other leadership requisites set as standard for U.S.N. long ago by Paul Jones. "It is by no means enough that an officer of the Navy should be a capable mariner. He should be as well a gentleman of liberal education, punctilious courtesy, the nicest honor."

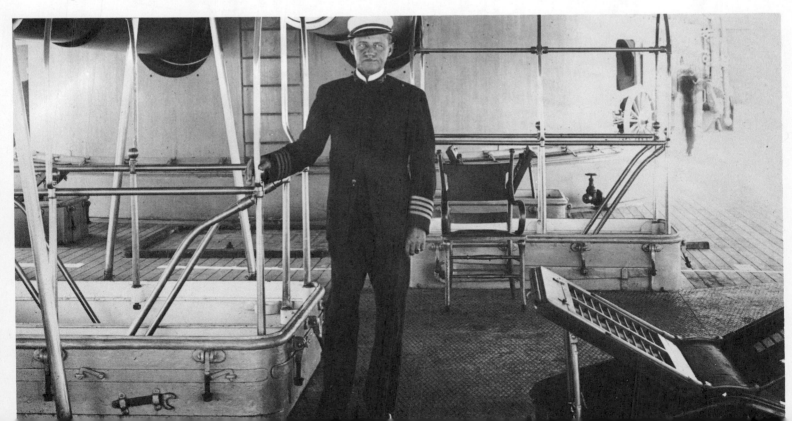

F I N I S

special
acknowledgments

First, I should like to thank Howard I. Chapelle for use of material from his two magnificent and monumental works, THE HISTORY OF AMERICAN SAILING SHIPS and THE HISTORY OF THE AMERICAN SAILING NAVY, without which no nautical library is worthy of the name. Also, to Katherine Barnard, editor, and W. W. Norton and Co., New York, publishers of Chapelle's works, go my thanks for their permission (and expressions of good will) to use this material. Seven of Mr. Chapelle's plans and reconstructions are reproduced herein and accompany the following text numbers: 20, 110, 111, 112, 275, 353, 507. In addition, I drew heavily on Mr. Chapelle's plans in the construction of my own drawings (if there are mistakes therein they are mine and not Mr. Chapelle's).

Secondly, my thanks go to Captain P. V. H. Weems and the Weems System of Navigation of Annapolis, Maryland, publisher. Captain Weems' enthusiastic letter of encouragement was as much appreciated as his permission to use any and all material from the splendid little volume, A SHORT HISTORY OF NAVIGATION written by W. J. V. Branch, R.A.F.V.R. and Captain E. Brook-Williams, M.M. with pictures by courtesy of the National Maritime Museum and Messrs. Henry Hughes and Sons Limited of London, England. For the sections "Seamanship in Sail" and "Development of Navigation" (text numbers 449 through 453.4 in our book), I offer special thanks to Mr. Peter Marsh Stanford, brilliant young naval historian, author of the excellent biography of Sir Julian Corbett (Naval Institute Proceedings, January 1951) and other naval works for his assistance to me.

To the Training Activity of the Bureau of Personnel of the U.S. Navy, appreciation is extended for the 23 small drawings used herein from the book YOUR NAVY. This little volume, prepared under the direction of Rear Admiral J. M. Will, USN and Captain Lot Ensey, USN as a training book for enlisted personnel, was written by Theodore Roscoe and designed and illustrated in the Illustration Unit of the Training Books Section. This unit was then under the direction of Lt. Fred Freeman, USNR and numbered thirty young enlisted men, Waves and Civil Servants, very few of whom had had previous illustrating experience or training. Since these drawings were joint efforts of the director and other personnel, now widely scattered, it is not possible to credit these drawings to individuals.

My thanks go to the Mattatuck Historical Society of Waterbury, Connecticut, for allowing the use of my painting of the *Independence*, Texas Navy, #507, and to the donor, the Scoville Manufacturing Company, also of Waterbury, Connecticut, for whom the painting was originally made. Also, thanks are given to the Charles Pfizer Co., of New London, Connecticut, for permission to use my painting of the Monitor-Merrimack Battle #710. And to Little, Brown and Company, publishers, Boston, go thanks for permitting me to use the quotations from THE INFLUENCE OF SEA POWER ON HISTORY by Alfred Thayer Mahan (accompanying text #616).

To the Coast Guard Academy at New London go my thanks for allowing me to disrupt their model room and for assistance in photographing their excellent model of the cutter *Morris* which I used in the reconstruction of *Independence* for our section on the Mexican War. And to the New York Yacht Club for use of its little known but magnificent marine library goes my appreciation.

To Captain and Mrs. F. Walter Rowe, USNR, and to Mr. E. E. Dickinson III and to Mrs. J. W. Halliday of Essex, Connecticut, go my thanks for use of their Naval Libraries, papers, scrapbooks and ship models. To Mr. Edward P. Foster, Jr. of McLean, Virginia, many thanks for his manuscript on the first American naval battle.

A pleasant surprise has been to receive warm interest and extensive collateral research when seeking permission to use material. People who must be very busy otherwise have taken time to correspond at length giving detailed information on picture background. I, personally, would like to extend thanks to the following: Charles H. P. Copeland, Curator of Maritime History, Peabody Museum, Salem, Massachusetts; Agnes Gray, City Art Museum of St. Louis; RAdm. John B. Heffernan, USN (Ret.), Director of Naval History, Department of the Navy; Mitchell A. Wilder, director, Williamsburg, Virginia; Edith Gregor Halpert, director, The Downtown Gallery, New York; Ernest S. Dodge, director, Peabody Museum, Salem, Massachusetts; Robert L. Harley, The Old Print Shop, New York; Sara Mazo, assistant to the curator, Museum of Modern Art, New York; James W. Foster, director, Maryland Historical Society, Baltimore, Maryland; C. E. Turner, London Electrotype Agency Ltd., London; Doris Doland, Manager, public relations, LOOK Magazine, New York; and R. W. Haddon, director, Mattatuck Historical Society, Waterbury, Connecticut.

Acknowledgments and thanks go, with full measure, to those artists and others who assisted me in the actual production of the book; to Arthur Strecker who, for 23 months, worked at my side, rendering layouts, researching charts, specifying type, cropping and servicing pictures; to Robert Bride, promising young artist, for restoring and retouching pictures, and rendering charts and mechanicals; to Eugene Heiffel and Oviatt Welcome, both of whom are artists and art directors in their own right, who executed 384 mechanicals (1 for each page in the book); to Howard Kenngott who rendered most of the charts and whose splendid work is always fresh and stimulating; to Robert Peterson, constructor of mock-ups and back-grounds extraordinary; and to my son Bill, for his many helpful and unsung services. Also thanks go to those natives of Essex, Connecticut, largely sea-farers, who doubled as models and were hung up in ropes, struggled with one another, twisted and rolled on the floor in outlandish costumes; to Harold Wilder, Capt. Jeremiah Whitaker, Mortimer Johns, Thomas Ford, Robert Peterson, Arthur Strecker, and Bill Freeman among others. And to the Regina Brothers, Harry and Mike, and Clemente Perrucci, appreciation is extended for miraculously producing usable and even excellent pictures from hopelessly bad copy by their skill and mastery of the art of photo-printing.

Thanks from me go, also, to Mr. George McCorkle of Charles Scribner's Sons for his invaluable aid and advice on technical matters and for giving generously of his time and interest. Also, to Mr. Joseph Poli of Scribners thanks are given for his assistance over the many production hurdles. And to Margareta F. Lyons, assistant Art Editor, I am grateful for her wise counsel and excellent taste. Her suggestions were most valuable to me.

To the Murray Printing Company, and particularly to Mr. Fred Walker and Mr. K. E. Adams, I should like to extend thanks for the patience and skill with which our material was handled.

Core and catalyst of this volume has been Mr. Burroughs Mitchell, editor for Charles Scribner's Sons. It is difficult to see how his task could have been a happy one, but his sound judgment, his unfailing aura of well-being and his genial common sense breed first confidence and finally absolute trust.

Lastly, to my collaborator, Mr. Theodore Roscoe, I wish to make special acknowledgment. The idea for the book was his. He planned the structure of the work. He had written the book and collected and researched by far the greatest proportion of the pictures, herein, before my part of the job was started. He cut and revised his text throughout the book twice to fit the layout of the material, both times with thoroughness and good will. If there is fundamental merit in the work it belongs to him. **F. F.**

R O S C O E

For professional assistance in the research of historical data and pictorial material, I remain personally indebted to many qualified experts and authorities who went out of their way to lend a helping hand.

To Mr. Milton Kaplan and Miss Virginia Daiker of the Prints and Photographs Division, Library of Congress, recognized experts in the pictorial field, who provided this researcher with an invaluable introduction to the Library's Brady, Detroit Photo and Currier & Ives collections.

To Messrs. Joe Doan Thomas, Howard T. Gardner and Thomas W. Ray of the Still Pictures Section, the National Archives, who enthusiastically aided this researcher with advice and suggestions. And to Miss Josephine Cobb, head of the Still Pictures Section, who permitted her staff to comb the files in this researcher's behalf.

To Mr. W. Douglas McKay, Assistant to the Curator, Mystic Seaport Marine Historical Association, Mystic, Connecticut, who extended valuable aid to this researcher and provided several rare and hitherto unpublished naval pictures for reproduction in this volume.

To Mr. Donald Shepard, Librarian, the Submarine Library, Electric Boat Division of the General Dynamics Corporation, Groton, Connecticut, who furnished much background material on pioneer submarine warfare.

To Mr. Irving S. Olds, former Chairman of the Board of U.S. Steel, who generously contributed the negatives of a number of rare naval prints from the fine iconographic collection published in his magnificent BITS AND PIECES OF AMERICAN HISTORY.

To Captain Charles West, Secretary, Company of Military Collectors and Historians, New York City, and to Mrs. John Nicholas Brown of Providence, for detailed information on the uniforms and dress of Confederate Navy men. Also to Mrs. Brown for her generous offer to provide pictures from her C. M. Robinson Collection.

To Mr. H. H. Kynett of Philadelphia for permission to reproduce four of the Wales marine paintings currently exhibited by the Mystic Seaport Marine Historical Association, Mystic, Connecticut.

To artist Lynd Ward for permission to reproduce several of his fine illustrations from AMERICA'S PAUL REVERE.

To artist G. B. Mitchell for permission to reproduce his dramatic painting, *The Battle of Stonington,* and for much detailed information on that historic episode.

To historian Edwin Valentine Mitchell for permission to reproduce several rare collector's items from his NEWGATE CALENDAR and a generous offer to furnish background material from the privately owned letter-books of Naval Secretary Gideon Welles.

To author Jay Monaghan for permission to reproduce the masthead of *Ned Buntline's Own* from his best-seller Buntline biography, THE GREAT RASCAL.

To Charles G. Davis of Port Washington, New York, for permission to use a photograph of his ship model of a British East Indiaman.

To Rear Admiral Thomas L. Wattles, U.S.N. (Rtd.), for data on early American privateering.

To Rear Admiral Elmer E. Duvall, U.S.N. (Rtd.), for the contribution of several dramatic pictures and information on the naval writings of James Fenimore Cooper.

To Commander Henri Behic, F.N., Assistant French Naval Attache in Washington, and Capitaine de Frégate Rostand, Chef du Service Historique de la Marine, in Paris, for information on the French naval forces under Count d'Estaing and Admiral de Ternay.

To Commander Roy de S. Horn, U.S.N. (Rtd.), Editor, and Mr. H. O. Werner, Associate Editor, of the U.S. Naval Institute, for assistance in procuring pictures.

To Lieutenant Commander John Hessian, U.S.N.R., of the Training Division, Bureau of Naval Personnel, for friendly assistance in picture research.

To Sr. Rafael Nieto, Minister Counselor of the Mexican Embassy in Washington, for information on Mexican ironclads *Moctezuma* and *Guadalupe.*

To Mr. Charles Storey and Miss Norma Ritchie of Washington, D. C. (with additional thanks to the Misses Harriet Putnam and Carolyn Boaz) for the original McPherson & Oliver photograph which, found in an attic in Richmond, may be the only surviving group photo of Confederate Navy enlisted men.

To photographer Herb Schaeffer of the *Rochester Democrat & Chronicle* (with additional thanks to columnist Henry W. Clune) for the fine photograph of the Civil War Soldiers and Sailors Monument in Rochester, New York.

To Mrs. Anna Anderson and Carleton Anderson of Block Island, Rhode Island, for permission to use illustrations from rare historical volumes in their possession.

To Mr. James R. Sirlouis of the Smithsonian Institution; Mr. Arthur B. Carlson of the New York Historical Society; Mr. William Williamson of the Museum of the City of New York; Mr. Sylvester Vigilante and Miss Elizabeth Roth of the New York Public Library, and Mr. Edward Stewart and Captain R. E. Gardener, U.S.N., of the Office of Naval History—all of whom personally aided this researcher.

I must also acknowledge the professional services of Mr. Joel D. Thacker, Marine Corps Historian, Headquarters U.S. Marine Corps, Washington, D. C.; Captain Wade de Weese, U.S.N. (Rtd.), of the U.S. Naval Academy Museum, Annapolis, Maryland; Miss P. Sichel of the National Maritime Museum, London, England; Mrs. Muriel D. Taylor, Librarian of the Masonic Temple in Boston, and Miss Llerena Friend, Librarian, Barker Texas History Center, the University of Texas.

Thanks are also due to historian, librarians and archivists at the Franklin D. Roosevelt Library, Hyde Park, New York; the Newberry Library of Chicago; the Texas State Library of Austin; the Mariners' Museum, Newport News, Virginia; the Historical Society of Pennsylvania; Pennsylvania Society, Sons of the American Revolution; the Independence National Historical Park Project, Philadelphia; the Colonial National Historical Park of Yorktown, Virginia; the Rhode Island Historical Society; the Marine Museum of Newport; the Stonington Historical Society; the Peabody Museum of Salem, and the Confederate Museums of Richmond, Virginia, and Charleston, South Carolina.

Further acknowledgments go to Harper & Bros.; Little, Brown & Co., the Houghton Mifflin Company; McGraw-Hill Co.; the Garden City Publishing Co., Inc.; the Columbia University Press; Charles Scribner's Sons; the Du Pont Powder Co., the United States Naval Institute; and the publishers of *The New York Times,* the *D.A.R. Magazine* and *Steelways* for permission (as credited in the picture credits) to use material under their copyright.

The writer must also make special acknowledgment to Mr. Fred Freeman, whose naval experience lends professional authority and meticulous authenticity to the original art work executed for this volume. In addition to creating fine illustrations and book design, Mr. Freeman wrote the one-line captions for many of the small SPOTS, authored the captions for two of his major illustrations (Nos. 378 and 711), and wrote the sections on Seamanship and Navigation in Chapter IV (Nos. 449 through 453.4).

Finally, I must express indebtedness to Mr. Charles Scribner for his interest in the production of this picture-history. I am also indebted to Burroughs Mitchell and others on the Scribner editorial staff for their constructive efforts in the volume's behalf. In dealing with a difficult book-making project, editor and publisher exerted a patience and forebearance far above and beyond the call of routine publishing. **T. R.**

PICTURE Credits

Listed below, numbered and in the order in which they appear in the book, are the captions of the pictures and the sources from which the pictures were obtained. The small pictures, which do not have numbered captions are listed as SPOTS and credits for these may be found with the numbered captions to which they are adjacent. Every effort has been made to identify the originators of the pictures, as well as the sources; however, where such identification has not been possible the originator has been omitted. Where prints or originals are in the possession of one of the collaborators, the source is indicated by his initials.

JACKET DRAWING. "Paul Jones at Sea." *Artist* Fred Freeman. *Calligrapher* Sam Marsh.
COVER DRAWING. *Artist* Fred Freeman. *Calligrapher* Sam Marsh.
END PAPER PAINTING. *Artist* Fred Freeman. Courtesy of Esquire Magazine.
BASTARD TITLE PAGE DRAWING. *Artist* Fred Freeman. *Calligrapher* Sam Marsh.
FRONTISPIECE DRAWING. *Artist* Fred Freeman.
TITLE PAGE DRAWING. *Artist* Fred Freeman. *Calligrapher* Sam Marsh.
DEDICATION PAGE DRAWING. *Artist* Fred Freeman.
CONTENTS PAGE DRAWING. *Artist* Fred Freeman.

CHAPTER I

CHAPTER I HEADING DRAWING. *Artist* Fred Freeman.
1.FIRST MAP OF UNITED STATES. *Cartographer* Abel Buell, **N. Y. Public Library.** (*SPOT,* lower left.) (FF)
2.TYPICAL SAIL PLAN. *Artist* Arthur Strecker.
3.LINE-OF-BATTLE SHIP. From "Kedge-Anchor." (*SPOTS,* lower left, *Ship-of-War,* dressed with Flags, lower right, *Ship-of-the-line, Starboard Tack,* from "Kedge-Anchor.")
4.FRIGATE. From "Kedge-Anchor." (*SPOT,* top right, *Frigate Drying Sails,* from "Kedge-Anchor.")
5.SLOOP-OF-WAR. From "Kedge-Anchor." (*SPOT,* at right, *Frigate under Full Sail,* from "Kedge-Anchor.")
6.WAR-BRIG. From "Kedge-Anchor." (*SPOT,* at right, *Sloop of War Under Sail,* from "Kedge-Anchor.")
7.NAVAL SCHOONER. From "Kedge-Anchor." (*SPOT,* at right, *Sloop-of-War Hove to,* from "Kedge-Anchor.")
8.CORNER OF CAPTAIN'S CABIN. From National Park Service, Colonial National Historical Park, Yorktown, Va. (*SPOTS,* at right, *Brig-of-War under full sail,* below, *Schooner-of-War getting under weigh,* from "Kedge-Anchor.")
9.BROADSIDE BATTERY. From National Park Service, Colonial National Historical Park, Yorktown, Va.
10.TYPICAL NAVAL GUN MOUNT. From National Park Service, Colonial National Historical Park, Yorktown, Va.
11.NAVAL MORTAR. From John R. Spears' "The History of Our Navy"; courtesy Charles Scribner's Sons. (*SPOT, Early Naval Button,* from Spears' "The History of Our Navy." *SPOT, Exercise of the Great Guns.*) (FF)
12.LINE-OF-BATTLE SHIPS IN COLUMN. *Artist* C. T. or A. W. Warren; courtesy Office of Naval Records and Library.
13.TACKING FOR "WEATHER GAUGE." *Artist* Thomas Birch; courtesy Office of Naval Records and Library.
14.STERN CHASE. From Spears' "The History of Our Navy."
15."RAKING." Courtesy Office of Naval Records and Library.
16."BOARDERS AWAY!" From "Your Navy."
17.YARD-ARM TO YARD-ARM. Courtesy Office of Naval Records and Library.
18.EARLY AMERICAN CRADLE. Ship model by Charles G. Davis; courtesy Mr. Davis, and Mystic Seaport, Marine Historical Association, Inc. (*PHOTOS,* below, *Views of model, 44-gun ship America.* Courtesy Peabody Museum.)
19.COLONIAL AMERICAN SEA CAPTAIN. (FF)
(At left), **MARITIME NEW YORK, 1718.** *Artist* Wm. Burgis; from Stokes Collection, N. Y. Public Library.
20.DRAUGHT OF COLONIAL FRIGATE *BOSTON*. *Artist* Howard I. Chapelle; from "History of the American Sailing Navy," W. W. Norton Co.
SEA CAPTAINS CAROUSING. *Artist* John Greenwood. Courtesy City Art Museum of St. Louis.
21.TROUBLE-MAKER OFF AMERICA'S EARLIEST LIGHTHOUSE. From Spears' "The History of Our Navy."
22.HERE COME THE RED COATS! *Artist* Paul Revere; N. Y. Public Library. (*SPOTS,* below left, *Faneuil Hall;* center, *Demolishing Statue of George III;* lower right, *Old Boston Building;* far right; *Tossing Tea Overboard.*) (FF)
23.GASPÉE EPISODE. *Artist* J. McKevin; N. Y. Public Library. (*SPOT,* above.) (FF)
24.BOSTON TEA PARTY. *Lithographer* Sarony & Major. Courtesy D.A.R.
25.FORCING COLUMBIA TO DRINK TEA. *Artist* Paul Revere; from Fiske's "History of the American Navy"; Library of Congress. (*SPOT,* below right. *Stamp Act Riots of New York.*) (FF)
26.MINUTE MAN. *Artist* F. O. C. Darley; Library of Congress.
27.HERE COME MORE RED COATS! *Artist* Lynd Ward; from "America's Paul Revere"; courtesy Houghton Mifflin Co. (*SPOT,* right, *Bunker Hill.*)- (FF)
28.BATTLE OF BUNKER HILL. Old Print; courtesy D.A.R. (*Chart:* lower left, *Battle of Breed's Hill.*) *Cartographer* Arthur Strecker.
29.ANSWER AT MACHIAS, MAINE. *Artist* Charles Turner Warren or Alfred William Warren; courtesy Office of Naval Records & Library. (*SPOT,* below from "Your Navy.")
30.ANSWER AT NEWPORT, R. I. *Artist* W. C. Jackson; from Blue Jackets of '76; Library of Congress.
31.ANSWER FROM AMERICAN PRIVATEERS. *Artist* Henry Reuterdahl; courtesy Charles Scribner's Sons.
32.CONGRESS—FATHER OF AMERICAN NAVY. (FF)
33.SHORE BOMBARDMENT, ROYAL NAVY STYLE. Old Print (probably picturing attack on Porto Bello); courtesy "U.S. Naval Institute Proceedings."
34.BURNING OF FALMOUTH. Old woodcut; from Fiske's "The American Revolution"; Library of Congress.
35.FLAG OF NAVY OF UNITED COLONIES. From Spears' "The History of Our Navy."
36.GENERAL GEORGE WASHINGTON. Old Print; probably engraved by Illman Bros. Collection of Miss Minnie Rose Hackett.
37.JOHN ADAMS. *Artist* J. S. Copley; National Archives.
38.COMMODORE ESEK HOPKINS. *Artist* Thomas Hart; from Spears' "The History of Our Navy."
39.IDEALIZED PORTRAIT OF ESEK HOPKINS. (Evidently a revision of Hart painting); from Spears' "The History of Our Navy."
40.CAPTAIN JOHN BARRY. *Artist* Alonzo Chappel; from Spears' "The History of Our Navy."
41.HIS MAJESTY GEORGE III. *Artist* Wynne Ryland; courtesy Kegan, Paul, Trench, Trubner & Co., Ltd.
42.LORD NORTH. From Fiske's "The American Revolution"; Library of Congress.
43.JOHN MONTAGU, EARL OF SANDWICH. *Artist* G. Knapton; N. Y. Public Library.
44.LORD GEORGE GERMAIN. *Artist* G. Romney; from contemporary "European Magazine." N. Y. Public Library. (*SPOT,* center, *Divertissement. Artist* John Collet.) (FF)
45.CAPTAIN ABRAHAM WHIPPLE. Courtesy "U. S. Naval Institute Proceedings." (*SPOT,* right, *Seaman in Rigging;* from Fiske's "The American Revolution; Library of Congress.
46.CAPTAIN NICHOLAS BIDDLE. *Artist* Schuessele from Peale; Historical Society of Pennsylvania.
47.CAPTAIN JAMES NICHOLSON. Courtesy Naval History Division, CNO. (*SPOT,* below, *Artist* C. E. Turner; courtesy Illustrated London News.)
48.CAPTAIN LAMBERT WICKES. (No picture available)
49.CAPTAIN JOHN PECK RATHBURN. (No picture available)
50.LIEUTENANT JOSHUA BARNEY. *Artist* Isahey; courtesy Naval History Division, CNO.
51.BENEDICT ARNOLD. *Artist* Du Simitière; (drawn from a medal Arnold never received); Library of Congress. (*SPOT,* below right, *Death of General Warren.*) (FF)
52.VICE ADMIRAL HOWE. *Artist* Copeley; from Spears' "The History of Our Navy."
53.VICE ADMIRAL RODNEY. *Artist* Gainsborough; from Spears' "The History of Our Navy."
54.REAR ADMIRAL ARBUTHNOT. *Artist* Rising; N. Y. Public Library.
55."BUTTERFLY FROM MAGGOT." From Spears' "The History of Our Navy."
56.REAR ADMIRAL HOOD. *Artist* Hoppner; courtesy "U. S. Naval Institute Proceedings."
57.REAR ADMIRAL PARKER. *Engraver* T. Blood; from "European Magazine"; N. Y. Public Library.
58.JOHN PAUL JONES. *Artist* Cecilia Beaux; courtesy "U. S. Naval Institute Proceedings."
59.AMERICA VERSUS BRITAIN. From Spears' "The History of Our Navy."
60.RECRUITING, 1776. *Artist* W. C. Jackson; from "Blue Jackets of '76"; Library of Congress.
61.AMERICAN GUN CREW, 1776. *Artist* W. C. Jackson; from "Blue Jackets of '76"; Library of Congress.
62.FLOGGING IN ROYAL NAVY. From "Your Navy."
63.BRITISH TARS, GEORGIAN ERA. *Artist* W. C. Jackson; from "Blue Jackets of '76"; Library of Congress.
64.IMPRESSMENT. From Fiske's "The American Revolution"; Library of Congress.
65.JUNIOR OFFICER, R.N. From Spears' "The History of Our Navy."
66.AMERICAN FRIGATE *ALFRED*. *Artist* Harry W. Carpenter; courtesy Naval History Division, CNO.
67.FIRST ALL-AMERICAN FRIGATE TO SEA (*Randolph*). *Artist* C. R. Patterson; courtesy "U. S. Naval Institute Proceedings."
68.MODEL FRIGATE *RALEIGH*. Courtesy Franklin D. Roosevelt Library.
69.AMERICAN WAR-SLOOP *RANGER*. *Artist* C. Chapman; courtesy Office of Naval Records and Library.
70.AMERICAN LIGHT FRIGATE *BOSTON*. Courtesy Office of Naval Records and Library.
71.H.M.S. *VICTORY*. Old print; courtesy Harry Shaw Newman. (*SPOT,* right, *Sailors Aloft.*) (FF)
72.H.M. FRIGATE *ALARM*. *Engraver* Carrington Bowles. Courtesy National Maritime Museum, Greenwich, England. (*SPOT,* left, *The Frigate ROSE; Artist* Sir James Wallace; courtesy of Naval Records and Library.
73.H.M. WAR SLOOP *DRUID*. *Artist* T. Mellish; courtesy Harry Shaw Newman. (*SPOT,* right, *Early Carronade;* courtesy Office of Naval Records and Library.)
74.PLAN DRAWING, NAVAL GUN MOUNT. National Archives.
75.HOLD, SLOOP OF WAR. Old Print; Library of Congress. (*SPOT, Getting Guns on Board.* From "Kedge-Anchor." *SPOT, Shot Gets Loose.* From "Kedge-Anchor." *SPOT, Frigate Hove Down to Dock.* From 'Kedge-Anchor.")
76.BRITISH FIRE POWER. *Engraver* Gouaz; courtesy National Maritime Museum, Greenwich, England.
Below, **LOWER GUN DECK OF H.M.S. *VICTORY*.** *Artist* C. E. Turner. Courtesy Illustrated News. (*SPOT,* above, from "Kedge-Anchor.")
77.FISHING SCHOONER *HANNAH*. *Artist* Halsoll; courtesy of Naval Records and Library. (*SPOT,* left, *"Setting the Jib."* From "Kedge-Anchor.")
78.ATTACK ON CONVOY OFF BOSTON. *Artist* C. T. or A. W. Warren; courtesy Office of Naval Records and Library.
79.FLAG RAISING ON BOARD *ALFRED*. *Artist* N. C. Wyeth; courtesy U. S. Naval Academy Museum.
80.COMMO. "ROBERT" HOPKINS. From Spears' "The History of Our Navy."
81.COMMANDER-IN-CHIEF COMES ABOARD. From "Your Navy."
82.ATTACK ON NASSAU. From "Your Navy." (*SPOT,* below, *The Intrepid Lieutenant Hall.*) (FF)
83.BATTLE OFF BLOCK ISLAND. *Artist* C. T. or A. W. Warren. Courtesy Office of Naval Records and Library.
84.DISCIPLINE FOR NAVY. From "Your Navy."
85.RED COATS EVACUATE BOSTON. *Artist* M. A. Wageman; N. Y. Public Library.
86.SEA BATTLE OF *LEXINGTON*. National Archives. (*SPOT,* right, *The Lexington;* National Archives.)
87.PHILADELPHIA BLOCKADE. *Artist* C. T. or A. W. Warren; courtesy Office of Naval Records and Library.
88.RED COATS RIDDLED AT CHARLESTON. *Artist* J. A. Oertel; N. Y. Public Library. (*SPOTS,* below, *Sergeant Jasper Rescuing American Flag at Charleston.*) (FF)
89.BATTLE OF FORT MOULTRIE. (Above and below) *Artist* Lt. Henry Gray, 2nd (Moultrie's) Regt.; courtesy Office of Naval Records and Library.
90.NEW YORK HARBOR, 1776. From Fiske's "The American Revolution"; Library of Congress. (*SPOT,* center left, *Battery of New York.*)
91.WATCHING BRITISH SHIP, BOSTON HARBOR. (Subject: *Cerberus.*) *Artist* Lynd Ward. From "America's Paul Revere." Courtesy Houghton Mifflin Co.
92.FORCED MARCH. National Archives. (*CHART, Battle of Long Island, Cartographer* Howard Kenngott.)
93.NEW YORK CAMPAIGN. Howes in Action; *artist* C. T. or A. W. Warren; courtesy Office of Naval Records and Library. (*SPOT,* center right, *Revolutionary Officers.*) (FF)
94.BATTLE OF LONG ISLAND. *Artist* Lossing Barritt; N. Y. Public Library.
95.HESSIANS INVADING NEW JERSEY. "Drawn by British Officer"; N. Y. Public Library.
96.ACTION AT SPUYTEN DUYVILL. *Artist* Dominique Serres; courtesy Office of Naval Records and Library.
97.REDCOATS AT ANCHOR. "After sketch by British Officer"; N. Y. Public Library. (*SPOT,* below, *The Beekman Mansion.*) (FF)
98.PRISON SHIP "OLD JERSEY." *Artist* W. C. Jackson; from "Blue Jackets of '76"; Library of Congress. (*SPOT,* left, "Old Sugar House.") (FF)
99.WAR-SLOOP *PROVIDENCE* AT SEA. Old print; courtesy Naval History Division, CNO. (*SPOT,* center left. Old woodcut; from "Newgate Calendar"; courtesy Edwin Valentine Mitchell.)
100.PAUL JONES' COMMISSION. National Archives.
101.*ALFRED* AND *PROVIDENCE* TRAP *MELLISH*. *Artist* C. T. or A. W. Warren; courtesy Office of Naval Records and Library.
102.PROVIDENCE BLOCKADE—HOPKINS STRANDED. Courtesy Office of Naval Records and Library.
103.NAVAL LEADER, 1777. *Sculptor* Niehaus; courtesy Naval History Division, CNO. (*SPOT,* center right, *Marine on Poop Deck of Alfred;* from "Your Navy.")
104.NAVY MAN WITH MIGHTY PEN. From "Your Navy."
105.PAUL JONES SIGNATURE.
106.ROBERT MORRIS. By Bass Otis after Stuart; the Historical Society of Pennsylvania.
107.PIONEER DEFENDER — SCHOONER *ROYAL SAVAGE*. N. Y. Public Library. (*SPOT,* left, *General Benedict Arnold;* old woodcut.) (FF)
108.BATTLE OF VALCOUR ISLAND. Attributed to Warren; courtesy Naval History Division, CNO.
109.GEORGE III AS "MAN IN MOON." From Spears' "The History of Our Navy."
110.(above) BATTLE OF LAKE CHAMPLAIN. *Artist* Warren Sheppard; from Ellis, "Standard History of the U.S."; (below) courtesy Canadian Government and Office of Naval Records and Library. (*SPOT,* top right, *Galley Washington. Artist* Henry Rusk, from Chapelle's "History of the American Sailing Navy," W. W. Norton.)
111.CHART: BATTLE OF VALCOUR BAY. Courtesy Map Division, Library of Congress.
112.CHAMPLAIN CLIMAX. *Artist* C. Chapman; courtesy "U.S. Naval Institute Proceedings." (*DRAWINGS,* left, *Draught of Radeau Thunderer,* center, *Plan of Gundalow Philadelphia. Artist* Howard I. Chapelle, from "History of the American Sailing Navy," W. W. Norton.)
113.BEAUMARCHAIS. From Fiske's "The American Revolution"; Library of Congress.
114.LOGISTICS LIFELINE, 1777. "Hazard of Salem"; *Artist* George Ropes; courtesy Naval Historical Foundation. (*CHART: Logistics Lifeline, 1777.* Prepared by Arthur Strecker and Fred Freeman; *cartographer* Howard Kenngott.) (*SPOT,* right, *Privateer WASP.*) (FF)
115.*LEXINGTON* CAPTURED BY *PEARLE*. *Artist* C. T. or A. W. Warren; courtesy Office of Naval Records and Library.
116.*ANDREW DORIA* CAPTURES *RACEHORSE*. *Artist* C. T. or A. W. Warren; courtesy Office of Naval Records and Library.
117.MARINE *TURTLE*. National Archives.
118.WORLD'S FIRST SUBMARINE ATTACK. *Artist* Anton Otto Fisher; from "Steelways"; courtesy American Iron and Steel Institute.
119.TORPEDO STRIKE! *Artist* W. C. Jackson. From "Blue Jackets of '76"; Library of Congress.
120.COMMISSION FOR EZRA LEE. National Archives. (*SPOT,* center left, *Men in Smallboat.*) (FF)
121.HANDWRITING ON BRITAIN'S WALL. (Wickes Letter) National Archives.
122.*REPRISAL* DODGES *BURFORD*. From Frost's "The Book of the Navy"; Library of Congress.
123.LOSS OF *LEXINGTON*. *Artist* C. T. or A. W. Warren; Library of Congress.
124.GUSTAVUS CONYNGHAM. From "Captain Gustavus Conynham"; courtesy Pennsylvania Society, Sons of the American Revolution.
125.END OF *REPRISAL*. *Artist* W. C. Jackson; from "Blue Jackets of '76"; Library of Congress.
126.TAKEN BY *SURPRISE*. *Artist* L. Robelle; from "Captain Gustavus Conyngham"; courtesy Pennsylvania Society, Sons of the American Revolution. (*SPOT,* left, from "Your Navy.")
127.*REVENGE* IN ENGLISH CHANNEL. *Artist* John Benson Willobank; courtesy Office of Naval Records and Library.
128.SABOTAGE IN ENGLAND. From "Newgate Calendae"; courtesy Edwin Valentine Mitchell.
129."CAP'N" CONYNGHAM IN BRITISH EYES. Contemporary British Print; from "Captain Gustavus Conyngham"; courtesy Pennsylvania Society, Sons of the American Revolution.
130.FRIGATE *HANCOCK*. *Artist* Geo. C. Wales; Mystic Seaport, Marine Historical Association, Inc. (*SPOT,* left, *Ships in Battle.*) (FF)
131.*HANCOCK* AND *BOSTON* TRAP *FOX*. *Artist* C. T. or A. W. Warren; courtesy Office of Naval Records and Library.
132.*HANCOCK* AND *BOSTON* VS. *RAINBOW* AND *FLORA*. *Artist* Butterworth; courtesy Office of Naval Records and Library.
133.LOSS OF *HANCOCK*. *Artist* C. T. or A. W. Warren; courtesy Office of Naval Records and Library. (*SPOT,* center right, *Hancock After Battle;* from "Your Navy.")
134.DRIVE ON REVOLUTIONARY CAPITAL. *Artist* C. T. or A. W. Warren; courtesy Naval History Division, CNO.
135.BATTLE IN DELAWARE RIVER. *Artist* Lt. W. W. Elliot, R.N.; courtesy "U.S. Naval Institute Proceedings."
136.LOSS OF FRIGATE *DELAWARE*. From Frost's "The Book of the Navy"; Library of Congress.
137.BATTLE IN DELAWARE RIVER. *Artist* J. M. Probst, Library of Congress.
138.LOSS OF *ANDREW DORIA*. *Artist* Warren Sheppard, from Ellis' "Standard History of the U.S." (*CHART: Operations in the Delaware, Oct.-Nov. 1777.* National Archives.)

645.C.S. IRONCLAD RAM *PALMETTO STATE.* *Artist* Clary Ray; from "Official Records of the Union and Confederate Navies in the War of the Rebellion."

646.C.S. GUNBOAT *PATRICK HENRY.* *Same as above.*

647.CONFEDERATE BLOCKADE RUNNER. *Photographer* probably Brady; National Archives.

648.C.S. RAM *GENERAL STERLING PRICE.* *Artist* Clary Ray; from "Official Records of the Union and Confederate Navies in the War of the Rebellion."

649.CONFEDERATE COAST ARTILLERY. *Photo.* N. O. or J. D. Edwards; National Archives.

650.GUARDING VITAL HARBORS. Library of Congress.

651.GUNS AT FORT JOHNSON, S. C. *Photographer* S. R. Seibert; National Archives. (*SPOT*, below, *Confederate Mortar Battery*; from *B. & L.)

652.PARROTT GUNS. *Artist* W. Taber; from *B. & L.

653.U.S.S. *NEW IRONSIDES.* *Artist* W. A. K. Martin; National Archives.

654.TYPICAL UNION MONITOR. *Photographer* probably Brady; Library of Congress.

655.U.S. IRONCLAD GUNBOAT *CINCINNATI.* National Archives.

656.BEHIND UNION FIREPOWER. *Artist* Adams; courtesy Du Pont Company.

657.BEHIND THE DIXIE DEFENSE. *Photographer* Geo. N. Barnard & James Gibson; courtesy Library of Congress.

658.CONFEDERATE MINE-TORPEDO. From "History of the Confederate Navy."

659.WASHINGTON NAVY YARD. *Artist* Alfred Waud; Library of Congress.

660.HOLOCAUST AT NORFOLK. From *Harper's P. H. (Below, *Artist* J. O. Davidson; from *B. & L.)

661.U.S.S. *PENNSYLVANIA.* *Artist* W. A. K. Martin; National Archives.

662.U.S.S. *DELAWARE.* Courtesy "U.S. Naval Institute Proceedings."

663.RUINS OF NORFOLK NAVY YARD. Library of Congress.

664.BURNING OF U.S.S. *MERRIMACK.* *Artist* J. O. Davidson; from *B. & L.

665.U.S. GUNBOAT *THOMAS FREEBORN.* From Miller's "Photographic History of the Civil War"; Library of Congress.

666.COMMANDER JAMES HARMON WARD, U.S.N. From Miller's "Photographic History of the Civil War"; Library of Congress.

667.SOAPBOX BLOCKADE. *Litho.* Currier & Ives; Library of Congress.

668.CIVIL WAR MEDAL OF HONOR. From "The Blue and the Gray"; courtesy Mrs. Anna Anderson. (*SPOT, Dead Sailor. Artist* Fred Freeman.)

669.TO GET AT THE KERNEL. *Lithographer* Currier & Ives; Library of Congress. (Left, *Eagle*; courtesy the Downtown Gallery, N. Y.)

670.PORT ROYAL. *Artist* C. Parsons; Library of Congress.

671.CONFEDERATE BATTERIES, PORT ROYAL. Library of Congress.

672.FIRST NAVAL AIRCRAFT CARRIER. The Smithsonian Inst.

673.MISSISSIPPI CHART. *Prepared by* Arthur Strecker *and* Fred Freeman; *Cartog.* Howard Kenngott.

674.COMMANDER JOHN RODGERS II, U.S.N. *Photographer* Brady; National Archives. (Below, *Commo. Foote's Gunboat Flotilla*; from *Harper's P. H.)

675.U.S. "TIMBERCLAD *CONESTOGA.* Library of Congress. (*SPOT*, above, *Water Battery*; from *Harper's P. H.)

676.U.S. GUNBOAT *ST. LOUIS.* National Archives.

677.U.S. GUNBOAT *LOUISVILLE.* *Artist* J. Muller; from "Official Records of the Union and Confederate Navies in the War of the Rebellion."

678.COMMO. ANDREW H. FOOTE, U.S.N. *Photographer* probably Brady; National Archives.

679.U.S. GUNBOAT *PITTSBURG.* National Archives.

680.U.S. "TIMBERCLAD" *TYLER.* *Artist* J. Muller; Library of Congress.

681.U.S. RIVER IRONCLAD *ESSEX.* Library of Congress.

682.CANNON WHEELS. (TR)

683.TRANSPORT DUTY. (TR)

684.MULES, MIRE, IMMOBILITY. *Artist* W. H. Shelton; from *B. & L.

685.SUPPLY BOAT. Library of Congress.

686.CREW OF GUNBOAT *CARONDELET.* (TR)

687.GENERAL FLOOD. National Archives.

688.SAWING A CHANNEL. *Artist* W. Tabor; from *B. & L. (*SPOT, Navy Mortar Boats. Artist* E. J. Meeker; from *B. & L.; *Chart*, below, *Island No. 10; prepared by* Arthur Strecker *and* Fred Freeman; *Cartog.* Howard Kenngott.)

689.CONFEDERATE SHARPSHOOTERS. *Artist* A. C. Redwood; from *B. & L.

690."TURTLES" BOMBARDING ISLAND 10. *Lithographer* Currier & Ives; Library of Congress. (*SPOT*, left, *Walke's Sketch of Carondelet*; from *B. & L.)

691.U.S.S. *RED ROVER.* *Artist* J. O. Davidson; from *B. & L.

692.PITTSBURG LANDING. *Artist* J. O. Davidson; from *B. & L. (*SPOT, Commissary Depot*; from *Harper's P. H.)

693.SHILOH! *Artist* A. F. Mathews; Library of Congress. (*SPOT*, center, *Death of Carson.*) (FF) (*Left, Chart, prepared by* Arthur Strecker *and* Fred Freeman; *Cartog.* Howard Kenngott.)

694.BATTLE FOR ROANOKE ISLAND. *Artist* A. Chappel; courtesy "U.S. Naval Institute Proceedings."

695.CAPTURE OF NEW BERNE, N. C. *Artist* Combe; Library of Congress. (*SPOT*, below, *Goldsborough's Expedition.*) (FF)

696.THE *MERRIMACK*—REBUILDING AT GOSPORT YARD. *Artist* J. O. Davidson; from *B. & L. (*SPOTS*, above left, *Merrimack Before Conversion; Artist* J. O. Davidson. Center, *Cross-Section of C.S. Virginia; Artist* J. L. Porter, constructor. Above right, *Merrimack After Conversion; Artist* Lt. B. L. Blackford, C.S.N. All from *B. & L.)

697.PLANS FOR *MONITOR.* *Artist* Ericsson and associates; from *B. & L.

698.INSIDE *MONITOR.* *Artist* Ericsson and associates; from *B. & L. (*SPOT, Passing Craney Is.; Artist* J. O. Davidson; from *B. & L.)

699.CROSS-SECTION *MONITOR.* *Artist* Wright, Ericsson *and* associates; from *B. & L. (*SPOTS*, at left, *Inside Monitor Turret; Turret Machinery; Captain's Cabin of Monitor*; center, *Launching the Monitor*; below, *Engine Room of the Monitor*; lower right, *Monitor in Storm; Berth Deck on Monitor; Pumping and Bailing En Route to Battle.* All from *Harper's P. H.; center, *Plan of Monitor Berth Deck; Artist* Ericsson and associates; from *B. & L.)

700.*MONITOR'S* CREW. *Photographer* probably Brady; Naval Records Library.

701.*MONITOR* MEN AT MESS. *Photographer* James F. Gibson; Library of Congress.

702.*MERRIMACK* RAMMING *CUMBERLAND.* *Artist* J. O. Davidson; from *B. & L. (*SPOT*, above right, *Lt. G. V. Morris*; from *same.*)

703.*CUMBERLAND* GOES DOWN. *Lithographer* N. Currier; Library of Congress.

704.MASSACRE OF *CONGRESS.* *Artist* C. Klackner. (*SPOTS*, center, *Lt. J. B. Smith of Congress*; lower left, *Explosion of Congress. Artist* J. O. Davidson; both from *B. & L.)

705.NORTHERN HEADLINES. Courtesy "The New York Times." (*SPOT*, above right, *On Gun Deck of the Virginia. Artist* W. Taber; from *B. & L.)

706.*MONITOR* ARRIVES. *Lithographer* Kurz & Allison; Library of Congress.

707.*MONITOR* VS. *MERRIMACK.* *Lithographer* Calvert Co.; Library of Congress. (*SPOT*, below, *Panoramic View. Artist* J. O. Davidson; from *B. & L.)

708."*MONITOR* AND *MERRIMACK.*" *Lithographer* T. Sinclair; contemp. Music Folio; Library of Congress. (*SPOT*, left, *In Monitor's Turret. Artist* Henry Sandham; from *B. & L.)

709.TURRET VS. CASEMATE. *Artist* J. O. Davidson; from *B. & L.

710.BATTLE OF THE IRONCLADS. *Artist* Fred Freeman; courtesy Chas. Pfizer Co., New London, Conn.

711.POINT BLANK HIT! *Artist* Fred Freeman. (*SPOT*, above, from *Harper's P. H.; *SPOTS*, below, all from *B. & L.)

712.OFFICERS OF. U.S.S. *MONITOR.* *Photographer* probably Gardner; Library of Congress.

713.INSPECTING *MONITOR'S* TURRET. *Photographer* Gardner; Library of Congress. (*SPOT*, below, *S. D. Greene*; from *B. & L.)

714.FIRST FIGHTERS OF THE TURRET—*MONITOR'S* CREW. *Photographer* Gardner; Library of Congress. (*Chart*, right, *prepared by* Arthur Strecker *and* Fred Freeman; *Cartog.* Howard Kenngott.)

715.TURRET PLAN OF LATER *MONITOR.* *Artist* Wright of Ericsson and Associates; from *B. & L.

716.U.S.S. *KEOKUK.* *Artist* C. H. Corbett; courtesy N. Y. Historical Society.

717.BUILDING THE *KEOKUK.* *Artist* T. Bonar; Naval Records and Library.

718.DOUBLE-TURRET MONITOR *ONONDAGA.* *Lithographer* Endicott & Company; Naval Records and Library.

719.U.S.S. *WEEHAWKEN.* *Artist* Granville Perkins; from *B. & L.

720.U.S.S. *ROANOKE.* Courtesy "U.S. Naval Institute Proceedings."

721.FARRAGUT ON BOARD *HARTFORD.* *Photographer* Brady; National Archives. (*SPOT*, left, from *A. & I.)

722.U.S. STEAM SLOOP *HARTFORD.* Naval Records and Library.

723.DEFENDING NEW ORLEANS. (Seacoast Cannon.) *Photographer* Brady; National Archives.

724.PARROTT RIFLES. *Artist* A. Waud; from *B. & L.

725.ROUND SHOT AND GRAPE. (TR)

726.TYPICAL HOT-SHOT FURNACE. (TR)

727.C.S.S. *STONEWALL JACKSON.* *Artist* J. O. Davidson; from *B. & L.

728.UNION MORTAR SCHOONER. *Photographer* Brady; Library of Congress. (Center, *Mortar Schooners in Action. Artist* J. O. Davidson; from *B. & L.)

729.GABIONS. Library of Congress.

730.ABATIS. National Archives.

731.CHAIN ARMOR. From *B. & L. (*SPOT*, left, *C.S. Ironclad "Louisiana"; Artist* W. Taber; from *B. & L. Right, *Plan of "Louisiana"; Artist* Cdr. J. K. Mitchell, C.S.N.; from *B. & L.)

732.CHANNEL BOOMS (and rope obstructions). From *B. & L.

733.PASSING THE DELTA FORTS. *Lithographer* Currier & Ives; Library of Congress. (*Chart*, above, *prepared by* Arthur Strecker *and* Fred Freeman; *Cartog.* Howard Kenngott.)

734.FIRING THROUGH THEIR OWN BOW. *Artist* J. O. Davidson; from *B. & L.

735.SHELL-HIT ON U.S. GUNBOAT *IROQUOIS.* Library of Congress.

736.MIDGET RAM *MANASSAS.* *Artist* J. O. Davidson; from *B. & L.

737.*MANASSAS* MAULS U.S.S. *MISSISSIPPI.* *Artist* J. D. Gleason; from "Autobiography of George Dewey"; courtesy Charles Scribner's Sons.

738.GENERAL "BEN" BUTLER, U.S.A. *Photographer* probably Brady; National Archives.

739.BATTLE OF NEW ORLEANS. *Artist* J. O. Davidson; Library of Congress.

740.FEDERAL HEADQUARTERS (New Orleans). National Archives.

741.STRIPPED FOR ACTION (*Hartford* and *Brooklyn*). *Artist* J. O. Davidson; from *B. & L. (*Chart*, left, *prepared by* Arthur Strecker *and* Fred Freeman; *Cartog.* Howard Kenngott.)

742.RAMS VS. "TURTLES." *Lithographer* Currier & Ives; courtesy Charles Scribner's Sons.

743.BATTLE FOR MEMPHIS. From *Harper's P. H.

744.FARRAGUT'S GUNNERS OFF VICKSBURG. *Artist* A. C. Redwood; from *B. & L. (*SPOT*, below, *"I would willingly give my other leg!"* from *A. & I.)

745.MEMPHIS CAPTURED. From *Harper's P. H.

746.MEN WHO RAN VICKSBURG GANTLET. From "Pictorial History of the Civil War"; courtesy Office of Naval Records and Library.

747.*ARKANSAS* ESCAPES. *Artist* J. O. Davidson; from *B. & L.

748.FEDERAL SHIPS IN HAMPTON ROADS. National Archives.

749.PEACEFUL JAMES RIVER. Probably Gibson; National Archives.

750.THROUGH DISMAL SWAMP. *Artist* H. L. Wait; from *B. & L. (*Chart*, left, *prepared by* Arthur Strecker and Fred Freeman; *Cartog.* Howard Kenngott.)

751.BLUEJACKETS ON JAMES RIVER. *Photographer* probably Brady; Library of Congress.

752.UNION MORTARS AT YORKTOWN. *Photographer* Brady; Library of Congress.

753.BOUND FOR RICHMOND. *Photographer* Brady; National Archives.

754.WAITING UP THE JAMES—GUNS AT FORT DARLING. Library of Congress. (*SPOTS*, left, from *B. & L.)

755.McCLELLAN COMING UP—AT HAMPTON, VA. *Artist* A. or W. Waud; Library of Congress.

756.U.S.S. *GALENA.* *Photographer* Brady; Library of Congress.

757.CONFEDERATE GUNBOAT *TEAZER.* *Photographer* Brady; Library of Congress.

758.HARVEST OF DEFEAT. *Photographer* Brady; Library of Congress. (*SPOT*, left, *Retreat from Malvern Hill*; from *Harper's P. H.)

759.NAVY AT MALVERN HILL. *Artist* C. Parsons; *lithographer* Virtue, Yorston & Co.; Library of Congress.

760.McCLELLAN COMING DOWN. *Artist* W. T. Treza; courtesy Rear Adm. E. E. DuVall, U.S.N. (Ret'd.).

761.U.S.S. *WYOMING.* *Artist* Clary Ray; courtesy "U.S. Naval Institute Proceedings."

762.FEDERAL BLOCKADER. (TR)

763.C.S. RAIDER *ALABAMA.* From "History of the Confederate States Navy"; Library of Congress.

764.SOUTHERN BLOCKADE RUNNER (under British Flag). Library of Congress.

765.THE *R. E. LEE.* Library of Congress.

766.BLOCKADE-RUNNER *VANCE.* Library of Congress.

767.*ALABAMA* SINKING U.S.S. *HATTERAS.* *Artist* F. Gutekunst; Naval Records and Library.

768.U.S.S. *SANTIAGO DE CUBA.* Library of Congress.

769.RACING YACHT *AMERICA.* Courtesy Charles Scribner's Sons.

770.THE CONSCRIPT BILL. National Archives.

771."KING COTTON." Library of Congress. (*SPOT*, below, *Growman*; from *A. & I.)

772."OLD MAN RIVER." From *Harper's P. H. (*SPOT*, below, from *same.*)

773.DAVID DIXON PORTER. *Photographer* Brady; National Archives.

774.CARTOON BY ADMIRAL PORTER. Courtesy N. Y. Historical Society.

775.MOUND CITY. Library of Congress.

776.U.S.S. *BLACK HAWK.* *Artist* F. B. Schell; from *B. & L.

777.MISSISSIPPI FLOTILLA. *Photographer* Brady; National Archives.

778.MAN-O-WAR'S MEN. *Photographer* Brady; National Archives.

779.U.S.S. *CAIRO.* *Photographer* Brady; National Archives.

780.GENERAL ULYSSES S. GRANT, U.S.A. National Archives.

781.VICKSBURG DEFENDER—"WHISTLING DICK." *Photographer* Brady; National Archives.

782."IRONCLAD" *CHOCTAW.* (TR)

783.JUBILO!—THE GUNBOATS. Library of Congress.

VICKSBURG. (*Chart, prepared by* Arthur Strecker *and* Fred Freeman; *Cartog.* Howard Kenngott.)

784.YAZOO MORASS. From "Frank Leslie's Illustrated Newspaper"; Library of Congress.

785.AMPHIBIOUS TRESTLE. (TR)

786.FAKE IRONCLAD. *Artist* W. C. Jackson; from "Blue Jackets of '61"; Library of Congress. (*SPOT*, left, *Bress de Lord!"* from *A. & I.)

787.POUNDING PORT HUDSON. Library of Congress.

788."TURTLES" VS. VICKSBURG. *Lithographer* Currier & Ives; Library of Congress.

789.BOMBARDING GRAND GULF. *Artist* Thomas Nast; courtesy U.S. Naval Academy Museum.

790.TRUCE TO BURY DEAD. *Artist* Gaul; from *B. & L.; Library of Congress.

791.TRENCHES BEFORE VICKSBURG. From Miller's "Photographic History of the Civil War"; Library of Congress.

792.VICKSBURG LEVEE. From Miller's "Photographic History of the Civil War"; Library of Congress.

793."UNVEXED TO THE SEA."—MISSISSIPPI MAIL BOAT. *Lithographer* Currier & Ives; Library of Congress.

794.NAPOLEON III. Library of Congress.

795.RUSSIAN ADMIRAL LESSOVSKY. *Photographer* Brady; National Archives.

796.RUSSIAN FLEET IN NEW YORK HARBOR. From "Harper's Weekly."

797.HOLDING U.S.N. AT BAY—AT CHARLESTON. National Archives.

798.GUN DECK OF U.S.S. *PAWNEE.* Library of Congress.

799.POWDER MONKEY ON U.S.S. *NEW HAMPSHIRE.* Library of Congress.

800."PET PARROT ESCAPES ON U.S. VESSEL." (U.S.S. *RICHMOND.*) From "Harper's Weekly"; Library of Congress.

801.CHARLESTON RAMS VS. BLOCKADER. *Artist* Xanthus Smith; from "The Blue and the Gray"; courtesy Mrs. Anna Anderson.

802.MONITOR *MONTAUK* DESTROYS NASHVILLE. *Artist* J. O. Davidson; from *B. & L.

803.U.S. IRON FLEET OFF CHARLESTON. *Artist* Smyth; from "Illustrated London News"; Library of Congress.

804.DIVINE SERVICE—ON BOARD *PASSAIC.* *Photographer* Sam'l. A. Cooley, 10th Army Corps; National Archives.

805.ASSAULT ON CHARLESTON FORTS. *Artist* A. R. Waud. (TR)

806.DAHLGREN WITH STAFF. *Photographer* Brady; National Archives.

807.MONITOR *WEEHAWKEN* VS. RAM *ATLANTA.* *Artist* J. O. Davidson; from *B. & L. (*Chart*, below, *prepared by* Arthur Strecker *and* Fred Freeman; *Cartog.* Howard Kenngott, *made over a print from* *Harper's P. H.)

808.CAPTURED RAM *ATLANTA.* Library of Congress.

809.MONITOR *CATSKILL* OFF CHARLESTON. *Photographer* Brady; National Archives.

810.UNION SAILORS IN FORT WAGNER. *Photographer* Haas and Peale; Library of Congress.

811.THE *ALLIGATOR.* Above, from "Les Bateaux Sous-Marins"; Library of Congress. Below, from "La Navigation Sous-Marins"; Library of Congress.

812.RAM AND SPAR TORPEDO (Confederate design). From "History of the Confederate Navy"; Library of Congress.

813.CONFEDERATE SUBMERSIBLE. *After plan by* Dr. St. Julian Ravenal. (TR)

814.AMAZING CONFEDERATE SUB. *Photographer* Brady; Library of Congress.

815.C.S.S. *HUNLEY.* *Artist* R. G. Skerritt, *after painting by* Conrad Wise Chapman; National Archives.

816."DAVID" SUB IN CHARLESTON HARBOR. From "Official Records of the Union and Confederate Navies in the War of the Rebellion." (*SPOT*, below, *"River Devils"*; from *A. & I.)

817.RECRUITING CONFEDERATE LADIES. Facsimile of original in Confederate Museum, Richmond.

818.COMIC VALENTINE, CIVIL WAR. Courtesy John B. Hapgood; N. Y. Public Library.

819.UNION ADMIRAL'S HAT. Courtesy The Marine Museum of the City of New York.

820.C.S. RAIDER *CHICAMAUGA.* *Artist* Clary Ray; from "Official Records of the Union and Confederate Navies in the War of the Rebellion." (*SPOT, Commodore Duncan Ingraham, C.S.N.*; Naval History Division, CNO.)

821.U.S. TURRET STEAMER *OUACHITA.* *Artist* J. Muller; from "Official Records of the Union and Confederate Navies in the War of the Rebellion."

822.U.S. RIVER RAM *VINDICATOR.* *Artist* J. Muller; from "Official Records of the Union and Confederate Navies in the War of the Rebellion."

823.U.S. DOUBLE-TURRET RIVER MONITOR *KICKAPOO.* *Artist* Wm. Jefferson; "Official Records of the Union and Confederate Navies in the War of the Rebellion."

824.PORTER'S SQUADRON UP RED RIVER. Library of Congress.

825.U.S. "TIMBERCLAD" *LEXINGTON.* National Archives.

826.U.S. RIVER MONITOR *OSAGE.* *Photographer* Brady; National Archives.